About the Author

Michael Norton is the founder, and was until 1995 the Director, of Directory of Social Change, the UK's leading agency providing information, training and support to voluntary organisations. In 1995, he founded the Centre for Innovation in Voluntary Action (CIVA – www.civa.org.uk) to promote innovation and new thinking on the role of charities.

CIVA's current projects include developing banks in schools run by the students themselves (to be called MyBnk), which will encourage saving and make small loans; starting a campaign to encourage young people to lead more sustainable lifestyles; the creation of a young achievers national awards scheme; and village publishing and libraries in India.

Michael Norton established Changemakers, which challenges young people to design and manage their own community projects. He is also the founder of YouthBank UK, which enables young people to make grants in their local communities.

In 2002, he set up an international summer school for young activists: YOUNG PEOPLE change the world! This has now become an annual event, planned and run entirely by young people, which brings together around 250 people from all over the world.

He is a Founder and Trustee of unLTD – the Foundation for Social Entrepreneurs, which received an endowment of £100 million from the Millennium Commission, and makes awards to over 1,000 individuals in the UK each year who wish to create change in their communities.

He is author of numerous books on fundraising and charitable status, including *Writing Better Fundraising Applications*, *The WorldWide Fundraiser's Handbook* and *The Complete Fundraising Handbook*, all published by Directory of Social Change, as well as *Getting Started in Fundraising* and *Getting Started in Communication*.

Visit www.AuthorTracker.co.uk for exclusive information on your favourite HarperCollins authors.

How to make the world a better place every day

Michael Norton

HARPER PERENNIAL
London, New York, Toronto and Sydney

Harper Perennial
An imprint of HarperCollins*Publishers*
77-85 Fulham Palace Road
Hammersmith
London W6 8JB

www.harperperennial.co.uk

This updated edition published by Harper Perennial 2006

987654321

First published in the UK in 2005 by Myriad Editions

All the author's royalties are going to charity to help fuel the campaign to change the world

A catalogue record for this book is available from the British Library

ISBN-13 978-0-00-724230-6
ISBN-10 0-00-724230-1

Set in Rotis Semi Sans
Edited and designed by mam publishing
Editor: Nina Sharman
Designer: Martin Hendry
Proof reader: Anne Rieley
Illustrations for themes: Geoff Westby
Printed and bound in Great Britain by Clays Ltd, St Ives plc

This book is proudly printed on paper which which contains wood from well managed forests, certified in accordance with the rules of the Forest Stewardship Council. For more information about FSC, please visit www.fsc-uk.org

Contents

Acknowledgements

The idea for this book had been in the back of my mind for some time, but it was only after discussing it with Vicki Saunders, a Canadian social entrepreneur, and her telling me to get on and do it, that I felt able to get started. Christen Eddy got the original website going to solicit ideas, arranged brainstorm evenings and got a team of young volunteers involved. Particular thanks should go to Victoria Stanski for agreeing to contribute to, and edit, the Peace section, and to all the named contributors who submitted material for the book:

Before you get started: Christen Eddy
7 February: Shane Messer
8 February: Victoria Stanski
15 May: Greg Buhrman
22 June: Peter Sweatman
4 July: Peter Tatchell
10 July: Victoria Stanski
14 July: Toby Lloyd
17 August: Jillian Frumkin
5 September: Victoria Stanski
20 September: Victoria Stanski
3 November: Victoria Stanski
4 November: Kathryn Blume
25 November: Margaret Murray
7 December: Rebecca Sherman
9 December: Bob Barclay
10 December: Victoria Stanski

Thanks to the following for permission to use ideas from their publications:
18 July: Gray & Company for *365 Ways to Meet People in Cleveland* (Gray & Co., 2001) by Miriam Carey
29 September: Pan MacMillan for *Crap Towns: The 50 Worst Places to Live in the UK* (Boxtree, 2003) by Sam Jordison, Dan Kieran and *The Idler* magazine
27 November: Pan MacMillan for *This Diary Will Change your Life* (Boxtree, 2005) by Bendrik Ltd.

Thanks also to my literary agents Mary Clemmey and Niamh Walsh, and all at Harper Perennial, especially Paul, Essie and Lizzie.

Introduction

What's the big idea? The world is full of all sorts of problems, including:

- **HIV/AIDS** which is infecting more and more of the world's population
- **A widening North–South divide**
- **War and terror** (and the 'War on Terror')
- **All the 'isms'** (racism, sexism, etc) that deny people opportunities
- **Environmental degradation** and pollution
- **A scarcity of water**
- **Hunger** for far too many of the world's population
- **A lack of universal primary education**
- **Corruption and bad governance** in too much of the world
- **Abuse of human rights** (including slavery and torture)
- **Global warming**, which will have an impact on almost everything

... and many more besides.

Everyone has their own ideas about what's wrong with the world. They'll argue about which are the most important issues. But they'll all agree that things could be a lot better than they are, and that something does need to be done. But then what? Do we just leave it to governments and international institutions? Or are there things we can do that will actually make a difference?

The issues that confront us may seem so huge, so difficult to deal with that it's hard to believe that anything we can do will have a meaningful impact. But there are a lot of us in the world. A lot of people doing a lot of little things could have a huge impact. And by doing something, we are also demonstrating that lots of people really do care.

Together we can change the world. That is the idea underlying this book. Through the way we live, the adjustments we make in our lives, and the action we take on issues that really concern us, we can begin to make a difference.

This book has an idea-a-day for changing the world. Most are quite simple, can be done from home (access to the internet will be useful), and will not take up that much time. Some require a bit more time, energy and commitment.

Get going on changing the world. You can make a start at any time. Just open the book at today's date, read, enjoy and be inspired to action.

Visit www.365act.com – a website that includes all the 365 ideas and many more. Click on the weblinks to go straight to the sources of information listed in the book.

This book is just a starting point for an ideas bank for changing the world. We need your help, ideas, and feedback from what you have done in order to help us make our dream, of people everywhere doing all they can to change the world, a reality.

Themes

Community and neighbourhood
Getting to know your neighbourhood or city, ways of brightening it up, bringing fun and laughter into local life, working with socially excluded people and with prisoners.

Culture and creativity
Connecting up with people, new ideas for getting your message across, communicating through language and stories, listening in to get inspired.

Democracy and human rights
Fighting for freedom of information, participating in elections, lobbying your elected representatives, human rights and human wrongs around the world.

Discrimination
Fighting for disability rights, tackling racism and sexism (and all the other -isms in society), dealing with violence and abuse.

Enterprise and co-operation
Sharing skills and resources, open-access software, internet collaboration, social enterprise, micro-credit.

Environment
Global warming, pollution, pesticides and toxins, conservation of species and resources, trees and forests, sustainable living, waste and recycling, transport.

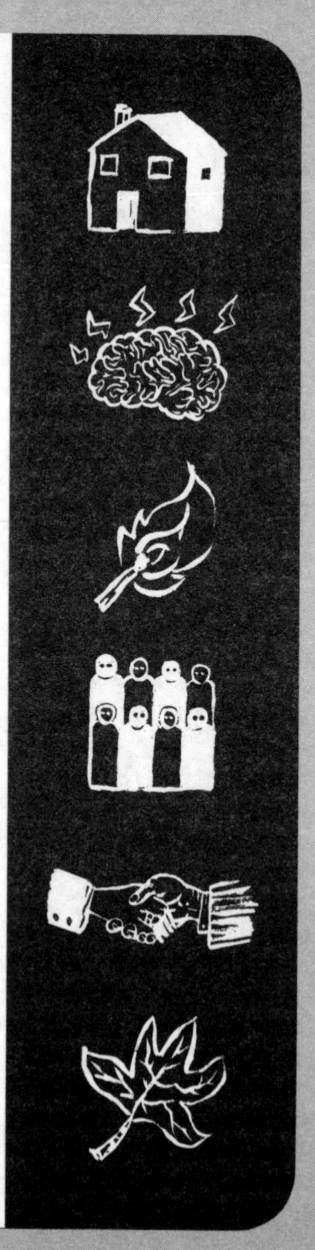

Globalisation and consumerism
Multinationals and responsible business practice, fairer trade and ethical consumption, consuming less.

Health
Battling HIV/AIDS, malaria and other global diseases, water and sanitation, better health, sport and fitness, hunger and obesity, food and diet.

International development
Addressing inequality and social injustice in the world with skills, money and ideas, recycling to benefit the world's poor, paying off foreign debt, enhancing livelihoods and using appropriate technology.

Peace
Ridding the world of weapons, waging war on war, promoting peace, preventing genocide.

Volunteering and citizenship
Getting your message across, being nice to others, gearing up for action, having the right attitudes, donating cash and raising money, giving in kind, volunteering your time.

Young people
Improving education and schools, fighting for children's rights, supporting children in need, dealing with child abuse, providing opportunities for play and exercise, being a young activist.

Before you start

You watch the news every night. You turn off your television set, disturbed by what you've seen and wondering what, if anything, you can do to make a difference. The fact that you picked up this book is evidence that you want to do something positive for the planet.

Before you eradicate AIDS, end the illegal arms trade and abolish world debt, take a brief look at your own lifestyle. There are things you should be doing on a regular basis. Some of these, even the most selfish idiot knows are 'the right thing to do'. Some are saintly, others fun.

Find out if you are 'eco-sinner' or 'socially minded saint'. Tick each thing you do on a regular basis:

- ☐ Turn off lights when you leave a room.
- ☐ Fill up your kettle with only as much water as you need.
- ☐ Don't leave the tap running when you're not using the water.
- ☐ Take a shower instead of a bath, or share your bath with a friend.
- ☐ Hang your clothes out to dry in the summer, rather than use a tumble drier.
- ☐ Put on a sweater in the house if you're cold, instead of cranking up the heat.
- ☐ Don't drop your litter or throw it out of the car window. This includes cigarette butts and gum.
- ☐ Pick up rubbish in the street.
- ☐ You spread a little happiness – smile at everyone and chat with neighbours.
- ☐ Perform an occasional random act of kindness to a complete stranger.
- ☐ Recycle everything that is recyclable.
- ☐ Make a compost pile with your food waste, and invite worms to feast on it.
- ☐ Walk or ride a bike for short journeys, instead of using a car.
- ☐ Support local small businesses.
- ☐ Do things for the community or for others. You volunteer two hours a week.
- ☐ Take your own bags when shopping.
- ☐ Buy fairtrade tea and coffee.
- ☐ Try to stop the barrage of junk mail by signing off from bulk mailing lists.
- ☐ Vote at election time; speak out on issues; lobby your local representative about anything important.
- ☐ Have never smoked, or have now quit smoking.

Now it's Judgement Day, the moment when you discover if Mother Earth will banish you to the molten core, or give you a palace in the clouds. Award yourself one point for each tick.

Score: 0–5 You are a hopeless barbaric eco-hating hooligan.

Score: 6–10 You are not a hopeless case, but you need to wise up.

Score: 10–15 You are a credit to the planet. Pat yourself on the back, but don't be too smug.

Score: 16–20 You are the saviour of the planet. You deserve a throne next to Gandhi and Mother Theresa.

What next? It's pretty obvious, isn't it? You should start living more responsibly and also start reading this book. Do one thing each day to make a better world.

New Year's revolution

The best way to predict the future is to invent it.
Alan Kay

New Year's Day is a time for looking forward, when we resolve to make a fresh start, do better and try harder. But all too often these resolutions evaporate by the time we have cleared up the remains of the previous night's party and by the time we get into work the next day. And if nothing is changing in the world, and the same old problems – war, famine, injustice, torture, poverty, disease – are in the news daily, it feels as though there is little point in giving up smoking, losing weight, or walking to work. So, instead of watching guiltily, as world events unfold on your TV, bring about a New Year's Revolution. Change your life by resolving to change the world.

Once you've got started, everything will get a lot easier. So, today, commit yourself to taking that first crucial step. Once you have resolved to make poverty history, to stop global warming (or whatever it is you want to do), the first thing you need is a plan of action. Make a plan and set targets. Be ambitious, but make sure that your plan is achievable.

At the end of the year, you will want to review your progress and assess whether you achieved your goals. You will want to see how much impact you have had on the issue and learn from your experience. Then you need to plan what to do next.

Resolve to change the world

Make a New Year's Resolution. Go to www.tomphillips.co.uk/portrait/sbec and download the portrait of Samuel Beckett which is ringed by the quotation:

No matter
Try again
Fail again
Fail better

Cut this picture out, frame it and put it somewhere you will see it every day. Let Samuel Beckett's words become your motto for the efforts you will be making to change the world.

For advice about making resolutions, visit: www.mygoals.com/about/NewYearsTips.html

Don't be frightened of failure

Do something, and always try your best to succeed.

But even if you don't, you will have shown that you care enough to want to do something, you will probably have made some difference, and you will have learnt a lot from the experience – which you can put into practice next time.

January 2

Make amends

Do it today!

Pick up the phone, write a letter, or send an email to someone you have hurt, or someone you have lost contact with. It doesn't matter whether it is your fault or theirs that you are no longer speaking. It doesn't matter if they choose not to respond. You've taken the first step. That's what's important:

- **What you need: a little humility**
- **Time invested: about 10 minutes**
- **The pay-off: a clean conscience**

Greensboro Truth and Community Reconciliation Project: www.gtcrp.org

It is almost certain that there is someone you've done wrong to, had a huge argument with, insulted, let things get to a point where you are not speaking, lost contact with. You've thought about this person more times than you can count, but for some reason, you've never made an effort to wipe the slate clean.

Make amends. Bury the past by apologising for what you've done. Admit responsibility. Heal the situation. In doing this, you will have done good – and it will be one less thing to worry about.

Even communities can make amends. In Greensboro, North Carolina, on 3 November 1979, members of the Ku Klux Klan and the American Nazi Party killed five people and wounded ten others, as activists gathered for a rally and conference for racial and social justice.

Twenty-five years later, the City of Greensboro decided to confront the past in the style of the Truth and Reconciliation Commission that Nelson Mandela so successfully instituted for post-Apartheid South Africa. The past can never be erased, but people and communities can move forward.

Pavel's story

Forced to work in a carpentry shop by day, locked in barracks at night, Pavel Kotlyarov will never forget the hunger and the hardship. Pavel, a Ukrainian, was one of millions forced into slave labour by the Nazis.

Fifty years later, some German students in Gersthofen, the town where Pavel was enslaved, tried to make amends for the past. They sent Pavel and other former slaves from Kiev a letter of apology and money they had collected as a gesture of compensation.

The German government has paid compensation of $1,000 to Ukraine's 600,000 surviving former slaves, but the students, as well as many others in Germany, feel the need to do more.

Cities have been sponsoring trips to Germany and raising money to provide aid packages for former slaves, who are now mostly in their 80s or older.

Stop climate change

The world's climate is a cause for intense concern. Heat waves, droughts, monsoons and hurricanes are breaking all records. These are already proving costly in terms of human life, but there are others that are more surreptitious and likely to be even more deadly.

In the Antarctic peninsula, vast areas of ice-sheet are disintegrating. In parts of Canada, Alaska, Siberia, the melting of the permafrost is undermining roads, airports, and buildings. There are signs that the huge ice-sheet over Greenland is starting to thin, releasing millions of cubic kilometres of fresh water into the north Atlantic. Mountain glaciers in temperate zones are retreating, and as they shrink, water flows will start to drop, creating severe shortages of water for irrigation and power in areas that rely on mountain watersheds. Melting ice that causes sea water to expand, is likely to lead to a rise in sea-level of about 92 cm over the next 100 years. Some low-lying areas will cease to exist; others will experience flooding.

These climate changes are being caused by the emission of greenhouse gases. Government action will be required if climate change is to be slowed down. But it is the sum of our own individual choices and actions that is causing the problem.

Halve it!

In the UK, George Marshall did everything he could to reduce his personal carbon emissions. In just one year he achieved a reduction of 50 per cent through energy saving and changes to his lifestyle. To encourage others and even whole communities to do the same, he set up COIN – Climate Outreach Information Network. One of their ideas is Carbon Pioneers, a group of 100 people who commit to reducing their emissions, and then encourage and support each other through the process.

Lick Global Warming: www.lickglobalwarming.org

COIN – Climate Outreach Information Network: www.coinet.org.uk

Stop it now

The average European emits directly and indirectly around 12 tonnes of carbon a year into the atmosphere. Pledge to save 5–10 per cent of your carbon emissions.

- Replace three standard bulbs with low-energy bulbs and save 136 kg a year.
- Turn the thermostat down by 2°C and save 272 kg a year.
- Install a modern programmable thermostat and save 453 kg a year.
- Travel 15 miles fewer each week by car and save 408 kg a year.
- Pledge to cut your personal consumption by at least 1 tonne (2,240 lb) a year; explore the options at: www.lickglobalwarming.org/pledge.cfm

The price of a cuppa

This is how the money you spend on a take-out cup of coffee gets shared around:

30 per cent corporate costs and profit
18 per cent labour
16 per cent outlet expenses on rent etc.
15 per cent tax
5 per cent cup and lid
5 per cent other packaging and sugar
5 per cent dairy
5 per cent the coffee itself!

Oxfam have launched a chain of fairtrade coffee shops called Progreso. The first two are in London's Covent Garden and Portobello Road: www.progreso.org.uk

Coffee at a fair price

Fairtrade coffee provides greater security for small producers than is offered by the fluctuating world market. The current fairtrade price is more than double the market price. In 1994 coffee reached a high of $4.40 per kg, caused by frost and drought in Brazil, but by 2001 prices had fallen to $1.10 – where it has mostly remained. The impact of low coffee prices is felt by small family producers, who depend on this crop for their living. In Ethiopia, Uganda and Honduras, coffee is an important export commodity – a slump in prices can depress the whole economy.

Recently more coffee is being produced than is being consumed, much of it funded by agricultural development schemes. The price has dropped as a result. New technology is being used to remove the bitterness from the lower-priced Robusta variety. This means more Robusta coffee is being consumed. It is grown intensively, on large estates, with increasing mechanisation, considerably reducing the need for labour. What 1,000 people might achieve on a small estate in Guatemala, can be achieved by 12 people on a state-of-the-art mechanised farm in Brazil.

Enjoy the taste of doing good

Buy and drink fairtrade coffee. The higher price will help small farmers. But ask whether a fairtrade cup of coffee is really a fairly traded cup of coffee. Roasted ground coffee wholesales at around £5 per kg; 1 kg is sufficient to make 100 cups of coffee. In a coffee shop, the coffee costs about 5p. The consumer will be paying £1 upwards. The grower will get only about 2p of this, even at fairtrade prices. Fairtrade coffee represents 1 per cent of the US and 2 per cent of the UK market. Write to the Managing Directors of Starbucks, Costa, Caffè Nero and ask them to:

- Sell only fairtrade coffee.
- Include a voluntary premium of 5p per cup to be added to your bill and paid to the Fairtrade Foundation to benefit small coffee producers.

Start drinking

When you have a drink with your friends, there are a number of things you can do to support the local economy and help the environment.

- Reduce your beer miles. This is the distance the beer has travelled from the brewery to get to you, the consumer. Support your local brewer – and your local whisky distiller and winemaker.
- Choose bottles that have natural cork stoppers. Oak corks bio-degrade. The oak cork woodlands in Portugal and Spain produce over 80 per cent of natural cork. These woodlands support a huge population of wildlife and are at risk of being felled to create even more intensively farmed fields when they no longer fulfil an economic purpose.
- Recycle all your bottles and cans.
- Buy organic beer and wine. Organic producers don't use pesticides that can harm wildlife and contaminate water sources. Organic beer and wine will contain fewer additives so you won't have such a killer headache when you wake up.
- Drink real ale, and keep traditional breweries in business. And why not brew your own?

Brew your own

Try brewing your own beer. You could start simple, or try one of the exotic varieties listed below, which were compiled to celebrate the first ten years of *Brew Your Own* magazine.

Or, if that is too daunting, make a point of drinking local beers. If your local doesn't offer any, ask why not.

Campaign for Real Ale: www.camra.org.uk

How to brew your own beer – all you need to know from Brew Your Own: www.byo.com

What's brewing?

The Brew Your Own website has some adventurous recipes:

- Black Pear Oyster Stout uses oysters. There's no strong oyster flavour, but it does have a slight salty/briny character.
- Wild Rice Helles Bock, a strong light-coloured beer made with wild rice.
- Original Hempen Ale is a dark ale made with roasted hemp seeds, which contain a trace of THC, which is the active ingredient in marijuana. But hemp is completely legit!
- Smoked Maple Amber Ale uses maple sap (you can improvise by adding water to maple syrup). For a strong smoky flavour, use hickory smoke.
- Stonehenge Stein Beer uses hot stones to heat the wort and caramelise the sugars; it requires heat-resistant tongs and some ingenuity to make it.

January 6

At the double

Human rights violations are as numerous today as when Amnesty was founded. Two simple things you can do:

- **Download a screensaver from the Amnesty website and remind yourself every day that human rights are the foundation of freedom, justice and peace in the world.**
- **Join Amnesty's Urgent Action Network and participate in campaigns: http://web.amnesty.org/pages/ua-index-eng**

Resources for activists:
Amnesty International: www.amnesty.org
Human Rights Watch: hrw.org
Human Rights Network International: www.hrni.org
International Service for Human Rights: www.ishr.ch

Human rights and wrongs

Open your newspaper ... and you will find a report from somewhere in the world of someone being imprisoned, tortured or executed because his opinions or religion are unacceptable to his government. The reader feels a sickening sense of impotence. Yet if these feelings of disgust all over the world could be united into common action, something effective could be done. Peter Benenson

Amnesty International was started in 1961 by Peter Benenson, a British lawyer, after he read about the imprisonment of two Portuguese students who had drunk a toast to liberty in a Lisbon restaurant, during Portugal's 32-year rule by right-wing dictator, Dr Antonio Salazar. He wanted to harness the enthusiasm of people all over the world concerned about human rights abuse. Supporters were asked to adopt three 'prisoners of conscience', one from the West, one from the Soviet bloc and one from the non-aligned world. They energetically campaigned for the release of their prisoners by writing letters, mobilising political support and showing the jailers (and the prisoner) that the prisoner had not been forgotten.

Amnesty Urgent Action Network

A peasant activist 'disappears' in Mexico. In Turkey, a journalist is arrested and at risk of torture. Environmentalists in Kenya are imprisoned and beaten. An elderly political prisoner in Indonesia is denied insulin for his diabetes.

Every day Amnesty receives this sort of information. If an immediate response is needed to deal with a specific human rights violation, the Urgent Action Network is set in motion. Members of the Network send a flood of letters to try to right the wrong. They may be trying to save someone from torture or death, from an unfair trial, or political killing, or from forcible repatriation to a country where they may be at risk of further human rights abuse.

Visit the hunger site

Twenty-four thousand people die every day from hunger. Three-quarters of the deaths are children under the age of five. A website that focuses the power of the internet on the eradication of world hunger was launched in June 1999. A visitor to 'The Hunger Site' just clicks the 'Give Free Food' button and a cup of food is donated to feed a hungry person. The food donation is paid for by a sponsor, and the cost of running the site is paid for by the advertisements of up to ten sponsors and the sale of merchandise (such as jewellery, crafts and T-shirts).

More than 200 million visitors gave more than 300 million cups of food in the site's first five years. In a typical month in 2005, 3.2 million people visited the site, and 3.6 million cups of food, weighing a total of 207 tonnes, were distributed as a result of this online clicking. The food is distributed to those in need by Mercy Corps (through food donations and food for work programmes in over 70 countries in Africa, Asia, Eastern Europe, the Middle East and Latin America) and America's Second Harvest (which collects food to help feed an estimated 26 million hungry people in the USA).

Provide a square meal

Visit the Hunger Site daily and trigger a donation. It will cost you nothing, but you will be feeding a hungry person. There is a facility on the site for you to be sent a reminder each day.

Develop a start-up routine for your computer that automatically gets your computer (or all the computers in your office) to visit the Hunger Site each morning and trigger a donation.

Tell all your friends. There is a facility on the site to do this or you can send them an e-card by clicking 'Tell a Friend' on this weblink:. www.thehungersite.com/seasonoflight.swf

January 7

Hunger in the world

Ten per cent of children in developing countries die before they are five. (CARE)

The majority of hunger deaths are caused by chronic malnutrition. Families are simply not getting enough to eat because of their extreme poverty. Famine and wars cause just 10 per cent of hunger deaths. (The Institute for Food and Development Policy)

Chronic malnutrition causes impaired vision, listlessness, stunted growth and greatly increased susceptibility to disease. (United Nations World Food Programme)

A few simple resources, such as seeds, tools, access to water and improvements in farming techniques would help impoverished people to grow enough food to become self-sufficient. (Oxfam)

Help to pay

Sierra Leone is the poorest country in the world. Until recently it has been in the grip of civil war. It was ranked lowest on the Human Development Index.

Put what you can afford in an envelope (cash or money order) and send it to the Bank of Sierra Leone, Siaka Stevens Street, Freetown, Western Area, Sierra Leone. Mark it for attention of the Governor, Dr J D Rogers. Indicate that it is to help repay the country's debt and you would like a receipt.

Visit these websites:
www.jubileedebtcampaign.org.uk
African Forum and Network on Debt and Development: www.afrodad.org
Paris Club (third world debt): www.clubdeparis.org/en/

Foreign debt ... send cash

During the 1970s and 1980s, the world's poorest countries were encouraged to borrow so as to invest in projects that would produce an economic return. This did not happen. Instead they got saddled with a huge amount of debt. 'Jubilee Year' in the Bible is a time to wipe out outstanding debts. The Jubilee Debt Campaign focused on 2000 as a date to clear the debts of the world's poorest countries.

The Heavily Indebted Poor Countries initiative was set up in 1996 by the World Bank and International Monetary Fund. The original debt of the world's fifty-two poorest and most indebted countries totalled $375 billion. The initiative aimed to write off $100 billion. In return, countries would spend the debt relief on health, education and development. Forty-two countries were eligible; of these, fifteen completed the process – $46 billion was written off.

The Jubilee Debt Campaign continued to press for 100 per cent cancellation of unpayable debt for every poor country. At the G8 summit in July 2005, leaders of the world's richest nations agreed to write off all World Bank, IMF and African Development Bank debt for the eighteen poorest African nations.

Third-world debt burden

- Total external debt of low-income countries: $523 billion, of which $300 billion relates to Africa.
- Debt service being paid every day by low-income countries: $100 million. For every $1 received in grants, they pay $2.30 to service debt.

Debt cancellation/relief works:

- In Benin, 54 per cent of the money saved has been spent on health.
- In Tanzania, debt relief enabled primary school fees to be abolished, which led to a 66 per cent increase in school attendance.
- In Mozambique, it enabled all children to be offered free immunisation.
- In Uganda, debt relief enabled 2.2 million people to gain access to water.

Fax your MP

I used your service to fax my MP a week ago, and today I received an email reply from her, which is fantastic! I never even knew who my MP was, let alone knew how to contact her directly, and even less expected to receive a reply.

Your Member of Parliament is there to represent you. So make your views known on the Iraq war; on ethnic cleansing in Sudan; on GM foods; on local gangs and school bullying; on the level of government aid being offered to tsunami victims; and on whatever concerns you. Get them to act for you and in the people's interest. Ask them to ask a Parliamentary Question. That's democracy! New technology is transforming the democratic process and will make elected representatives a lot more accountable.

Visit www.writetothem.com – the UK website that enables you to fax your elected representative. Originally intended as a way of contacting UK MPs, you can now use this service to contact Members of the European Parliament, Members of the Scottish Parliament and Welsh Assembly, and local councillors. To write to your elected representative you simply type in your UK postcode and choose which one you want to contact. Write your letter and hit the 'submit' button. You will receive an email asking you to confirm that you wish to send the fax. Click the link you are given and that's it! And it's completely free. You should get a reply within about two weeks.

Find out who your MP is and how they have performed in Parliament by going to www.theywork foryou.com and typing in your postcode.

Make your views known

Fax your MP today. If their answer is unsatisfactory, then fax them again.

Telephone their office to find out when their next 'surgery' is. Book an appointment or just turn up.

Write To Them: www.writetothem.com

They Work For You: www.theyworkforyou.com

Join your constituency mailing list: www.hearfromyourmp.com

MP watch

Find out more about what your MP is doing by joining your constituency mailing list, organised by MySociety.org project. Enter your details. When enough have signed up, the MP will be sent an email saying '20 (50 or 500) of your constituents want to hear about what you are up to'. When they reply, you will be able to join a forum to discuss what they have said.

Our beliefs

- Buddhism
- Christianity
- Confucianism
- Hinduism
- Islam
- Jainism
- Judaism
- Mormonism
- Quakerism
- Sikhism

But there are differences within religions, such as those between Catholic, Protestant and Evangelical Christianity, or between Sunni and Shiite Muslims.

Virtual Religion Index, hyperlinks to a wealth of resources on religions: virtualreligion.net/vri/

Dietary practices and beliefs of nine religions: www.faithandfood.com

Seeing is understanding

There is much common ground between religions, but it is the differences that are highlighted. Religions seem to have grown from similar impulses – the desire to understand the place of human beings in the universe, the need to comprehend the mysteries of life and death, and the wish to experience meaning and happiness in the face of suffering. The troubles between Unionists and Nationalists (Protestants and Catholics) in Northern Ireland, the continuing conflict in Israel and Palestine (Jews and Arabs), the Kashmir problem between India and Pakistan (Hindus and Muslims), and the Tamil Tiger separatist movement in Sri Lanka (the Hindu minority in a largely Buddhist country) may all be based on very real grievances, but they all demonstrate how religious differences can create divisions within communities and societies, and how this can perpetuate intolerance and lead to violence.

The world would be a better place if there were greater religious tolerance.

Promote religious tolerance

Develop a better understanding of the world's religions. Get a group of friends together. Each person should research one religion (on the internet, read the main text, and talk to people of that faith). Then go to the services of as many religions as you can and observe the different practices. First, contact the church, temple or mosque to confirm whether outsiders are welcome and to find out about dress/behaviour/protocol.

Some questions to ask yourselves:

- What are the basic religious tenets?
- How are concepts of peace and non-violence highlighted?
- Has the process confirmed or dismissed any preconceptions held?
- Does the religion promote tolerance of other religious beliefs? And does it see itself as the only true religion?
- How are women treated?
- What does it say about forgiveness?

What's the big idea

Do you bore your friends endlessly by going on about the best way to deal with the burning issue of the day? Or maybe you are something of a lateral thinker, for whom simple everyday problems have elegant and imaginative solutions. Instead of keeping your good ideas to yourself, you now have a chance to share them with the wired-world.

The Idea-a-Day website was launched in August 2000, and one original idea has been published on this site every day since then. Arrange for the idea of the day to be sent to you simply by submitting your name and email address. You also can submit your own ideas, and they will be posted on the site if they are imaginative enough. All ideas posted on the site since its inception remain on the site, and it is the intention that the site will continue for ever.

One a day

Subscribe to the Idea-a-Day website and receive an idea a day. This should set you thinking about things you could do to change the world. Then come up with your very own brilliant idea – and submit it to: www.idea-a-day.com

500 of the best ideas have been published in *The Big Idea Book*, by David Owen, founder of the Idea-a-Day website – details of this book are on the website.

Ideas from the website

- Meeting posts in city centres. There could be twelve posts set out in a big circle in a public square in the city centre. The post at due north would be 12 o'clock. Going clockwise around the circle, the posts would be 1 o'clock, 2 o'clock, etc. You could then say to a friend: 'Hey, let's meet for a drink after work, at 6 o'clock ...' You would have agreed when and where.
- Being able to vote against a candidate in an election. You would still have just one vote, but you could use this either to vote for or against a particular candidate. This would make it much easier to run a campaign against a person or a party that you don't want to see in power.
- Cordoning off places of natural beauty or which have some cultural significance. The police will use 'Do not cross this line' tape not just at a crime scene, but for an ancient manhole cover or where an IRA bomb was detonated or where David Beckham proposed to Posh Spice.
- The 'International Language of Love': a language school which is also a dating agency. You get paired up with someone for some 'intimate tete-a-tete conversation'. By talking together, you each learn the other's language.

January 12

Show that you care

- Buy a wristband and wear it with pride. Tell other people why the cause is important.
- Selling wristbands can be a good way of fundraising. Try to get a celebrity to wear yours, for publicity.
- To order wristbands, go to BAND-ITS.com at: www.mpglink.com/bands or find other suppliers on Google.

Wear a wristband

Wristbands are a way of showing that you support a particular cause. Since Lance Armstrong's 'LiveStrong' campaign for cancer survivors, which was run in association with Nike, they have replaced 'ribbons' as the must-have fashion accessory. For some wristbands, the demand has been so high, because of celebrity endorsement, that they have become virtually unobtainable. Most cost around £2. Try to buy direct from a charity rather than from a commercial supplier; then all proceeds will be going to the cause.

Keep a Child Alive, AIDS drugs for children in Africa, *red*: www.keepachildalive.org

Make Poverty History, a campaign to end global poverty, *white*: www.makepovertyhistory.org

LiveStrong with Lance Armstrong, surviving cancer, *yellow*: www.livestrong.org

Someone you know has Lupus, lupus awareness, *purple*: www.lupus.org

Orange Ukraine, solidarity with Ukraine's 'orange revolution', *orange*: orangeukraine.squarespace.com

Stand Up Speak Up, against racism in football, *one black and one white*: www.standupspeakup.com

Get in the Pink, the fight against women's cancers, *pink*: www.breastcancercare.org.uk

Beat bullying

An anti-bullying campaign, run by BBC Radio 1 and the Department for Education and Skills in 2004, produced a bright-blue wristband for young people to wear in solidarity with the campaign. They got celebrities such as footballers Wayne Rooney and Rio Ferdinand, and music acts such as Franz Ferdinand and Scissor Sisters, to support the campaign and be seen wearing the wristband. This created a huge demand, not all of which could be met. Eventually, 1 million were handed out before the campaign was closed. They were so popular that some were being traded for up to £30 on eBay.

Virtual activism

The internet brings thousands of people together for a common purpose. It enables you to contact lots of people quickly, allowing them to make an immediate response. And you don't have to spend money on printing and postage. The anti-World Trade Organization demonstration in Seattle in 1999 first awoke the world to the power of internet activism. Ideas and information had spread around the world with a click of a mouse, and people had come to Seattle in huge numbers to fight for fairer trading arrangements for the developing world.

The starting point for internet activism is to create an email list of individuals and organisations that might be interested in what you are doing.

Collect the email addresses of as many friends, colleagues and supporters as possible. Research the media, potential funders, and anyone else you would like to influence and communicate with regularly. Include a space for email addresses in all your material, so that anyone interested can let you know.

Produce a regular e-newsletter to let people know what you are doing in an electronic format.

Internet activism

Learn the skills of internet activism. Read the training materials on:

- **NetAction: www.netaction.org/training**
- **Backspace.com: www.backspace.com/action/all.php**
- **A picture gallery of Seattle 1999: www.globalarcade.org/wto/photo.html**
- **The World Trade Organization History Project: depts.washington.edu/wtohist**
- **Read Liz Highleyman's account of Seattle N30: www.black-rose.com (and see below).**

Eyewitness at Seattle

Tuesday 30 November 1999 ... dawned gray and cloudy as I made my way up Pike Street to Victor Steinbrueck Park on the Seattle waterfront. By the time I arrived at 7.00 a.m., over 1,000 demonstrators had gathered ... Soon the crowd began to march toward the Seattle Convention Center, site of the meeting of the World Trade Organization ... government representatives who set the international rules regarding trade and tariffs. WTO delegates were scheduled to attend an opening ceremony ... at the historic Paramount Theater at 8th and Pine, but protesters were determined that WTO business did not proceed as usual. As delegates arrived, demonstrators – some in sea turtle costumes and others carrying giant puppets – formed a human barrier to deny them entry.

Contributions welcome

Contribute a panel to commemorate someone you know who has died of AIDS, or to an unknown victim of AIDS – just like the Tomb of the Unknown Soldier, which provides a remembrance to all those who might otherwise be forgotten.

Contributing a panel is absolutely free, but donations are welcome. The organisers (the NAMES Project) suggest a voluntary contribution of $100 a year to process and care for each panel, and $200 to add a new panel to the Quilt.

The NAMES Project Foundation and the AIDS Memorial Quilt: www.aidsquilt.org

AIDS Memorial Quilt

In June 1987, a small group of people came together in San Francisco. Their aim was to create a memorial for those who had died of AIDS, and to promote a better understanding of the disease. This meeting led to the foundation of the AIDS Memorial Quilt. Since that day, more than 44,000 individual memorial panels have been sewn – each commemorating the life of someone who has died of AIDS and contributed by friends, lovers or family members. The Quilt is exhibited from time to time, either as a whole or just a part. All the panels contributed will eventually be put on a database and form a 'virtual quilt'.

The Quilt is a creative way of remembering a life cut short; it provides a strong visual illustration of the scale of the AIDS pandemic: it creates public awareness of HIV and AIDS; and it raises funds for the fight against AIDS.

You don't have to be an artist or a sewing expert to contribute a panel. You can use paint, needlework, iron-on transfers or appliqué – whatever technique you like. You can create a panel privately, or you might follow the tradition of 'quilting bees' by involving friends, family and colleagues.

How to design a panel

The finished, hemmed panel must be exactly 3 x 6 ft (90 x 180 cm). Add 3 in (7 cm) on each side for the hem.

- Use a panel to commemorate just one individual.
- Include the name of the person you are commemorating, and additional information such as date of birth and death, hometown, special talents, etc.
- Use medium-weight, non-stretch fabric (such as a cotton or poplin).
- Sew things on. Don't glue them – as glue will deteriorate.

If you want to include a photo or a letter, the best idea is to photocopy this onto an iron-on transfer, iron this onto a piece of cotton fabric, and then sew this onto your panel.

Uncover your hidden bias

Even though you are consciously committed to egalitarianism and strive to behave without prejudice, you might still possess strong hidden negative prejudices or stereotypes. Psychologists at Harvard, the University of Virginia and the University of Washington have created Project Implicit, and launched a series of tests on the internet – Implicit Association Tests – that aim to detect any hidden bias in people's attitudes.

The test on racial bias: the first task is to sort faces identifiable racially as either black or white. The second task is to sort words associated with positive qualities (peace, pleasure, friend) or negative qualities (violent, failure, awful). Next, participants are asked to sort words into combined categories, assigning positive words and white faces to one column, and negative words and black faces into the other. As the items flash on the screen – peace, white face, awful, black face, friend – the vast majority of people continue to have little trouble doing the sorting. The signals of bias appear in the next step, when people are asked to reverse the process: to group positive words with black faces, and negative words with white faces. Theoretically, this task should have precisely the same level of difficulty as the previous step. However, most test-takers take longer and make more errors when trying to group good qualities with blacks (and in other versions of the test, with other socially excluded groups). Over 3 million tests have been completed. Consistently, the test shows bias against stigmatised groups, whether they be Aboriginals in Australia or Turks in Germany.

In other versions of the test, people show strong preferences for young versus old. And both men and women have far more difficulty grouping women's names with words having to do with science (chemistry, biology), than with arts (drama, poetry).

Tools for tolerance

www.tolerance.org is a website for people interested in countering bigotry and promoting diversity, whether at home, at school, in the workplace or in the community. It supports anti-bias activism through its online resource bank and downloadable announcements. It gives ten ways to fight hate and provides 101 tools for tolerance.

Project Implicit: implicit.harvard.edu

A website about race, racism and life: www.britkid.org

Self-test

Take a Demonstration Test at Project Implicit to test your bias. Each test takes around ten minutes to complete. At the end, you will be given a summary of your results.

After taking the test on race, read the tolerance.org tutorial to learn more about stereotypes and prejudice and the impact of these.

Making sandals just for you

Buy a great pair of beaded sandals (either flip flops or proper sandals), made for you by ex-street kids of Kisumu. Draw an outline of your foot on a piece of paper. Send this with £30 or $50 in cash or a money order and your address to the Hart Foundation, 196 Icknield Way, Letchworth Garden City, Hertfordshire SG6 4AE, UK.

Your support will create work for them, pay for postage anywhere in the world, and provide a bit more to support James's work with street children (see below).

Find out about street children and the organisations working for them: www.streetchildren.org.uk

Kenyan street children

Jonathan and Flick Hart support schools and children in Kisumu, on the shores of Lake Victoria, Kenya. Both retired teachers, they visit Kisumu several times a year. Here is their account of what they do.

'We help an orphanage for street children that houses 45 children aged between 6 and 18. The home consists of a large dilapidated house with a concrete yard. There are several crowded bedrooms; the oldest boys sleep in a leaky garage. There is no water supply – every drop has to be paid for and collected by handcart. Food is basic, and cooked by the children on an outdoor wood stove.

Health is a big problem. A pile of rags on a bed turned out to be a child suffering from TB. Treatment for TB is free, but all other medicines are expensive. One problem is convincing people to keep taking the TB medication once they feel better. We found malaria, malnutrition, worms and all sorts of infections. The concept of keeping wounds clean is difficult to explain and achieve, particularly with no clean water supply.

We are also supporting links between schools in the UK and Kisumu. With money we have raised and donations from the UK schools, we had 140 desks made for three schools where previously children had been sitting on the earth floor to do their lessons.'

James's story

'James works with the street children. When we were introduced, we asked him where his office was. He replied, "On the street, with the children". He deals sensitively with the children, who call him "teacher". He also works to create a life for them off the streets. Some of his ex-street boys work on a market stall, making and selling sandals from recycled tyres. The sandals are made in a variety of styles, and decorated with beads and studs.'

News on the street

Street papers being sold by homeless or socially excluded people are a familiar sight in many of our cities. Vendors buy bulk copies at a 50–60 per cent discount, and then re-sell them, keeping the profit. They are given some training and identification, allocated a 'pitch' and asked to comply with a code of conduct. The organisers aim to:

- Help homeless people help themselves, by providing them with a means of earning an income and a dignified alternative to begging.
- Support their re-integration into society, through a philosophy of 'a hand up, not a handout'. Any profit made is used to support homeless people.

The *Big Issue* in London was inspired by the first street paper, *Street News* in New York. There are more than 400 vendors, who between them sell 131,000 copies of each issue. There are separate *Big Issues* for the North, the South West, Scotland and Wales. In the last ten years, the Big Issue Foundation has worked with 5,398 people, of whom 407 have gone into further education or attended a course, 281 have been re-housed, and 75 have been helped into permanent employment.

The International Network of Street Newspapers has 55 members in 28 countries, with a combined annual circulation of 26 million copies.

Read all about it

Buy a copy of your city's street paper. Do this on a regular basis, and smile when you do it. Why not engage in small talk with the vendor? When you get to know your local vendor, why not take him or her out for a coffee at your local café.

The vendor code of conduct states:

- **No begging**
- **No drinking**
- **No swearing**
- **No harassment of the public**

Big Issue website: www.bigissue.com

Download *Street Papers, a Guide to Getting Started* from the International Network of Street Papers (INSP) website: www.street-papers.com

January 17

John's story

Aged 33 and after losing his job and splitting up with his partner, John found himself homeless, friendless and jobless. He started selling the *Big Issue* to earn money, but wanted to go back to education. The Big Issue Foundation helped him enrol on a suitable course and provided a grant towards tuition fees. 'Two years ago I was living on the streets in a cardboard box. Now I'm a mature student at the University of London.' (From the Big Issue Foundation)

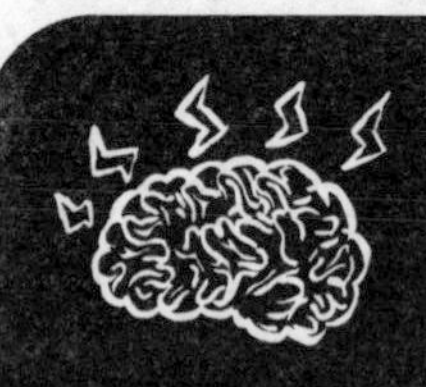

Money talks

Money matters

Explore the world of banknotes at: www.banknotes.com

Find out all about money at: en.wikipedia.org/wiki/Money

Everyone uses money. Even if you are a serious credit-card addict, you will almost certainly have some banknotes in your purse or wallet. Money speaks to the masses. It promises food in your stomach, a warm home, entertainment and enjoyment and a better tomorrow. But you can also make your money serve a different purpose from just buying you a cup of coffee and a doughnut.

You can make your money speak to the world. People pay attention to money – and to red ink. So use red ink to put messages on your money, which will be passed from person to person.

Some hard-hitting facts to inscribe on your notes:

- Over one billion people have to survive on less than a dollar a day.
- 842 million people across the world will go to bed hungry tonight.
- One in five women experience a rape or attempted rape in their lifetime.
- Guns kill 34,000 Americans every year.
- Wear a condom. Today 14,000 people will become infected with HIV/AIDS.
- Perform a random act of kindness today.
- Give this money to someone who really needs it.
- Make amends with someone – say sorry.
- Spread a little happiness. Smile at a stranger.

Give money a voice

Use your money to spread the word:

- Take all the banknotes in your wallet and write a simple, but hard-hitting, fact on each side. Don't write all over the note, or someone might not be able to use it. Write round the edges.
- Your message will be spread to everyone who gets possession of the money. Try to make it lively and interesting – so that people will want to read it. You could even direct the reader to a website.

Think long term

Ten thousand years is about as long as the history of human technology. We have fragments of pots that old. But geographically it is a blink of an eye. I cannot imagine the future, but I care about it. I know I am part of a story that starts long before I can remember and continues long beyond when anyone will remember me. I sense that I am alive at a time of important change, and I feel a responsibility to make sure that the change comes out well. I have hope for the future. Danny Hills

Progress is often measured by how quickly things happen and how cheap things become. It has been nearly 10,000 years since the end of the last Ice Age and the beginnings of civilisation. The Long Now Foundation was established in the year 01996 [*sic*]. It seeks to promote slower and better thinking, and to foster creativity within a framework of the next 10,000 years.

One of the projects of The Long Now Foundation is a clock that will tick only once a year, the century hand will advance once every 100 years, and a cuckoo will come out at each millennium. The clock will last for 10,000 years. It is being built by Danny Hills, and a prototype is exhibited at London's Science Museum.

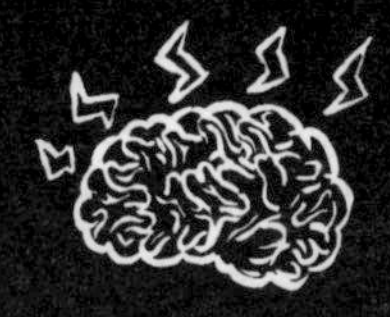

Future ideas

The World Future Society is a neutral clearing-house for ideas about the future. These ideas will help people to anticipate what may happen in the years ahead. When people can visualise a better future, then they can start to create it. The society has branches in over 100 cities.

These are some forecasts from the Society:

- **More emphasis will be placed on skills that cannot be automated, such as caring, ethics, intuition, inspiration, friendliness and imagination.**
- **With global climate change, coral reefs will see greater changes in the next 50 years than they have faced in the last half million years.**

World Future Society: www.wfs.org

Long Now Foundation: www.longnow.org

Predict the future

Make a long-term prediction about the future on the Long Now website. To do this costs $50. You can also challenge a predictor with a bet of at least $200 that their prediction will not come true – whoever wins, donates their winnings to charity. Bet at: www.longbets.org

Some predictions to bet on:

- By 2020 bioterror or bioerror will lead to 1 million casualties in a single event.
- By 2020 solar energy will be as cheap or cheaper than that of fossil fuels.
- By 2060 the total human population will be less than what it was in 2004.

Computer aid

Discover a vaccine

Over 5 million people will contract HIV/AIDS in 2006. Don't you think it's time to come up with a vaccine? Well why don't you help in the search?

Download the free Scripps program and follow some simple instructions. There are over 10,000 computers working on this project.

Download the Scripps program: fightaidsathome. scripps.edu/help.html

The United Nations Programme on AIDS: www.unaids.org

Avert: a good source of information on AIDS: www.avert.org

The most obvious way to fight HIV/AIDS is to wear a condom. But we're not all having crazy, fun sex all the time. Regardless of whether you are or not, you can be fighting HIV/AIDS. The people working at the Scripps Research Institute have put their geeky brains together and come up with an easy way for you to help in the search for an HIV/AIDS vaccine.

It takes an unimaginable amount of computer power to conduct the data searches necessary to create a new vaccine. Yet your computer often sits idle, with its power not being used, while it could be helping in this search. Scripps has devised a computer program – FightAIDS@Home – which you can download. The program puts your computer to work when you aren't using it. When your computer has completed a computation, the results are packed up and sent back to Scripps, ready for its researchers to analyse. If you need your computer for personal use, the FightAIDS@Home program automatically turns the power to the task you are doing.

AIDS around the world

According to UNAIDS, over 60 million people have been infected with HIV since the epidemic began in the 1980s. In the 45 most affected countries, it is projected that 68 million people will die prematurely as a result of AIDS between 2000 and 2020. The projected toll is greatest in Sub-Saharan Africa - 55 million more deaths are expected.

The average life expectancy in Sub-Saharan Africa is currently 47 years. Without AIDS, it would have been 62 years. Life expectancy at birth in Botswana (which, at 38.8 per cent, has the world's highest adult prevalence rate) has dropped below 40 years – a level not seen there since before 1950.

Current HIV prevalence levels only hint at the much greater lifetime probability of becoming infected. In Lesotho, for example, it is estimated that a 15-year-old in 2000 has a 74 per cent chance of becoming infected with HIV by his or her 50th birthday.

News reporting

In his book *We the Media*, Dan Gillmor, writes: 'Big media ... treated the news as a lecture. We told you what the news was. You bought it, or you didn't. ... Tomorrow's news reporting and production will be more of a conversation or a seminar. The lines will blur between producers and consumers, changing the role of both in ways we're only beginning to grasp. The communication network itself will be a medium for everyone's voice, not just the few who can afford to buy multimillion-dollar printing presses, launch satellites, or win the government's permission to squat on the public airways.'

Dan's book discusses some momentous changes that are taking place. Here are three examples:

OhMyNews – in Korea everyone can be a reporter. When launched in 2000, the website OhMyNews had 727 citizen reporters called 'guerrillas', who posted news based on their own informed perspectives, which was usually anti-establishment. Immediately, huge numbers of people wanted to report the news, and OhMyNews changed from a weekly to a daily format. By 2004, some 32,000 people had registered as citizen reporters. OhMyNewsInternational, English version: english.ohmynews.com

The Memory Hole in the USA disseminates and preserves material that is in danger of being lost, or hard to find or not widely known. For example, it used the Freedom of Information Act to get photos of dead US soldiers being brought back from Iraq in flag-draped caskets into the public domain – www.thememoryhole.org

Indymedia is a global network of independent and alternative media activists and organisations, offering grassroots coverage of important social and political issues. There is now a network of Indymedia organisations spanning the globe and providing a passionate telling of the truth – www.indymedia.org

Anyone can do it

Subscribe to Indymedia and SchNEWS for a different slant on the news.

Report the news. When you have something important to contribute, ring up a journalist; write a letter to the editor; call a phone-in show.

Download Dan Gillmor's book free on the We the Media website: wethemedia.oreilly.com

Read SchNEWS

For details of direct action events in your area – a peace festival, a human rights lecture – SchNEWS' *Party & Protest* is the activist's version of *Time Out*. See www.schnews.org.uk for news reports on subjects from animal rights to Zimbabwe via GATS and WTO. Order a free weekly email subscription, read back issues online, use the yellow pages directory, or buy a copy of the SchNEWS annual.

Quality of life

Do something

- Assess how you feel about your own quality of life. Is there any way you can improve it?
- Do something to improve the quality of life in your country. You can't do anything about your climate (heating it up by contributing to global warming doesn't count), but there may be lots of other things you can do through campaigning or direct action.
- Do something for the people of Zimbabwe or Haiti. Go to the Human Rights Watch website to find out about some of their problems: hrw.org

Quality of Life Index: www.economist.com/media/pdf/QUALITY_OF_LIFE.pdf

The Economist Intelligence Unit has devised a Quality of Life Index, which tries to measure how good a country is to live in. In 2005, 111 countries were surveyed in respect of nine different areas:

Material wellbeing: GDP per person
Health: life expectancy at birth
Political stability and security: EIU ratings
Quality of family life: divorce rate
Community life and social cohesion: rate of church attendance or trade union membership
Climate and geography: geographical latitude, to distinguish between warmer and colder climates
Job security: unemployment rate
Political freedom: index devised by Freedom House
Gender equality: ratio of male and female earnings

Ireland comes out top, because: 'it successfully combines the most desirable elements of the new (high GDP per head, low unemployment, political liberties) with the preservation of elements of the old, such as stable family and community life.' Zimbabwe comes bottom. With widespread food shortages, one of the world's highest HIV/AIDS infection rates, 200 per cent inflation, 70 per cent unemployment, a complete erosion of political freedom, life has become very tough for its citizens.

Ireland 8.3, Zimbabwe 3.8

The scores out of ten for the countries ranked top and bottom were:

Top 6 countries
1 Ireland (8.333)
2 Switzerland (8.068)
3 Norway (8.051)
4 Luxembourg (8.015)
5 Sweden (7.937)
6 Australia (7.925)

Bottom 6 countries
106 Tajikistan (4.754)
107 Tanzania (4.753)
108 Nigeria (4.505)
109 Botswana (4.313)
110 Haiti (4.090)
111 Zimbabwe (3.892)

Other rankings include USA 13, UK 29, China 60, India 73, South Africa 92 and Russia 105.

Lost in translation

Do you want to send out a message in many different languages? Maybe you need to mount some text on a website, produce multi-lingual leaflets about a campaign, or publish a manifesto setting out your ideas – all in a range of languages. If you are working in the USA, you might want to translate some practical advice into Spanish for the local Hispanic community. You could find an English speaker who is fluent in other languages to do the translation for you. But there is now another way. The Altavista Babel Fish Translation program will translate web pages or 150-word blocks of text at the click of your mouse. It will translate from English into:

- Chinese
- Dutch
- French
- German
- Greek
- Italian
- Japanese
- Korean
- Portuguese
- Spanish

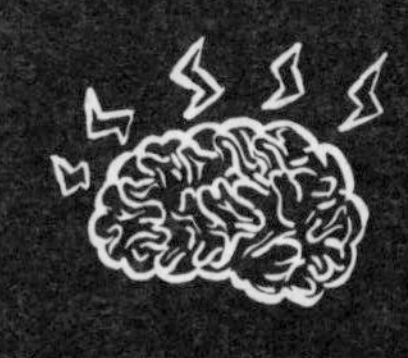

Free service

It's a free service – although you can purchase more advanced software from Altavista. You will need to load special fonts onto your computer for translating into Chinese, Japanese, Korean and Greek.

Babel Fish works best when the text you wish to translate uses the correct grammar. Slang, misspelled words, bad punctuation and complex or lengthy sentences can all cause a page to be translated incorrectly. If you want a polished translation, the computer-generated text will need to be properly edited.

Babel Fish: world.altavista.com

Give it a try

Go to the Babel Fish website at world.altavista.com and translate a leaflet or a page of your website into another language.

Allez au site Web de Poissons de Babel à world.altavista.com et traduisez un prospectus ou une page de votre site Web dans une autre langue.

Vaya al Web Site de los Pescados de Babel en world.altavista.com y traduzca un prospecto o las páginas de su web site a otra lengua.

Gehen Sie zur Babel Fisch Web site auf world.altavista.com und übersetzen Sie ein Faltblatt oder die Seiten ihrer Website in eine andere Sprache.

Next time you travel abroad, write down 20 or 25 useful phrases which you might need to use (such as 'Which restaurant sells the best pizza in town?' or 'I want to email my mother. Where is the nearest internet café?') and translate them into the languages of all the countries you will be visiting.

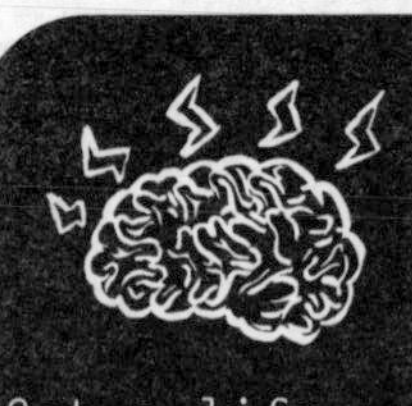

Get a life

- Test your addiction to the internet at: www.netaddiction.com/resources/internet_addiction_test.htm
- Switch off your computer on Internet-Free Day – which is the last Sunday in January. And keep it switched off for the whole day! To find out about the next Internet-Free Day, go to: www.globalideasbank.org
- Organise your very own internet-free day in your office, at your college, or in your community.

The internet switch-off

We are basically trying to persuade people for just one day to do something, do anything, that involves the real world – meeting people, walking, cycling or just getting out. By all means use email to prearrange to meet up with people – but do turn it off on the day itself. The Global Ideas Bank

The internet is wonderful in so many different ways. It has transformed the way we live. We can contact people instantly, wherever they are. We can involve large groups of people in discussions, and capture their ideas. We can plan things together, without ever needing to meet. We have access to a world of information at the click of a mouse. We can download films and music ...

But on the other hand, the internet glues us to our computer monitors, isolates us from our fellow human beings. Large offices have become eerily silent. We will now email someone a message, rather than ring them up or walk ten metres to the next office to say hello.

We need to create a balance between the world wide web and the real wide world. Turn your computer off for one day a week, leave your laptop at home, get out into the real world and get a life!
Internet-Free Day is the last Sunday in January

End of the internet?

If you type into Google 'end of internet', you get about 118 million English pages alone– www.turnofftheinternet.com is one of the first:

The End of the Internet
Congratulations! This is the last page.
Thank you for visiting the End of the Internet.
There are no more links.
You must now turn off your computer and go do something productive.
Go read a book, for Pete's sake.

Tackle Africa

Let us not equivocate. AIDS today in Africa is claiming more lives than the sum total of all wars, famines and floods, and the ravages of such deadly diseases as malaria. It is devastating families and communities. Nelson Mandela

TackleAfrica uses old-fashioned football to educate local African communities about HIV/AIDS. It organises football tours in Sub-Saharan Africa. Matches and mini-tournaments are set up in collaboration with local charities, and then form a focal point for wider HIV/AIDS awareness events. It was founded in 2002 by a group of young people from the UK who had either lived or worked in Africa, and felt driven to do something to stop the spread of a disease that was bringing increasing devastation to a continent that they knew and loved.

TackleAfrica provides information about HIV/AIDS and its impact on local communities. It explains how to reduce the risks of contracting the virus, and promotes acceptance of people who are living with HIV. It works with Christian Aid, one of the UK's leading international development agencies.

In 2005 over 40 million people were living with HIV/AIDS. Every 9 seconds one more person becomes infected. Every 13 seconds one more person dies.

Football aid

TackleAfrica needs any football-related goods you can donate. This includes: footballs, shirts, training bibs, corner flags, goal nets, balls, boots. Most young people in Sub-Saharan Africa will never have the money to buy equipment. Donated shirts and shoes are worn with pride.

Send your sports equipment to The Kit Amnesty, TackleAfrica, Meadham Cottage, Hannington, Tadley, Hampshire RG26 5UA.

Go to Africa for six months, play in a football match and help spread the word about HIV/AIDS. You'll need to raise a participation fee of £2,500. Contact: volunteer@tackleafrica.org

TackleAfrica: www.tackleafrica.org

Christian Aid: www.christianaid.org.uk/tackleafrica

The first football tour

The first TackleAfrica football tour took place in 2003–04, and visited eleven countries in West and East Africa. The team included 20 young players aged 21–30 (from students to bankers) four of whom were women. They travelled by truck and played 45 matches during the six-month tour, making 28 school visits and playing to a combined audience of 50,000. The pitch in Burkino Faso had a tree growing in the middle until villagers burned it down in time for kick off.

A better outlook

Donate your spectacles. In the UK, go into your local optician and ask if they act as a Vision Aid collecting point. Or wherever you live, pack up your old spectacles and send them to Vision Aid Overseas, Crawley RH10 2FZ, UK. Enclose contact details so that they can thank you.

Vision Aid requests that all frames should be in good condition, and have two unscratched lenses. Bifocals are of no use to them.

Vision Aid Overseas: www.vao.org.uk

Unite for Sight: www.uniteforsight.org

Old specs, new owner

A pair of spectacles could mean a much easier life for 200 million people living in the developing world. Many of these people live in rural areas where there is no eye care available. Most are too poor to afford an eye test and a pair of spectacles. So they have to live their lives in a haze of half sight.

If they can afford to, people change their spectacles as their eyesight changes. Some people buy the latest designer brands. This means that millions of pairs of perfectly usable spectacles are discarded each year – around 10 million pairs a year in Europe and North America. These could help people to see in the developing world, but only if a simple way could be found of recycling them.

So why not start a collection in your community. Ask all your friends and workmates to hand you their spectacles. Get publicity in the local media. You might be able to collect lots of pairs. Doing this could make an unbelievable impact on the lives of others.

Vision Aid Overseas

In 1985, a group of UK optometrists and dispensing opticians took a two-week holiday, ran eye clinics in a developing country and dispensed spectacles that they had collected in the UK. They now send teams of volunteers each year to countries such as Ghana, India, Kenya, Malawi, Uganda and Vietnam. Each team consists of between four and eight professionals who go for two weeks and take with them thousands of pairs of carefully sorted, recycled spectacles.

Rotary Clubs, schools and churches all help to collect unwanted spectacles. Most opticians in the UK now act as collecting points.

Prisoners in seven prisons sort and grade the spectacles.

Vision Aid Overseas does not simply distribute spectacles; it runs 'eye camps', to check people's eyesight so that the correct lenses can be prescribed. It also acts as a centre of expertise and runs training workshops to teach optical skills to local health workers.

Holocaust memorial day

First they came for the Jews, and I did not speak out – because I was not a Jew. Then they came for the communists, and I did not speak out – because I was not a communist. Then they came for the trade unionists, and I did not speak out – because I was not a trade unionist. Then they came for me – and by then there was no one left to speak out for me. Pastor Martin Niemoller, victim of Nazism

In 2005, the United Nations declared that International Holocaust Remembrance Day be celebrated annually on 27 January. Some facts about the Holocaust:

- January 1940: The first experimental gassing of Jews.
- 27 April 1940: Himmler establishes the infamous death camp at Auschwitz-Birkenau, Poland.
- 20 January 1942: The Wannsee Conference was set up to establish the framework for the 'Final Solution' to the Jewish problem.
- 27 January 1945: Soviet army liberates Auschwitz.
- 6 million Jews were murdered between 1939–1942.
- A further 7 million plus non-Jews were also exterminated, including communists, homosexuals, Romany people, and physically and mentally handicapped people; but also 3 million non-Jewish Poles, 3 million Soviet prisoners and 700,000 Serbs.

Take action

On January 27, wear a paper clip to commemorate International Holocaust Memorial Day.

Start your own paper clip collection. Aim to get 6,000 to start with.

See the Whitwell Middle School Paper Clips Project: www.marionschools.org/holocaust

Read 'Six Million Paper Clips: The Making of a Children's Holocaust Memorial', available from www.amazon.com

See the film: www.paperclipsmovie.com

International Holocaust Memorial Day: www.un.org/holocaustremembrance

Holocaust facts: http://en.wikipedia.org/wiki/Holocaust and www.holocaustforgotten.com

The paper clips memorial

Eighth-grade schoolchildren in Whitwell, Tennessee created a monument to the Holocaust. They collected six million paper clips – one for each Jew who had been killed. The children had learned that Europeans had worn paper clips on lapels to protest against the Nazis. This symbol of resistance commemorated Johann Valer, the Norwegian inventor, who was Jewish. The students purchased a cattle car which had been used to transport Holocaust victims to death camps. This was lined with Plexiglas so the paper clips would provide a visible, lasting holocaust.

Houses for sustainability

Home help

In the UK, the Peabody Housing Trust built a Zero (fossil) Energy Development (ZED) of low-cost housing in South London, and has published a handbook, *From A to ZED*, setting out basic green principles.

Find out about ZED buildings at: www.zedfactory.com

Take a virtual tour and visit a green building without leaving your home. Find out about some of the key design concepts that make it green. You can visit the Tree People Center, the Cleveland Environmental Center and other green buildings. There's no charge!

Go to: http://tours.virtuallygreen.com

After your visit, think about making your home greener.

The Tree People Center in Los Angeles is a building with lots of green features. These include:

Extensive landscaping and a 'green roof' planted with native vegetation, which reduces heat absorption.

Bicycle storage and changing facilities so as to encourage cycle use.

A 'water harvesting' storage tank and filtration to collect rainwater with which to irrigate the gardens.

Low-flow plumbing and waterless fixtures to reduce water use.

Renewable energy supply for at least half of the building's energy consumption.

On-site solar panels, producing 20 per cent of the building's electricity requirements.

Insulated floors, walls and roofs, which reduce heat loss in winter and heat gain in summer.

Recycled building materials, produced locally or from sustainable sources, wherever possible.

Low-fume-emitting paints, coatings, adhesives, carpets and sealants used for decoration, which improves indoor air quality.

Daylight illumination, where possible, to avoid having to use artificial light.

Create a greener home

You can't change the design of an existing building, but you can do things to make it greener. Using lessons from the Tree People Center, you might improve the way your house deals with:

Water: Store your roof-water run-off, or use it to recharge the ground water. Use more water-efficient home appliances. What about installing a composting toilet? Plant a garden on a flat roof, collect and use rainwater to water it.

Energy: Make sure that your roof and hot water tank are properly insulated, and use draught-excluders on windows and doors to reduce heat loss. Make sure that curtains do not obstruct daylight, and paint walls white or in a light colour to maximise natural light.

Fight the 4x4 menace

Do you live in the depths of the country and frequently have to drive off-road? If not, then you have little need to drive a 4x4 or SUV (Sport Utility Vehicle). Nevertheless, these huge cars are very popular, despite being dangerous both for pedestrians and the environment. One in four vehicles sold in the USA is an SUV. The same trend is apparent in Europe.

The 4x4 is seen as a passport to freedom and the great outdoors. TV commercials depict them climbing snow-capped mountains, or tearing through desert sand dunes. In reality, the only off-road action most of these vehicles are likely to see is when they are accidentally driven across a grass verge!

They are the most polluting form of transport. Every gallon of petrol burned emits more than 12 kg of carbon dioxide, and 4x4s have huge appetites. Some do as little as 13 mpg in town, and not much more on the open road. This makes them a major contributor to climate change. Their engines spew out twice as much carbon monoxide, hydrocarbons and nitrogen dioxide as 'greener' cars. These chemicals cause ozone and other pollutants to build up, leading to poor air quality, which in turn causes people to suffer from headaches, eye and throat irritation and, in the long term, lung damage.

Get off-roads off the road

Download fake parking tickets for some of the London boroughs and for use elsewhere in the UK. Put these under the windscreen wipers of 4x4s. The information they contain will show everything that's wrong with a 4x4.

Download your parking tickets from the Alliance Against Urban 4x4s website: www.stopurban4x4s.org.uk

The USA Friends of the Earth website dedicated to SUVs is: www.suv.org

January 29

Buy a cleaner car

When you choose your next car, do some research. There is a huge range of different models and they vary enormously in their environmental impact. Pay attention to fuel-emission ratings, miles per gallon in the city and on the highway. Cars powered by non-carbon fuels are gaining in popularity, with rising petrol prices and fears of global warming. Consider buying an electric car or a hybrid, or using a carpool. www.eta.co.uk/news/car-buyers-guide.asp will help you choose the 'greenest car' for your needs.

Sloths slowing down

Join the club

The Sloth Club was created to protect the animal's habitat and to change our way of thinking and living. It promotes the concept of doing less, living simply and finding joy in our life without consuming an endless chain of meaningless things.
Sloth Club objectives:

- **Establish a sloth sanctuary in Ecuador.**
- **Create a fund to help protect and restore the forests where sloths live.**
- **Support communities in those forests to improve the quality of their lives.**
- **Lead a cultural movement inspired by the sloth's low-energy, cyclical, symbiotic and non-violent lifestyle.**
- **Promote 'Sloth Businesses' – those that are ecologically and socially conscious.**

www.slothclub.org

What does it mean to be a sloth? Is a sloth lazy, dirty, stupid and slow? You will be surprised to find out how sloths actually live, and why we could all benefit from emulating them. An incident in the coastal jungle of Ecuador inspired the creation of the Sloth Club. A group of eco-tourists encountered a three-toed sloth, tied up in a cage in a kitchen, awaiting the time when it would be killed and eaten. Anja Light, singer/activist with the Australian Rainforest Information Centre, and several members of the Japanese Action for Mangrove Reforestation were moved by the defencelessness of the sloth.

They saw the injustice and suffering in the world reflected in the act of binding a harmless animal for three days and killing it for a tiny amount of meat: the torture of prisoners of conscience, children in poor countries starving while the rich world doesn't notice, abuse of animals, senseless warfare and degradation of the planet. The sloth is also a symbol of the forest, and the Ecuadorian forest is being destroyed at a frightening pace. It suddenly became very important for these people to find a way to release the sloth, in order to try to lessen the amount of suffering in the world, if only for a moment. So they paid about $5 for it, and released it down river.

The three-toed sloth

This harmless vegetarian lives in the rainforests of Central and South America and spends most of its life upside-down about 30 metres above the ground. It has only half the muscle weight of other animals of the same size. Although it can only move very slowly, it is light enough to climb thin branches and, therefore, is less likely to be attacked by predators. The sloth lives in harmony with the environment. Its fur even grows green-blue algae that support many species of insect. No wonder it has such a beatific smile.

Technology can help

You scratch. Then it becomes like malaria, you get a high fever. If the fly has previously bitten a rabid animal, and it bites you, you could get rabies. Ndith

This is the worst kind of insect bite. Ndith lives in Kathekani in southern Kenya. Cattle are also affected. Her neighbour lost all his cows to trypanosomiasis, a disease carried by the bloodsucking tsetse fly.

If the tsetse fly is allowed to spread unchecked, it will devastate the lives and livelihoods of many thousands more Kenyan farmers. Much of Kenya is dry, and crops fail three out of four years. Many families raise animals such as chickens, goats and cows. It is the one way they can meet their basic needs. Twenty years ago, the tsetse fly wiped out 80 per cent of the livestock in Kathekani. Across Africa, 55 million people and their livestock are under threat.

But there is a solution. Tsetse fly traps can eliminate 99 per cent of flies. Farmers work together to build 'barriers' of fly traps, which are erected in key locations. In Kathekani, ten traps kill 20,000 flies every day. One trap costs $40 to build. The trap looks enough like a cow to trick the tsetse fly. The flies are lured to the trap by the smell of cow's urine contained in a bottle. They fly towards the blue cloth on either side of the trap. The black cloth in the middle invites the flies to settle. They then fall into the trap and die. The tsetse fly trap is one of many technological solutions developed by Practical Action. Other ideas that have been turned into action include:

- Building roads in Sri Lanka.
- Harnessing local river power in Zimbabwe.
- Water harvesting, terracing, using donkey ploughs, damp-proof grain storage in Sudan.
- Solar dryers to preserve food and earthquake-proof housing in Nepal.
- Solar lanterns in Kenya.

Some simple solutions

- **Practical Action supporters have cycled the world, run the Andes and other incredible things to raise money for ITDG. Take a year or two off and do the same. www.practicalaction.org**
- **Design a machine for turning sea water into drinking water. Of all the Earth's water, 97 per cent is salt water found in oceans and seas; 2 per cent is frozen; only 1 per cent is drinking water. Your invention could transform the world.**

Small size

Intermediate Technology Development Group (now Practical Action) was set up following the 1973 publication of E. F. Schumacher's book, *Small is Beautiful: economics as if people mattered.* Small-scale water harvesting instead of big dams is a good example of his pioneering idea of small-scale solutions to problems.

February 1

Give up apathy

First steps

This is your own personal five-step action plan:

1 Admit that a life addicted to apathy is a life half lived.
2 Come to believe that the power to change things and restore society lies within every one of us.
3 Ponder the question, 'What can I do?' And while you're at it, list some answers.
4 Make a list of the things you do in your everyday life that cause stress to the planet and to society.
5 Act on your discoveries. Find alternatives, or just stop doing the things that cause harm.

Adapted from Anti-Apathy's 12 steps to personal recovery. Anti-Apathy: www.antiapathy.org

If the sheer weight of the world's problems induces apathy, and you don't know where to direct your energies (assuming you have any), there is a website just for you. It saves you the trouble of trawling the internet, providing 'one-stop shopping' for anyone wanting to make a difference.

The Anti-Apathy movement starts with the idea that we should all be engaged in doing something for a better world, and our apathy is one of the reasons why things are not changing for the better. Anti-Apathy aims to get cynical and disengaged people to connect with key issues and organisations by showing them how they can help create a more just, more democratic and more sustainable world through their awareness and action. The website provides a list of 24 key organisations. All you have to do is express an interest in five of them, and act on the information they send you.

On the Anti-Apathy website

Amnesty International human rights
The Big Issue Foundation homelessness
Centre for Alternative Technology low-energy technologies
Fair Trade Foundation fair trade
Friends of the Earth environment
Grass Roots Collective arts and media
Let's Kick Racism Out of Football anti-racism
Slow Food responsible eating and living
Soil Association organic agriculture
Space Hijackers use of public spaces
Surfers against Sewage marine and river pollution
Survival International tribal peoples around the world
World Development Movement tackling global poverty

The seven deadly sins

Things used to be so cut and dried. Medieval Christianity laid down what constituted a sin and let people know what punishment awaited them in Hell.

Sin	Punishment in Hell
• Pride or vanity	Torture on a large stone wheel.
• Envy	Immersion in freezing water.
• Gluttony or greed	Enforced consumption of rats, toads and snakes.
• Lust	Being burnt alive.
• Anger or wrath	Having arms and legs chopped off.
• Greed or avarice	Immersion in boiling oil.
• Sloth or idleness	Thrown into a snake pit.

Mahatma Gandhi drew up a different list of deadly sins that he felt were appropriate for the modern world. These are more complex, and well worth pondering:

- Wealth without work
- Pleasure without conscience
- Science without humanity
- Knowledge without character
- Politics without principle
- Commerce without morality
- Worship without sacrifice

Clear your conscience

Biblical teaching also provides us with the seven heavenly virtues:

- **Faith**
- **Hope**
- **Charity**
- **Courage**
- **Justice**
- **Temperance**
- **Prudence**

The medieval Church also stipulated The Seven Works of Mercy:

- **Feed the hungry**
- **Give drink to the thirsty**
- **Give shelter to strangers**
- **Clothe the naked**
- **Visit the sick**
- **Minister to prisoners**
- **Bury the dead**

For more on the sins and virtues, go to: www.deadlysins.com

Have mercy

- Try to commit one less sin than you would otherwise have done. And be grateful for the punishment you won't have to suffer!
- Do one work of mercy today. Visit someone who needs company, cook a meal for someone who'd welcome it, or take some old clothes to a charity shop. You'll end up with some benefit yourself – even if it is just emptier cupboards.

February 3

Airports for all

Bring Wi-Fi to your locality

Get connected to the internet by setting up your own Wi-Fi connection.

- **Join with your neighbours to set up a wireless base station that all of you can use. Share the costs.**
- **Use the money you save to do something to bridge the digital divide.**
- **Subscribe to www.bytesforall.org – an online magazine on IT and development.**

Find out more about the infothela bicycle rickshaw at: www.iitk.ac.in/MLAsia/infothela.htm

The Nepal Wireless Networking Project: nepal wireless.net

Wi-Fi (wireless internet) hotspots are springing up in public spaces all over the developed world, giving us internet access wherever we go. But the people who stand to benefit most from the Wi-Fi revolution are those in the developing world, where roads and telephones are basic, rare, or nonexistent.

Wi-Fi comes brightly painted. A bicycle rickshaw, decorated like a Hindu temple carriage, but carrying a computer with a Wi-Fi connection, travels round villages in Uttar Pradesh, India. The driver, a computer instructor, gives classes to young and old, providing villagers with the skills to run their own webcam, in turn enabling them to participate in online learning. The rickshaw can also carry medical diagnostic equipment.

Wi-Fi helps isolated communities stay in contact. Yak farmers in remotest Nepal are using a Wi-Fi connection to stay in touch with families, get help with health problems, and trade online. The project was started by teacher Mahabir Pun; he'd been given some computers for his school, but with no telephone link couldn't get on line. He adopted a wireless solution. Signals are sent from a server 30 miles away, to a solar-powered relay station on a tree up the mountainside. Via another relay station the signal is then distributed to five villages.

The MagicBike

The MagicBike marries internet connectivity and two wheels. The MagicBike was developed by Yury Gitman in New York. It is a mobile Wi-Fi hotspot that gives free internet connectivity wherever the bicycle is ridden or parked. It is ideal for art and culture events, emergency access, public demonstrations, and for the use of communities who are at the struggling end of the digital divide. For more information: http://yuryg.com/yury

Mind the Gap

Keeping costs down and profits up is the name of the game for fashion and sport retailers. One way of achieving this is to use sweatshop workers to produce their goods. Sweatshops range in size from hi-tech factories with 10,000 workers to individuals working from home. What they have in common is that the workers fulfil long hours for low wages, often in unhealthy and unsafe conditions.

Over 23.6 million people work in sweatshops, in 160 countries around the world. Many of them are young women and teenagers, producing cheap clothing for Western consumers. About 80 per cent work in conditions that violate local and international laws. Some firms have pledged to clean up their act, but in reality the situation is getting worse as poor countries compete for low wage jobs. With complex production systems, involving thousands of suppliers, work is often subcontracted to sweatshops, which remain 'off the books', hidden from view.

Now is the time to demand that retailers eliminate the sweatshop system. They control the industry, and they can end it. But we consumers may have to forgo the pleasure of purchasing dirt-cheap clothes.

No sweat

Next time you shop, ask the store the following:

- **Do you have a list of the factories that make your products, with information on wages and working conditions?**
- **Does your store guarantee that the workers who made this product were paid a living wage?**
- **Does your store have a code of conduct on human rights, forbidding child labour and unsafe conditions in factories that make your products?**

No Sweat, the UK anti-sweatshop campaign: www.nosweat.org.uk

Behind the Label, a US union-sponsored campaign: www.behindthelabel.org

PeopleTree Fairtrade clothing now sold by Top Shop: www.ptree.co.uk

February 4

Look behind the label

In 2003 David Beckham 'earned' £15.5 million by endorsing companies like Adidas. Indonesian sweatshop workers producing for Adidas earn the equivalent of £400 a year.

Workers in Tower Hamlets, London, produced jackets for Top Shop in hot and dangerous working conditions, for as little as £3.70 an hour. Philip Green, owner of Top Shop denied knowledge of this transgression of his company's code of conduct.

Women sewing \$17.99 Disney shirts in Bangladesh are paid just 5 cents for each shirt they sew, while Disney boss Michael Eisner makes about \$63,000 per hour.

Loos for schools

Give a toilet

If everybody with a toilet helped get one for someone without, the problem would be solved. Development agencies are working on sanitation. Find a scheme you like, and start raising money for it. According to WaterAid:

- **£8 pays for enough cement to produce four latrine slabs in Malawi.**
- **£15 buys an ecological sanitation latrine in Mozambique.**
- **£350 pays for a school sanitation block for 150 boys and girls in India.**

At your workplace provide collecting boxes in the men's and women's toilet, with a poster inviting people to drop a coin in every time they use the toilet.

WaterAid: www.wateraid.org

IRC International Water and Sanitation Centre: www.irc.nl

Most of us take a flushing toilet for granted. Yet more than half the people in the world have no access to any kind of toilet at all, let alone one we would consider acceptable. It is important to prevent other people, animals, and in particular insects from coming into contact with human waste for that is how many diseases are spread. Diarrhoea kills over 2 million children a year. Many of these deaths could be prevented by proper sanitation.

Lack of sanitation is also a gender issue. Boys and men find it much easier, and less embarrassing, to urinate and even defecate in public. Women dare not be caught relieving themselves. They either have to get up before dawn, or wait until nightfall, which can be bad for their health, as well as being uncomfortable.

Many schools in the developing world have no toilets at all – even large secondary schools with several thousand pupils. This is unpleasant for all concerned, but especially difficult for teenage girls. Many agencies recognise that latrines in schools are key to the education of girls. And that well-educated young women are, in turn, key to the social and economic development of some of the world's poorest nations. So, the answer to many of the world's problems is more toilets in schools ...

Keeping it simple

The simplest pit latrine is a hole in the ground, with a cover to prevent insects from entering, some having ventilation pipes to take away odour and insects.

A more luxurious version is a pour-flush latrine, which has a u-bend kept continually full of water to create a seal. Each user takes water in with them to pour down the latrine.

These simple devices have to be properly managed, and resited when they become full.

Hole-in-the-wall education

Mere curiosity will lead groups of children to explore, and this will result in them learning.

Dr Sugata Mitra of NIIT – a leading computer training and software company in India – came up with the idea of Minimally Invasive Education (MIE). The NIIT office was located next to a slum, where none of the children had access to computers, nor were particularly familiar with the English language. A hole was made in the wall of the office, and a computer was installed there with a monitor and a mouse, accessible from the street through this 'hole-in-the-wall'.

Within three months, the children had achieved a certain level of computer skills without any instruction at all. They were able to browse the internet, download songs, go to cartoon sites, work on MS Paint. They even invented their own vocabulary to define terms on the computer, for example, *sui* (needle) for the cursor, *channels* for websites and *damru* (Shiva's drum) for the hourglass (busy) symbol. By the fourth month, the children were able to accomplish tasks such as creating folders, cutting and pasting, creating shortcuts, moving/resizing windows and using MS Word to create short messages, which they were able to do without using a keyboard.

Kiosk of learning

Ten more MIE kiosks have been set up in towns and cities across India, and 100 are planned. When the idea of removing the original kiosk was discussed, parents and children strongly opposed this. The kiosk is still there, and approximately 80 children use it daily.

Read about the Hole-In-The-Wall project at www.hole-in-the-wall.com

Helping develop MIE

- Find out as much as you can about the Hole-In-The-Wall project. Write a simple manual about it.
- Bring the idea to the attention of organisations working in education and urban issues – in your own country as well as in the developing world.
- And next time you travel, try to find an organisation working in a slum and discuss with them how they might set up a Hole-In-The-Wall project in their community (with your support?).

Fight corruption

Transparency International produces Toolkits for fighting corruption (downloadable free from their website), country surveys and an annual corruption report: www.transparency.org

Find out about corruption in your own country. Find out about corruption worldwide. Do something about it.

Transparency International: CORIS, Corruption Online Research and Information System: www.corisweb.org

Get Banana Republic from: www.benco-boardgames.com/bananarepublic game.htm

Run a banana republic

General Sani Abacha, military dictator of Nigeria from 1993 until his death in 1995, is estimated to have stolen between $2–5 billion of his country's wealth – 10 per cent of Nigeria's total oil revenues.

Corruption is a fact of life in many countries, leaders stealing natural resources and taking bribes from companies, with dire consequences:

- It traps millions of people in poverty and misery.
- It undermines democracy and the rule of law.
- It distorts national and international trade.
- It jeopardises good governance and business ethics.
- It hinders social and economic development.
- It threatens over-exploitation of natural resources.
- It breeds social, economic and political crisis.

Transparency International is fighting for a world free of corruption. It compiles a Corruption Perceptions Index.

In 2005, the 12 most corrupt countries in the world were Angola, Bangladesh, Chad, Equatorial Guinea, Haiti, Ivory Coast, Myanmar (Burma), Nigeria, Somalia, Sudan, Tajikistan, Turkmenistan.

Play at being a dictator

You will need 2–5 other people to play Banana Republic. Your goal is to become President-for-Life.

You are Jomo Amin, rebel leader of the Southern Swamp. You have 40 soldiers, 30 rifles, 8,000 voters and 10,000 dollars.

Question: A famine is sweeping the province of the ruling President. Relief agencies want to transport aid through your province. What will you do?

1 Hijack the supply trucks and distribute the food amongst your own voters?

2 Declare a cease-fire to allow the supplies to reach the people who need them?

3 Refuse to allow the supplies to move through your territory in the hope that this will weaken the President?

If you understand the issues, you will be better equipped to fight corruption.

Name a species

The framework for naming plants and animals is based on the 250-year-old Linnaean binomial system, which gives a genus name to the larger group, and a species name to the members within it.

While an ordinary person uses a common name like 'tent caterpillar' to identify an insect eating tree leaves, entomologists and botanists are much more specific. The 'forest tent caterpillar' (*Malacosoma disstria*) eats a variety of trees including quaking aspen (*Populus tremuloides*) and red maple (*Acer rubrum*). The 'eastern tent caterpillar' (*Malacosoma americanum*) feeds primarily on wild black cherry (*Prunus serotina*).

New mammal discoveries are rare, but occur occasionally. Canadian gaming site GoldenPalace.com paid $650,000 at auction for the right to name a monkey – *callicebus audeipalatii* – purely as a publicity stunt.

There is much more scope for naming insects and plants, as these comprise 80 per cent of all living things. There are possibly 10 million invertebrates and 125,000 plant forms still to be scientifically described.

The name game

Discover a new comet or a new species, and have it named after you. Or just pay to have a rose named after you.

International Commission on Zoological Nomenclature publishes a code: www.iczn.org

International Association for Plant Taxonomy: www.botanik.univie.ac.at/iapt/index_layer.php

Name-your-own-rose: www.name-your-own-rose.com

Central Bureau for Astronomical Telegrams, guidelines for naming comets: http://cfa-www.harvard.edu/icq/cometnames.html

Information on comet-naming: www.ss.astro.umd.edu/IAU/csbn/cnames.shtmlne

The George W. Bush Slime-Mold Beetle

Entomologists Quentin Wheeler and Kelly Miller had 65 new species of slime-mold beetle to name. They started with descriptive names, then their wives, then pop characters such as Darth Vader (who resembles a beetle) ... and then political heroes. Wheeler is a fan of President George W. Bush, so he named beetles for Bush, Cheney, and Rumsfeld. He got a thank-you call from Bush himself. 'He seemed to understand that the honor was in having a whole new life-form named after you, not necessarily what its eating preferences are.'

February 9

Donate your organs

Register now

In the UK in the year to 31 March 2005:

- **2,242 organ transplants were carried out as a result of the generosity of 752 organ donors following their death.**
- **A further 2,375 people had their sight restored through a cornea transplant.**
- **More than 1 million people added their names to the National Organ Donor Register.**
- **Organs that can be donated include: heart, lungs, kidneys, pancreas, liver, small bowel**

Register online as an organ donor at: www.uktransplant.org.uk

Transplants save lives – but there is a desperate need for more organs. More than 5,500 people in the UK are waiting for an organ, and around 400 people die each year while waiting for a transplant.

Transplants depend entirely on the generosity of donors and their families. You can donate your organs – but only if you have expressed a wish in writing (or orally in front of two witnesses), or if the person in possession of your body at the time of your death is willing to donate your organs and has no reason to believe you would have wished otherwise. The law differs from country to country, but there are two basic models: 'Opt-in' (the UK model), whereby individuals are asked to register their consent, or 'Opt-out', which assumes that individuals consent unless they register an objection.

Corneas can be transplanted to restore the sight of a person who has a severe eye disease or injury.

Bone and tendons are used for reconstruction after an injury or in joint replacement surgery. A bone transplant can prevent limb amputation in bone cancer patients. Tendons can restore mobility.

Heart valves help children born with heart defects and adults with diseased or damaged valves.

Skin grafts are used as protective dressings to help save the lives of people with severe burns.

It costs nothing

- Make known your wish to be an organ donor. Tell your partner, your family and your friends. Tell your doctor.
- Join the NHS Organ Donor Register and carry an Organ Donor Card. This will alert those who are dealing with you in an emergency situation.
- Get nine of your friends and family to register too. This is a gift of life that costs you nothing, but will help to tackle an international shortage of donors.

Collect your small change

Loose change in your pocket really does 'burn a hole' – or at least wears away at your pocket linings. And bulky purses full of change only add to the weight most of us end up lugging around with us. The only thing to do is offload it. Empty your pockets or your purse each night and bung it in a jar, a piggy bank, under your mattress, or wherever takes your fancy.

You'll be amazed at how quickly your spare change mounts up. And you probably won't even miss it! At the end of the year – or whenever the container gets full – you will then have the pleasure of deciding which project to donate the money to. You might decide to give it to a project near to home, or to respond to one of the many charitable appeals in the media. Even small sums of money can make a huge difference.

Give online

Here are some of the good online giving websites.

Global Giving: for high impact social and economic development projects around the world: www.globalgiving.com

Give India: lots of different types of project, and many give you several options for giving. Surf the site, and you might end up by building a well, sponsoring a child's education, helping provide eye operations: www.giveindia.org

Just Giving: an Anglo-US website with lots of options for giving both at home and abroad: www.justgiving.com

February 10

Donate a fortune

What a difference your small change can make! There are all sorts of interesting things you can donate to. Put your money to work changing the world. You could give:

- £5 to send four carefully selected books to Africa: www.bookaid.org
- £17 for an adult cataract operation: www.sightsavers.org
- £200 for an 'elephant pump': www.pumpaid.org

Or you could be more ambitious and choose a longer-term project on the Global Giving website. Here are two examples in El Salvador:

- Enable one farming family to buy the land that they are working. Cost $7,535
- Save the El Imposible rainforest, helping over 50 volunteers working with SalvaNATURA to ensure that the trees don't get cut down. Cost $10,000.

These are suggestions just to illustrate the good that you could be doing with your money. Make a big change with your small change!

Top tools

The tools most requested are for:

- **woodworking**
- **blacksmithing**
- **building and plumbing**
- **shoemaking and leather working**
- **car and bicycle repairing**
- **metal working and tin smithing**

Shipping costs are the same for good tools or bad tools, so wherever possible only the best are sent.

Tools for Self Reliance: www.tfsr.org

Tools in the right hands

My African people have great skills, initiative and energy. They work so hard to develop their communities and their continent, against such heavy odds. But you cannot work with bare hands.
Archbishop Desmond Tutu speaking to the BBC about Tools for Self Reliance

Giving a tool enables people to make a living for themselves and their family – it is the same principle as teaching a hungry person how to fish, rather than just handing out fish. In countries such as Tanzania and Ghana, it can be incredibly difficult and far too expensive for people to buy the tools they need to make a living. This is tough for the people involved. But there's an imaginative solution.

Tools for Self Reliance (TFSR) collects and sends over half a million pounds' worth of high-quality tools every year to six countries in Africa. The tools they send are used by skilled craftspeople to earn a living. TSFR also trains people how to use and take care of their tools. The organisation has over one hundred collection points across the UK. You can join a local TFSR group, or just collect some tools, which TFSR will ship to people in some of the poorest parts of Africa.

A tool collection drive

Organise a collection drive amongst your friends and family:

- Contact Tools for Self Reliance. They will supply you with a list of needed tools as well as a nearby collection point.
- Contact your friends, family, and local businesses. Tell them what you are doing and what you need. Ask them to donate tools.
- Take all the tools to the drop-off location.

Organise a FlashMob

FlashMobs are designed to amuse and to bemuse. A FalshMob seems to be a spontaneous gathering, but has actually been organised in secret by email or text message. It requires meticulous timing if it is to be effective. Large groups of people converge at a public (or semi-public) place for a brief period of time. The mob is formed, and then just as quickly the mob disperses again. At a pre-set time, all members depart in different directions.

The FlashMob phenomenon started in New York City in 2003. The craze quickly spread across America and migrated to Asia and Europe. Germany is now the FlashMob centre of the world. There are groups registered in 21 cities and FlashMobs are staged every night of the week.

What's the point?

A FlashMob is a seemingly pointless activity, but it doesn't have to be so. A FlashMob will be talked about by those who participated and also by those who hear about it. So it could be a creative way of getting across an important message – even if only subliminally.

FlashMobs in the UK and around the world: www.flashmob.co.uk

A capital idea

London's first FlashMob took place at precisely 6.30pm on August 7, 2003. Sofas UK in central London was besieged by 250 people speaking English without using the letter 'o'. Emails had been sent to people who had signed on to the LondonMob website, with instructions to meet in one of three pubs at exactly 6.17pm, when more information would be given. When the mob arrived at Sofas UK they found that the Manager had closed early to go for a drink – it was a hot day! But he was persuaded to open up, the mob congratulating him on the quality of the furniture before departing.

On another occasion, 200 people with umbrellas sang in the sunshine to the accompaniment of their mobile phones in the courtyard fountains of Somerset House, London's former public record office. The mob arrived at precisely 6.25pm from pubs around the West End. Participants were asked to text a mate en route to the venue with the message 'call me at 6:30' in order to provide a ringing accompaniment to the FlashMob's choral efforts. Mobsters were also asked to click their fingers every time they heard or spoke the letter 'Y' and to compliment strangers as they departed from the mob.

Press the green switch

You can switch to green electricity online. Check out www.ecotricity.com, which sells electricity direct to the end user. You can visit its Swaffham wind turbine in Suffolk. It has a viewing platform 60 metres high up a 300-step spiral staircase.

Most importantly, try to reduce your electricity consumption in every way possible.

Friends of the Earth, campaigning on green energy: www.foe.co.uk – click on 'climate' and then 'green energy'.

Information on green electricity from Green Electricity Marketplace: www.greenelectricity.org/domestic.html

Switch your supplier?

About 30 per cent of CO_2 emissions are produced by the burning of fossil fuels to generate electricity. Green electricity (which is electricity produced from renewable sources such as wind or wave power) produces no CO_2 at all. How does this work? Electricity generators in the UK are required by law to generate 3 per cent of their electricity (rising to 15 per cent by 2015) from green (renewable) sources. Some other countries have similar requirements. The generating companies obtain a certificate showing that they have produced a certain quantity of green electricity. But if they produce more than their quota, they are allowed to sell certificates for the surplus to other electricity companies – which then use these rather than generating their own green electricity.

Demand and supply. The best way of encouraging the generating companies to produce more green electricity is for consumers to demand more of it, and to purchase it from a supplier that is generating electricity above its quota and is not selling all its surplus certificates.

Electricity sources

Bright green Wind turbines, solar-electric, solar heating, hydro-electric and wave power all use natural sources of energy, producing no carbon emissions.

Pale green Biomass takes plant material and burns it. Landfill sites and sewage produce methane, which can then be burned. Carbon taken from the atmosphere is returned to it – which is better than ...

Conventional Burning oil, coal and gas. Burning non-renewable fossil fuel is the major factor in increasing carbon in the atmosphere.

Nuclear No carbon is produced, but disposal of the waste is a problem.

Sign up for a new language

Sign is the primary means of communication for many profoundly deaf people. It is in effect their first language. Sign uses hand gestures that are interpreted visually. Each word has its own gesture. There are also signs for each letter of the alphabet. There are two different versions of sign: British Sign Language (BSL) and American Sign Language (ASL). And, just as with spoken language, there are colloquialisms and slang.

Social inclusion is one of the dominant ideas of our age – finding ways of including people whatever their difficulties or disabilities. For example, enabling people with learning difficulties to attend regular schools, making public buildings accessible for wheelchairs, and so on. If you meet a profoundly deaf person, find out how they prefer to communicate. Learning to sign will show your commitment to a just, tolerant and inclusive society.

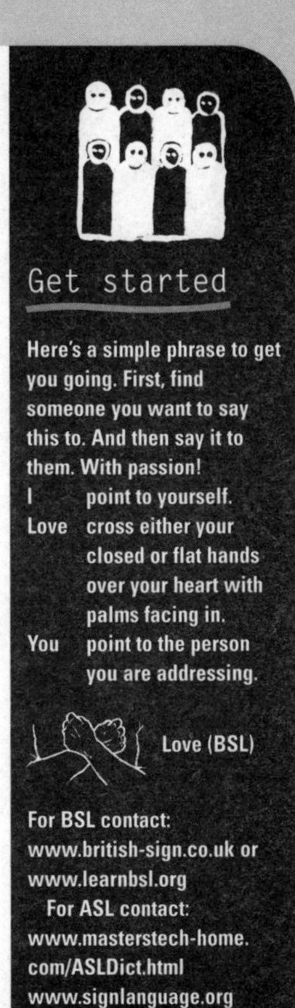

Get started

Here's a simple phrase to get you going. First, find someone you want to say this to. And then say it to them. With passion!

I point to yourself.
Love cross either your closed or flat hands over your heart with palms facing in.
You point to the person you are addressing.

Love (BSL)

For BSL contact: www.british-sign.co.uk or www.learnbsl.org

For ASL contact: www.masterstech-home.com/ASLDict.html www.signlanguage.org

Speak to deaf people

It isn't hard – many words are based on gestures which reflect the essence of the word. For example:

How are you? Open your hands and touch your chest with them, then move them outwards, making them into fists with raised thumbs.

Hungry With a clenched fist draw a circle on your stomach. Exactly the same sign actions are used to indicate the country, Hungary.

Thank you With straight fingers put your hand to your chin and gently bring it forward, once or twice.

February 15

Knitting cast off

Purl for peace

If you've never knitted, now's the time to learn.

- **Order some Peace Fleece wool and make a woolly jumper.**
- **Or use the yarn to try out some of the wackier ideas on the Cast Off website. They include: a dishcloth, shoe-laces, a first aid kit, a blindfold, a deluxe lipstick, an exfoliating sponge cover, a knitted willy, and even a knitted hand-grenade that doubles as a purse.**

Peace Fleece: www.peacefleece.com

Cast Off: www.castoff.info/shop.asp

Peace Fleece seeks to find a common ground across political and religious divides. It was started by Peter Hagerty and Marty Tracy in 1985 when they bought wool from the Soviet Union in the hope that through trade they could help defuse the threat of nuclear war. Since then they have created links with shepherds in Russia, Kyrgyzia, Israel and Palestine, Montana, Ohio, Texas and Maine, developing mutual understanding and economic interdependence.

Combining wools from around the world into one yarn symbolises peace. In response to the Iraq war, Peace Fleece came up with 'Baghdad Blue', a vibrant new Peace Fleece colour as bright as the desert sky. All profits from the sale of Baghdad Blue are donated to Neve Shalom/Wahat al Salaam, an international community in Israel, founded by a Dominican monk, Father Bruno Hussar.

Knitting can itself be a political act, about self-sufficiency and designing-it-yourself, as an alternative to responding to the whims of the fashion industry and buying garments made in sweatshops. Boys who knit challenge gender stereotypes. So believes Cast Off, a guerrilla knitting group launched in the UK in 2000 by designer Rachael Matthews and artist Amy Plant.

School for peace

In Neve Shalom peace village, Jews, Christians and Muslims live in peace, each practising their own faith while respecting others. It's the setting for a school for peace. The inspiration is the biblical quotation: 'Nation shall not lift up sword against nation, neither shall they learn war any more'. Peace is an art. It doesn't happen spontaneously; peace-making has to be learnt. You can go to Neve Shalom/Wahat al Salaam as a volunteer. For more information about the village and the peace school, go to www.nswas.com

The one-straw revolution

My method of 'do-nothing' farming is based on four major principles:
1 No cultivation (that is, no ploughing and no hoeing)
2 No fertiliser
3 No weeding
4 No pesticides
I will admit that I have had my share of failures during the forty years that I have been at it. But because I was headed basically in the right direction, I now have yields that are at least equal to or better than those of crops grown scientifically in every respect. And most importantly my method succeeds at only a tiny fraction of the labor and costs of scientific farming, and my goal is to bring this down to zero.

At no point in the process of cultivation or in my crops is there any element that generates pollution, in addition to which my soil remains eternally fertile ... and I guarantee that anyone can farm this way. Masanobu Fukuoka, author of *The One-Straw Revolution*

Masanobu Fukuoka is a Japanese farmer who devised a revolutionary method of farming. Ploughing the land, large-scale monoculture, and chemical fertilisers and pesticides were all discarded. To everybody's surprise, year by year his yields rose, eventually exceeding those obtained using modern farming techniques. Disciples all over the world continue to experiment with Fukuoka's methods of natural farming. These challenge the whole basis of the world's agricultural policies. Fukuoka believes they can also be used to transform the arid lands of Africa. *The One-Straw Revolution* is available from: www.amazon.co.uk .

Nature's way

There is more information on Fukuoka and natural farming at: www.seedballs.com/2seedpa.html

Book in here

Other books that have revolutionised thinking:
Gaia by James Lovelock. Natural self-regulation will save the planet in the long term.
Small is Beautiful by E F Schumacher, the inspiration for appropriate technology.
Pedagogy of the Oppressed by Paolo Friere, on the role of education in the fight for social justice.
Rules for Radicals by Saul Alinsky, practical ideas for effective organising.
Limits to Medicine and **De-schooling Society** both by Ivan Illich, two books that show the need for radical ideas in the two public services that most affect us.

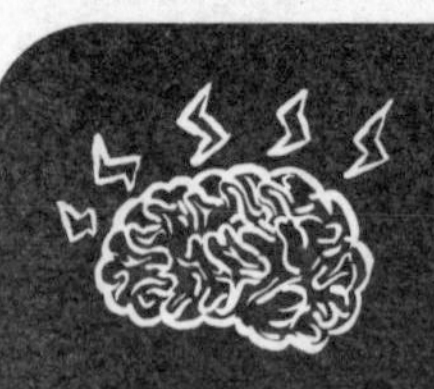

Join up

Join a Meetup near you that brings a group together around a topic that interests you. If there isn't one, start your own group.

Or if you care about the environment and like drinking, why not join a Green Drinks group to meet, talk and do things together?

Meetup: www.meetup.com

Green Drinks: www.greendrinks.org

Meeting up is fun

Meetup.com helps people find others who share their interest or cause. This can be a starting point for creating or joining a lasting and influential local community group. Meetups are usually informal, held monthly, open to anyone and held in public places such as cafès and parks, although some take place in offices or private houses. Some Meetups are based on activities like knitting or speaking a foreign language; others focus on a cause – such as planning a women's rights march or getting a political candidate elected; others are self-help groups at which people can swap information and stories.

There are literally thousands of local Meetup Groups all over the world. There are Meetups for: Spanish speakers, Elvis fans, Atkins dieters, Red Sox supporters, Alternative-energy bores, Wine lovers, Quit-smoking optimists, Poker-playing nuts, Quilting sororities, Pekinese dog walkers, Harry Potter aficionados, Pregnant women, Bloggers with attitude, Environment savers ... the list is endless.

Over 1 million people worldwide have joined local Meetup Groups, which have brought communities together, shaken up politics, given people a voice ... and provided a lot of fun. United we Meetup!

The right way

The Meetup Bill of Rights for members:

- The right to meet: free, local monthly Meetups should be open to all.
- The right to privacy: email addresses will not be shared without permission.
- The right not to get annoying ads: no pop-up ads, no spam.
- The right to meet about almost anything: Meetup.com is non-partisan and non-denominational. There should be access to a Meetup Group about anything (except hate and obscenity).
- The right to choose where to meet: Meetups can take place anywhere. If it is a place of business, buy a drink to thank your host location!

Stop eating prawns

Prawns are produced in huge quantities in developing countries. More than 4 million tonnes are shipped annually for consumption by the rich world, causing major environmental problems in the poor world.

Prawn fishing is a major threat to marine life and ecosystems. 75 per cent of prawns are fished, mostly by boats dragging huge nets over estuaries, bays and continental shelves, scooping up whatever lies in their path. About 10 kg of dead fish, turtles and other species are discarded for every kilo of prawns caught. Prawn fishing represents 33 per cent of the world's discarded catch, but yields less than 2 per cent of seafood.

Nor is prawn farming the answer. When fishponds are built, chemicals, fertiliser and salt water leach into the soil, degrading the land and making it unusable for agriculture. The average prawn farm provides 15 jobs on the farm and 50 for security around the farm, while displacing up to 50,000 people through loss of traditional fishing and agriculture. Nearly 25 per cent of the world's mangrove forests have been destroyed over the past 20 years, most making way for prawn farms. Each kilo of farmed prawn requires 2 to 4 kg of fish protein, mainly derived from captured wild fish.

Prawn pledge

Pledge to stop eating prawns. For every 1,000 people who stop eating prawns, this will save more than 5.4 tonnes of marine life per year.

Grassroots environmental groups are working with international activists to develop more ecologically sound prawn farming. In Sri Lanka for example, the Small Fishers Federation and the Mangrove Action Project (www.earthisland.org/map/) work with prawn farmers to curb mangrove destruction and protect fish habitat.

Find out more from the WorldWatch Institute: www.worldwatch.org/pubs/goodstuff/shrimp

The Ecuador experience

Ecuador's prawn industry has taken up 500,000 acres of former mangrove forests, salt flats and agriculture land over the past thirty years.

Corrupt officials and prawn producers rob coastal people of their fishing and food-gathering lands, preventing mangrove forestry activities such as charcoal-making and wood production.

Coastal villagers wanted to evict illegal producers and reforest the mangrove areas around Muisne. Supported by Greenpeace and Fundecol, and using only shovels, pieces of wood and bare hands, they cut a breach in an illegal prawn pond, drained the water and planted mangrove seedlings to restore what had been destroyed.

February 19

Send an email to Bill Gates

Dear Bill ...

Email Bill Gates and tell him you are fed up with porno emails, Nigerian fund-transfer scams and ads for Viagra, and expect Microsoft to find a workable solution.

The Microsoft website does have tips for hiding your address from spammers, avoiding phishing and other email scams, blocking junk mail, and reporting spammers to the authorities: www.microsoft.com

Email Bill at: billg@microsoft.com or askbill@microsoft.com

The unofficial Bill Gates website: www.zpub.com/un/bill

Microsoft Corporation: www.microsoft.com

Bill Gates receives about four million emails a day. Much of this is spam – unwanted, unsolicited mail. This is being sent to him because of his wealth, or because some people believe he exercises too much control on the virtual world, or simply because he is Bill Gates III.

All this unwanted email should focus his mind on the fact that spam is a major internet problem – as well as a time-consuming nuisance. Up to 80 per cent of all email traffic is spam, much of it trying to sell pornography or aids to increase your sexual performance, or some sort of scam that aims to part greedy fools from their money.

As the biggest software company in the world, Microsoft is in a position to take action – to protect all of us from receiving spam and to stop it being sent. Bill Gates has a department that sifts through the mountain of email he gets each day. So he won't actually read what you send him. But if his mail mountain continues to rise, perhaps this could spur him into action.

Foundation work

Today's problems are solvable. While the world around us fuels our sense of urgency, it also fuels our optimism. We believe that by increasing equity and opportunity, the world will become a better place for generations to come ... As the years ahead bring more advances in health and learning, we share the global responsibility to ensure that they reach the people who need them most.
Bill Gates and Melinda French Gates

Bill and Melinda put their money where their mouth is. Their Foundation has an endowment of $27 billion and funds initiatives in global health, libraries and US schools – and community initiatives in the USA's Pacific North West, where Microsoft is located. Bill is not only the richest person on the planet, but also the most philanthropic.
The Bill and Melinda Gates Foundation: www.gatesfoundation.org

Non-violent direct action

Non-violent direct action is often misrepresented as being too 'radical', too 'political', or even 'illegal'.

It is certainly radical, often political and it may even challenge the law, but has a long tradition of success: The Boston Tea Party, when tea was dumped into the sea, heralded American independence. Gandhi's Salt Marches highlighted the injustice of British rule in India and mobilised popular support for the Quit India campaign. And Gandhi successfully built non-violent direct action into a political philosophy. Peter Hain (subsequently a British cabinet minister) led the Anti-Apartheid campaign to stop South African sportsmen touring the UK by digging up rugby pitches. The US Civil Rights Movement involved sit-ins and boycotts to end segregation. Friends of the Earth in the UK started by returning non-returnable bottles to Schweppes' head office. Stunts such as this are now a common campaigning technique.

The environmental movement has incorporated components of direct action in its campaigns against nuclear power, to save ancient forests, to achieve a global ban on high-seas drift-net fishing and to end dumping on the high seas. Ditto the anti-war movement, the Campaign for Nuclear Disarmament and the efforts to stop the growing of GM crops.

Get spanking

The Ruckus Society, a resource centre for organisers, runs training camps in the USA – you can make a donation of $100, but nobody is refused for lack of funds. They also have direct action resources, including an Action Planning Manual and a guide to Hanging yourself from a Billboard – downloadable free from their website.

If you want to campaign for the environment, join Greenpeace. They use direct action effectively. Visit their website, and play games on themes such as GM foods, toxic chemicals, oil discharges, nuclear waste, global warming, wind farms and Spank Esso! And you might decide to get involved.

Greenpeace: www.greenpeace.org

Ruckus Society: ruckus.org

Challenge creating change

The functions of direct action:

Alarm to get attention to a burning problem or issue.

Reinforcement to get publicity to support your campaign.

Planned escalation to raise the stakes and show you mean business.

Morale to raise spirits and renew energy.

Before you take action, you need to clearly define the issue, who is responsible and what you want to achieve. You need to design an action that will have impact. You also need to know the law and what your rights are.

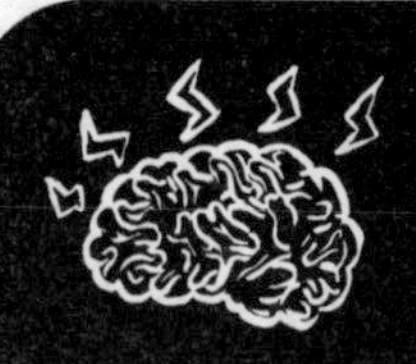

Save a tongue

Investigate the languages indigenous to your region.

Take a course in an endangered language.

Go to www.word2word.com/coursead.html to learn 100 different languages online.

Foundation for Endangered Languages: www.ogmios.org

Ethnologue, resource on lesser-known languages: www.ethnologue.com

International Mother Language Day is UNESCO's campaign to highlight the importance of linguistic diversity: www.un.org/depts/dhl/language

Free Online Language Courses: www.word2word.com/coursead.html

Can you say Adios in Ainu?

Only eight elderly people spoke Ainu on Hokkaido Island, Japan by the late 1980s. But when something was done about it, the language was revived. Cornish died out in 1777. Using old documents, descendants of Cornish speakers learned the language, teaching it to their children. Now, road signs appear in Cornish and English, and about 2,000 people speak Cornish.

Without words to express things, knowledge and ideas begin to disappear. The loss of any language means a reduction in the sum of human thought and knowledge. It's predicted that at least half the world's 6,000 or so languages still in existence will be dead or near death by 2050. An *Atlas of Endangered Languages* reports that 50 European languages are in danger, with France having 14 near death. In Siberia, in the Russian Federation, nearly all the 40 or so local languages are disappearing. Languages are becoming extinct at twice the rate of endangered mammals and four times the rate of endangered birds. While there are huge campaigns to preserve animal and plant species, there is far less concern about preserving the world's languages.

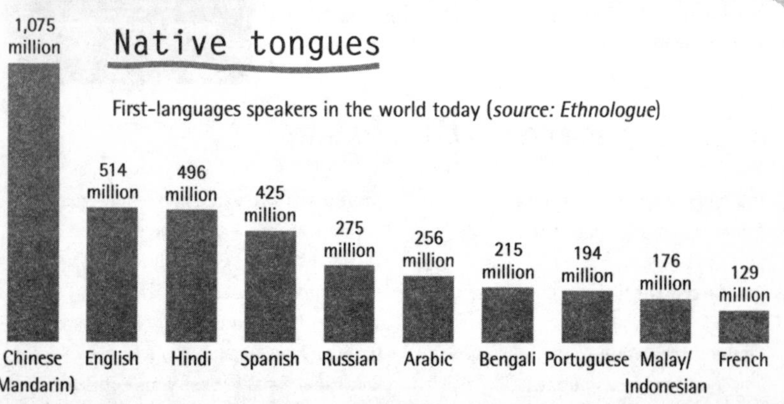

Say no to plastic bags

Bags used for just a few minutes may last for between 15 and 1,000 years. Every time you accept a plastic bag in a shop, it harms the environment – even biodegradable bags take years to degrade.

Plastic bag litter creates huge problems. The bags can trap birds or kill livestock (if eaten). An Australian farmer found eight plastic bags in the stomach of a dead calf – the loss cost him around $500. And when a dead animal decays, the plastic bags will be re-ingested by other animals, the cycle continuing for many years. Plastic bags can block drains and foul waterways. They can accumulate along the roadside or on beaches, a blot on the landscape as well as an environmental hazard.

Governments can help. In Ireland, a 2002 law taxed retailers on non-reusable bags they issued, and plastic check-out bag use was reduced by 90 per cent. That saved nearly 1 billion bags in just a year. In Australia, retailers had to reduce their use of plastic bags by 25 per cent during 2004 and 50 per cent by 2005.

Customers also need to act. Use reusable bags when you go shopping. Recycle any plastic bags you take home with you as bin liners or freezer bags.

Shopping for alternatives

Just say No! to plastic bags. Buy cloth bags, jute bags, straw bags, bags made out of recycled bottle tops. Use these instead. Take one with you whenever you go out shopping. And use it again and again and again.

Planet Ark organises anti-plastic bag campaigns in Australia and the UK. Its book, *Greeniology – how to live well, be green and make a difference*, shows how to change your ways without sacrificing your lifestyle: www.planetark.com

Onelessplasticbag, a fabric bag that folds up to put in your pockets: www.oneless.co.uk

February 22

Plastic pollution

- There are now over 46,000 pieces of plastic waste in every square mile of the world's oceans. Bag litter kills 100,000 birds, whales, seals and turtles annually.
- During the manufacture of plastic bags, benzene gas, a known carcinogen, enters the atmosphere.
- Plastic can take centuries to decompose. When it is burned, poisonous dioxins and hydrogen cyanide enter the soil and natural water supply.
- In Australia at least 80 million bags end up as litter each year.
- In China, plastic bags blowing around are called 'white pollution'.
- In South Africa, there are so many bags in the countryside that they have become known as the 'national flower'.

Survey the scene

Do a 'Liveability Survey' to see where you live or shop scores on the 10 points. Score each point out of 10, and the total out of 100. Are you satisfied with the result? If not, come up with some ideas for what to do.

The Living Streets campaign: www.livingstreets.org.uk

Reclaim the Streets campaign: http://rts.gn.apc.org

Network control

'On Saturday 21 August, a little bit of Cardiff's busy road network was liberated from the sound of traffic and the smell of petrol fumes for a few hours. For one afternoon only, the streets were filled with the sounds of free-spirited souls partying and the smell of ... well ... free-spirited souls partying!' – a local Reclaim the Streets event, a 'disorganisation for a people-centred world'.

Streets for people

Streets traditionally accommodated a full range of human activity. They were places for trading, socialising, playing, entertaining, meeting and demonstrating in. They were also routes for travel and the movement of goods, and all this was kept in balance. Today the balance has been lost. Streets have become traffic corridors, cutting swathes through local communities. Traffic management is more important than the quality of local life. Streets are dirty and dangerous, and communities suffer.

Let's give the streets back to the people. Let them be living streets. This 10-point manifesto has been adapted from the Pedestrian Association's Living Streets campaign:

1. Streets need people living on them, walking down them and overlooking them, with a mix of housing, shops, offices, pubs, schools and places of worship within reasonable walking distance.
2. Streets have become ugly and intimidating for pedestrians. Streets should be designed for people as well as for traffic.
3. Traffic volume and speed should not be too high. Traffic kills people, and too much traffic kills communities.
4. People are being squeezed out by 'street furniture' on pavements between buildings and traffic.
5. Streets need to be properly managed to get rid of litter, dog fouling, vandalism and graffiti.
6. Safe and well-lit streets. If people don't feel safe, they won't use the streets.
7. Facilities like benches where people can relax.
8. The street environment should be attractive and interesting.
9. Access in and out should be made easy.
10. Maps and signs for pedestrians should be informative and helpful.

Change the next world

Thou shalt laugh at this website! New York Times

Ship of Fools, which calls itself 'the magazine of Christian unrest', is a 'serious and satirical, entertaining and thought-provoking' Christian web-zine inviting believers to 'do some head-scratching about their faith and sceptics to take a second look'. At the Ship of Fools online store find:

Get to know the Bible Suck a 'Testamint'. Each sweet is individually wrapped in one of 40 different verses from the Old and New Testaments. Share the Good Chews at $19.95.

Wash away your sins Can't shift Catholic guilt? Why not try the 'Wash Away Your Sins' soap? Make 'cleanliness is next to godliness' a reality for $8.00.

Make praying easier Shaped like a credit card, out goes the traditional string of beads; in comes the Credit Card Rosary with embossed points, stashed away in your wallet between your gold Amex and your driver's licence, ready for immediate use. There is an entry-level plastic card, a brass-embossed card for middle-income earners, and a top-end gold version studded with diamonds.

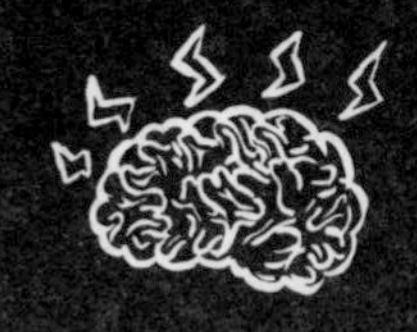

Be a good Samaritan

Help someone in dire need. Good Samaritan laws protect you from liability if you act reasonably and without payment where you do not have a pre-existing duty of care. Continue to provide aid until you call in medical assistance, or somebody more competent comes on the scene, or providing aid becomes unsafe (for example, exposing yourself to the risk of HIV).

Read about the Good Samaritan in the Bible, St Luke (Chapter 10, Verses 25–37).

Ship of Fools – the website's Fruitcake Zone provides links to websites that put the 'fun' back into fundamentalism: http://ship-of-fools.com

A plague at your fingertips

Re-live the ten plagues using finger puppets – 'This little boil went to market. This little locust stayed at home. And this little plague sneaks into bedrooms in the middle of the night and smites children of your age – on purely racial grounds.'

All the ten plagues are here, including flies, thunder, hail, gnats, darkness.

For just $16.95 from the Ship of Fools online store you can scare the daylights out of your first-born with the story of the Passover and Exodus out of Egypt.

February 25

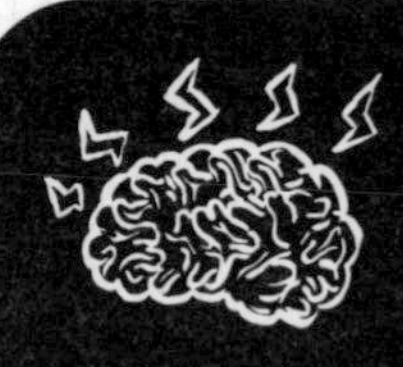

Influence the media

Blog blag

These are some good examples of political blogs:

www.andrewsullivan – Andrew is a British-born gay republican with great sources and a sharp outlook on American politics.

Baghdad Burning, an award winning blog from where it's happening: http://riverbendblog.blogspot.com

www.instapundit.com – a hyperactive blogger who focuses on the intersection between technology and individual liberty.

You ask me what I came into the world to do. I came to live out loud. Emile Zola

The internet has provided us all with an opportunity to make our views known. Political 'blogging' is an effective way of keeping democracy alive using the latest technology. Use your freedom of expression as an individual to keep government transparent and accountable – locally or nationally. Even if you live under a tyrannical government, the internet may still provide a space for you to express your views.

'Blog' is short for 'web-log' – an internet diary reflecting the ideas, experiences and views of the blogger, often linked to other web-based information. People blog for every reason under the sun. Some just do it to keep a diary, some because they are keen to share their ideas or expertise. And some do it for a political purpose. Some people just want to share their secrets. One of the most visited websites, and a web publishing sensation, is a web-log of a call girl known as 'Belle de Jour': belledejour-uk.blogspot.com

Become a political blogger

Become a blogger. A free basic blogging service that will help you get started is: www.blogspot.com. Setting up a blog will take you less than five minutes. Then how much time and energy you put into making it really good and in finding readers is up to you.

Are there issues in your community that no one is addressing: traffic, homelessness, gangs, police brutality? Become the voice that brings this issue to the forefront so it can no longer be ignored.

Provide the latest news. Praise and criticise government officials. See that they live up to the promises that got them elected. Research the candidates running in the next election. Find out about their campaigning platforms and their stance on important issues.

Give up Group Think

Do you ever find yourself listening to a group discussion, disagreeing with what is being said, but afraid to speak up? It is quite likely that others are feeling the same way. This is Group Think.

We will all find ourselves in a Group Think situation. It may be about a tiny issue, or something more important. Whatever it is, get your point of view heard, influence the discussion and the decision.

Six symptoms of Group Think:

1 Believing there are good reasons for what you know are poor decisions, and explaining away facts that do not support the line of thought.
2 Believing what you are doing is morally correct, even when the evidence suggests otherwise.
3 Using shared negative and positive stereotypes to inform the decision.
4 Exercising direct and indirect pressure on those of the group who hold contrary views.
5 Self-censorship: failure to speak up means that your views remain hidden.
6 Maintaining an illusion of unanimity, where silence is taken for assent.

And six ways to avoid Group Think:

1 Understand how Group Think affects decision making.
2 Find someone neutral to chair the group.
3 Give space for everyone to express their views.
4 Always compare the proposed decision with a less popular alternative. Ask someone to play devil's advocate.
5 After reaching what seems to be a consensus, encourage people to express their doubts.
6 Break into several smaller groups to discuss the issue and suggest a course of action. Then try to reach a consensus.

Speak up

In a meeting don't remain silent, speak up. Others may also not be happy with how the discussion is going and will welcome your comments.

If you are chairing a group, encourage everyone to say what they think, and make sure everyone's view is respected. Sharing ideas leads to better decisions – and better decisions are needed for a better world.

Fictional Group Think

- *1984* by George Orwell – a frightening parable of Stalinist Russia and a couple's attempt not to conform: www.online-literature.com/orwell1984
- *12 Angry Men* – an Oscar-winning film in which the Henry Fonda character is the only juror to believe that the defendant is not guilty: www.filmsite.org/twelve.html

February 27

At your disposal

Check if there is a local Freecycling group for your city, town or neighbourhood. If there is, join it. Dispose of your old stuff and get new stuff by Freecycling. Enjoy!

If there isn't a local Freecycling group, then start one. The Freecycle website tells you what you need to do to get started. It essentially means moderating a Yahoo group whilst being a passionate advocate for recycling. Freecycle: freecycle.org

Freecycle for fun

'Think globally, recycle locally'– the Freecycling Network has been set up for those who want to recycle things, rather than throw them away. Whether it's a chair, a fax machine, a piano or an old door, your local Freecycling group will provide you with an opportunity to advertise the things you no longer need in the hope that you can find someone who would like them. Or if you're looking to acquire something yourself, this is a good place to start.

Freecycling helps keep good stuff out of landfills. It is a virtual response to a global problem. There is just one rule – everything that is advertised must be free. There are now over 1,500 cities all over the world with a Freecycling group, with over 525,000 members in total. The largest group is in Portland, Oregon, with over 10,000 members. There are 120 groups in the UK. Freecycling can be started in any city, and is open to anyone who wants to participate. Groups are run by a local volunteer, who facilitates the group. The Freecycling Network gives itself a pat on the back: 'This is grassroots action at its best!'

The Freecycling Oath of Honour

- I, ... (your name) ... , pledge to be a really nice and patient person when moderating our new Freecycle webpage.
- I promise to use the Freecycle name only for our non-commercial Yahoo group.
- I will remain open to the occasional democratic discussion on our webpage, but will know when to make the tough calls and decisions in order to spare the rest the long debates.
- With great honour I shall also keep spam, ads and money-makers out of my group with the 'two strikes, you're out' rule.
- I'll suggest people give preference to nonprofits when giving stuff away.
- And, finally, I shall come clean of my rat pack ways and clean out my own garage before asking the same of others.

Be a good neighbour

In these days of high-speed communications, you can feel close to someone thousands of miles away. The sense of a 'global village' is being used by NABUUR, a Dutch Foundation, to help give urban and rural communities in developing countries (which they call 'villages') access to the resources they need.

This is how NABUUR.com works:

1 After an assessment, a village in need of help is given a page on NABUUR.com.
2 People who want to help sign up as virtual neighbours of that village.
3 The best solutions are then put forward to the village. A neighbourhood representative discusses these with the community.
4 The community decides what to do, and the solutions are implemented.
5 A new question may then be put forward; and the process starts all over again.

The neighbours mainly help by searching for information on the internet, contacting organisations that could be helpful, using their creativity and other skills, and providing specific expertise and advice.

NABUUR.com is the brainchild of Siegfried Woldhek, previously the Chief Executive of WWF Netherlands.

Neighbourly action

Choose from around 60 villages in Africa, Asia and Latin America with problems covering community development, income generation, education, environment, sanitation, agriculture, health and much else.

Go to NABUUR.com and select a village that interests you. Become a good neighbour of that village. Get to work. Post your answers and ideas on the discussion board for that village.

NABUUR Foundation: www.nabuur.com

Help a village in need

Welcome to Chimaltenango, Guatemala: The Kaqchikel Maya there are direct descendants of the precolumbian Maya. The majority are peasant farmers, growing maize, beans and vegetables. The population has grown rapidly in recent years, leading to deforestation. To stem the tide, the community wants to develop ecotourism. The area has much to offer: beautiful forests (despite the deforestation), volcanoes, ancient temples and indigenous arts and crafts. The community needs information on what tourists find interesting, what activities could be developed and how to promote the area as an ecotourist destination.

Web-wise

Check out the following ideas websites.

Why not?: www.whynot.net

Global Ideas Bank: www.globalideasbank.org

Idea Explore: www.ideaexplore.net

Idea a Day: www.idea-a-day.com

Creativity Pool: www.creativitypool.com

Premises Premises: www.premisespremises.com

ShouldExist:: www.shouldexist.org

Half Bakery: www.halfbakery.com

The Innovation Tools website catalogues the best resources for innovation, creativity and brainstorming: www.innovationtools.com

Clear your head

Today is an extra day added to the calendar to keep it aligned with the seasons. Why not mark it by taking the day off and doing something out of the ordinary, something you've been meaning to do for four years? And this could include thinking up some great ideas for changing the world. Here are some suggestions, but don't feel pressured to do any of them!

Soak in a hot tub Relax and start thinking about how to change the world.

Ask your friends to come round and celebrate Leap Day with you. Ask them to bring a bottle and one good idea.

Take your local Big Issue seller for a cup of coffee and a chat. Ask him or her to give you one idea for doing something about homelessness.

Surf the internet Type in two or three words that describe the issue you're interested in, and see what appears. Follow up any interesting links suggested.

Write to your head of government (or any other famous person), and ask him or her to give you one good idea for what you and other people can do to make the world a better place.

Make room for new ideas

Organise an 'Ideas Party' for changing the world. Decide on an issue you care about, identify some of the problems. For each problem, ask everyone to come up with a practical idea. List all the ideas, selecting those that are simple and likely to have some impact. At the end of the evening, review all the good ideas, asking each person to do one thing from the list. Eat, drink, be merry – and get your creative juices flowing. These ideas blogs may be of use to you:

Global Ideas Bank blog: www.globalideasblog.com

World Changing: www.worldchanging.com

The Demos Greenhouse: www.demosgreenhouse.co.uk

The New Cafè: http://newcafe.org

Keep up with the news

There's so much information on the web, and so little time to sift through the billions of web pages. Keeping up to date with the news can be extremely time-consuming.

How about getting the latest news and features delivered to your desktop? Now news updates can be sent straight to your computer using a service called RSS. No more hopping from site to site looking for new information updates – RSS sends it to you direct.

RSS stands for Really Simple Syndication. It enables you to choose websites you're interested in, and get their news delivered to your computer or BlackBerry. RSS makes it easy for people to access multiple blogs and news websites simultaneously. Instead of surfing 20 web pages, RSS shows new content on your favourite sites at the click of a button. To use RSS, simply install an RSS reader and log your favourite websites. Then click the update button, and your RSS reader lists all new items on your preferred websites by headline, brief description, date and time.

A growing number of websites offer RSS, including news providers such as *The Guardian*, Reuters, the BBC and CNN. As Really Simple Syndication becomes more widely used, more information providers will offer the service.

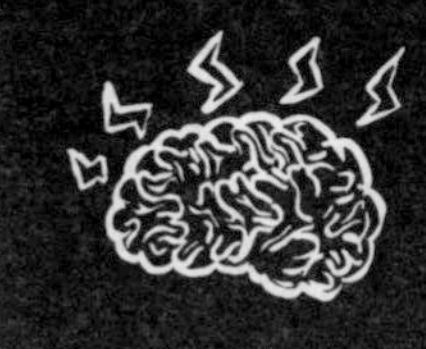

Free delivery

Here are a few websites already offering RSS:

- **National Public Radio: www.npr.org/rss/index.html**
- **BBC: news.bbc.co.uk/1/hi/help/rss/default.stm**
- **CNN: www.cnn.com/services/rss/**
- **Reuters: today.reuters.com/rss/newsrss.aspx**
- ***The Guardian*: guardian.co.uk/webfeeds**
- **Wired: www.wired.com/support/rss_instructions.html**

RSS News Reader Downloads for Windows: www.newzcrawler.com

Downloads for Mac: http://ranchero.com

RSS at How Stuff Works, interesting facts about almost everything: www.howstuffworks.com/rss-feeds.htm

March 1

Really Simple Syndication

Get a News Reader. One may be included in your browser software, or you can download one from the internet. There are lots of programs available, although the free versions generally have fewer features.

Check your favourite website for an RSS link. If it has one, click on the link and choose the categories you want to be updated on. Then follow instructions on how to hook up, and get news updates from this site to your computer.

Junking the junk

Make junk mail more environmentally friendly. The following websites tell you how:

Mail Preference Service. UK: www.mpsonline.org.uk US: www.the-dma.org/consumers/offmailinglist.html

Do-it-yourself – stop junk mail, email and phone calls – a free guide: www.obviously.com/junkmail

New American Dream: www.newdream.org

Forest Ethics: www.forestethics.org/

Stamp out waste

Everyone gets junk mail – the endless stream of unsolicited letters and leaflets arriving through the mailbox each day: loan invitations, credit card applications, mail order catalogues, offers of fabulous prizes, etc. As soon as we recognise junk letters we throw them away unopened.

Junk mail is a complete waste of paper, extra weight for the postman to carry and extra rubbish for the refuse collector to cart away, not to mention personal aggravation for us.

New American Dream and Forest Ethics are asking five of the USA's biggest catalogue companies (all of whom use little or no recycled paper) to start greening the 600 million catalogues they print each year.

Help persuade mail order catalogues to be more environmentally friendly. Write a letter urging companies sending you mail to reduce the frequency of their mailings, and start printing on at least 10 per cent recycled content immediately. Ask them to commit to improving this to 50–60 per cent over the next five years. Tell your friends to do the same.

Stopping junk mail

If you're fed up with junk mail, you can do something about it:

- Contact the Mail Preference Service and tell them you don't want to get unsolicited mail. Mailing list organisations servicing the direct marketing industry will delete your name from the addresses sold to marketers. Your name will be removed for five years and you should start to notice a reduction in junk mail after three months. It's much better to stop junk mail at the source rather than recycle.
- Tick the box on any reply form you fill in stating you do not want information about future offers.
- Do not fill in the warranty applications for consumer goods as these are often used as a way of collecting names and addresses. Your rights are protected under law.

Cities of contrast

Google Earth provides aerial maps of the whole world. Here are two interesting cities to visit.

Mumbai

The commercial capital of India. It had a population of 18.3 million in 2005, and is the home of India's major financial institutions. It is also the centre of India's Bollywood film industry. Mumbai attracts migrants from all over India.

Dharavi is near the airport. It's known as Asia's largest slum, housing around 1 million people. Its squalid conditions are in stark contrast with the wealth of Mumbai. Yet Dharavi is a hub of energy, industry, enterprise ... and hope for a better tomorrow.

Los Angeles

The second largest city in the USA, with a population of 3.95 million, and 17.5 million in the wider metropolitan area. The hub of the Hollywood film industry, immigrants are attracted by the promise of the 'American Dream', and LA has a large and growing Mexican and Chicano population.

Near the luxury mansions of Beverly Hills is 18th Street East, the centre of LA's gangland culture, with its daily gun crime, drugs scene and carjackings.

Where on earth

Visit Google Earth at: www.earth.google.com

Understand gangland culture: www.streetgangs.com/18thstreet.html

www.aliciapatterson.org/APF1602/Rodriguez/Rodriguez.html

Catch up with the latest Bollywood news: www.planetbollywood.com

Catch up with the latest Hollywood news: www.hollywoodreporter.com

See the iconic HOLLYWOOD sign at: www.hollywoodsign.org

An eye on the world

1 Visit Dharavi on Google Earth. Read: *Rediscovering Dharavi: Stories from Asia's Largest Slum*, by Kalpana Sharma, Penguin Books, India, 2000

2 Visit LA's18th Street on Google Earth. Find out more about gangland culture on 18th Street.

3 Visit your home town on Google Earth; go to where you live.

Find out as much as you can about the people living in these three locations. Think about what you can do to reduce inequalities in your community and in the wider world.

Toxins in your television

Do the Toxic Tech Test

Go to the Greenpeace website:
- **Do the Toxic Tech Test.**
- **Send a letter to the manufacturer of the electronic product you have just bought. The site provides a form letter, with space for you to fill in your details.**

Toxic Tech Test is at the GreenpeaceWeb.org website: www.greenpeaceweb.org/consumingchemicals/ddtest.asp

Many electronic products contain toxic chemicals. Small amounts of these chemicals can cause widespread pollution once the product has reached the end of its useful life and is discarded.

What is being done? One solution is to put pressure on the manufacturers to remove toxic chemicals from their products. Samsung, Nokia, Sony and Philips have all promised to do this as soon as they realistically can.

- If your cellphone is made by Motorola, Panasonic, Sharp, Siemens or Sony Ericsson
- If your TV is made by Akai, Bang & Olufsen, Daewoo, Grundig, JVC, Panasonic or Sharp
- If your computer is an Acer, Apple, Dell, Fujitsu-Siemens, HP/Compaq, IBM, Panasonic, Toshiba or Tulip

... then your pressure could push these companies to follow the good example of those that have already made a decision to phase out toxic chemicals.

Pen power

Form letter you could send to a manufacturer:

Dear Sir/Madam,

I have a product from your company (*insert the company's name*). I am asking if the computer/electronic equipment (*insert the item and model*) I have bought from you contains toxic chemicals.

Toxic chemicals, if used in the production of these products, would cause damage to the environment and to people. I am particularly concerned about brominated flame retardants and phthalates.

Many companies are phasing out all these toxic chemicals in their products and production. If your products contain toxic chemicals, are you planning to phase these out or not?

If you do not plan to phase out all these toxic chemicals, then I will consider buying from a different company next time.

Yours sincerely,

(*name, email address*)

Divide up your day

In 19th-century Europe, working conditions were unregulated. The health, welfare and morale of working people suffered, and child labour was common. The working day could range from 10–16 hours for six days a week. Religious sentiment ensured a day off for the Sabbath.

Robert Owen, a socialist pioneer, demanded a ten-hour day in 1810, which he instituted in his model industrial community of New Lanark. In 1817, he demanded an eight-hour day using the slogan: 'Eight hours labour, Eight hours recreation, Eight hours rest.'

Despite some initial successes in achieving an eight-hour day for skilled workers in New Zealand and Australia in the 1840s and 1850s, most employees in the industrialised world had to wait until the 20th century for an eight-hour day to be widely achieved.

In Europe today, the working week for many people is just 35 hours, with up to 6 weeks of annual holiday, and the Working Time Directive seeks to limit the maximum number of hours worked per week to 48. In developing countries, workers are not so lucky, where child labour, a long working day and sweatshop conditions are often the norm.

Managing time

Keep a diary of what you do. How much time are you spending on what each day?

For example: travel to work, working, eating, study, reading, hobbies, sport, housework, shopping, cooking, sitting in front of the TV, and doing things for others and the community.

Is your life in balance? How much time are you wasting? Could you be doing more for the community and for a better world?

Trade Unions have been at the forefront of the fight for better working conditions:

International Confederation of Free Trade Unions: www.icftu.org

Cyber Picket Line, links to unions around the world: www.cf.ac.uk/socsi/union/links.htm

China's great leap forward (1958-61)

Mao Zedong demanded that the people work at fever pitch. They had to run carrying heavy loads, whether it was freezing cold or blazing hot. They had to carry water up winding paths to irrigate the terraced fields. They had to keep the backyard steel furnaces going night and day. They literally had to move mountains. Work was good, and Mao hoped it would transform China. Mao set this out as the daily norm for workers and peasants: 8 hours sleeping; 4 hours eating and breaks; 2 hours studying (good Communist thought); 10 hours working.

Under this 8-4-2-10 regime, workers were allowed two days off a month (five for women). Mao called this way of working the 'Communist Spirit.'

Brew up some great ideas

Set up your own coffee house challenge for your city, town or neighbourhood.

Organise a regular meeting, perhaps once a month. Find a local coffee house that will make a great venue and talk to the manager about your plans. Select the subjects for discussion. Invite a speaker to kick off the proceedings and find a moderator to make sure everything runs smoothly.

Publicise the event in the local press, and wait to see who turns up. The rest will depend on the ideas and the energy of the group.

The Royal Society of Arts: www.thersa.org/250/chc.asp

Converse over a coffee

When people get together over a cup of coffee, they put the world to rights. Chatting informally with others is a great way to generate ideas, solve problems and get to know others better. But these days it feels like nobody has the time to listen or swap thoughts.

In Rawthmell's Coffee House in London in 1774, a group of friends decided to take time to talk. They wanted to discuss all kinds of problems, and to see how, together, they could do something to make the world a better place. They set up an organisation now known as the Royal Society of Arts (RSA).

To celebrate its 250th anniversary, the RSA teamed up with Starbucks to organise coffee house gatherings so that people could exchange thoughts and come up with great ideas to see the world through its next 250 years.

The Knights of The Square Table

Right in the centre of Bangalore, at Koshy's coffee house, a group called The Knights of the Square Table meet every morning from 11 am to 12 pm. Prem Koshy explains how it began:

'A few of us used to sit at this table, discussing everything under the sun. One of us might mention someone who needed help. This might be to do with drugs, alcohol, food or another health problem. One of the group could always find an answer. We've helped an 11-year-old boy who was paralysed, taught hypnosis to a man suffering chronic pain, and helped someone with edinoma (a growth on the lung). Our services are completely gratis. Our policy is no demands, no expectations.'

They aren't trying to save the world, but they are trying to help people.

Save the rainforest

Originally there were 6 million square miles of tropical rainforest worldwide. Today, as a result of deforestation, just over 2 million square miles remain. The rainforest continues to shrink rapidly: almost two acres disappear every second. This leads to soil erosion, loss of biodiversity and an increase in carbon dioxide in the atmosphere.

But you can do something to help. You can save acres of the rainforest by visiting one of the many 'click to donate' sites. Click and make a donation to the rainforest (and many other good causes) in seconds. You can buy acres of rainforest much more cheaply than you can buy land in the UK. For a donation of £25 through World Land Trust you can buy an acre in the Amazon Basin in Ecuador. For a donation of just £150 you can save 1,500 rainforest trees.

- To save the rainforest for free, visit: www.therain forestsite.com
- Or visit www.worldlandtrust.org to buy acres of rainforest.

March 7

Click to donate sites

There are many opportunities to donate to good causes.

The Hunger Site: www.thehungersite.com

The Literacy Site: www.theliteracysite.com

Race for the Rainforest: rainforest.care2.com

Race for the Ocean: oceans.care2.com

Race for the Primates: primates.care2.com

The Ecology Fund: ecologyfund.com

WildGlobe: www.wildglobe.com

Solve Poverty (education for young people): www.solvepoverty.com

PovertyFighters (microcredit): www.povertyfighters.com

For an up-to-date listing of click and donate sites, see: www.thenonprofits.com

Let a mouse do the work

Visit the Rainforest Site daily at www.therainforestsite.com and save an area of rainforest land for free. Just click on the 'Save Our Rainforests' button. Your click triggers a donation from the sponsors of the site. Each click saves a square metre of rainforest – about the space you occupy at your computer. So far, visitors' clicks have preserved more than 17,000 acres in the following areas:

- The Atlantic Rainforest Preserve in Paraguay.
- The Calkumal Bio-Reserve in Mexico.
- The Reserva Comunal Tanshiyacu Tahuayo in Peru.
- Brazil's Atlantic Forest.

Take the lead

Do three things to promote the achievements of women:

- **Spend 15 minutes researching a current woman leader who has impressed you.**
- **Interview a woman in your community who is doing fantastic things. This could be a person of power or a cleaning lady. What's important is what they are doing to change the world.**
- **Tell at least five people about this amazing woman and what she has achieved.**

International Women's Day: www.un.org/events/women/iwd

Putting women first

In 1909, after a declaration by the Socialist Party of America, the first US National Woman's Day was held on 28 February.

In 1910, the Socialist International meeting in Copenhagen established an International Women's Day, the first being held on 19 March 1911.

In 1913, as part of the peace movement on the eve of World War I, Russian women observed their first International Women's Day on the last Sunday of February. In 1917, Russian women again chose the last Sunday in February to strike for 'bread and peace'. Four days later the Czar abdicated and the new Provisional Government granted women the right to vote. That Sunday fell on 23 February on the Julian calendar then used in Russia, 8 March on the Gregorian calendar used elsewhere.

International Women's Day has become a global opportunity to celebrate acts of courage by ordinary women in the advancement of women's rights.

Women of peace

The Nobel Peace Prize has been awarded to 12 women since founded in 1901:

Bertha von Suttner (Austria) 1905, who helped set up the Nobel Peace Prize.

Jane Addams (USA) 1931, leader of the women's suffrage movement.

Emily Balch (USA) 1946, co-founder of the Women's International League for Peace and Freedom.

Mairead Corrigan and **Betty Williams** (Northern Ireland) 1976, peace activists.

Mother Teresa (Calcutta, India) 1979, working with the most marginalised.

Alva Myrdal (Sweden) 1982, campaigner for nuclear disarmament.

Aung San Suu Kyi (Burma) 1991, opposition leader, prisoner of conscience.

Rigoberta Menchú (Guatemala) 1992, protecting the rights of indigenous peoples.

Jody Williams (USA) 1997, banning and clearing landmines.

Shirin Ebadi (Iran) 2003, improving the status of women and children in Iran.

Wangari Maathai (Kenya) 2004, tree planting.

Down with tobacco

Tobacco is the cause of 1 in 10 adult deaths worldwide (around 5 million people a year), and this is projected to double by 2020 if current smoking trends continue. Half those who smoke today (around 650 million people) will be killed by tobacco.

Many smokers live in developing countries, where the international tobacco companies are now concentrating their marketing. Smoking and poverty are closely linked, poor people spending a greater proportion of their income on tobacco – which means that they have less to spend on health, education and nutrition.

More than 160 countries so far have signed the UN Framework Convention on Tobacco Control, and are committed to protecting non-smokers and banning tobacco advertising. The States of New York, Delaware and California were the first in the USA to ban smoking in places like bars, restaurants and even – in California – in prisons.

Bhutan aims to become the first country to be completely tobacco-free. The sale of tobacco products, and smoking in public places in this tiny Himalayan kingdom have already been banned in 19 of the country's 20 Districts, and the Ministry of Health provides support for anyone wanting to give up.

No Smoking Day is the second Wednesday in March

March 9

Give it up

Be a pain in the bum. Tell everyone you know who smokes, and any smoker whose smoke is curling into your face how harmful smoking is to them, and how unpleasant and dangerous to those around them.

Download information on smoking and pregnancy. Hand this out to friends and colleagues who are or intend to become pregnant. You'll be giving a baby a better chance of good health.

Talk to the manager in bars and restaurants about providing smoke-free zones, where these aren't yet provided.

Action on Smoking and Health: www.ash.org.uk

No Smoking Day in the UK: www.nosmokingday.org.uk

The killer facts

- 5,600 billion cigarettes are smoked every year. That's 875 for every person in the world.
- There are 1.1 billion smokers, only 15 per cent living in rich countries. And 30 per cent of adults still smoke in North America, Europe and Japan.
- There are 4.8 million premature deaths a year from smoking-related illnesses. WorldWatch predicts that smoking will become the world's biggest killer by 2030, with over 10 million deaths a year.

Build your own website

Design matters

If you don't know how to design a website, you can:
- **Find a professional website designer.**
- **Visit WebSpawner.com and teach yourself.**
- **Find a virtual volunteer.**

Seven steps to setting up a website: www.havingmyownwebsite.net

Virtually Ignorant, an online web design course for beginners: www.virtuallyignorant.com

WebSpawner.com, a free and easy way to create your own webpage: www.webspawner.com

Do you really exist? French philosopher Rene Descartes declared: 'Cogito ergo sum', which is Latin for, 'I think, therefore I am'. He was looking for certainties in life. One thing he was absolutely certain about was that he was thinking. And this led him to another certainty – that in order to think, he must exist.

'I don't have a website, therefore I don't exist.' If someone wants to find out more about you, your ideas, your organisation and the cause you are involved with, the first thing they will do is type your name into Google. If the search comes up with nothing, then as far as the searcher is concerned you just don't exist. In the internet age, you need a virtual web identity.

You could have a website:
- For yourself
- For your community
- For the organisation or ideas you are putting your energies into.

Free websites for good causes

Charity Focus was founded in 1999 by 23-year-old Nipun Mehta, and four of his friends from the San Francisco Bay Area. They decided that most non-profit organisations at that time couldn't afford to create good websites, so they offered to build websites free for charities. Quite soon demand began to grow exponentially. Charity Focus now receives around 40 requests a week. It can't help everybody, so it concentrates on smaller organisations without a current web presence. The service is volunteer-run and completely free, apart from domain and web hosting charges (which have to be paid to third parties).

Charity Focus has developed a pledging system, a charity shop facility for selling things from websites, enlightening banners of inspiring quotations instead of advertisements and a quote-for-the-day email service (charityfocus.org)

Sell books online

GreenMetropolis.com is an online bookstore for recycling books. If you are a buyer, you can find the book you've been looking for at a great price. All paperbacks sell for £3.75. There is no minimum order and no postage to pay. Browse the bookstore to see if they've got what you want to read.

If you are a seller, you can turn the books you've read and no longer want into cash. Just log on to GreenMetropolis.com, and enter the book's ISBN number (usually printed on the back of the book) and its condition. Once the book is sold, you are notified by email of where to send the book and your account is credited with £3.00. You have to pay postage and packing costs.

GreenMetropolis.com also donates 5p for every book sold to the Woodland Trust's Plant a Tree scheme, so you are helping grow wood to make more paper.

Another alternative is to sell your old books on Amazon, where you pay a fixed fee (75p in the UK) and 15 per cent of the selling price. When you are notified of a sale, you send the book to the purchaser. You are given a credit towards the postage costs, and the proceeds are credited to your account.

Second hand

What should you do with your old books and magazines?

Recycle all the books you no longer need. Get your books into the hands of new readers (this will save trees), and use any cash you raise to support a good cause.

Advice from the World Environmental Organization:

- **Donate books to a library.**
- **Sell study books directly to other students – let them save a ton of money.**
- **Set up a table at your community centre where people can drop off old magazines for others to buy. Then donate the money to charity.**

World Environmental Organization: www.world.org/reuse/Books

Green Metropolis: www.greenmetropolis.com

Oxfam: www.oxfam.org.uk

Amazon: www.amazon.co.uk

March 11

Donating books to charity

If none of the above appeals to you, you can always donate your books to a charity shop. Oxfam is the largest retailer of second-hand books in Europe, selling around 11 million books per year. Most of the 750 or more Oxfam shops in the UK sell books, and over 70 are specialist bookstores. Take your unwanted books into an Oxfam shop, or use one of the 1,000 plus Oxfam 'Book Banks' around the country, usually found next to glass and newspaper recycling bins.

March 12

Say no to the death penalty

Champion human rights

- Become a pen friend of a prisoner on death row.
- Help Reprieve, based in the UK, fight for people facing the death penalty. They offer internships for people wishing to spend time in a law office in the USA or Caribbean helping out on cases.

Organisations to check out:
Reprieve:
www.reprieve.org.uk
Human Writes:
www.humanwrites.org
Cyberspace Inmates:
www.green.colossus.net/cyberspace-inmates/death.htm
Receive execution alerts from the National Coalition to Abolish the Death Penalty:
www.ncadp.org/execution_alerts.html

Governments all over the world are ending capital punishment. Each year since 1976, three more countries have abolished the death penalty. But judicial killing continues to be used in some parts of the world. The USA, China, Iran and Saudi Arabia today account for over 80 per cent of recorded executions. The USA has executed over 800 people since 1976, and over 3,700 men and women are held on death row. Despite popular support for the death penalty, it does not stop violence. Other reasons for pressing for its abolition are that it affects poor and black people disproportionately, and that it is irreversible (and evidence can turn up when it is too late, proving the innocence of an executed prisoner).

Befriending a person on death row by writing to them regularly allows an element of humanity to enter an inhumane system. Organisations exist to advise you about what is involved, and tell you whether they feel you are suitable as a pen friend. All being well, they put you in contact with a prisoner who is under sentence of death.

Ernest Willis's story

Ernest Willis was the 117th death row prisoner to be freed in the USA since 1973. He had been sentenced to death 17 years earlier, for allegedly setting a house on fire that killed two people. The District Judge held that the State had administered medically inappropriate anti-psychotic drugs without Willis's consent, had suppressed evidence favourable to Willis, and had provided ineffective legal representation at his trial. The District Attorney hired a fire expert to examine the evidence, and his conclusion was that there was not a single item of physical evidence supporting a finding of arson.

Reason to dream

The words spoken by Gandhi, 'be the change you wish to see in the world', means to us living according to our values. We know that everything we do has an impact on the world, and because we truly want a sustainable future, we question every single one of our personal actions ...

From getting dressed, to grabbing a coffee and transporting ourselves to school or work, we know that we can either be contributing to child labour, the exploitation of people and natural resources, pollution and climate change ... or we can contribute to alternative income projects, fair trade, sustainable agriculture and an emissions-free bicycle culture.

Two 21-year-olds Jocelyn Land-Murphy and Jessica Lax founded The Otesha Project ('Otesha' is 'reason to dream' in Swahili) in 2002 to take the message to young Canadians. In 2003, they organised a 5,500-mile cycle ride across Canada, reaching over 12,000 people with their presentations and performancesThey continue to spread the word by organising cycling tours throughout Canada.

March 13

Wake up to a better world

If you're stuck for ideas on what to do, then:

- **Get the funky inspiring *Otesha Book* – download it free, or order a copy. It comes in two versions: a traditional paperback, or bound in recycled cardboard packaging (suggested donation $20).**
- **Read *101 Ways for a More Sustainable World* on the Otesha website: www.otesha.ca/being+the +change/101+ways... en.html**

Wake up call: listen to Irving Berlin's 'Oh, how I hate to get up in the morning': www.scoutsongs.com/lyrics/ hatetogetup.html

Morning Choices

The Otesha Project's *Morning Choices* comedy shows how people can make a positive impact on the world through what they do when they get up. It features the Careless Consumer, the Hopeful Hooligan, Mother Earth and a variety of live props to connect actions in an hour of a typical morning with global problems – including using the bathroom, getting dressed, drinking coffee, packing lunch and getting to school.

What are your morning choices going to be regarding your use of water, the clothes you will wear, the newspaper or TV that will inform you, the breakfast you will have, your packed lunch, and how you will get to college or work?

See what you can do during this one hour of the day – today and every day – that will help create a better world.

Organise your own toxic tour

Action plan

- Visit any of the following: a local sewage treatment facility, a landfill site, a municipal recycling centre, a hospital to look at medical waste disposal, a manufacturer to see how they dispose of effluent, and a battery chicken farm or a pig production unit.
- Discuss the problem, and develop a plan of action to do something about it.

Friends of the Earth, campaigning against incineration, landfill and toxic waste: www.foe.co.uk/resource/briefings/toxic_tips.html

Play a Toxic Waste Team-building exercise: www.wilderdom.com/games/descriptions/ToxicWaste.html

Our society spews out unbelievable quantities of effluent and waste, all of which has to be disposed of. But mostly this process is kept hidden from us. What we see are rows of attractively designed products on the shelf, not the factories manufacturing either the packaging or the contents, nor the solid waste they produce and the chemicals they discharge.

We don't see the mountains of garbage collected from our houses and piled up in landfills. Nor do we see human waste and how that's disposed of. This is the hidden backside of our society. If we knew the mess we were causing, we might choose to live differently and be a lot more environmentally conscious.

Organise a Toxic Tour to raise community awareness and to stimulate action on pollutants and those who are generating them. Take members of the public and local decision-makers to see how waste is disposed of in and around your town or city. You will all be intrigued and horrified at how much we waste and how our waste is disposed of.

International dumping of toxic waste

In November 1998, the cargo ship *Chang Shun* slipped into Cambodia's southern port of Sihanoukville. The cargo was unloaded and dumped 15 km away. Soon, villagers nearby started to complain of diarrhoea, headaches and vomiting.

Dumping toxic waste is a serious problem for poor countries, who may need the money but do not have the resources for proper waste treatment or public safety. The Basel Convention controlling shipments of toxic waste was adopted in 1989. The Basel Action Network (BAN) campaigns on toxic waste issues, including ship breaking, electronic waste, mercury pollution and ratification of the Basel ban on exporting hazardous waste from rich to poor countries.

Green babies

Seven million trees are felled to manufacture the nearly 3 billion disposable nappies that are needed to supply the UK market each year. And all those nappies, each of which takes between 200 and 500 years to decompose, have to be disposed of. Because of the huge environmental impact of disposable nappies, there is now active encouragement for parents to try reusable nappies instead.

In the USA, the story is much the same – only on an even grander scale. Each year, parents and babysitters dispose of about 18 billion disposable nappies, which consume nearly 100,000 tonnes of plastic and 800,000 tons of tree pulp in the process. The estimated cost of disposal is $350 million a year.

Things have moved on. A modern, fitted, reusable nappy is far better than anything available just a few years ago. You will find that you can pamper your baby without buying Pampers, and you will save money at the same time. The cost of kitting out a baby with reusable nappies can be as little as £50. Even if you add the cost of washing them, you'll save around £500 for each baby.

Real Nappy Networks are run by mums experienced in using cloth nappies and are valuable sources of impartial information and advice.

For suppliers of reusable nappies, go on the internet. Babygroe produces a catalogue of green, recycled, organic and ethical products: www.babygroe.co.uk.

March 15

Come clean

The Women's Environment Network encourages the use of washable cotton nappies and co-ordinates Real Nappy Week, which is held in the UK at the end of March each year and acts as a focus for its campaigning: www.wen.org.uk/rnw

Join a 'Real Nappy Network'; check on Google to see if there is a local network near you.

Nappy facts

- Find out the facts on the environmental impact of disposable diapers. Go to www.wen.org.uk/nappies/cost_comparison.htm for a cost comparison.
- Tell every expectant parent you know about the benefits of reusable nappies. Produce and hand out a leaflet to every parent with a baby you come across in the street.
- Participate in Real Nappy Week. Help the organisers with their annual stunt.

March 16

Fight big oil

The Stop Esso Campaign also suggests lobbying customers and staff.

Download the Alternative Staff Magazine from the Stop Esso Campaign, and give it out to Esso staff at service stations.

The Stop Esso Campaign can provide you with a full how-to briefing.

The Corporate Watch website on Exxon/Mobil: www.corporatewatch.org.uk/?lid=292

The Stop Esso Campaign is organised by Greenpeace, Friends of the Earth and People and Planet: www.greenpeace.org.uk/climate/climatecriminals/esso

Ten new action ideas to stop Esso: www.peopleandplanet.org/stopesso/action.php

Esso stopped

Exxon/Mobil, trading in the UK as Esso, is the world's largest non-state-owned oil company. It played a significant role lobbying the US government against Kyoto, and promoting the idea there is no provable link between carbon emissions and global warming. *The Economist* has described Exxon/Mobil as 'the world's most powerful climate change sceptic'.

Exxon/Mobil has also done much less than it could in investing in renewable energy technologies. The Esso UK website says: 'As a citizen, sometimes direct action is necessary to make a positive contribution to something you care about.' The Stop Esso Campaign replies: 'Esso chooses to wreck the climate. We can choose not to buy Esso's products. Don't buy Esso!'

Consumer power can change corporate attitudes. According to the Stop Esso Campaign, one million people are now boycotting Esso in the UK (MORI poll). Since its launch in May 2001, the Campaign has spread to the USA, Germany, Canada, Austria, Australia, France, Norway, Luxembourg and Slovakia. The second Stop Esso Day saw 400 Esso stations with protests outside. A leading oil analyst has said that the Campaign 'has to be considered a brand risk'.

Quietly taking on Esso

This plan of action is probably best done when there is a full moon!

See if you can find yourself an Esso (or Exxon) station on a long stretch of road.

Make yourself posters saying:
ESSO Garage 100m ahead, PLEASE DO NOT USE!
ESSO Garage 50m ahead, DEFINITELY DO NOT USE!!
ESSO Garage 25m ahead, AVOID AT ALL COSTS – DRIVE ON!!!

Once you have prepared these signs, go out at night and place the signs at the required distances. (The originator of this idea is unknown.)

Check out the Ideas Bank

The Global Ideas Bank contains a mixture of weird and wonderful ideas for changing the world. Some have been tested in practice, some are work in progress, others are just good ideas. You can vote on the ideas and add your own comments.

Here are some of the ideas:

Mayor on a park bench The mayor turns up each week to discuss the city and its problems with local residents.

A web page for every prescription drug This could be used for information and patient discussions. The best advice comes from users rather than experts.

A pig in every neighbourhood People in inner cities have virtually no exposure to animals other than domestic pets. This cuts them off from nature.

Free wireless internet access Canada is currently installing wireless access throughout its library network – this idea is a must!

Print statistics on toilet paper This will grab people's attention, and inform them about an interesting problem they did not know about.

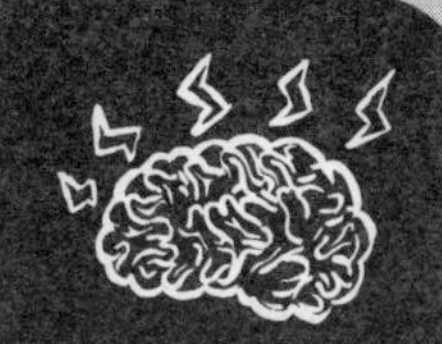

Contribute a great idea

- Send in your ideas to the Global Ideas Bank: www.globalideasbank.org
- Read *The Problem Solving Pocketbook: An introduction to creativity techniques for the budding social inventor*, from the Global Ideas Bank, £3.50.
- Visit the Enterprise Insight website, which has a manual for turning your ideas into action. You can find it on the web at www.starttalkingideas.org
- Enter The World Challenge, run by BBC World and Newsweek, and aims to find individuals and groups who have made a difference to their communities. See: www.theworldchallenge.co.uk

March 17

Ask Jack

Committees, decision-making groups and governments may think they know what they are talking about, but they hide it in fancy language. I suggest that at every meeting of any decision-making group (e.g. at 10 Downing Street, The White House, the local pub darts team, etc.), there is a cardboard cut-out of an 11-year-old. My boy is called Jack.

Then as the meeting continues, everyone has to check that Jack understands what they are talking about, and if he is getting bored and fidgety. If Jack can understand and is interested, then the meeting is going well, and it is likely that more sensible decisions will be made. *An idea submitted to the Global Ideas Bank by Dr G Caldwell*

March 18

It's a wind-up

Radio waves

Give the gift of a radio. A gift of just one radio can make a positive difference to a family, a classroom or a whole community for years to come. Through the Freeplay Foundation it costs just £35 to bring a radio to a family or a community. Save up the money, and donate it. It'll make a wonderful gift.

Freeplay Energy Group: www.freeplayenergy.com

Freeplay Foundation: www.freeplayfoundation.org

Or take your used postage stamps to ASDA; they will sell them to the Salvation Army and donate the proceeds towards buying Lifeline radios.

How can you listen to the radio if you have no source of power? British inventor Trevor Baylis came up with the Clockwork Radio, to be used for spreading the word about safe sex, and combating AIDS in Africa.

Clockwork technology can be used for other electronic gadgets, as Chris Staines and Rory Stear have shown with the Freeplay Energy Group. As well as radios, the Freeplay range now includes torches, mobile phone chargers and stand-by power units.

The Freeplay Foundation was created by Freeplay Energy in 1998, to ensure that the technology reached those who needed it most. Over 300,000 Freeplay radios have been brought into communities in more than 40 developing countries, benefiting over 6 million people directly by enabling them to listen to radio for pleasure and information.

The Foundation created the Lifeline radio in 2003, based on feedback from children orphaned by AIDS and conflict in Kenya, Rwanda and South Africa. The Lifeline is the first radio created specifically for humanitarian projects, especially children living alone.

Radio can help children learn. The Zambia Education Project donates radios to community schools, enabling children not having formal schooling to receive primary-level education.

Listen here

In Malawi, the Ministry of Agriculture distributed 9,100 Freeplay radios to farmers' clubs in remote areas. Each of the clubs, or listening groups, elected a chairperson responsible for the use and care of the radio and for notifying club members of the broadcasts.

In Madagascar, a radio drama series for women's listening clubs is aimed at improving health education, family planning and AIDS prevention. Wind-up radios, funded by the Rotary Club, have been distributed to clubs, who provide regular feedback on the programmes.

Global sisterhood

GSN provides regularly updated information including critical comment and displays of newspaper and journal articles that reinforce patriarchy/misogyny, but have attracted sparse attention and/or comment as the world moves closer to un-democracy. The Global Sisterhood Network

If you want to know how women's lives are changing around the world, then visit the Global Sisterhood Network. This organisation monitors electronic and print media for developments likely to have a direct impact on women's lives. These include agriculture, economics, employment, environment, health, law, militarism, politics, technology, trade and science.

Sisters can sign in here

Global Sisterhood Network (GSN): www.global-sisterhood-network.org

Subscribe to Global Sisterhood Network List for daily online feminist comment and information: http://groups.yahoo.com/group/GSN

Research Foundation: vshiva.net

March 19

For a feminist perspective ...

Visit the GSN website, click on Links to:
Afghan Women's Mission (USA), supporting Afghan women refugee projects: afghanwomensmission.org
Friends of the River Narmada, supporting Narmada Bachao Andolan, India, which is protesting the construction of a big dam: www.narmada.org
Gramya, female infanticide prevention in Andhra Pradesh: home.vicnet.net.au/-gramya
Revolutionary Association of the Women of Afghanistan, Afghan women for human rights and social justice: www.rawa.org
Link to the following groups associated with the Global Sisterhood Network:
Feminism on Line, feminist links: home.wanadoo.nl/-vidabo/Feminism On-Line.html
Feminist Peace Network, ending violence towards women and children: www.feministpeacenetwork.org
International Women's Tribune Centre, connecting women globally for social change: www.iwtc.org
Organisation of Women's Freedom in Iraq: www.equalityiniraq.com/english.htm
Saidit Online, feminist news, culture and politics: saidit.org
WINGS, women's voices on radio worldwide: www.wings.org
Women's International League for Peace and Freedom: www.wilpf.int.ch

Earth Day

Help the planet

Sign the pledge at the Earth Day website:

I will act as a Trustee of the Earth by:

- **Promoting actions to preserve peace and planet.**
- **Conserving nature and its resources.**
- **Encouraging environmental stewardship.**
- **Asking others to do the same.**

Earth Day Network: www.earthday.net

Earth Day site: www.earthsite.org

The one thing we all have in common is our planet. So let's pledge our lives and fortunes to aid the great task of the earth's rejuvenation, and each do our part as a trustee of the earth to take charge and take care of the planet.
John McConnell, founder of Earth Day

Earth Day is dedicated to celebrating the wonder of life on the planet, and making a pledge to ensure a sustainable future for all its inhabitants. It is held each year at the Spring Equinox.

The Earth Day Network was founded by the organisers of Earth Day, promoting environmental citizenship and year-round action. At the website you can find ideas for action on: animals and plants; clean air and water; food and agriculture; forests and wilderness; global warming and clean energy; nuclear and toxic waste; planes, trains and automobiles; recycling and waste; urban growth and more.

Spring Equinox falls on 20 or 21 March

'I Will Not'

Today on Earth Day we are celebrating by making promises, but I will not:
I will not stop throwing paper on the ground.
I will not stop using plastic bags
I will not go to clean the beaches
I will not stop polluting
I will not do all these things because I am not polluting the world
It is the grown-ups who are dropping bombs
It is the grown-ups who have to stop
One bomb destroys more than all the paper and plastic that I can throw in all my life
It is the grown-ups who should get together and talk to each other
They should solve problems and stop fighting and stop wars
They are making acid rain and a hole in the ozone layer
I will not listen to the grown-ups!

A poem by a student of class 5 of Karachi High School for Earth Day 1991

Eliminate racism

21 March is International Day for the Elimination of Racial Discrimination – a time to think of the millions of people all over the world being persecuted as a result of extreme prejudice. They are denied rights and opportunities because of their race, their gender, their religion or some physical disability. Don't just sit there and do nothing!

How can we stop racism? Consider the case of Mal Hussein, an Asian, and his partner Linda Livingstone, who bought the Ryelands Mini-Market corner shop on the Ryelands Estate near Lancaster in June 1991. They were subjected to a 24/7 campaign of intense racial harassment, including death threats, stoning, firebombing, physical attack, graffiti and verbal abuse. Their shop was routinely attacked and customers threatened. They have now sold their shop and moved away. Such behaviour in a civilised society should be completely unacceptable. Citizens need to take a stand against racial violence, and bring pressure to bear on the police and the judicial system to intervene more fairly and more effectively.

You can help

When you come face to face with racism or discrimination, you can:

- **Intervene personally – but do so with caution – showing solidarity with the victim.**
- **Report the matter to the police, the local Council for Racial Equality, your MP, and ask them to act.**
- **Publicise the incident in your local newspaper.**

Friends of Mal Hussein Campaign: www.naar.org.uk/family/mal.asp

Justice for Jay: www.naar.org.uk/family/jay.asp

National Assembly Against Racism: www.naar.org.uk

Commission for Racial Equality, working for a society free from prejudice: www.cre.gov.uk

Jay's story

Jay Abatan, a 42-year-old black man, was attacked by a gang in Brighton on 24 January 1999. He died five days later from severe head injuries. His brother Michael and a friend were also attacked. Two men were arrested and charged with manslaughter, but at the trial were only charged with affray and Actual Bodily Harm to Michael because of a lack of witnesses. The jury was not allowed to hear of Jay's death as the judge ruled that this would prejudice the trial. No one has yet been tried for Jay's murder.

This investigation was the subject of an inquiry by Essex police, after which the original investigating team was replaced. The murder was now being treated as racist, two years after it happened. The family are still campaigning for the release of this second report.

Catch all

Design a rainwater-catching system to harvest all the water that falls onto the roof of your house. Use the rainwater to water your garden and your pot plants, and to wash your dog and your car. You would need to filter it to make it drinkable.

Produce a simple design manual and circulate it to your friends. Your ideas might even help solve the water crisis in the world!

Two good sites which are dedicated to rainwater harvesting: Harvest H2O: www.harvesth2o.com The Rainwater Harvesting Network: www.rainwater harvesting.org

A 'how to' guide, with simple drawings and photos of harvesting projects: www.dot.co.pima.az.us/flood /wh/index.html

Harvest the rain

Rainwater comes direct to you whenever it rains. If your house sits on a 400-square-metre plot and a storm dumps 2 centimetres of rain, you've just received 8,000 litres (1,750 gallons) of water on your house and garden. This water is largely clean and chemical-free. Most people don't utilise this rainwater – they just let it run away. But in countries where rain comes seasonally or where there is simply not enough of it, communities will set up elaborate water-catching systems to collect rainwater and stop it running off into the sea.

This is called rainwater harvesting. It can include storing and utilising the water that falls on roofs, building dams, ponds and other systems for stopping the water running away, and using the rainfall to recharge the ground water. Harvesting rainwater and using water sensibly are crucial in a world running short of water. Parts of the UK are coming under water stress, particularly the South East, where there are now regular hosepipe bans.

Think of others on World Water Day

Any time we need water in the rich world, we just turn on a tap. You probably give little thought to the amount of water you use, or to how it's brought to your home. But for billions of people around the world, getting enough clean water to meet their daily needs is a major struggle. Women and children may have to walk hours every day to get to their local water source – which might be a lake or a pond. They may have to make several trips just to meet their family's daily water needs, and this water is not always clean.

Face up to global warming

Climate change poses a bigger threat to the world than terrorism. David King, UK Government Chief Scientific Adviser

Since the beginning of time, the Earth has been warmed by sunlight, which penetrates the insulating atmosphere of carbon dioxide, water vapour, ozone, methane and nitrous oxide. This atmosphere traps heat on the Earth, creating the greenhouse effect and keeping the climate stable enough to sustain life. Without it, Earth would be too cold for living things.

Since the industrial revolution, the burning of fossil fuels has increased greenhouse gas emissions. These gases trap heat which would otherwise escape into space. Unless something is done, the world will become too hot for life as we know it.

Do your bit

- **Make a 24-hour personal energy log to see how much you are consuming.**
- **Plant one tree. This will consume more than enough CO_2 to offset the CO_2 you are breathing out.**
- **Live lite. Go on a carbon diet. Change your lifestyle to cut down on your emissions.**
- **Log your energy use at: http://fp.arizona.edu/khirschboeck/nats101gc/energy_log.htm**

March 23

World Meteorological Day

The world in 2050?

The best scenario

New Year's Eve 2049 is being celebrated around the world. 2050 was the deadline set by the United Nations for the global economy to switch away from burning fossil fuels. And to everyone's surprise, the target has been met – but only just.

The breakthrough was the 2025 International Climate Treaty, signed after the breakdown of the Kyoto agreement, under which the populations of countries declared uninhabitable by the UN were offered residence in Europe and North America – reversing years of immigration policies designed to keep environmental refugees out of rich countries.

The worst scenario

With a global temperature 3°C higher than in 2000, the world is a very different place. Millions have fled from the low-lying Pacific atolls of Tuvalu, Kiribati and the Marshall Islands because of an 80 cm rise in sea levels. The Alps lost their snow; only the biggest glaciers remain, and skiing ended 20 years ago. The Himalayas have lost about a third of their ice cap, and last year the Ganges ran dry. Panic swept through India and Bangladesh; in the biggest migration in history, nearly 300 million people are moving towards Europe. *Adapted from www.outtherenews.org May 2001*

March 24

Dubble agents for chocolate

On a mission

Sign up to become a fully-fledged Dubble Agent and receive your free choc-secret Mission Pack.

Become a Stock the Choc Sleuth. Your mission is to help get fairtrade chocolate more widely distributed and properly displayed in stores. Visit local Dubble stockists as often as possible and check Dubble chocolate bars are on the shelf and displayed in a prominent position. If your local shop, school or work canteen doesn't stock Dubble, try to persuade them to do so.

Throw a Dubble Agent party. Invite friends to dress up as Dubble Agents or Dubble lookalikes, sample some chocolate and plan tactics for promoting fairtrade chocolate.

The Dubble website: www.dubble.co.uk

Divine Chocolate: www.divinechocolate.com

Cocoa production in Ghana is suffering. In the 75 years up to 1976, Ghana was the world's leading cocoa producer, contributing nearly 40 per cent of world output. There are still around 1.6 million people in Ghana involved in growing cocoa, and many more work in associated industries. In the late 1970s the world market price for cocoa plummeted by two-thirds. Ghanaian cocoa farmers were receiving less than 40 per cent of the world market price from the State Purchasing Board, so many stopped producing cocoa altogether. The situation got even worse after the droughts and bush fires of the early 1980s: cocoa production in Ghana fell from one-third of the world's total in 1972 to just 12 per cent by 2005.

The Kuapa Kokoo co-operative are trying to change things in Ghana. They are a group of farmers, who formed a co-operative in 1993 to sell cocoa for the benefit of its members. The Kuapa Kokoo co-operative now has a membership of 35,000 and sells about 1,000 tonnes of cocoa annually to the European fairtrade market. They currently receive $1,600 a tonne, plus a $150 fairtrade premium for their cocoa, whilst the world price has been around $1,000. This additional income makes a huge difference to the lives of the farmers and their families.

Divine fairtrade

Kuapa Kokoo decided that another way to increase farmers' income was to produce their own brand of chocolate to sell in Western markets. In 1998 they founded the Day Chocolate Company in partnership with Twin Trading and international development agencies, and launched Divine fairtrade milk chocolate, which is now available in UK supermarkets nationwide. The Dubble Bar is part of the Divine range, and is a fun bar aimed primarily at children.

Become a zoo checker

March 25

An adult lion's roar can be heard up to five miles away. One of the few places you can still hear the sound is at your local zoo. There are approximately 1,500 zoos around the world, providing an amazing opportunity for people (and especially children) to experience the diversity of animal life existing on our planet. But if you think the lions and tigers and bears living in zoos are happy campers, you are wrong.

Some zoo animals are kept in quite appalling conditions. It's a tragedy when creatures are treated badly, and animal abuse may also be occurring in circuses, magic shows, dolphinaria and other tourist attractions where performing animals are used. Many establishments do not provide their animals with adequate living conditions. A lion's roar of distress may not bother some zookeepers, but if you care enough you should try to do something.

Grass on animal-abusers

The Born Free organisation has set up the Zoo Check and Travellers' Alert systems to report animal maltreatment.

If you see animals being badly treated or kept in bad conditions at your local zoo or at a tourist attraction (at home, or on holiday abroad), take photographs or make video evidence of the conditions in which the animals are being kept.

Send your evidence to Zoo Checker, and a campaign will be started to improve the treatment of these animals.

Sign up to be a Zoo Checker: www.bornfree.org.uk/zoocheck/zoo20.htm

Did you know?

An albatross can sleep while it flies. It apparently dozes while cruising at 25 miles per hour.

Clams can change sex. All start out as males, but some decide to become females later in life.

Elephants have a gestation period of over 20 months.

Mockingbirds can imitate any sound from a squeaking door to a cat meowing.

Sharks are apparently the only animals that never get sick. Current research suggests they are immune to every known disease, including cancer.

The Kiwi can't fly, lives in a hole in the ground, is almost blind and lays only one egg each year. Yet it has survived for 70 million years.

The poison-arrow frog has enough poison to kill about 2,200 people.

You can see all these animals and many more in a zoo.

Local issues

See if there is an Architecture for Humanity group near you. Everyone is welcome.

Check out the latest competition. Your design could be featured in a top architectural magazine and exhibited in international design shows, not to mention help to solve a humanitarian crisis and save thousands of lives.

Go to the People We Like section of the Architecture for Humanity website – it offers information on interesting people and organisations promoting socially responsible design.

Architecture for Humanity: www.architecturefor humanity.org

Designer ambitions

Architecture for Humanity is a non-profit organisation founded by Cameron Sinclair, a London-trained architect. It promotes architectural and design solutions to global, social and humanitarian problems, and brings design services to communities in need.

Architecture for Humanity runs design competitions, open to everyone. These competitions don't focus on designing the next Trump hotel. The aim is to obtain designs of low-cost structures for international communities in crisis. Entrants are provided with a list of materials and costs local to the area where the winning project will be built. They are then asked to formulate a design, taking into consideration factors such as how to get water, what resources are available locally, whether there is electricity, and the budget. If your design is selected, they build it.

Some major projects

2002 A design competition for mobile health clinics to provide healthcare, health education and AIDS/HIV testing in Sub-Saharan Africa. Architecture for Humanity is also working on mine clearance, building playgrounds in the Balkans and refugee housing on the borders of Afghanistan.

2004 A competition to design a football pitch in Somkhele, an area in South Africa with one of the highest rates of HIV in the world. It also had to offer a place to learn about HIV/AIDS, and a mobile healthcare facility.

2004 and ongoing Rebuilding Bam in Iran. Architecture for Humanity is working with Relief International to provide permanent housing for the many thousands left homeless by an earthquake that killed over 41,000 people.

Become a protest singer

Songs are enormously important for peace or protest.

Songs of peace

- Bob Marley & The Wailers 'War' (*Rastaman Vibration*, 1976)
- Faithless 'Mass Destruction' (*No Roots*, 2004)
- Boogie Down Productions 'Stop the Violence' (*By All Means Necessary*, 1988)
- Curtis Mayfield 'We've got to have Peace' (*Roots*, 1972)
- Spearhead 'Piece O'Peace' (*Home*, 1994)
- Basement Jaxx (featuring Yellowman) 'Love is the Answer' (*Peace Songs*, 2004)

Songs of protest

- Public Enemy 'Fight the Power' (*Fear Of A Black Planet*, 1994)
- Levellers 'Liberty Song' (*Levelling The Land*, 1992)
- Johnny Cash 'I Shall not be Moved' (*My Mother's Hymn Book*, 2004)
- Chumbawumba 'Enough is Enough' (*Anarchy*, 1998)
- The Pogues 'Streets of Sorrow/Birmingham Six' (*If I Should Fall From Grace With God*, 1987)
- Jimmy Cliff 'Viet Nam' (*Wonderful World, Beautiful People*, 1970)

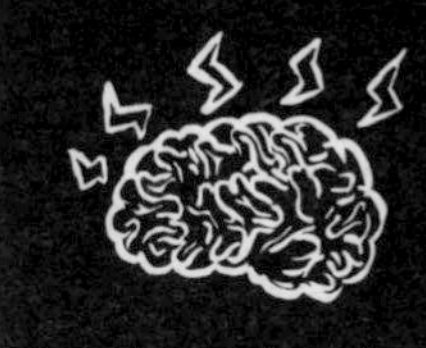

Be inspired

Download these songs onto your iPod, listen and be inspired.

And if you'd like to, write your own song or poem for peace and post it on the 365 Ways to Change the World website. www.365act.com

Anti-war songs at: www.lacarte.org/songs/anti-war/index.html

Peace songs at: www.newsongsforpeace.org and www.songs4peace.com

March 27

Singing the changes

The Smithsonian Museum (www.folkways.si.edu) publishes folk songs, some of which are classics of peace and protest, including Pete Seeger's 'Songs of Protest and Struggle', Woody Guthrie's 'Struggle', 'Good Morning Vietnam' and 'Poems for Peace'. *Amaze Me: Songs in the Key of Peace* is a peace CD featuring female musicians from across the USA. All of the proceeds are being donated to peace organisations, such as Women Against Military Madness, DemocracyNow and CodePINK. For more information, go to: www.rubberneckrecords.com/bio

Flushed with success?

Poo with a view

- The Humanure Handbook is a guide to composting human manure. The authors claim that 'after reading this book, you will never flush a toilet with indifference again'.
Buy the Humanure Handbook at www.amazon.co.uk
- Build your own composting toilet using wood and sawdust. A simple design will cost you only £15 to build. Get the plans from www.jenkinspublishing.com/sawdustoilet.html
- Composting Toilet World, which describes itself as 'the official website of composting toilets': www.compostingtoilet.org

We take the disposal of human waste for granted, flushing the toilet and watching it disappear. Most human waste is disposed of through the sewerage system. But there are problems with this. Raw sewage starts to break down, using oxygen dissolved in the water. But once the oxygen is used up, micro-organisms continue the process anaerobically (without oxygen). This produces a nutrient-rich effluent (which could be used as fertiliser) and methane gas (which could be used as a fuel). But the untreated effluent is often left to run into rivers and ends up in the sea. The nutrients cause algae to bloom; and when they die they decompose, which uses up dissolved oxygen in the water. The reduction of oxygen in the water kills marine animals.

To ensure sustainability, everything taken from the land needs to be put back. Otherwise the natural fertilisers in the soil diminish, to be replaced with chemical fertiliser. These chemicals run off into rivers and lakes, and pollute the water table. Clean water is piped to us, often over hundreds of miles, and 40 per cent of it is flushed down the toilet. There has to be a better way. Composting toilets are the answer.

Composting toilets

Composting toilets use little or no water; they are not connected to a sewage system; they cause no damage to the environment; and they produce compost as a by-product, which you can use in your garden – or sell.

There are two ways of composting. The batch system uses a container, which is filled, then replaced with an empty container. The composting is completed inside the filled container. In a continual process system, the waste moves downwards and is harvested as compost after about six months.

If your carpentry skills aren't good enough, then think about buying a composting toilet. For advice go to the Composting Toilet World website.

Disability rights

We are not the source of the problems; we are the resources needed to solve them. We are not expenses; we are investments. We are citizens of this world. Andrew Biyinzika, Ugandan Disability Rights Activist

This is Andrew's Story: 'I am Andrew Biyinzika. I move with the help of a wheelchair. During my education I faced a lot of challenges in the schools I attended. The classrooms, toilets and labs were totally unfriendly environments for persons with disabilities. It was not easy, but I had no alternative. I encountered many difficult situations, which had a big psychological influence on my life. But I wouldn't give up. I started an organisation called RENYAD (Reach the Needs of Youth and Young People with Disabilities) with the aim of fighting for the fundamental rights of people with disabilities. It is vital for disabled people to be given equal opportunities in all aspects of life. Until the world accepts its responsibility to us, I will continue to fight for our rights. I have the will, knowledge, sensitivity and dedication to do this.'

Andrew's suggestions for making a difference to those with disabilities include:

- Join a campaign to support the right to human dignity of people with disabilities. Force governments to implement measures to ensure that disabled people are able to realise their full potential. This is a human rights issue.
- Counter negative attitudes towards disabled people and stop judging people by their appearance.
- Stop governments going to war. War increases the number of disabled people in the world.

Use your radar

Find out how you can get involved at:
RADAR, the UK's disability network: www.radar.org.uk
Disability rights in the UK: www.direct.gov.uk/DisabledPeople/fs/en
Action on Disability and Development: www.add.org.uk

An end to inequality

Identify a problem that a disabled person might encounter. Maybe the local bank has no disabled access, or the traffic lights don't emit a sound to let a visually-impaired person know when it is safe to cross. Discuss the problem with disabled people, then set about solving it.

Write letters to the bank. Meet a local official to point out the traffic light problem. Many things can improve the lives of the disabled, and you can help make them happen.

Hitchhiker's guide

Join the Morocco Hitch during the spring holiday period. The registration fee of £25 gets you a t-shirt and a Rough Guide. A minimum fundraising target is only £300, and each £250 raised provides a development grant for one school. For every £500 you raise you can claim back £75 towards the cost of your trip. Travel in a group of two or three people, and get to Morocco however you can. Average journey time from London is four to five days. When you get to Morocco, you might even visit a school or two.

Link Community Development:: www.lcd.org.uk

Morocco Hitch: www.lcd.org.uk/events/hitch

Camfed, extending girls' access to education in Africa: www.camfed.org

The road to Morocco

Imagine a classroom, but take away the books, desks, chairs, and windows. Remove the roof as well for good measure. Next put an under-trained teacher in charge of too many children – some of whom have walked 5 km to school, or had no proper breakfast, or both. These are the conditions in which many children in the world today are trying to get an education. It is not their fault that they were born in a country without the resources for a decent education system.

Without education, it is hard for any community to escape from poverty. But things can be done. Link Community Development is based in South Africa, and also works in Ghana and Uganda. It supports head teachers implementing development plans for their schools. It trains teachers, helps schools raise money for improvements, twins schools in Africa with schools in the UK, and provides educational electives for UK teachers to share their expertise with an African school.

Link has helped improve education for over 500,000 children. Only 700 organisations like Link would be able to improve education for all of Africa's children.

Dance classes in Morocco

While working as a Peace Corps Volunteer in Morocco, I noticed that instead of going to school, girls stayed at home to do household chores while their mothers wove carpets to sell at the market. I wanted to give young girls an opportunity to be themselves, express their creativity, and have fun! I started a series of dance classes. Wrapped in headscarves and long skirts, we twisted, turned and let loose. This increased the girls' self-esteem and gave them something to look forward to. *Kari Detwiler, New York*

Become a football fan

March 31

Street League uses the power of sport to transform people's lives – people from underprivileged, poorly educated and socially excluded communities. This includes the homeless, people in drug and alcohol rehabilitation, refugees, long-term unemployed and others. Founder Damian Hatton says, 'As well as the structure given to their lives through practice and match timetables, players might be motivated to make positive changes in their life through a desire to improve their sporting performance.' Anyone can participate, regardless of footballing ability. There are weekly training sessions with qualified coaches, monthly match days and a cup competition.

Street League was founded in 2001, by Dr Damian Hatton (whilst doing a stint on an infectious disease ward in a London hospital). The idea grew. There are now more than 850 players in Street League teams across the UK, in cities as far apart as London and Glasgow. The Homeless World Cup brings together teams from national Street Leagues and homeless football projects in 26 countries. It is organised through the International Network of Street Newspapers. The World Cup provides a shared international goal, and also great publicity for the homeless football movement.

The action on the street

- **Support a side and watch them play.**
- **Sponsor a side – £300 gets your name on team shirts and £30 pays for a Cup: www.goodgifts.org**

Homeless World Cup: www.streetsoccer.org

Street League: www.streetleague.co.uk

Organisations promoting anti-racism football tournaments: www.mondialiantirazzisti.org www.progettoultra.it www.farenet.org

Football promotion amongst young people in developing countries: globall.streetfootballworld.org www.playsoccer-nonprofit.org

Jose's story

Drug dependency lost 42-year-old Jose everything – his job, his family, his home. After seven years of sleeping rough, watching friends die from AIDS or go to prison, he started rehab. Now he's got an apartment, attends college and is reconnected with his children. The credit 'goes to God – and to soccer'. Jose was a member of the US team that competed in the first Homeless World Cup in 2003. He didn't actually get to Austria, as he had to complete his rehab. But the training helped him clean out his body and open his mind.

Masturbate for peace

Today is All Fools Day aka April Fool's Day. Is this website a joke? Go to www.masturbateforpeace.com and see. This is their mission statement:

> There's no greater antidote for war than love. Feelings of hatred and distrust form the necessary basis of armed confrontation. Replace those negative feelings with love and you're halfway towards resolution of any conflict.
>
> However, any real love must start from within. You can't love others without loving yourself first. And, of course, masturbation is the greatest expression of self-love. So it's natural that we, the citizens of the world, are joining together to masturbate for peace.
>
> As we begin with this act of self-love, we encourage others to do the same, to take pleasure in life and to share masturbation's positive energy with a world in need.
>
> Joining this movement is simple. Just masturbate in your own way, focusing your thoughts and energy towards love and peace. Encourage others to do the same. Also, please fill out our petition and tell us how you intend to masturbate for peace.

Slogans for peace

- **Anything war can do, peace can do better**
- **Collateral damage is HUMAN LIFE!**
- **Drop Bush, not Bombs**
- **Go solar, not ballistic**
- **How many lives per gallon?**
- **If you can't pronounce it, don't bomb it!**
- **War is expensive; peace is priceless**
- **War is so 20th century!**

Slogans from the Unrepentant Liberal: liberal.home.comcast.net/slogans.htm

Top April Fool's Day hoaxes of all time: www.museumofhoaxes.com/hoax/aprilfool

Self-love, not war

- Make and distribute bumper stickers on the theme Make Love, Not War.
- Masturbate for Peace is an international movement for peace, with over 17,000 petitions from 91 countries and all 50 states of the USA. You can sign their petition, and in your own words say why making love (even if it's with yourself) is better than making war.
- Remember, testosterone is potentially the world's most dangerous chemical. We should all try to do something for peace.

Guerrilla gardening

Armed with trowels, seeds and vision, you can garden everywhere. Anywhere. Guerrilla Gardeners

Our cities are a sad concrete mess. More parking lots than parks. More traffic signs than trees. Whilst you're looking at the cityscape, ask yourself: Does it have to be like this? Guerrilla Gardeners are people who anonymously plant herbs, flowers and vegetables on vacant land and by the sides of roads and paths.

Planting-as-protest began in the 1970s with a New York group called the Green Guerrillas. These urban horticulturalists lobbed seed grenades (Christmas tree ornaments filled with soil and wildflower seeds) into hundreds of abandoned building sites, which eventually became hundreds of beautiful flower- and vegetable-filled community gardens. Their slogan was: 'Resistance Is Fertile'.

Why not become a guerrilla gardener? Start to sow the seeds of change. Start to reclaim the urban environment for nature. All you need is:

- Some seeds and a small bag of soil.
- A trowel and a watering can.
- Used packaging – recycled of course.
- Some friends (doing it with others is always more fun).
- As much creativity as you can muster.

Start sowing

Walk around and look for good places to start planting. It could be just a crack in the concrete to start your planting.

You can plant seeds and cuttings in spring and summer, and bulbs in the autumn. Plant flowers, vegetables, shrubs and trees. If you're planting seeds, allow them to grow for four to eight weeks at home, before planting them out at your site.

Protect your new plants for the first few days; cut the tops and bottoms off plastic water bottles and put these over the plants.

Primal Seeds, a network protecting biodiversity: www.primalseeds.org

Guerrilla gardening and reclaiming public space: www.publicspace.ca

April 2

Plant for peace

The most revolutionary action is to plant in a spirit of peace. 'Plant for peace' is the Mission Statement of the Toronto Peace Gardeners (May 2003). Join us as we reclaim Ecology Park beside the subway as a place for community and peace. Community includes all the birds, the sky, trees, people, little animals, stones, plants, and insects. Peace means a place to sit, smile, breathe and enjoy the treasures of the present moment. Guerrilla Gardening is a revolutionary idea - the way to peace.

Locks of love

April 3

Donate your hair

- **Grow your hair to more than 10 in long, then get it cut off. Send it to Locks of Love.**
- **If you have a wig you no longer use, donate it to Wig Bank.**

Wig Bank: wigbank.com
Locks of Love: www.locksoflove.org

Agnes's story

Agnes Lennox was diagnosed with breast cancer in January 2003, subsequently losing her hair during chemotherapy. A National Health Service prescription wig is expensive – £53 for a synthetic wig and £204 for one made of human hair. So Annie decided to set up a Wig Bank to help others.

Donated wigs are washed and reconditioned, then sold for £10–£20, with £5 from each transaction going to Maggie's Cancer Caring Centre. Agnes has set up a network of Wig Banks throughout the UK.

Alopecia Aresta has no known cause or cure, and many children suffer from it. Locks of Love provides hairpieces to children in North America aged 18 or younger who are suffering any form of medical hair loss and who are in financial need. Other recipients are cancer patients undergoing chemotherapy. This restores self-esteem, and helps them have better relationships with their peers.

Wigs made from human hair are not always an option for cancer patients, for two reasons. The wigs are made to order, and this can take two months – but most people don't know two months beforehand that they are going to have chemotherapy. And human hair wigs are expensive; if your hair is going to grow again, it may seem a bit of a luxury.

Anyone can donate their hair to Locks of Love from anywhere, provided these conditions are met:

- 10-in (25-cm) minimum hair length (tip to tip). Pull curly hair straight to measure its length.
- Hair supplied bundled as a ponytail or braid. Layered hair may be divided into multiple ponytails for donation.
- Hair to be clean, dry, placed in a plastic bag, and then in a padded envelope.
- Hair can be from men as well as women, young and old, all colours.
- Hair may be coloured or permed, but must not be bleached or chemically damaged (if unsure, ask your stylist).
- Hair swept off the floor is not usable.
- Hair cut years ago is usable if it has been kept in a ponytail or braid.
- Hair that is short, grey, or unsuitable for children will be separated out and sold at market value, which will offset the cost of manufacturing.
- Most hair donated to Locks of Love comes from children wishing to help other children.

Emulate Gandhi

Apply the following test: recall the face of the poorest and the weakest man [or woman] whom you may have seen, and ask yourself if the step you contemplate is going to be of any use to him. Will he gain anything by it? Will it restore him to a control over his own life and destiny?
Mahatma Gandhi

Reading this book makes you a very fortunate person. You have the resources to buy it. You can take the time to read it. You are literate, you can understand what the words mean. And you can see with your eyes, helped perhaps by contact lenses or spectacles. All this makes you one of the world's more fortunate.

Every day you probably walk past people down on their luck. Your natural instinct, most likely, is to ignore people sitting in the street begging for a few pennies. For you, this is a moment of discomfort that you shrug off when you get round the next corner.

There are many reasons why people are living rough. But it is always hard and often lonely. A small act could transform their whole day – a smile, a little conversation, a coin or two from your pocket that you can well afford. For you this could be insignificant; for them it could mean everything.

April 4

Do something today

Practise the Gandhi principle. He believed no day was worth living unless by the end of the day you could say that you had done something to help someone less fortunate than you.

Today, when you are out doing whatever you do, stop when you pass someone begging. Take them for a pizza, ask how their day is going. Listen to their dreams for the future. Share ideas about the state of the world.

Find out about Gandhi, his life and his ideas from:

Mahatma Gandhi Foundation: web.mahatma.org.in

Gandhian Institute: www.mkgandhi.org

Kamat's Mahatma Gandhi album: www.kamat.com/mmgandhi/iink.htm

Who was Mahatma Gandhi?

Mahatma means 'Great Soul', a title given to Gandhi as a mark of respect. Mohandas Gandhi was born in 1869 in Western India. He went to London to study law, and qualified as a barrister in 1891. He then went to South Africa, where he was appalled by the conditions and lack of human rights of immigrant Indians, and he set out to change their lives, developing the idea of non-violent resistance as a protest tool.

He remained committed throughout his life to religious tolerance and to improving the lives of the very poorest.

Go skinny-dipping

Find a tempting river or lake, and take the plunge. Do it in a swimming costume, or go skinnydipping if you dare. Do it at the height of summer, or in the middle of winter. Go early or go late, or any time in between. Just do it. Assert your right to swim. You'll feel all the better for it.

The Right to Swim: www.righttoswim.co.uk

River and Lake Swimming Association: www.river-swimming.co.uk

Assert the right to swim

In April 2005, a group of hardy swimmers won a battle to bathe outdoors on winter mornings in the natural ponds on London's Hampstead Heath without lifeguards having to be present. Hampstead Heath Winter Swimming Club won a court case against the Corporation of London, which had claimed that it risked prosecution by the Health and Safety Executive if it allowed unsupervised dips.

In many countries, over-regulation in the name of public health and safety, or a fear of prosecution for damages in the event of an accident, is making it harder for people to swim in lakes, ponds and rivers. At the same time, government is trying to encourage exercise. The environmental impact of swimming in rivers and lakes is nil. But swimming pools use chemicals to disinfect the water, and the energy for heating the water and the building, and for lighting.

Now the courts are upholding the idea that people should be able to do things at their own risk, and public authorities are being forced to keep open pools and ponds they have been seeking to close.

Where to swim

In the UK, there is a right to swim in most tidal waters, in many stretches of rivers which are not tidal, and in lakes where there is an established use by the public. You can also swim where there are public navigation rights over the water. Swimming is not allowed in canals or in most reservoirs. And if access to the river or lake is privately owned, the landowner may object to you trespassing on their land.

Bathing in rivers and lakes does not create a high level of risk of drowning. These are the deaths of children from drowning for the UK in 1998–99:

- River, canal, lake: 31
- Bath: 25
- Garden pond: 21
- Private and public pools: 11
- The sea: 10
- Other: 6

Source: British Medical Journal

Remember Rwanda

Genocide occurs, and we say 'Never again'. But it still happens. So, with Rwanda, Kosovo, and Darfur fresh in our minds, and with violence between Hindus and Muslims rising in India, it's a good time to act. The Rwandan genocide started on 7 April 1994. A million people were massacred in 100 days. We must work to stop anything like this ever happening again.

The first step is awareness. Educate yourself about what is happening on the planet. Often major media sources do not cover the atrocities which are happening. Know where injustice is occurring. Mary Kayitesi Blewitt, originally from Rwanda, founded SURF (the Survivors Fund) after losing 50 family members herself during the Rwandan genocide. SURF helps survivors deal with and recover from the tragedies of 1994. Remember Rwanda preserves the memory of the Rwandan genocide by remembering its victims and those who tried to aid them, and via education on the Rwandan and other genocides.

The Elie Wiesel Foundation for Humanity creates forums for the consideration of urgent ethical issues, being particularly concerned with hate, intolerance and injustice. It organises an annual essay contest for US undergraduates (read what they have to say).

Stop genocide

Learn about the tragedies of Rwanda. Download the personal testaments of Rwandan genocide survivors being collected by the Memory and Remembrance Project of the Survivors Fund (SURF) at: www.survivors-fund.org.uk/remember/index.htm

Print out the photos at the Remember Rwanda website collected as a 10th-anniversary memorial: www.visiontv.ca/RememberRwanda/main_pf.htm

Create your own mini-exhibition to 'Remember Rwanda'.

Visit: www.preventgenocide.org

SURF: www.survivors-fund.org.uk

Elie Wiesel Foundation: www.eliewieselfoundation.org

Assumpta's story

I was 18 at the time of genocide. I lost my mother, father, brothers and sisters and 30 other relatives, and suffered rape and beatings. My surviving sister went back to our village after the genocide and was attacked again with machetes by the killers of my family. She was in a coma for months. She lost her hearing ability and she lives with constant headache and mental problems. I have tried to commit suicide twice but failed to die. I live in the shadow of genocide. Sometimes I imagine meeting my mother on the street. Sometimes I see people wearing similar clothes like my dead relatives, and I follow them and tap on their shoulders ...

Make polio history

Get writing

Write to the Chairs of Sanofi-Aventis and the Chiron Corporation. Congratulate them on the support they have given to the Global Initiative, and request them to continue this support until polio is eradicated. Ask that they also make a similar commitment to address other important health issues in the developing world.

Jean-François Dehecq, Président-Directeur Général, Sanofi-Aventis, 174 Avenue de France, 75013 Paris, France: www.sanofi-aventis.com

Howard Pien, President, Chief Executive Officer and Chairman of the Board

Chiron Corporation, 4560 Horton Street, Emeryville, CA 94608-2916, USA: www.chiron.com

World Health Organization: www.polioeradication.org

Rotary International: www.rotary.org/foundation/polioplus/

Polio is one of a few diseases that can be totally eradicated. As it only affects humans, an inexpensive vaccine exists, and immunity is life-long. Polio will die out through mass immunisation. In 1988, the Global Polio Eradication Initiative was launched, spearheaded by the World Health Organization, Rotary International (who have provided volunteers and fundraised worldwide), Centre for Disease Control and Prevention (CDC) and UNICEF. The effort has so far involved over 200 countries, 20 million volunteers, and international investment of $3 billion. The number of polio cases worldwide has decreased from 350,000 in 1988, to fewer than 800 in 2003.

An estimated 5 million people are able to walk due to this initiative. The campaign has also strengthened health delivery in many countries, with hundreds of thousands of health workers trained, and millions of volunteers supporting immunisation campaigns.

Polio is endemic in only six countries: Afghanistan, Egypt, Niger, Nigeria, India and Pakistan. All have pledged to end the disease. The success of the world's largest public health campaign is now within reach. If the world can end polio, no child will ever again experience the crippling effects of this devastating disease. And drug companies could play a stronger role in helping combat malaria and the spread of HIV, and in extending the lives of those living with AIDS.

Helping eradication

- Sanofi-Pasteur, the vaccines business of the Sanofi-Aventis Group and the world's third largest pharmaceutical company, had donated 120 million doses of their polio vaccine to the polio eradication programme by 2005.
- Chiron Vaccines gave more than 20 million doses of polio vaccine between 1997 and 1998. In 2002, it made a second donation of 9.5 million doses.

Time for tithing?

Tithing means giving away 10 per cent of your annual income to charity. The idea of giving a proportion of your income to charity, and the idea of this specific amount – 10 per cent – comes from the Old Testament. But many religions encourage tithing.

There are lots of good reasons for giving to charity:

- If you have more than enough money, you can help others who don't.
- If you have more than enough things, buying more is a waste.
- Using your money creatively to help others or to change the world can be a lot of fun.

You might not be willing to give 10 per cent just now. In which case give a smaller proportion of your income. And increase your level of giving as your income rises and as you start to enjoy what you are achieving with your money. And you don't have to be limited to 10 per cent. You can give more!

If you feel already over-committed financially, you might consider donating your time or talents to a charitable cause instead.

Decision time

If you want to give your money away, there are a number of decisions to make.

How much to give away? Is this to be a proportion of your income, a fixed annual sum, or some other amount?

Are you setting aside a monthly or annual sum into a separate bank account?

How to give tax-effectively, so you benefit from tax reliefs on offer.

To calculate how much a tithe is per annum, per month, per week or per day, put in the figure for your annual income and use the tithe calculator at: www.nacba.net/tithe.htm

To donate tax-effectively in the UK, open a Charities Aid Foundation charity account: www.cafonline.org

Choose a tithe or time donation

Start giving a portion of your income or of your time to charity:

- Calculate how much money you actually need to live at the standard you want. Then donate everything in excess of this.
- Tithe your time instead of your money. Cash might be tight, so you may be able to give your time instead. 10 per cent of your work time equals four hours a week. Donate that by volunteering.
- Tithe your talent instead of your money. Do you have a skill or an expertise or a talent which you can donate?
- Donate a valuable item which you don't really want, or no longer need. Or sell it on eBay and donate the proceeds.
- Get a part-time job specifically to donate your earnings from. You could baby-sit, work as a bartender, or mow someone's lawn through the summer.

Elections make a difference

Make a stand

At the next election if you meet the criteria, decide to run for office.

Your friends will vote for you. If you campaign vigorously, other people might too. You may not get elected, but you could get a great deal of publicity for an important cause.

For how to stand, see: www.electoralcommission.org.uk

You can stand for election. You need to be aged at least 21 and be a citizen of the UK, the Republic of Ireland or a Commonwealth country. Peers, bishops, members of the police and armed forces, prisoners serving sentences of more than one year and bankrupts cannot stand.

You need ten people to nominate you, and must put up a deposit of £500 (returned if you get at least 5 per cent of the vote). You can send one letter (not more than 60 grammes) free of charge to everyone on the Electoral Roll – this could save up to £10,000 in stamps, but you have to pay for the leaflet.

Screaming Lord Sutch founded the Monster Raving Loony Party in 1983. He contested over 40 elections, often getting a respectable number of votes. Sutch (who was not a proper Lord, but a UK pop singer), was easily recognised by his flamboyant clothes. Shortly after he polled several hundred votes in Margaret Thatcher's Finchley constituency in 1983, the deposit paid by candidates was raised from £150 to £500. This did little to deter the deposit-losing Sutch, who increased the number of rock concerts he performed to pay for his mock political campaigns.

Pitting his wits

William Pitt the Younger became Prime Minister of Britain in 1783 at the age of 24, whilst still technically a 'young person'. He'd gone to university at 14, entered parliament at 22 and was made Chancellor of the Exchequer at 23.

Pitt is remembered for his fight against corruption, taxation reform, and for shifting power towards the House of Commons. He was also responsible for the Act of Union 1800, which brought Ireland into the United Kingdom. This Act included Catholic emancipation, rejected by the King. Pitt resigned in protest in 1801.

Pitt was Prime Minister again in 1804 up to his death in 1806. He ran the country for a total of 20 years.

Ethical finance

Choose where to put your savings, and who you choose to borrow from. This can have an impact not just on the banks, but also on the companies they choose to invest and not to invest in. Financial companies such as banks rely on your money to keep them in profit. Many people bank with a regular commercial bank, such as Citibank (the world's largest) or HSBC (which advertises itself as 'The World's Local Bank').

An alternative is to use a bank which is a co-operative. This means the bank doesn't have to pay out dividends to its shareholders, and so has more commitment to invest locally and uphold socially responsible values.

Co-operative banking has a huge appeal to people who want to bank ethically. In the UK, the Co-operative Bank is part of the Co-operative movement, together with its Smile online banking operation. Other UK ethical banks are Triodos and the Ecology Building Society.

Money matters

Swap your credit card for an affinity card, and bank with an ethical bank.

If you have stocks and shares (or a pension fund), invest ethically – putting your money in companies which do not degrade the planet or exploit their workers.

There is a good deal of advice available on ethical investing. There are specialist unit trusts for the ethical investor. Some ethical shares are traded on Ethex: www.triodos.co.uk

Websites for socially responsible investors:

Social Investment Forum: www.uksif.org

Ethical Investment Research and Information Service (with free online magazine): www.eiris.org

Affinity cards

Credit cards provide another opportunity to do good with your money. Some are issued by a financial institution in partnership with a charity, which gets an upfront fee for every new customer plus a small percentage of the amount spent on the card. These are known as 'Affinity Cards'. If you are interested in an Affinity Card, think about four things:

- Are you prepared to forgo other benefits, such as Air Miles, that are available on other credit cards?
- Are the interest charges fair?
- Does the card give enough to the charity? Some give more than others.
- Do you believe enough in the cause to want to support it through an Affinity Card?

April 11

The village pharmacy

Tree power

Go neem! Buy neem soap, neem shampoo, neem mosquito and insect repellant, and neem treatment for head lice.

Big drug companies have become interested in identifying the active ingredients of neem and patenting them. But the neem tree is part of India's indigenous knowledge base. For bio-piracy issues around the attempts to patent neem, go to: www.american.edu/TED/neemtree.htm

The Neem Foundation promotes the growing and use of neem: www.neemfoundation.org

Where to get neem products: www.neemco.co.uk

The neem tree is known as the 'Village Pharmacy' in India because of its many healing properties. It is the source of a large number of natural medicines. It helps protect crops against insect pests and people against disease-carrying mosquitoes. Its twigs are used as a toothbrush and toothpaste all in one.

The neem tree was largely unknown to the rest of the world until 1959, when a German scientist witnessed a locust swarm in Sudan. After the swarm had passed by, the only tree left untouched was a neem tree. On closer investigation it was concluded that the locusts did indeed land on neem trees, but they always left without feeding.

There has been worldwide scientific interest in neem since then, and intense research into its many properties. We now know that the tree contains many active ingredients which make it resistant to more than 300 different types of insects, as well as to fungi, bacteria, and even viruses. These chemical defences are not only useful in protecting neem trees, but can be used as the basis for natural medicines.

The properties of the neem tree

Healing and soothing Leaves from the neem tree can be used to ease a variety of skin conditions, complaints and wounds. In India, neem leaf poultices and infusions and neem oil are widely used to treat skin and nail complaints.

Insect repellant Neem is also a powerful insect repellant. The oil was extensively tested in Scotland on the Highland midge by a team of leading experts. Neem seed extract, which is highly concentrated, is a powerful way of eliminating insects, particularly head lice.

Economic fuel Neem has a huge potential for solving global agricultural, public health, population and environmental pollution problems. The demand for neem products, especially the seed as the basic raw material, is set to increase, and with it income generation and job opportunities.

World heritage to visit

Heritage is our legacy from the past, and what we pass on to future generations. Our cultural and natural heritage are both irreplaceable sources of life and inspiration. Places as unique and diverse as the wilds of East Africa's Serengeti, the Pyramids of Egypt, the Great Barrier Reef in Australia and the Baroque cathedrals of Latin America make up our world's heritage.

What makes the concept of World Heritage exceptional is its universal application. World Heritage Sites belong to all the peoples of the world, irrespective of the territory on which they are located.

World Heritage Sites encourage the preservation of cultural and natural heritage around the world. This is embodied in an international treaty called the Convention Concerning the Protection of the World Cultural and Natural Heritage, adopted by UNESCO in 1972.

Plan your visit

If you are planning a visit to a World Heritage Site:

- **Prepare a picnic. No pre-prepared foods; no packaging; no plastic bags, cans, or plastic bottles. Just good friends, real food, proper plates and cutlery. Make sure that everything but the food is re-usable. Have a great day out.**
- **Visit every World Heritage Site in your country.**
- **Go on a conservation holiday with Earthwatch to help save World Heritage Sites. No experience is necessary – just a passion to make a real contribution to heritage conservation.**

The UNESCO World Heritage Centre: whc.unesco.org

In our back yard

Some World Heritage Sites to visit in the United Kingdom:

- Giant's Causeway and Causeway Coast
- Durham Castle and Cathedral
- Ironbridge Gorge
- Stonehenge, Avebury and Associated Sites
- St Kilda
- Blenheim Palace
- Westminster Palace
- City of Bath
- Hadrian's Wall
- Tower of London
- Canterbury Cathedral
- Old and New Towns of Edinburgh
- Maritime Greenwich
- Heart of Neolithic Orkney
- Blaenavon Industrial Landscape
- Dorset and East Devon Coast
- Derwent Valley Mills
- Royal Botanic Gardens, Kew
- Liverpool - Maritime Mercantile City

Make democracy work for you

Taking action

Find out about what is happening in Zimbabwe, a once prosperous country now suffering famine and hyperinflation.

If you are a Zimbabwean, vote at the next election. Form your own voter bloc, finding 10 people who agree to vote your way. Ask each of them to find 10 more people. Each person you persuade is one extra vote.

MDC (Movement for Democratic Change): www.mdczimbabwe.org

Zanu-PF: www.zanupfpub.co.zw

The Zimbabwean opposition leader, Morgan Tsvangirai of the MDC (Movement for Democratic Change), said that there was no point in contesting the 2005 elections for the Senate because the government would rig them – and anyway the Senate had no real power. The MDC claimed that previous elections were seriously rigged, and that opposition politicians and supporters had been harassed, imprisoned and even murdered. The spokesman for the ruling Zanu-PF party, Comrade Webster Shamu said: 'We would like to congratulate the people of Zimbabwe for once again showing their commitment to Zanu-PF and what the party and leadership stand for. The elections and the results have once again demonstrated that the people of Zimbabwe cannot be bought or sold.'

How to rig an election in Zimbabwe

- Install cronies to oversee the poll. Mugabe chose Justice Chiweshe to chair the Election Commission.
- Manipulate constituency boundaries. Justice Chiweshe redrew the electoral map to favour ZANU-PF.
- Ban likely opponents from voting. Up to 3.4 million Zimbabweans living abroad were unable to vote.
- Ensure all likely supporters vote. Senior ranks of the army, air force, police and prisons service were rewarded, junior ranks threatened with the sack if they voted MDC.
- Reduce independent election scrutiny. Western inspectors were banned. Those from Iran, China and Russia were admitted.
- Fill the electoral roll with the names of dead people. There appeared to have been 1 million dead electors.
- Double the number of polling booths and place them in regime strongholds difficult to monitor.
- If all else fails, falsify the result. Votes were counted in polling booths, results phoned to a Constituency Centre then a National Logistics Centre in Harare. Mugabe loyalists ran the whole process.

Plant a tree

- Trees renew our air supply by absorbing carbon dioxide and producing oxygen. Just two mature trees can provide enough oxygen for a family of four.
- One tree produces nearly 118 kg of oxygen each year.
- One acre of trees removes up to 2.6 tonnes of carbon dioxide each year.
- Shade trees can protect against fierce sunlight and make buildings up to 10°C cooler in the summer.
- Trees cool the air by evaporating water in their leaves.
- Tree roots stabilise the soil and prevent erosion.
- Trees improve water quality by slowing and filtering rainwater, as well as protecting aquifers and watersheds.

Adapted from 'Fun Facts' on the Trees Are Good website of the International Society of Arboriculture. Trees Are Good has information on trees and caring for them: www.treesaregood.com

Grow your own

Go to your local ice cream shop and ask them for some large empty cartons. Find some seeds (acorns if you want to plant oak trees), and plant the seeds in the cartons. Put the tubs in a sunny window, water from time to time, and add some plant food if you feel that your trees are getting hungry. Transplant into a bigger pot as your trees grow.

Find a suitable spot to plant out your trees: on a bit of waste land, the canal towpath, the edge of an existing grove of trees.

Visit your trees. Take pride in what you have done.

Trees for Cities: www.treesforcities.org

Tree Aid: www.treeaid.org.uk

April 14

Tree charities plant trees for you

Charities such as Trees for Cities plant trees in cities in return for donations of around £15 a year. They also have a partnership with Ben & Jerry's, whereby they supply free tree-planting kits (in a Ben & Jerry's ice cream tub of course).

Trees for Cities also operates overseas, and you can plant banana, lemon or avocado trees in somewhere exciting such as Addis Ababa.

Trees for Cities runs a number of interesting training courses, including: 'How to operate a chain saw', and 'How to hang from a tree'.

Tree Aid runs tree nurseries, plants trees and manages woodlands in Ethiopia, Mali, Burkina Faso, Niger and Northern Ghana, all in the arid zone of central Africa. Help regenerate the desert by getting Tree Aid to plant a tree.

Imagining peace

Imagine ... John Lennon

Imagine peace. Think about what peace means to you. Here are some ideas to reflect on:

- If soldiers fought for peace instead of going to war, what would they be doing?
- If all guns were replaced with flowers, what would the world look like?
- How can we get rid of hate and violence in the world? In your neighbourhood?
- Listen to the song 'Imagine' by John Lennon. Make a drawing of what you imagined.
- What animal represents peace? What animal represents violence? Why are they different? How are they similar?
- If peace grew from a tree, what would it look like?
- What ingredients would you use to make a 'peace meal'? Write a recipe for this.
- If peace could be embodied in a person, who would that person be?

Organise an art show

Organise a local art show on the theme of peace. Maybe to commemorate those who died in a conflict that has touched your community.

- **Contact schoolteachers and after-school programme organisers.**
- **Find a venue – a space such as a library, town hall or shopping mall.**
- **Have an official opening. Ask the young artists to bring family and friends.**
- **Get a sponsor and offer prizes for everyone.**

Read the full text of 'Imagine' at: www.merseyworld.com/imagine/lyrics/imagine.htm

Art for peace

Young people can teach us a lot. As future adults and even future leaders of the world, their visions of the future and their ideas for dealing with the world's problems are important.

Enabling young people to express their ideas for peace through art is a step closer towards making peace a reality. It can inspire young people to share their dreams, and even to take action for a better world. Young people can express their views in a variety of media (drawing, painting, sculpture, an installation, a happening).

Ask the young artists to use their imagination. It is important to remove the idea of competitiveness from the event, as the purpose is to promote peace and co-operation, which means respecting everyone's views and ideas.

Focusing on peace creates optimism. Focusing on the terrorist threat only makes us more afraid.

Super computing

ChessBrain was the first distributed network to play a game against a single human opponent. On 30 January 2004 this earned an official World Record for the largest networked chess computer in history. One chess Grand Master competed against 2,070 PCs from over 50 countries. The game ended in a draw ...

Some projects require too much computing power to solve. Using a large number of small computers via the internet in a 'distributed network' is a way of overcoming this problem.

Small parts of the problem are given to lots of different computers, the solution being combined from the component parts. Distributed computing projects use hundreds of thousands of volunteers all over the world. Besides playing chess, projects include:

- Prime numbers: finding larger ones – now with more than 10 million digits.
- Extraterrestrial radio signals: the search continues.
- Exploring protein folding to try to find treatments for Alzheimers, Huntingtons Chorea and such.
- Finding new and more effective drugs to fight cancer and AIDS.
- Mapping the World Wide Web at grub.org

April 16

Start your networking

Join a distributed network. This will involve your visiting a website and downloading some software whilst keeping your computer connected to the internet.

After that you won't notice a thing. Your computer will be using its unused storage and processing capacity to solve some of the world's big problems, which are either too large or too expensive for a supercomputer to manage on its own.

Choose the project that interests you the most. Go to: http://distributedcomputing.info/projects.html

Monkey business ...

Help test the Shakespeare monkey theory: 'If you have enough monkeys typing randomly, they will eventually type the works of William Shakespeare'.

The current record is the first 24 letters of *Henry IV part 2*, which was typed after 2,737,850 million billion billion billion monkey-years, on 3 January 2005. To participate, display the project web page in your web browser. A Java applet generates random pages of text and compares them to all of Shakespeare's plays, and displays any matches between the first however many characters of your random page and a Shakespeare play.

If you beat the record, you press the Submit Record button.

Visit the website: www.aardasnails.com

April 17

Make a wish come true

Help make a child's wish come true. Put a smile on their face. Help their recovery. Go to Make-A-Wish Foundation: www.worldwish.org

Donate your air miles to the Foundation. Participating airlines include: America West, American, British Airways, Continental, Delta, Northwest, Southwest, United, US Airways.

To donate air miles, go to: www.wish.org/home/giving/airmiles.htm

Ben's story

Ben Duskin was diagnosed with cancer aged five. His mother used a video game analogy to explain what was going on inside his body. Ben asked Make-A-Wish to create a game to help others battle cancer. Based on the idea that attitude gets you through cancer, in the game Ben skateboards around killing bad cancer cells.

Play the game at www.makewish.org/ben

Donate your air miles

Today, more than 120 million people worldwide belong to airline loyalty schemes. The Air Miles scheme awards air miles as a customer loyalty bonus in other retail sectors. According to *The Guardian*, air miles have become 'a new global currency'.

Frequent flyer schemes started in 1981. Almost 14 trillion frequent-flyer miles have been accumulated. Each mile is worth between two and ten cents. The total stock of air miles issued is worth more than $700 billion, which is more than the value of all dollar bills in circulation, and far more than the UK's £42 billion issued notes and coins. You can spend air miles on travel and other benefits. Some schemes allow you to donate them for use by a charity.

The Make-A-Wish Foundation grants wishes to children who have a life-threatening medical condition. Children over the age of two-and-a-half, and under the age of 18 at the time of referral, are potentially eligible to have their wish granted. The Foundation contacts the doctor treating the child to determine if the child is medically eligible for a wish (based on the Foundation's medical criteria), and that the child has not received a wish from another wish-granting organisation.

Most wishes fall into one of these categories:

- I wish to go somewhere ...
- To a favourite theme park, an exotic beach, go on a cruise, see snow for the first time, or attend a major sporting event or concert.
- I wish to be somebody ...
- To be someone for a day – a fireman, a police officer, a model.
- I wish to meet someone famous ...
- To meet a favourite athlete, recording artist, television personality, movie star, public figure.
- I wish to have something ... a computer, a shopping spree, something you've wanted for ages.

Use recycled toilet paper

Reducing the amount of paper you use and increasing the amount that is recycled, can help reduce the pressure on the world's timber resources. This saves energy as well as trees, as recycled paper manufacture only uses half the energy and water required for new paper.

Everyone in the UK uses about six trees' worth of paper every year. This is six times more than 50 years ago. Most paper in the UK has been imported, which adds to transport pollution. Making paper uses a huge amount of energy. To produce a tonne of paper requires the same energy as is used in producing a tonne of steel. New paper is often white, not because this is paper's natural colour, but because it's bleached. This bleach is a major cause of water pollution.

Toxic wastes, including dioxins and other waste, are discharged from pulp mills. Yet until recently there was little control of these discharges. Even though paper can be recycled and the amount being recycled has been increasing, more than half of all paper used is still thrown away. One in five of the world's trees is used to make paper. Check out your own dustbin. On average 30 per cent of your waste is paper and card. That's two trees' worth each year just caused by you!

April 18

Roll back waste

Buy recycled toilet paper. This is available from many supermarkets, and also from eco-shopping services.

Just for a challenge, see if you can cut down on the number of squares you use.

Start to use other recycled paper products – tissues, and kitchen rolls.

Paper facts and lots of other information from Wildlife Watch: www.wildlifewatch.org.uk/helpingwildlife

The ShitBegone website: www.shitbegone.com

ShitBegone

ShitBegone is 100 per cent recycled, because who wants to flush trees down the toilet? Only an asshole would sell people something made of trees when they don't need it. ShitBegone toilet paper is non-embossed. Instead of being puffed up with air, ShitBegone is wound tightly on the roll. This makes ShitBegone rolls smaller and harder than the rolls that other companies sell. But ShitBegone is just as soft, just as long-lasting, and cheaper too! ShitBegone expresses hope and belief that a better world is possible!
From the ShitBegone website

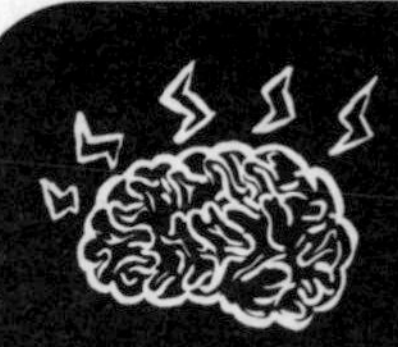

Connecting up cyberspace

See what can happen

Visit the websites below and find out as much as you can about these projects.

Let this be a spur to your imagination. Think up a project that will connect people in your community or across the world.

Take the first crucial step in developing your idea.

Keep going until your project is out there.

1000 Journals: 1000journals.com

Degree Confluence Project: www.confluence.org

PhotoTag: www.phototag.org

The internet creates all sorts of opportunities for connecting people, often in some intriguing projects.

The 1,000 Journals project consists of 1,000 journals, which travel at random through the world. Each person completes a page, and then sends it to another person. The first 700 journals were sent to people who asked for them, who then passed their journal to a friend. People add whatever they like to the journal that is in their possession before passing it on – writing, painting, bits and pieces. Sightings of all 1,000 journals are logged on the website. The first journal to return had travelled to 13 US states and also to Brazil and Ireland. The completed journal was exhibited on the 1,000 Journals website.

The Degree Confluence Project's aim is to visit each point on the surface of the earth where degrees of latitude longitude intersect, and for the person visiting each location to take a photo. The pictures and stories from the location are then posted on the website. So far 3,430 points have been photographed in 155 countries. There's an intersection point within 49 miles (79 km) of everyone, and a total of 12,737 points on dry land. Anyone can take part in the project.

Releasing cameras into the wild

This fun, not-for-profit venture captures the chance wanderings of disposable cameras, which are labelled and sent out with instructions for those who find them to take one picture and then pass the camera on. A pre-paid and addressed envelope is included with the camera so that it can be mailed back to PhotoTag when all the film has been used up. People who stumble upon a camera can log on to the PhotoTag website to update the progress of their particular camera. And when the camera is returned (if it ever is) then the photo-images are posted on the website. 40 cameras have been released since 2000, of which only 6 have so far been returned.

Link up with the slums

There are 923 million people around the world living in slums: 554 million in Asia, 187 million in Africa, 128 million in Latin America and the Caribbean and 54 million in the rich world. This represents nearly a third of the world's urban population, and 43 per cent of people in developing countries. In the next 30 years, this will increase to 2 billion if no action is taken.

The UN defines a slum as a household lacking:

- Access to sufficient and affordable water.
- Access to a private or shared toilet.
- Secure tenure without threat of eviction.
- A permanent and adequate structure in a non-hazardous location.
- Sufficient space – with not more than two people sharing a room.

Most slum dwellers live in homes of less than 150 square foot with no amenities. Instead of rent, they pay money to a 'local boss', who protects them from eviction by the authorities or the landowner. Sometimes a slum community will be resettled onto a site where they can build their own homes. But more often, they will be evicted with nowhere to go, and have to find somewhere to live all over again.

April 20

Home help

Contact one of the slum-dwellers associations listed on the SDI website. Organise fundraising on the theme of housing, such as:

- **A sponsored sleep-out on your street or in a garden, in home-made shelters.**
- **Raise sponsorship to spend 24 hours with no mains water, collecting all your water from at least 100 metres away.**
- **Make 'Shack Chic' objects (see Craig Fraser's photographs on: www.quivertree.co.za) and sell them on a stall.**

Slum/Shack Dwellers International: www.sdinet.org

UN Habitat, the United Nations Human Settlements programme: www.unhabitat.org

Shack attack

Shack/Slum Dwellers International is a forum for slum dwellers to report on what they are doing to improve their housing. The success stories include how they are:

- Advocating their needs, and obtaining basic rights.
- Obtaining land, designing and building their own housing.
- Developing income-generating activities.

You can read how the government in Thailand has approved a $470-million plan to upgrade housing in 2,000 communities in 2005–08. The people living in the communities will be the key actors and owners of the project, and will develop it collectively. Or you can keep up to date with darker developments in the slum-clearing in Zimbabwe.

April 21

Slow down

Start to relax

Sign up to slowing down.

Society for the Deceleration of Time: www.zeitverein.com (an English language version of this website is being created at a snail's pace!)

Tracey Smith's downshifting website: www.frenchentree.com/fe-downshifting

The National Downshifting Week website has lots of good links: www.downshiftingweek.com

In Praise of Slow: www.inpraiseofslow.com

The slow lane

In Praise of Slow by Carl Honore has chapters on: slow food, cities, mind and body, medicine, sex, work, leisure and childrearing. 'I am a speedaholic, and so this book is also a personal journey. I want to be free of the constant itch to go faster ... to be able to read to my son without watching the clock. I want to find a way to live better by striking a balance between fast and slow.'

Most people agree that modern life is lacking something. Life in the fast lane means stress, worries about status and money, and a feeling that you are somehow missing out. Here are two interesting reactions to an ever-faster world:

Downshifting Swapping a high-octane, stressed-out career for a more relaxed existence. An estimated 16 million people in Europe will have downshifted by 2007. Broadcaster and journalist Tracey Smith organises an annual National Downshifting Week in the last week of April to highlight ways in which people can live simpler and happier lives, while being kinder to the environment. Among her suggested activities are:

- Book half a day off work to spend entirely with someone you love.
- Cut up a credit card.
- Eliminate three non-essential purchases a week.

Slowing down The Society for the Deceleration of Time campaigns for slowness. Its 1,000 members contribute to a general process of deceleration, pausing for reflection wherever appropriate. It was founded in 1990 and is based in Klagenfurt, Austria. It organises talks and workshops, and an annual symposium. It also organises stunts to get publicity for the idea of deceleration. For example:

- Gold medals for the slowest competitor in Olympic events – an idea they put to the International Olympic Committee.
- Pedestrian 'speed traps', which time people over 50 metres. If the pedestrian takes under 37 seconds, they are asked to explain their haste. As a punishment they are then asked to walk a tortoise puppet along the same 50-metre stretch.

Be a backyard beekeeper

Bees are essential to life on earth. They transfer pollen from the male parts to the female parts of flowers. Without this process, many garden plants would not be pollinated and so would fail to produce the fruits, vegetables and flowers that we need and enjoy. Around 80 per cent of the food we eat comes from crops that have been pollinated by bees.

Beekeeping can be a lot of fun. The bees will do most of the work. To collect 454 grammes of honey, bees will need to visit over 2 million flowers. This means a journey of around 55,000 miles – the equivalent of more than twice round the world. A worker bee will visit up to 100 flowers each trip and make up to 15 trips each day.

To get started you will need:

- a hive
- some basic equipment
- protective clothing
- and, of course, some bees.

A typical hive will produce around 12 kg to 15 kg and possibly as much as 30 kg of honey each year.

April 22

Pollinate the world

Even in the concrete jungle, you can be a beekeeper. You'll be a friend of the earth, pollinator and food producer. There are around 40,000 beekeepers in the UK. Most are hobbyists rather than commercial producers.

You can sell the honey you produce to earn an income. Or you can distribute it amongst your friends.

Backyard Beekeeping – notes on keeping bees in urban neighbourhoods: outdoorplace.org/beekeeping/citybees.htm

Somerset Beekeepers has lots of practical information: www.somersetbeekeepers.org.uk

British Bee Keepers Association: www.bbka.org.uk

Where to put your bees

You don't even need your own garden, you can do it on your rooftop. Or arrange with a park or a landowner, or ask a local allotment gardener, to put your hive on their land. The bees will be doing a useful job for them, so they may welcome you.

You will need to put in around half an hour per week per hive from mid-April to August to look after your bees. You can buy a complete hive of bees, or you can obtain a swarm, when a bee colony divides into two, with half leaving to form a new colony elsewhere; or you can buy a nucleus and grow this into a colony.

According to the British Beekeeping Association you might need to invest £150–£230 for equipment and £80 for a second-hand hive with bees.

Copyright and copyleft

Left wanting to know more?

Check out these websites for more information:
The GNU General Public License project: www.gnu.org/copyleft/gpl.html
Free Software Foundation Copyleft site: www.gnu.org/copyleft/copyleft.html

Copyright creates ownership over intellectual property, a control over its use, and the right to demand income from any use of the material. It protects the written word, electronic data, music and graphic design. It may be owned by the originator, or it can be assigned or sold on: for example, Michael Jackson bought the copyright to a large number of Beatles' songs, and the copyright to *Peter Pan* was donated by J M Barrie to Great Ormond Street children's hospital. Copyright exists for 70 years from the original publication date or from the author's death, whichever is later. After this, the work can be used freely by anyone without payment.

Property is theft

There is an alternative: 'Copyleft', developed by the Free Software Foundation. It asserts the author's ownership, but allows it to be distributed free, and at the same time prevents anyone else claiming copyright over it.

Copyleft should be used by anyone wanting to promote free dissemination of any work, to set out the terms for doing this and as a commitment to the idea of sharing. In a world where genetic sequences, traditional medicines and foods are being patented, Copyleft shows that there is an alternative.

Add the following to anything and everything you write:

This work is 'Copyleft' as part of the author's commitment to a fair and sharing society. This means you are free to publish any part or all of it under the following licence:

Copyright © year of publication, author name.

Permission is granted to anyone to make or distribute verbatim copies of this work, in any medium, provided that this copyright notice and permission notice are preserved, and that the distributor and any subsequent distributor grants the recipient permission for further redistribution as permitted by this notice.

Modified versions may not be made except with the permission of the author.

Failure to comply with this may result in legal action to obtain financial compensation for the illegal use of the intellectual property.

April 24

Happiness Manifesto

Most people in the developed world and most middle class people everywhere are not as happy as they might be. Doing jobs they don't enjoy, travelling nose to bumper or crushed inside a bus to get to work, the strains of family life, 'I want, I want' but never having quite enough money to afford everything – all this makes life really stressful. Despite growing affluence, happiness levels remain fairly constant. Once people have the basic necessities, money does not make much of a difference. And the people who spend more time pursuing money are often less happy.

Slough, a town near London, participated in a programme called 'Making Slough Happy' made by Optomen Television for the BBC. The aim of the programme was to raise the level of happiness. They encouraged singing and dancing, communal art projects, visits to lottery winners to see if money made a difference. Even a trip to a graveyard: 'Reminding yourself that life is short can really boost your appreciation that it's wonderful just to be alive!'

Change your world

Before you change *the* world, you need to change *your* world.

Print out the Happiness Manifesto, pledge to do all 10 things for two months. Then see how you feel.

Circulate the Manifesto to your ten best friends – or to the first ten people you meet.

The BBC website for Making Slough Happy: www.bbc.co.uk/lifestyle/tv_and_radio/making_slough_happy

A Slough journalist's site: www.richardhill.co.uk/makingsloughhappy

The official website for Slough: www.slough.gov.uk

The Slough experience

Some of the happiness experts featured in the programme 'Making Slough Happy' drew up a Happiness Manifesto.

1. Get physical: Exercise for half an hour three times a week.
2. Count your blessings: At the end of the day, reflect on five things you're grateful for.
3. Make time to talk: An hour of uninterrupted conversation with your partner or closest friend each week.
4. Plant something: Even if it's a window box or pot plant. Then keep it alive!
5. Cut your TV viewing: By half at least.
6. Smile or say hello to a stranger: At least once each day.
7. Phone a friend: Make contact with a friend or relation you haven't seen for a while, and arrange to meet up.
8. Have a good laugh: At least once a day.
9. Give yourself a daily treat: Take time to really enjoy this.
10. Do a daily kindness: Do an extra good turn for someone each day.

April 25

Boycott bad companies

As a consumer you are in a powerful position. You can support companies that behave ethically, but you can also exercise your buying power to boycott companies who are behaving in unethical ways. 'Taking action' then involves doing nothing other than not buying products from suppliers you disapprove of.

Boycotts work. Canadian forests, Mexican salt marshes, whales and the seabed have all benefited from boycott activity in the past. Animal rights campaigners have also been sophisticated users of the boycott technique, with successes in the fields of live animal transport, hunting, pet shops and animal testing. Last but not least, human rights boycotts have also made a string of gains, most notably perhaps over corporate activity in Burma.

The power of not buying

Boycott companies and products you disapprove of.

See the boycott list at Ethical Consumer: www.ethicalconsumer.org

Find out about company practice at: www.responsibleshopper.org

Co-op America's boycott site includes a guide to organising a consumer boycott: www.coopamerica.org/programs/boycotts

Some ongoing campaigns

Boycott Bush has been called by Ethical Consumer because of Bush's rejection of the Kyoto Agreement. The top five brands to boycott are: Esso, Maxwell House, Microsoft, MBNA and Asda. Log on to: www.boycottbush.net to find out the ethical alternatives.

Boycott Coca-Cola is supported by the Colombia Solidarity Campaign and India Resource Centre following environment and human rights abuses. In Colombia, Coca-Cola stands accused of complicity in the assassination of eight trade union leaders since 1990. In India, the company has depleted and polluted groundwater in Kerala. Check out: www.colombiasolidarity.org.uk and www.indiaresource.org

Boycott De Beers has been called by Survival International in support of the Bushmen of the Kalahari in Botswana, forcibly evicted from their ancestral land to make way for future diamond mining. Support the Bushmen at www.survival-international.org

Boycott Nestlé is another long-running campaign, called by Baby Milk Action, originally in response to the marketing of breast-milk substitutes for babies. An estimated 1.5 million babies die each year because they are not breast fed. Go to: www.babymilkaction.org

High street diversity

Starbucks is one of just a few big corporations that are taking over our high streets. It may serve good coffee, support fairtrade and donate some of its profits to good causes, but it also drives local shops out of business and creates a uniform look to shopping centres in whichever city or country they are in.

Space Hijackers opposes the way that public space is being eroded and being replaced by corporate profit-making space. They want to reclaim public ownership for these spaces.

A particular target of Space Hijackers is Starbucks, which is massive in the USA and expanding fast in the UK – its second biggest market. In 1997, a 25-year-old Houston-based computer programmer called Winter started a quest to visit every Starbucks in the world and drink an espresso or a black coffee at each. By 2005, he had visited 4,765 Starbucks in North America, and 213 elsewhere. The problem is that Starbucks is opening, on average, 25 new outlets each week.

Play the game

Play Starbucks Musical Chairs:

- **Players separately make their way to a Starbucks.**
- **Each player smuggles in a drink disguised as a Starbucks beverage.**
- **Players move chairs each time two songs are played on the in-store stereo.**
- **Points are awarded, based on where a person is sitting (on the floor 5 points; sole occupant of an armchair 20 points).**
- **The first to reach 100 points stands up and says 'I've been Starbucked'.**
- **Other players curse themselves for losing and leave the store.**

Starbucks Musical Chairs: http://spacehijackers.co.uk/starbucks/index.html

Space Hijackers: http://spacehijackers.co.uk

Starbucks: www.starbucks.com

April 26

Starbucks Musical Chairs

You're sitting down in your local Starbucks. The people who sit next to you keep moving away to other seats. So you sniff yourself to check you don't smell. Suddenly, a girl stands up at the far end of the cafe and screams at the top of her voice 'I've been Starbucked'. Everyone else in the store simultaneously sighs with depression. The next thing you know, everyone in the store starts laughing, they all get up and leave at once. You and the staff are the only ones left, and they look as stunned as you ... everyone has been playing Starbucks Musical Chairs!

April 27

Petition the world

Sign up

Create your petition online. It's free!

After you have collected signatures, don't just let your petition sit and rot. Send it to politicians, companies, and leaders – whoever can help you work toward getting the change you want.

Here are two websites where you can set up and distribute your petition for free:

The Petition Site: www.thepetitionsite.com/create.html

PetitionOnline: www.petitiononline.com/petition.html

Words without actions are the assassins of idealism. Herbert Hoover

An effective way of getting attention and gathering support for an issue is a petition. The days of knocking on doors in residential neighbourhoods begging for signatures have passed. Not only is this hard work, it's only really appropriate for a neighbourhood campaign, when everyone has a vested interest in the subject. Nowadays, the advent of the internet has given us a fast and easy mechanism for collecting thousands of signatures.

What makes for a good petition? Explain exactly what the issue is, and what exactly you are asking people to sign up to. Do your research. Present the reader with concrete facts. Be brief. Don't write more than half a page.

How to collect more signatures than you ever dreamed possible:

- Send emails to your friends asking them to sign.
- Post links on relevant discussion boards.
- Contact relevant writers and journalists and tell them about your petition.
- Send out a press release announcing your petition.
- Talk about your petition in online chat rooms.
- Add a link to your petition in your email signature and your website.
- Ask special interest groups to add a link on their website or in their newsletters.
- Submit your petition page to search engines (it usually takes between three and four weeks to be indexed). Type into Google 'submit search engines' to find a way of reaching a lot of search engines for free.

Petition online

Some petitions on the PetitionOnline website:

Get softball back into the 2012 Olympics to the International Olympic Committee

Property rights in animals to the US Congress

Please Lindsay, eat! to Lindsay Lohan, teen actress

Experimental travel

Feeling like a day out? A long weekend away? A holiday of a lifetime? Why not do something really different, and at the same time, save energy, reduce your carbon emissions and see the world in a completely new perspective.

In 1990, Joel Henry started experimenting with travel as a form of conceptual art. He invited people in Strasbourg to travel to Zurich, view the city as a serious tourist and then bring back some memento of their visit. Each person paid his or her own costs and travelled independently. They met up on their return to discuss their visit. This was the start of Latourex, the laboratory of experimental travel.

Joel Henry teamed up with Rachel Antony to compile the *Lonely Planet Guide to Experimental Travel*. Below are some of the 40 ideas in the book.

April 28

Break away

You can use Rachel and Joel's book to give you ideas. Why not set up your own Experimental Travel Group, and plan one experimental tour each month?

Spend a day at the airport: enjoy the shopping, have a meal, wash and brush up, meet others awaiting their flight. And remember Merhan Karimi Nasseri, a stateless refugee from Iraq who has lived at Paris Charles de Gaulle airport since 1988 – the basis of theTom Hanks film *Terminal*.

Latourex: www.latourex.org

The Lonely Planet Guide to Experimental Travel: www.lonelyplanet.com/experimentaltravel

A very different holiday

A-to-Z travel Find the first street in a town that starts with the letter A and the last that starts with the letter Z, draw a line between the two. Walk as close to your line as the roads will allow you. That's your route for exploring the city.

Backpacking at home Go to the airport dressed as a backpacker. Take public transport back to the centre of the city, check into a hostel, and spend a few days doing backpacker things.

Chance travel Every time you come to a crossroads, flip a coin. If it's heads, you turn left; if tails, you turn right. See where chance will take you.

Eros-tourism Discover a city whilst looking for love. Arrange to take a holiday with your partner, but travel to the city independently with no plans for meeting up. Your task is to find your loved one.

Lonely Planet Guide to Experimental Travel

April 29

Community gardening

Green fingers

Turn the area in front of your home into a wonderful floral garden for everyone who passes by to enjoy.

If you don't have a front garden, put hanging baskets on the walls and window boxes on all the windowsills facing the street.

If there's a piece of vacant land, get together with others in your community to turn it into a community garden.

Cavendish Gardens: www.cgc.vze.com

Federation of City Farms and Community Gardens, for information and advice on community gardens, community orchards or city farms: www.farmgarden.org.uk

This is the story of Graham and Bob, who live in Cavendish Gardens, a low-rise housing estate built in the early 1970s by Walsall Council – near the M6 motorway just north of Birmingham.

In 1998, Graham and Bob planted a small tree in the communal area outside their apartment. They added herbaceous borders the next year and began to maintain the lawn. Soon other residents began to extend the garden and create new ones around the estate. In January 2002, a Gardening Co-operative was set up for the maintenance of the estate. The landlord provided all the equipment, including a lawn tractor, mowers, tools and storage. Most of the plants and garden furniture were provided by the residents.

The estate is now filled with gardens that the residents can sit in and enjoy, a real neighbourhood in what was a run-down enclave. Cavendish Gardens is a great example of how two people with energy and enthusiasm transformed their community, turning hard-to-let flats into desirable residences.

The good life

City Farms and Community Gardens are community-managed projects ranging from tiny wildlife gardens to fruit and vegetable plots on housing estates, to community polytunnels and large city farms. They exist mainly in urban areas, in response to a lack of access to green space, and a desire to encourage strong community relationships and an awareness of gardening and farming. City farms and community gardens are usually developed by local people. If you volunteer on a community farm or garden you might become involved in:

- Maintaining trees, livestock and crops.
- Pre-school and after-school clubs and special needs groups.
- Running a cafe or a shop.
- General maintenance and construction work.
- Administration, marketing and fundraising.

Get non-voters to the polls

April 30

All of us know people who don't vote at election time. Are they the kind of people who give long-winded speeches about how little difference their one vote will make? Are they completely fed up with politics and politicians of all parties, seeing them as corrupt windbags who promise a lot and then deliver nothing? Or are they just so lazy that they can't be bothered to get off the sofa?

Voting is the most direct route we have to our politicians. When someone doesn't vote, one less voice is heard and the democratic process is weakened. It is our opportunity to back someone we trust and whose ideas we like, someone whom we believe will do their best for the community they represent.

We have the chance at election time to engage with politicians. After they have been elected, hold them accountable to all the promises they made and ensure that they make their best efforts as our representatives. If they are performing poorly, then we can vote next time for someone better. You accomplish all of these things and more when you vote. The actual voting process only takes a few minutes.

Drag them out to the vote

Your vote can make a difference. If you are over 18, make sure you are registered to vote and that you vote on Election Day. Drag all your non-voting friends to the polling station.

Pledge that you will vote at the next election. Also that you will take five people to the polls who wouldn't otherwise vote. Have a party on election night just for people who voted. Do whatever it takes!

The Orange revolution in Ukraine: orangeukraine.squarespace.com

A guide to the Iraqi election: www.motherjones.com/news/update/2005/01/01_402.html

Find out about elections around the world: http://en.wikipedia.org/wiki/User:Electionworld/Electionworld

Why democracy?

Democracy is the recurrent suspicion that more than half the people are right more than half the time. E B White

Many societies do not enjoy what we would regard as true democracy. Fair and open elections are something that people have fought hard for and even died to establish. A recent example was in the former Soviet republic of Ukraine in 2004, when the protests of millions of people on the streets achieved a re-run of the first rigged election.

Captured on film

Kids with Cameras gave cameras to the children of sex workers working in Calcutta's brothels so that they could photograph their lives. An Oscar-nominated documentary was made about this project called 'Born into Brothels'.

Find out about how the children of sex workers see their lives: www.kids-with-cameras.org

International Union of Sex Workers: www.iusw.org

Network of Sex Work Projects, promoting health and human rights: www.nswp.org

Membership is free

Join the International Union of Sex Workers. Membership is free. No, you don't need to be a sex worker to join.

Do this as an act of solidarity. Find out what's going on. Help out if you can.

Join the sex workers union

Sex work is big business all over the world. People become sex workers because they see no other way of earning a living, to feed a drug habit, because they are forced into it as slaves, or out of choice.

Sex work has many dangers: the risk of violence, AIDS, prosecution, extortion and much else besides.

Sex workers conventions take place all over the world. Sex workers have banded together in the International Union of Sex Workers.

The Union's demands include:

- Decriminalisation of all aspects of sex work which involves consenting adults.
- The right to form and join professional associations or unions.
- The right to work on the same basis as other independent contractors and employers and to receive the same benefits as other self-employed or contracted workers.
- No taxation without such rights and representation.
- Zero-tolerance of coercion, violence, sexual abuse, child labour, rape and racism.
- Legal support for sex workers who want to sue those who exploit their labour.
- The right to travel across national boundaries and obtain work permits wherever the person is living.
- Clean and safe places to work.
- The right to choose whether to work alone or co-operatively with other sex workers.
- The absolute right to say 'No'.
- Access to training – sex workers' jobs require very special skills and professional standards.
- Access to health clinics where sex workers will not feel stigmatised.
- Re-training programmes for sex workers who want to leave the industry.
- An end to social attitudes which stigmatise those who are or who have been sex workers.

Go urban letterboxing

May 2

Letterboxing combines orienteering and treasure-hunting with craftsmanship and inventiveness. Traditionally, it has been a countryside rambling activity which has taken root in the USA, but it is now being developed by Space Hijackers in an urban form in the UK.

A funky way of exploring your city. A 'letterbox' is a weatherproof box which contains a unique rubber stamp and a log book. The box is hidden somewhere interesting. Letterboxers exchange clues to the location of the boxes. They then find and stamp the box's log book with their own personal stamp (to show that they've been there), and stamp their log book with the box's stamp (to show how many letterboxes they've hunted down).

Box clever

- **Make a personal stamp, construct your letterbox, and find somewhere to hide it. Put it somewhere that enhances perception of the urban (or rural) environment.**
- **Enter its location on the Urban Letterbox database on the letterboxing website.**
- **Then start letterboxing, using the locations and clues listed for other people's letterboxes.**

All about letterboxing: www.letterboxing.info

UK website for urban letterboxing: www.spacehijackers.co.uk/letterboxing

Dartmoor letterboxing (the original location): www.dartmoorletterboxing.org

Letterboxing: a short history

Letterboxing began in southwest England in 1854, when James Perrott hid his calling card in a jar in a remote area by Cranmere Pool on Dartmoor. Perrott was a guide on the moor, and he encouraged his clients to leave their cards in the jar as well.

Eventually, visitors began leaving a self-addressed postcard or note in the jar, hoping for them to be returned by mail by the next visitor. Later the current custom of using rubber stamps and visitors' log books came into use.

By the 1970s there were 15 boxes on the moor. In the 1980s letterboxing exploded on Dartmoor. Today there are more than 3,000 letterboxes in the 365 square miles of Dartmoor National Park.

Freedom of the press

Support its defenders

- Visit the Reporters Without Borders website.
- Find out about abuses of press freedom around the world.
- Sign and send petitions to try to free some of the world's imprisoned journalists. Just click and send. It will remind the oppressors that their victims have not been forgotten.

Reporters Without Borders: www.rsf.org

Today is World Press Freedom Day. In over a third of the world's countries there is no press freedom, with journalists being persecuted for telling the truth.

In 2003, 42 media professionals lost their lives for just doing their job. Around the world, 184 reporters, media assistants and cyber-dissidents are in prison.

Reporters Without Borders is an international network working to uphold press freedom by:

Monitoring press freedom around the world via a network of over 100 correspondents.

Publishing regular reports on press freedom. This includes an annual World Press Freedom Ranking. In 2003 at the bottom of the list were Burma, Cuba and North Korea.

Defending journalists who have been imprisoned or persecuted, and providing legal aid to get torturers and murderers of journalists brought to trial.

Campaigning to reduce censorship and oppose laws that restrict press freedom.

Working to improve the safety of journalists around the world, particularly in war zones.

Journalists in the front line

Persecuting journalists in Eritrea

In September 2001, the Eritrean government ordered all independent publications to close down. In the following days, the police arrested at least 15 journalists. They were accused of publishing interviews with political leaders calling for 'democratic reforms' in the country. Those leaders were also arrested. Today, ten of the journalists remain behind bars in Eritrea.

Shutting down a website in China

Police arrested Huang Qi at his home on 3 June 2000. Huang, founder of the website www.tianwang.com, waited three years before finding he had been sentenced to five years for 'subversion' and 'incitement to overthrow the government'. He has been tortured in prison. His website was closed down, and the domain name is for sale. Why not buy it as a memorial to his bravery?

May 4

Think of a title

Books can change the world. Tom Paine's *The Rights of Man* fuelled the American and French Revolutions. Alexander Solzhenitsyn exposed Stalin's prison camps in *The Gulag Archipelago*, heralding the collapse of communism. This is why people ban books, but banning books will not stop the flow of ideas. Even in the repressive Soviet Union, people copied by hand and circulated works in a process known as 'samizdat publishing'. Here are six titles in search of an author:

1. *How to be a Guru*: to inspire activists and build a movement that will change the world.
2. *The Layman's Guide to the Indian Highway Code*: a humorous look at behaviour on Indian roads and an insight into the Indian psyche.
3. *One-hundred-and-one ways to Rig an Election*: will be the standard work in teaching good governance.
4. *Twenty-five ways to say NO*: a practical manual for dealing with bureaucracy.
5. *How to Bribe an Official*: you never know when you might need to.
6. *Ten Things to do with Coca-Cola other than Drink It.*

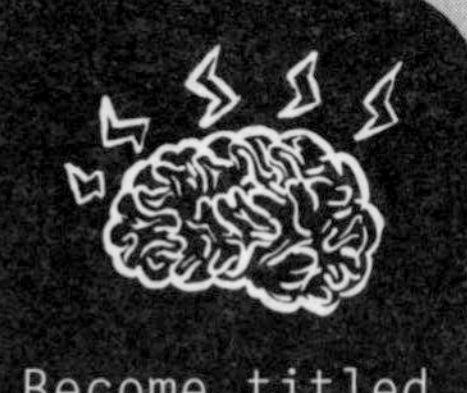

Become titled

Write your own book to change the world. Recognise the power of the written word.

First think up a great title (the fun part), then write your book.

Once it's written, put it on the web, publish it yourself or find a publisher.

Reports on anti-Cola campaigns in India: www.indiaresource.org/campaigns/coke/2004/cokespins.html

Some things to do with Coca-Cola

Centre for Science and Environment in Delhi claimed that the top 12 soft drink brands of Pepsi and Coca-Cola in India contained pesticides and insecticides in excess of limits set by the European Commission. Other campaigners claim that Indian cola bottling plants are extracting so much water that local wells are running dry, and that waste discharged by the factories is polluting local ground water.

Farmers in India are using Coca-Cola as a pesticide. Gotu Laxmaiah from Andhra Pradesh sprayed several hectares of cotton with the Real Thing: 'the pests began to die after the soft drink was sprayed on my cotton'.

'The properties of Coke have been discussed for years. It has been reported that it is a fine lavatory cleaner, a good windscreen wipe and an efficient rust spot remover.' *Guardian Unlimited*

Saving mothers

Speed dating

Organise a speed dating evening for safe motherhood. Maternity Worldwide will help. Every £12 you raise will sponsor a safe birth

About 25 single men and 25 single women are seated male/female. Each gets a few minutes to talk to the person next to them. Every few minutes they change seats. On a Speed Dating card they note who they'd like to see again. If ticks are mutual, what happens next is up to them ...

Maternity Worldwide: www.maternityworldwide.org

Safe Motherhood: www.safemotherhood.org

Marie Stopes International: www.mariestopes.org.uk

Royal College of Midwives: www.rcm.org.uk/data/international/data/safe.htm

Every year, 600,000 women die from complications during pregnancy and childbirth. Maternal deaths account for 25–30 per cent of all deaths among women of reproductive age. And there are huge differences across the world: a woman in Somalia is 700 times more likely to die in pregnancy or childbirth than a woman in the UK.

Safe Motherhood is an organisation that protects women throughout pregnancy and childbirth. Women everywhere should receive the care they need to be safe and healthy. This can be achieved by providing high-quality maternal health services to all women during pregnancy, childbirth, and the postpartum period, including:

- Care by skilled health personnel before, during, and after childbirth.
- Emergency care for life-threatening obstetric complications.
- Services to prevent and manage the complications of unsafe abortion.
- Family planning and health education.

Millennium Goal 5 is to improve maternal health. The target for 2015 is to reduce by 75 per cent the chances of women dying in childbirth (currently they are 1 in 48).

Speed dating for crickets

To find out whether male crickets were attractive, Megan Head organised 'dating tournaments'. Pairs of male and female crickets were timed to see how long it took for them to have sex. Males that got the females interested quickly were labelled 'attractive'.

Females who mated with attractive males died earlier and had slightly fewer children. But they had a greater number of attractive sons and their grandchildren were born much sooner. The result was that their genes were more likely to be passed down to future generations.

Plant your birth tree

Each day of the year has a particular tree associated with it. The tree for the day you were born is known as your 'birth tree'. Don't just plant any tree. Plant your birth tree. Or commemorate someone else's birthday by planting their birth tree.

Your birth tree confers a set of characteristics on you. For example, if you are born on 10 July your birth tree would be a Fir. You would then be likely to have all of the following characteristics: taste, dignity, cultivated airs, a love of anything beautiful, modesty, ambition, and many friends.

Happy birthday

Use the table to identify your birth tree.

Plant your birth tree to commemorate your next birthday. Do it yourself in your own garden, or on a plot of vacant land, or in a clearing in a wood or forest. Find somewhere that desperately needs a tree. Then plant one.

To find out about your birth tree go to: www.geocities.com/Athens/5341/tree.html and www.artistic.fadingwhispers.org/cornucopia/birthtree.html

Tree power

Use this table to check out how the date of your birth matches you up with your birth tree:

Date	Tree
Jan 02 to Jan 11	**Fir**
Jan 12 to Jan 24	**Elm**
Jan 25 to Feb 03	**Cypress**
Feb 04 to Feb 08	**Poplar**
Feb 09 to Feb 18	**Cedar**
Feb 19 to Feb 28	**Pine**
Mar 01 to Mar 10	**Weeping Willow**
Mar 11 to Mar 20	**Lime**
Mar 21	**Oak**
Mar 22 to Mar 31	**Hazelnut**
Apr 01 to Apr 10	**Rowan**
Apr 11 to Apr 20	**Maple**
Apr 21 to Apr 30	**Walnut**
May 01 to May 14	**Poplar**
May 15 to May 24	**Chestnut**
May 25 to Jun 03	**Ash**
Jun 04 to Jun 13	**Hornbeam**
Jun 14 to Jun 23	**Fig**
Jun 24	**Birch**
Jun 25 to Jul 04	**Apple**
Jul 05 to Jul 14	**Fir**
Jul 15 to Jul 25	**Elm**
Jul 26 to Aug 04	**Cypress**
Aug 05 to Aug 13	**Poplar**
Aug 14 to Aug 23	**Cedar**
Aug 24 to Sep 02	**Pine**
Sep 03 to Sep 12	**Weeping Willow**
Sep 13 to Sep 22	**Lime**
Sep 23	**Olive**
Sep 24 to Oct 03	**Hazelnut**
Oct 04 to Oct 13	**Rowan**
Oct 14 to Oct 23	**Maple**
Oct 24 to Nov 11	**Walnut**
Nov 12 to Nov 21	**Chestnut**
Nov 22 to Dec 01	**Ash**
Dec 02 to Dec 11	**Hornbeam**
Dec 12 to Dec 21	**Fig**
Dec 22	**Beech**
Dec 23 to Jan 01	**Apple**

May 7

Plant a sunflower

And enjoy the benefits

Click and sign the Sunflower Petition on the Sunflower Site.

Plant a sunflower in your garden, on waste land or wherever. The larger varieties grow up to 3.5 metres. After they have flowered, snack on the seeds. They're nutritious, containing 24 per cent protein and lots of minerals and vitamins.

The Sunflower Project: www.sunflowerproject.org and www.sunflower project.com

The scientific word for Sunflower is *Helianthus*, derived from *Helios* meaning sun and *Anthos* meaning flower. Its head follows the sun from sunrise until sunset, so as to gather the sun's rays. The sunflower is making a silent, simple and spontaneous statement about the importance of sunlight.

On 4 June 1996, the defence ministers of the USA, Russia and Ukraine met at the Pervomaisk missile base to celebrate Ukraine's transfer of its nuclear warheads to Russia for dismantling. The ministers planted sunflowers where missiles were once buried. US Secretary of Defense, William Perry, stated: 'Sunflowers instead of missiles in the soil would ensure peace for future generations.'

The Sunflower Project is dedicated to taking the 1996 Ukrainian missile gesture and fostering a worldwide campaign to encourage people everywhere to plant sunflowers throughout their cities, towns, communities, and countryside as living symbols of peace, celebrating our connection to nature.

The Sunflower Petition

The Sunflower Project is a global appeal to all people on planet earth concerned about nuclear war, pollution, violence, injustice, and threats to the balance of nature – to plant at least one sunflower seed in a sunny place where it will be noticed. This simple act of planting a seed will demonstrate the energy, simplicity, and practicality of nature. The incredible sunflower turns its head to follow the sun and provides seeds to eat, fibre for materials, medicine to heal, a golden yellow dye, and oil. It offers shade and beauty. It is a symbol of our hope for Nature and for Peace. We make a collective, conscious, and powerful statement planting sunflowers where they will be noticed – in vacant lots, fields, along roadways, streets, at schools, toxic waste sites, reservoirs, along stretches of railroad, parking lots, places of worship, playgrounds, and in gardens. We encourage all to plant a sunflower seed and watch it grow to become a majestic symbol – to summon harmony between humans, and with nature - toward peace on earth.

Send flowers

> *I, Woodrow Wilson, President of the United States of America do hereby direct the government officials to display the United States flag on all government buildings and do invite the people of the United States to display the flag at their homes or other suitable places on the second Sunday in May as a public expression of our love and reverence for the mothers of our country.*
> President Woodrow Wilson, 1914

Mother's Day started with the Greeks. Their spring festival honoured Rhea, mother of many gods. The Romans similarly honoured Cybele. Christians honoured Mary, mother of Christ, on the fourth Sunday of Lent, around the same time of year. In the UK this became Mothering Sunday. In the USA, the idea of Mother's Day was started by Anna Jarvis, who decided to campaign about the poor health of her community. To focus on this, she organised a 'Mother's Work Day'. After Anna's death, her daughter continued to campaign for a day dedicated to mothers. Then in 1914, Woodrow Wilson formally created Mother's Day as we now know it.
Mother's Day is the second Sunday in May

Flowers with a difference

On Mother's Day, send your mum some flowers. But send flowers with a difference – flowers which will also contribute to a better world.
Organic Bouquet: www.organicbouquet.com
Charity Flowers: www.charityflowers.co.uk
Order Charity Flowers through Practical Action: www.practicalaction.org/?id =flowers_by_post

May 8

Flowers for Charity

If you live in the UK, order flowers from Charity Flowers, sent direct from the growers in Guernsey. But if you place the order via the Practical Action website, 15 per cent is donated towards creating practical solutions to many of the poor world's problems using appropriate technology. Charity Flowers is owned by Age Concern, funding services for the elderly in the UK. In the US, order via Organic Bouquet. A proportion is donated to non-profit working for the environment and human and animal rights. If you have your own website, create a link to Organic Bouquet and get 15 per cent commission on any sales you generate.

May 9

Trade fairly

Buy to help

Look for the FAIRTRADE mark on products. Go out now and buy fairtrade chocolate and a packet of fairtrade tea or coffee.

Make a commitment to buy fairtrade whenever you can.

Make Trade Fair, a global campaign led by Oxfam: www.maketradefair.com

Fairtrade Labelling Organisations International: www.fairtrade.net

The Fairtrade Foundation: www.fairtrade.org.uk

International Fair Trade Association: www.ifat.org

World Fair Trade Day: www.wftday.org

Prices for agricultural produce from the south have not risen in real terms for 40 years, but the costs of fertilisers, pesticides and machinery have all increased. When the market price of commodities falls below production cost, it can force millions of small farmers into crippling debt. Farmers need fair prices for their products, and an assurance that they can sell what they produce. This is the basis of the fairtrade movement. Today in the UK you can buy over 1,000 FAIRTRADE products from coffee and tea to fresh fruits, in supermarkets, independent shops and cafés. Sales are growing by 40 per cent annually.

1 Out of every $100 generated by world exports, only $3 goes to low-income countries.
2 For every $1 given to poor countries in aid, $2 are lost via unfair trade, costing $100 billion a year.
3 If the third world share of world exports increased by just 1 per cent, it would lift 128 million people out of poverty.
4 Rich countries spend $1 billion a day on agricultural subsidies.

World Fairtrade Day is the second Sunday in May

Fairtrade Towns

In 2000, Garstang in Lancashire declared itself 'The world's first Fairtrade Town'. The idea has spread. To be a Fairtrade Town, five goals must be met:

1 The local council must support fairtrade, serve fairtrade coffee and tea at its meetings and in its offices.
2 Fairtrade products must be available in the town's shops, cafés and catering establishments.
3 Fairtrade products must be used by some local workplaces and community organisations.
4 The campaign should have popular support.
5 A committee must be formed.

Campaign to get your town declared a Fairtrade Town.

www.garstangfairtrade.org.uk
www.fairtrade.org.uk/towns.htm

Be a virtual volunteer

With virtual volunteering you can give practical help without leaving your home. Anyone who has the time available, who has regular, reliable access to a computer and the internet, and has skills that others might need is ideal for online volunteering. Your skill could be computer programming, writing, fundraising, project management or fluency in another language. More than 15,000 people have registered on the United Nations online website as interested in doing something. They work on anything from translating documents, editing press releases and research, to creating web pages, designing brochures, giving professional expertise and advice, and much more.

What it takes to be a good online volunteer:

- Attention to detail.
- Commitment to answer emails quickly.
- Commitment to stay with a project through to its completion.
- Enjoying working independently.
- A desire to learn, and a willingness to be flexible.
- Having a clear definition of what you want out of it.
- Being enthusiastic about the goals of the organisation you are helping.

Click away

Become an online volunteer today.

Go to www.onlinevolunteering.org and register (the website used to be called NetAid).

Or if you could use an online volunteer to help you change the world, then post your volunteering assignment on the website.

May 10

The Egyptian experience

Carlos Jimenez from Spain has been the driving online volunteer force behind the website of the Volunteer Network Egypt, a portal aimed at increasing awareness of volunteerism in Egypt. The portal was launched on International Volunteer Day (5 December) in 2004. Its success can be attributed to Carlos's committed co-ordination of a team of 11 online volunteers from seven countries, spread over the Arab region, Asia, Europe, and North America. Online volunteering gives us the opportunity to contribute – from our homes or workplaces – much more than a donation. We can actively participate in sustainable development.

May 11

Let's stop using money

Play LETSplay at www.letslinkuk.org
It shows you:

- **The difference between conventional and community money.**
- **The significance of that difference.**
- **The value of using both.**
- **How to use a community money system without risk.**

Start with a street party. Ask everyone to write things they need on a set of cards, and skills they could offer on another. Put them on a noticeboard and see what happens. All you need to know about LETS: www.gmlets.u-net.com
International LETS groups network: www.lets-linkup.com
LETS in the UK: www.letslinkuk.org

James's story

James Taris travelled the world without money for 400 days. He has created a website with free tips for living on LETS: www.travelwithoutmoney.com

Less is more

Imagine having enough money to meet all your needs. Now think about a society and economy operating without any of the problems caused by money and its unfair distribution: poverty, exploitation, homelessness, unemployment, fear, and stress. A world where everyone can afford what they need, where they can all work and have the time and facilities to play.

This is the dream of an 'Open Money Economy' where people within a community can freely exchange goods and services. LETS (Local Exchange Trading System) is a working example of an open money system. With LETS, members exchange goods and services with each other. A person receives credits for all the goods and services they provide. These can then be used to purchase other goods and services from within the LETS community. A credit cannot be exchanged for cash. A bookkeeper records all the transactions and keeps accounts for members, showing whether they are in credit or debit.

LETS relies on trust and co-operation amongst the community. If someone builds up a substantial credit and there is nothing they wish to purchase, then they will probably lose interest. If they go into debt because they have been on a 'spending spree' or because they can't provide things that other people want, then the LETS community has to sort the matter out with the person concerned. LETS really works. Around 40,000 people are involved in 450 LETS groups in the UK. LETS has a particular relevance for people who are out of work either through lack of employment opportunities, disability or retirement. LETS enables them to participate in economic life when they don't have a means of doing this within the formal economy.

Say no to billboards

Mobile billboards, trucks with an advertising hoarding on the back, drive around the city but don't go anywhere. They fill up road space and contribute to gridlock, spew out pollution but ignore the fact that they're inconveniencing everybody else. They're symptomatic of a selfish and wasteful society, and completely unnecessary. If people really want to advertise in the streets, they could use the sides of buses. Campaign against mobile billboards:

- Make a note of any mobile billboard you see. Write down where you saw it, its registration number, the company advertising and the date and time. If you have a camera, photograph it.
- Write to the company to complain. Tell them to be more environmentally sensitive. Tell them that you will stop buying their products if they don't change their policy. And tell them that you will tell all your friends to do the same.
- Try to get some really bad PR for the advertiser. Think of a creative and powerful way of getting media coverage for a 'Say NO to mobile billboards!' campaign.
- Don't buy from any company that advertises on mobile billboards. Don't vote for any politician or political party that uses a mobile billboard for campaigning.

Battle the boards

Here are two Canadian websites which should spur you on in your own battles with mobile billboards in your own country:
Stop Mobile Billboards: www3.sympatico.ca/alwaysweb/mobile_billboards.html
überculture's Montreal campaign: www.uberculture.org/projects/bad_trucks.html

May 12

Save our air

Say no to mobile billboards:

Ad Trucks are Bad Trucks. They're bad for the environment, bad for driving and pretty much illegal.
(überculture, Montreal)

This organisation in Montreal, Canada campaigns to reclaim public space. Downtown Montreal has over thirty billboard trucks each day, travelling 2.34 million kilometres a year, burning over 400,000 litres of gas and emitting 940,000 kg of carbon dioxide.

May 13

Gutenberg project

Bringing people books

- Read a Gutenberg book tonight.
- Send people books they might be interested in as a virtual birthday present.

Project Gutenberg: www.gutenberg.net

Michael Hart set up Project Gutenberg in 1971 when he was a student. His goal was to make available free electronic copies of out-of-copyright books, and books whose copyright had been donated. It became the world's first digital library. Michael himself typed in the first hundred books, but the project really took off with the internet and is now truly international.

Books are scanned electronically, though very old and fragile books are typed in manually. There are now a thousand volunteers all over the world helping with these processes. Any title can be downloaded for free from the Project Gutenberg website and then sent on to people who might be interested in reading it. Software on the website (which is still being tested) will allow users to convert books into other formats and eventually into Braille and voice.

The number of books available reached 11,000 by the start of 2004. And 350 new titles are added every month. Most titles are in English, but there are now books available in 25 languages, and the target is to extend the library to at least 100 languages. Michael Hart's dream is to have one million titles available by 2015.

Become a distributed proofreader

Go to the Project Gutenberg website, to the book you want to work on. Pages appear side by side in two forms: one the scanned image and the other the text produced by OCR (optical character recognition). You compare the two and make corrections. OCR is around 99 per cent accurate, making about ten corrections a page. Save each page. You can then stop or do another page. All the books are proofread twice (secondly by a professional) before being finally ready for distribution. Any further errors noted by readers can then be corrected. Proofreaders aren't given a quota, but it's suggested you do at least one page a day – a small contribution towards a library of a million books.

Commemorate a celebrity

The Blue Plaque Scheme was started in 1867 by the Royal Society of Arts. It was set up at the instigation of William Ewart MP as a way of honouring noteworthy people who had contributed in some way to society, history or to the local area. Initially the scheme placed more emphasis on the buildings, but more recently it has been adapted to become a way of developing an interest in local history.

Blue Plaques boost tourism. Visitors like to see where the artists, physicists, statesmen and literary figures of the past have been born, lived (for some period of their lives) and died. The scheme has spread from London to other cities in the UK, and the idea is now beginning to be exported to other countries.

To get a plaque in London, a person has to be nominated. They must have died more than 20 years ago, or been born more than 100 years ago, whichever is earlier. The criteria include: eminence; having made an important positive contribution; exceptional personalities; and deserving of national recognition. If a person meets these criteria, a plaque may be placed on a building linked to them.

Fame academy

Was someone famous born or lived in your locality? Find out who, and what you can about their life and their connection with your area.

Start a campaign to commemorate this person through the Blue Plaque scheme, with the help of your Local Council or completely unofficially.

How to get started in local history, advice from Local History magazine: www.local-history.co.uk/gettingstarted.html

Information on plaques in London: www.blueplaque.com

Information site on Blue Plaques in London with a 'Submit your Nomination' feature:www.blueplaque project.org

Put up a plaque

Commemorate a physicist The Director of the Institute of Physics has set up a scheme to erect blue plaques to commemorate famous scientists. Visit: groups.iop.org/HP/Bluepq/index.htm

Commemorate a Muslim There are not many plaques that commemorate Muslims in London, though there are many for people with an Islamic connection.

These three Muslims do have a plaque:

- Mohammed Ali Jinnah (1876–1948), Founder of Pakistan
- Syed Ahmed Khan (1817–1898), Muslim Reformer
- Mustapha Pasha Reschid (1800–1858), Turkish Statesman

Campaign for more plaques for Muslims: www.masud.co.uk/ISLAM/bmh/BMH-IRO-blue_plaque.htm

South African AIDS orphans

Put your heart into it

Organise a Dinner of Hope. Host a dinner at your home. Book a restaurant. Have a picnic. Throw a party. Invite as many people as you can.

Ask your guests to make a contribution. Every pound raised will help AIDS-orphaned children in South Africa. Find out more from www.starfishcharity.org which supports Heartbeat.

Find out about Heartbeat at www.austincommunityfoundation.org/?nd=invisible

Find out about Nkosi's Haven at nkosi.iafrica.com

The struggle against global AIDS is one of the great challenges of our time. And the suffering of children affected by AIDS is one of the issues that most demands our attention. Nowhere is the problem more evident than in South Africa, where there are nearly 1 million AIDS orphans. This is close to the number of children aged under five in the entire state of New York. Soon there will be 2 million AIDS orphans.

Africa's AIDS orphans have been described as 'an army in search of a leader'. Brought up without the protection of adults, basic material needs or moral guidance, these children are the most dispossessed.

Heartbeat works with 5,000 children in more than a dozen areas of South Africa. Home-based care workers serve as surrogate parents for AIDS orphans and other children who head a household. Heartbeat provides food, clothes, school fees and basic medicines to these children, and, just as importantly, supplies nurturing, attention and counselling. The care workers provide protection from sexual and physical abuse.

Nkosi's Haven

Nkosi Johnson died from AIDS in 2001 aged only 12. During his short life, he saw that little was being done to protect children from HIV, or to care for those born with HIV or provide for orphans. He also saw AIDS-discrimination when refused entry to school. Nkosi, with his foster mother Gail, set about doing something. He became the 'human face' of AIDS orphans in South Africa, gaining a huge amount of media attention. Nkosi and Gail set up Nkosi's Haven, a hostel for 11 mothers who are HIV positive or with full-blown AIDS, and 27 children (ten are HIV positive). A next-door property has also been purchased, doubling the capacity, and plans are being made to buy a 12-acre farm and a property with 13 self-contained cottages and flats, to set up residential communities for mothers and children living with AIDS.

May 16

Unite as Netizens

A 'Netizen' is a 'Citizen of the Internet', a member of a worldwide community. All Netizens should have rights, freedom and equality. But in order for the cyber-world to be a place for good, we need 'Responsible Netizenship'. Citizens Coalition for Economic Justice in Korea has drawn up a charter for good Netizenship. Netizens should:

- Voluntarily develop the cyber-world as an open and sound space for everyone.
- Respect and protect the human rights and privacy of others, valuing them as their own.
- Try to respect the work of others whilst having access to unlimited information.
- Protect the private information of others as if it were their own.
- Refrain from using vulgar or foul language.
- Use their real names, and take responsibility for their actions and comments.
- Not produce or disseminate incorrect information.
- Not engage in illegal actions, such as spreading a virus or cracking passwords.
- Participate positively in the cyber-world by watching out for and commenting on irresponsible actions.
- Contribute towards creating a positive internet culture by keeping and practising these principles.

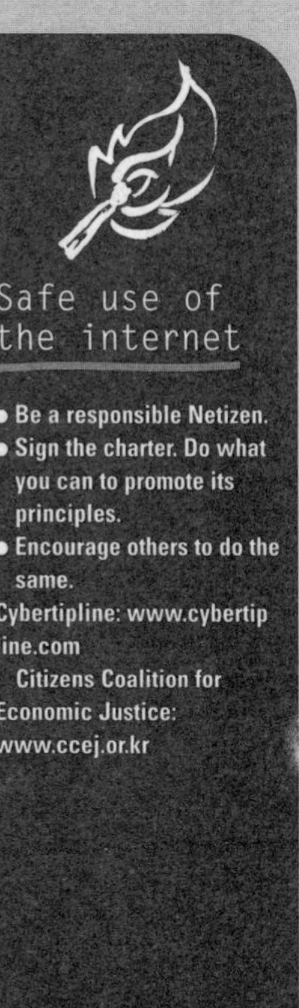

Safe use of the internet

- **Be a responsible Netizen.**
- **Sign the charter. Do what you can to promote its principles.**
- **Encourage others to do the same.**

Cybertipline: www.cybertipline.com

Citizens Coalition for Economic Justice: www.ccej.or.kr

Exploiting the Tsunami

A mass email sent out in January 2005 posing as a plea for aid to help the victims of the 26 December 2004 Asian tsunami disaster was in fact a vehicle for spreading a computer virus. The worm appeared with the subject line: 'Tsunami donation! Please help!' and invited recipients to open an attachment 'tsunami.exe'. If opened, this would then forward the virus to other internet users. Another worm said the tsunami was God's revenge on 'people who did bad on earth'.

Helpline volunteers

It's good to talk

Volunteer on a telephone helpline. Volunteer at a festival or an event.
The Festival Branch of Samaritans provides a 24-hour service at outdoor music festivals like Glastonbury, and also at biker, dance, surf, lesbian/gay and other gatherings. Contact: www.samaritans.org/~festival/volunteer.html

Telephone Helplines Association, supporting helplines in the UK: www.helplines.org.uk

Child Helpline International, promoting children's helplines internationally: www.childhelplineinternational.org

Samaritans: www.samaritans.org

and around the world: www.suicide-helplines.org

Helplines provide comfort and sometimes direct assistance to those in real need. Samaritans was started in 1953 by Chad Varah, a young London vicar. Chad had buried a 14-year-old girl who had taken her own life, having mistaken her periods for a sexually transmitted disease. He recognised the distress caused by having nobody to talk to about confidential issues, and decided to take action. Chad organised a network of people who would be at the other end of a telephone and could be asked anything. Around 4.6 million calls are now received each year in the UK by Samaritans.

ChildLine was started in 1986 by TV presenter Esther Rantzen for children experiencing problems such as sexual and physical abuse, bullying, serious family tensions, worries about friends' welfare and teenage pregnancy. Around 650,000 calls are answered each year.

The idea of telephone helplines has now spread around the world. The Befrienders International network, run by Samaritans, is a network for suicide lines, and Child Helpline International for children's helplines. The use of the internet, cellphones and broadcast television are all being explored as additional mechanisms of providing advice.

The Muslim Youth Helpline

This is an email received by the Muslim Youth Helpline:

'hi my name is youssef and i am a heroin addict and i need some help, i chase about 0.5 of a gram a day. if u can help me phone me on this number. A.S.A.P. cos am suffering every min of every hour of every day. salamo alaikum.'

The Muslim Youth Helpline was set up by 17-year-old Mohammed Mamdani in 2001. Young Muslims contact the Helpline by phone or email. Visit: www.myh.org.uk

Unwanted Styrofoam

In May 1971, 1,500 non-returnable bottles were returned to the Schweppes' Headquarters. Schweppes was then the UK's leading fizzy drinks manufacturer. This was done to protest against the switch from returnable bottles (with the customer paying a refundable deposit on purchase of the drink) to non-returnable bottles (which would just have one single use before being disposed of).

This stunt was used to launch the Friends of the Earth reuse and recycle campaign. Friends of the Earth now has 72,000 members and over 240 local groups in the UK alone. Since 1971, non-returnable bottles have become standard. But there are now easily accessible recycling points so that the glass can be collected, melted down and reused.

Most Styrofoam (polystyrene) packaging will end up in a landfill site. Until manufacturers are made aware by the purchasing public that Styrofoam packaging is not good for the environment, then goods will continue to be supplied in this way. But if manufacturers begin to get the point, then they might switch to more environmentally sensible packaging, or even come up with a way of collecting and reusing the Styrofoam.

Send it packing

Send Styrofoam packaging back to the manufacturer. Address your parcel to the Chairman at Head Office – find out the name and address from the company's website. Styrofoam may be bulky, but it's very light, so it won't cost that much in postage.

Include a polite and positive letter asking the company to think more carefully about the environmental impact of their packaging. Ask them to try to find a safe recycling solution or look for sensible alternative ways of packing their products.

International Foam Solutions offers a recycling scheme for schools in the USA, and produces equipment for the D-I-Y enthusiast: www.internationalfoamsolutions.com

Styrofoam is recyclable

You could reuse it for its original purpose. Cups and plates could be washed and used for another meal or drink. Packaging could also be collected by the manufacturer to be used again.

You can separate out the Styrofoam products from other trash, and shred it. It can then be dissolved in a solvent and moulded to make another product. This is not very cost-effective for mass production, so is not widely done.

May 19

Google Bombing

Widen the net

**Google Bombing will get your message out.
Try typing in a slogan, and see what comes up. For example:**

- **End Third World Debt gets you to an article on third world debt on the Socialist Workers Party website.**
- **Education, Education, Education gets you to the UNESCO website.**
- **Make Love Not War gets you to political posters from the Sixties Project.**

Try Google Bombing at www.google.co.uk

A 'Google Bomb' is an attempt to get a site ranked top when people search for it on Google. This is quite easy if you understand the way the Google Search Engine works. The key factors are the number of links and the use of particular words or phrases on many linked webpages.

The first Google Bomb to get publicity was in 1999. Typing in the words 'More evil than Satan' led to the Microsoft Home Page. Such was the interest in this, that now, typing in this phrase gets you to several articles on the discovery of Google Bombing.

Google Bombs come and go. Many get too well known, and mentions in popular web journals get these journals to the top spot. Google Bombing can be used to get your organisation or issue to the top, which should be an important goal for your PR.

Weapons of Mass Destruction

In 2004, by typing in 'Weapons of Mass Destruction' and clicking 'I'm feeling lucky' you got to: www.coxar.pwp.blue yonder.co.uk

This is what came up on your screen:

> These Weapons of Mass Destruction cannot be displayed. The weapons you are looking for are currently not available. The country might be experiencing difficulties, or you may need to adjust your weapons inspectors mandate. Please try the following:

- Click the 'Regime change' button, or try again later.
- If you are George Bush and typed the country's name in the address bar, make sure it's spelled correctly (IRAQ).
- To check your weapons inspector settings, click the 'UN' menu, then click 'Weapons Inspector Options'. On the 'Security Council' tab, click 'Consensus'. The settings should match those provided by your government or NATO.
- If the Security Council has enabled it, the USA can examine your country and automatically discover WMDs.
- If you would like to use the CIA to try and discover them, click 'Detect weapons'.
- Click the 'Bomb' button if you are Donald Rumsfeld.

Promote veggie sex

Try a veggie burger in the kitchen for a whopper in the bedroom! What could be more of a turn-on than snuggling up to someone who's both passionate and compassionate. Bruce Friedrich, Director of Vegan Campaigns, People for the Ethical Treatment of Animals (PETA)

In August 2004, PETA launched its 'Make Out Live' Campaign. On a popular Los Angeles corner, a couple made out all afternoon on a bed in plain view of everyone who walked by. They wanted to raise awareness for vegetarianism by proving their claim that 'vegetarians make better lovers'. Supporters held a banner next to the bed and handed out free vegetarian starter kits to passers-by. It's debatable how many people converted to vegetarianism, but they certainly got a lot of attention for the cause!

Do vegetarians have an advantage in the bedroom? Yes. They are likely to be more fit and have more stamina than people who stuff themselves with fat-laden meat, dairy products, and eggs. They don't have to rely on chemical potions like Viagra to be up for any task – the cholesterol in meat and other animal products causes hardening of the arteries, slowing the flow of blood to all the body's vital organs, not just the heart. And there's nothing sexy about turning a blind eye to the suffering of the animals who are raised and killed for food each year.

May 20

Start making out

Instead of organising a sit-in, stage a make-out.

Choose an important issue that is not getting enough attention. Get together some friends. Set up a bed in a very public place. Have a couple make out like mad while volunteers hold up signs and hand out leaflets to people gawking as they walk by. If you want to make it really spicy, get a dozen couples to make out at the same time.

Ask people to sign a petition. Suggest a simple action they can take.

Don't get too carried away. The police will arrest you if your spectacle turns to hardcore. You will find yourself in the news, but for the wrong reason.

Read about the case for vegetarianism at: www.peta.org

Don't abuse animals

PETA was founded in 1980, and now has more than 800,000 members. It subscribes to the basic principle that animals are not ours to eat, wear, experiment on, or use for entertainment. It campaigns on factory farming, laboratory use of animals, the fur trade, and the use of animals in the entertainment industry.

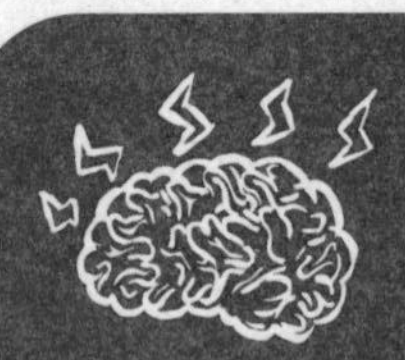

Spread the word by email

Compose a clear, simple message that promotes positive change. It can be about racism, sexism, war, peace, sex, inclusion – whatever inspires or infuriates you.

Create a simple weblink for people to access the message. Or just put it in an email.

Forward this to everyone you know, everyone in your address book. And ask them to forward it to everyone they know. Your message could reach the four corners of the globe in a single day. Who knows what its impact will be?

End Hate has a message to get your neurons moving: www.endhate.org

Speak to a Thai farmer

The theory of six degrees of separation states that any person is linked to any other person on Earth by only six ties. So a Hollywood mogul will be linked to a Mongolian shepherd through six people or fewer. You know someone, who knows someone, who knows someone, who knows someone, who knows someone, who knows the Mongolian shepherd. There are over 6 billion people covering our planet. Over 600 million have some form of internet access, the number rising day by day. So take advantage of the absurd simplicity of email to disseminate information to the growing number of people who can receive it.

If you can reach hundreds of people ... and they can reach hundreds of people ... and they can reach hundreds of people ... and they can reach hundreds of people ... and they can reach hundreds of people ... and they can reach hundreds of people (that's six degrees of separation) ... then your message can speak to a Mongolian shepherd, or a Thai chicken farmer ... or the President of a country.

Change can start with a simple message. Put forward an idea, give one or two key facts, and this could get people thinking about the world in a slightly different way – a first step in creating change.

Ending hate with email

What if we all decided, right now, that the colour of our skins didn't matter?
or religion?
or nationality?
or ideology?

What if we stopped being afraid? Think about it for a minute ... maybe it wouldn't be that hard to live in peace?

Maybe it's just that simple. It's estimated that there are 605,000,000 people on earth with internet access.

If 100,000,000 see this message can they make a difference?

Forward this.

Maybe it's just that simple: Maybe_its_that_simple@endhate.org

Endangered species

Some animals and plants are so sought-after that they are at risk of extinction. WWF compiles an annual most wanted list of species threatened by trade and consumer demand. For 2004, it included:
Humphead Wrasse: a bulbous-headed, coral-reef fish caught and displayed live in tanks for diners in East Asian restaurants.
Ramin: a tropical hardwood grown largely in peat swamp forests in Indonesia and Malaysia, used for mass-produced mouldings, doors and picture frames.
Tigers: over the last 100 years, numbers have been reduced by 95 per cent – with perhaps fewer than 5,000 left in the wild. They are poached for their skins, and for bone used in traditional Chinese medicines.
Great White Shark: the largest of the predatory sharks, they are poached for their jaws, teeth, and fins, which are in demand worldwide.
Irrawaddy Dolphins: these are entangled in fishing nets and injured by explosives used for dynamite fishing. Also in demand for display in zoos and aquaria.
Asian Elephant: poached for ivory and meat in many Asian countries. There are now only 35-50,000 Asian elephants in the wild, plus 15,000 in captivity.
Pig-Nosed Turtle: a giant freshwater turtle with a protruding snout, found in Papua New Guinea, northern Australia, and Indonesia, in demand by the international pet trade. Nests are robbed of eggs, which are either eaten or sold.
Yellow-Crested Cockatoo: fewer than 10,000 of these exotic-looking birds remain. They are in high demand by the international pet trade.
Leaf-tailed Gecko: these lizards found in Madagascar, with their bark-like appearance, are also in high demand by the international pet trade.

Trade in these species needs to be regulated and well-managed. Don't even think of getting a pig-nosed turtle or a yellow-crested cockatoo as a pet.

Extinction from greed

Campaign for wildlife conservation from your desktop.

Get a Panda Passport from www.panda.org. You will be asked to post letters or send emails, petitions or faxes to decision-makers.

You may be asked to make a personal commitment, such as buying wood products only made from FSC-certified wood or switching to renewable energy.

International office of WWF: www.panda.org

UK office of WWF: www.wwf.org.uk

Save our trees

Over 8,000 tree species, 10 per cent of the world's total, are facing extinction. They include the Monkey Puzzle Tree, Nubian Dragon Tree and Clanwilliam Cedar.

Find out about these and others at Global Trees Campaign: www.globaltrees.org

Publish it yourself

Get yourself published

Become a published author today. Get your manuscript out of the drawer where it has been gathering dust for years – or rather find it on your computer's hard drive. Give it an editorial once-over to make sure it makes sense and to remove all the typos (remember that rubbish in = rubbish out). Or write your soon-to-be a best-seller today on a subject that you're passionate about. Then upload your manuscript onto Lulu and follow the instructions: www.lulu.com

Read the *Publish-it-Yourself Handbook* by Bill Henderson, and be inspired by some of the extraordinary people who have done just that: www.amazon.com

Publish your own book for as little as $6! With the technology of print-on-demand where printing presses are set up to print individual copies, and an internet-based system for turning a typescript into a final design, www.lulu.com has created a cheap and simple way to publish a book.

Whether you want to publish just one copy, or 25 copies to give to friends next Christmas, or 500 to sell at book readings, or an e-book to send around the world, Lulu enables you to become a published author.

Founded in 2002 by Bob Young, Lulu is a website where you can publish and sell books, music, comics, photographs and movies. Lulu provides you with the tools, and you, the author, retain complete control over content and design.

There is no set-up fee or minimum order. With simple instructions for turning your text into a book, Lulu manages printing, delivery and customer service. You can take delivery of the books and sell them yourself, or you can set your own royalty and use Lulu for marketing. You will receive royalties at the end of each quarter, Lulu taking a percentage from each transaction to cover its costs.

What's in a name?

'Ever heard the phrase "Boy, that's a real Lulu"? Well, even if you haven't, think of the word "Lulu" as an old-fashioned term for a remarkable person, object or idea. That's exactly what Lulu is. Think of us as an open marketplace for digital content. An on-demand publishing tool for books, e-books, music, images, movies and calendars.' This is how Lulu describes itself. For a 64-page paperback 8.5 x 11 inches: a single copy costs $5.81; 50 copies cost $4.72 per copy; 100 copies cost $4.18 per copy. Books can be shipped world-wide, with free SuperSaver shipping on orders between $25 and $100.

Meet a centurion

In some societies, old people are seen as a nuisance – to be put in old people's homes and forgotten about. Abuse of the elderly is commonplace. But in others, old people are revered. They are seen as a source of wisdom, people to be consulted ... and listened to.

Old people have a wealth of experience to share. They carry traditional knowledge from one generation to the next. They can provide important information from the past for the benefit of future generations.

The Honeybee Network looks for rural innovations in India. They organise an annual walk through villages to speak to farmers and village elders. Their Centurion Project has interviewed several hundred people aged over 100. Honeybee uses these promising innovations to improve the lives of the poor.

Two centurions: Ismailbhai Gajan, a local veterinary healer, bemoaned the extinction of herbal plants, as this affected his providing treatment. Deviben Lakum spoke about treatments for animal disorders and diseases. The world would be worse off without the wisdom of Ismailbhai and Deviben and others similar!

Find your centurion

Go find somebody aged over 100. Interview them. Ask them about what life was like when they were young, what were the problems in their lives, and how they overcame them. Ask them about what they cooked and ate. Ask them about what they did to lead more healthy lives, and about going to the doctor for treatment. How are things different today? Are they better or worse? The Honeybee Network: www.sristi.org and www.sristi.org/honeybee.html

Derivations and definitions

'Centurion' is derived from the Latin *Centum* which means 'a hundred'. Some uses of the word include:

- A professional officer of the Roman army who commanded between 60 and 160 men.
- A British battle tank created at the end of World War 2.
- A town in South Africa between Johannesburg and Pretoria; cricket test matches are played at Centurion Park.
- A drinking game, involving the consumption of 100 one-ounce shots of beer. Power Hour is a variant where players drink one shot a minute for a whole hour.
- The most exclusive American Express card, available only on invitation. You have to spend $250,000 per annum.
- Someone over 100. A SuperCenturion is someone over 110, which is about one centurion in 1,000.

May 25

Help a family out of poverty

Buy a goat for a family, as a first step towards their self-sufficiency.

You just provide the money, and someone else does the necessary. Your bright new goat will be delivered to its proud new owner.

You won't even notice the £15-£25 it costs.

Send a Cow: www.sendacow.org.uk

Christian Aid: www.christianaid.org.uk/learn/goats

Goats for Peace: www.goodgifts.org

What's the cost

It takes £60 for Christian Aid to provide four goats for a goat bank in Bolivia or Burundi, £25 for Send a Cow to send a goat.

Goats for Peace is a scheme run by the Good Gifts Catalogue; it gives goats to widows and families in several areas, including to genocide survivors in Rwanda. £15 pays for one goat.

Help a goat revolution

Giving poor families an animal is a good starting point for helping them out of poverty. It used to be cows, but now it's other animals as well. Very poor people, with little land and few resources, sometimes find it difficult to manage a dairy cow.

Send a Cow has launched a new programme called StockAid. This scheme provides the poorest of the poor with smaller stock, such as goats, pigs or poultry. They are thus able to begin rearing livestock even where they are unable to provide the shelter or fodder needed for a cow. This is particularly helpful to families suffering the impact of drought, AIDS and conflict.

Christian Aid runs a revolving goat scheme. Here's how the scheme works:

Step 1 Goats are given to a goat bank.

Step 2 The goat bank lends a female goat to a family, possibly a widow and her children.

Step 3 The goat grazes on scrub land or eats up waste, and produces milk.

Step 4 The children have nutritious milk to drink, and any surplus is sold.

Step 5 The goat produces manure. If the widow has a plot of land, this fertilises the soil and the crop yield goes up. This represents more to eat or more money for the family.

Step 6 The goat gets pregnant, and produces more goats.

Step 7 One female is returned to the goat bank to pay off the loan, and the widow keeps the others.

Step 8 A goat is lent to another widow ... and so the process of getting families out of poverty will go on.

Start your own aid agency

Many people choose to run their own aid agencies. Often just ordinary people, motivated by what they see abroad. This may not be a best way of getting aid to the neediest, but it is direct, it involves no highly paid professionals, and it is done with a good heart.

The first step is to find out about local problems and needs. As an outsider it isn't always easy to know who or what to support. Ask around. Talk to a teacher or the village head. Work through existing institutions.

Support obvious immediate need: medicines for eye and ear infections can save sight or hearing.

Set up a hardship fund for distributing small grants to those in need after you've gone.

Support people with no income such as widows.

Help build facilities of obvious community benefit, such as a classroom, toilets, or village well.

Use your support to add to the energies and efforts of local people.

Be a friend in a hundred

Resolve to make a difference by:

- **Becoming one of Marc Gold's 100 Friends.**
- **Doing it yourself. Change the world whilst travelling.**
- **Do what Marc has done and set up your own 100 Friends Project. If you haven't got 100 friends, 50 should be fine.**

100 Friends Project: www.100friends.com

May 26

Marc's story

I am Marc Gold. I started the 100 Friends project in 1989. The idea is simple. Every year about 100 people contribute, and I take the money to Third World Countries and look for the neediest people. I put the money to work in the most compassionate, appropriate, culturally compatible, constructive and practical manner. I pay for my own travel expenses.

The project began when I visited India for the first time. I met a Tibetan woman in the Himalayas who had a terrible ear infection. I was able to save her life with antibiotics that cost about a dollar. For another $30 I purchased a hearing aid that restored her hearing. I was shocked to see that something so important could be accomplished with so little. *Marc Gold*

Over fifteen years Marc has made nine trips: to India, Thailand, Cambodia, Tibet, Nepal, Vietnam, Afghanistan, Bangladesh, South Africa, Mozambique and Turkey. He now distributes $18,000 a year.

'Ultimately you have to ask yourself: Is it better to sit around doing nothing, or to do something, however imperfect?'

May 27

Assist cancer survivors

Live strong

Nike launched the Wear Yellow campaign to support the Lance Armstrong Foundation promoting cancer survival. Nike donated $1 million, plus $5 million through the sale of yellow wristbands with the words 'Live Strong'.

They can be purchased for $1 each in quantities of 10, 100 or 1,200 from the Foundation's website.

Keep healthy. Stop smoking, eat five portions of fruit and vegetables daily, and go for cancer screening as recommended by your doctor.

The Live Strong website: www.livestrong.org

Find out more about cancer from CancerFacts: www.cancerfacts.com and from CancerHelp UK: www.cancerhelp.org.uk

The 'Big C' can strike anyone anywhere. One in three people will be diagnosed with cancer during their lifetime. Cancer is the second most likely cause of death, coming a close second after heart failure. The main types of cancer are: bladder, breast, cervical, colonic and rectal, endometrial (womb), oesophageal (throat), kidney, leukaemia, lung, lymphatic (Hodgkins disease and other lymphomas), melanoma (skin), multiple myeloma (bone marrow), oral (mouth cavity), ovarian, prostate, testicular, and uterine.

Over the last 50 years, deaths from cancer have not reduced. But death from heart disease has halved. For men the most common cancers are lung, prostate and colo-rectal; and for women, lung, breast and colo-rectal. Together these account for more than half the incidence of cancer. The overall survival rate for all cancers is 63 per cent. The highest levels of survival are prostate (98 per cent), melanoma (90 per cent), breast (87 per cent) and urinary tract (82 per cent).

Lance Armstrong's story

Lance was 25 when diagnosed with testicular cancer. This is treatable if detected early. But Lance ignored the warning signs, and the cancer spread to his abdomen, lungs and brain. Once diagnosed, and determined to live, he declared himself a cancer survivor rather than a victim. He underwent two surgeries (to remove a cancerous testicle, and two cancerous lesions on the brain) plus four chemotherapies. Lance survived the treatment, and went on to become the most successful cyclist ever, winning the Tour de France a record seven times in a row from 1999 to 2005.

Fight bio-piracy

Bio-pirates exploit patent and trademark laws for profit. Patents and trademarks exist to protect tangible property, such as inventions or brands. But in some cases they are used to make amoral proprietary claims. Examples include ripping off indigenous knowledge, monopolising genes, patenting plants, or even trademarking a patron saint.

Examples of bio-piracy include the following Captain Hook Awards:

The greediest Genetic Technologies (Australia) patented non-coded DNA (known as 'junk DNA') of all living creatures, including humans.

The worst corporate offender Monsanto holds a European patent on soft-milling, low-gluten wheat that is derived from a traditional Indian wheat variety.

The worst nano-pirate Mr Yang Mengjun (China) secured 466 patents on nanoscale versions of traditional Chinese medicinal herbs by turning the plants into fine powders, claiming a 'new' product.

Help the real owners

Bring the bio-pirates to justice. Shower RiceTec with rice.

Buy Basmati rice from India. Write to John Nelsen CEO, RiceTec Inc, 1925 FM Road, 2917 Alvin, TX 77511, enclose some rice and ask him to hand back the Basmati brand to its indigenous owners.

Nominate someone for a Captain Hook Award for bio-piracy: www.captainhookawards.org

For information on Vandana Shiva: www.navdanya.org

May 28

RiceTec

By patenting similar Basmati grains outside India, RiceTec has ended India's ownership of the Basmati brand. Basmati rice is no longer a product unique to the Himalayan foothills (unlike sherry, which can only be made in Spain, or scotch whisky, which can only come from Scotland).

Today, the world is on the brink of a biological diversity crisis. In India we are increasing awareness of the importance of conserving our valuable genetic heritage, while challenging and opposing the forces responsible for its rapid erosion. Join us in the struggle and research for sustainability and justice in these turbulent and uncertain times. Vandana Shiva

Vandana Shiva has been fighting the theft of indigenous knowledge by multinational companies, and has run a vocal campaign against RiceTec for securing US patents on Basmati rice, a major contributor to the Indian economy.

Peacemakers are stars

Know their work

Find out about these and other award winners. Be inspired by them. Learn from what they have done.

For Nobel Peace Prize Winners, go to nobelprize.org/peace

The Nobel Peace Prize has developed an online museum. Go to www.nobelpeacecenter.org

For Right Livelihood Winners, go to www.rightlivelihood.se

The Nobel Peace Prize has been running since 1901, honouring individuals and organisations for exceptional contributions to peace and justice.

There is now an 'alternative Nobel Peace Prize', known as the Right Livelihood Award, established in 1980. The idea of 'right livelihood' embodies the principle that each person should fully respect other people and the natural world. It means being responsible for our actions and taking only a fair share of the earth's resources.

The people honoured should be the stars in our human cosmos. Their work often entails huge sacrifice and being opposed or persecuted by forces around them. The Right Livelihood Award now has over 100 laureates from 48 countries.

Nobel Winners in recent years have included:

2003: Shirin Ebadi, Iranian human rights activist.

2002: Jimmy Carter, since relinquishing the US presidency has devoted himself to peace and conflict resolution through the Carter Institute.

1999: Médecins sans Frontières, for their medical work in areas of conflict.

1998: John Hume (with **David Trimble**), who was the architect of the peace process in Northern Ireland.

The alternative peace prize winners

Right Livelihood Award Winners in 2003 and 2004 included:

Walden Bello and Nicanor Perlas (Philippines), for efforts in educating civil society about the effects of corporate globalisation.

The Citizens' Coalition for Economic Justice (South Korea), for its efforts to bring social justice to South Korea, and for aiding reconciliation with the North.

Bianca Jagger (Nicaragua), for her human rights campaigning.

Memorial (Russia), for prompting civil society, revealing truth about the past.

The art of non-violence

Many computer games involve zapping the enemy. Ivan Marovic, a founder of the Serbian student resistance group Otpor!, has worked with the International Center on Nonviolent Conflict to develop a video game called A Force More Powerful, which teaches non-violent tactics, rather than shoot-to-kill.

The game teaches you how to defeat real-world adversaries by non-military non-violent means. It features 10 scenarios inspired by recent history – to show the potential of 'weapons' of non-violence.

A Force More Powerful focuses on abstract ideas, rather than depending on reflexes, co-ordination and quick thinking. Players learn strategic planning, formulation of goals (such as ensuring free elections), as well as the tactics to use to achieve success.

Tactics include leafleting, protests, strikes, boycotts, civil disobedience and non-co-operation. The scenarios are fictional, but based on successes in Russia, Chile, Poland, the Philippines and elsewhere. Groups are the game's basic political units, representing the interests and agendas common to every struggle.

Recruiting characters and building alliances is a principal game activity, involving labour, business, government, agriculture, academics and professionals, the media, religion and the military.

Play the game

Learn how to change the world using non-violence. Play A Force More Powerful. The game sells for $19.95 plus shipping, or 10 or more at $10 each, plus shipping. Order online at www.afmpgame.com (for PC platform) and www.aforcemorepowerful.org/game/index.htm

Individuals active internationally in campaigns to win rights and freedom who wish to obtain copies should direct requests to game@nonviolent-conflict.org

Otpor, the Serbian resistance movement: www.unesco.org/courier/2001_03/uk/droits.htm

International Center on Nonviolent Conflict, advocating and promoting non-violence to achieve social and political goals: www.nonviolent-conflict.org

May 30

Otpor! (Resistance!)

This pro-democracy Serbian youth movement was formed at Belgrade University in October 1998 as a response to repressive university and media laws introduced that year. Following the NATO airstrikes against Yugoslavia during the Kosovo war, Otpor! started a campaign against the Yugoslav President, which resulted in 2,000 Otpor! activists being arrested. During the presidential election in September 2000, Otpor! launched its 'He's finished' campaign which galvanised public discontent and contributed to Milošević's defeat and trial for war crimes.

Tobacco sucks

Avoid passive smoking

Passive smoking:

- **Increases the risk of heart disease to about one quarter of that faced by an active smoker.**
- **Increases the risk of lung cancer by 20 per cent to 30 per cent.**
- **Aggravates asthma and other existing respiratory complaints.**
- **Increases coughing, wheezing and phlegm.**

ASH, the UK's anti-smoking campaign: www.ash.org.uk

Big Tobacco Sucks, the California campaign against the tobacco industry: www.bigtobaccosucks.org

Two giant corporations dominate the world cigarette market: Philip Morris (owned by Altria) and British American Tobacco (BAT). They stand accused of promoting a product which is addictive and injurious to health, and of doing little to discourage underage smoking. Passive smokers are also at risk, as are foetuses if the mother-to-be is a smoker.

Public attitudes are changing. Banning smoking on public transport and in public places (such as restaurants and bars) is becoming the norm. Tobacco advertising has been banned throughout the European Union, including motor racing sponsorship.

Smoking has more than 50 ways of making you ill and more than 20 ways of killing you. Around 364,000 patients are hospitalised each year in England due to smoking-related illness. Half the teenagers who smoke will die from diseases caused by tobacco if they continue to smoke; those dying before 70 will lose an average 21 years of life. Between 1950 and 2000, 60 million people worldwide died from tobacco related diseases.

In the workplace

Get a sensible smoking policy introduced at your workplace. This will benefit smokers and non-smokers alike, and productivity could increase by as much as 3 per cent in a clean-air environment.

A workplace smoking policy should state the following:

- Principles such as the rights of non-smokers and compliance with government legislation.
- Where and when smoking is allowed, and if there are smoking areas.
- How it applies to visitors.
- Any contractual obligations, such as time off allowed for smoking breaks.
- What support is available for smokers who wish to quit.
- What physical improvements are needed, such as improved ventilation.
- Procedures for reviewing the policy, and resolving any disputes.

Go unshopping

In a throwaway convenience world, we buy so many things we don't need. The principle of unshopping involves unlearning all the bad habits of our consumer society, shopping more responsibly and thinking about the future of the planet.

Coop America has come up with a list of ten things you should never buy:

Styrofoam cups Polystyrene is forever – it's not biodegradable. Americans use enough Styrofoam cups each year to circle the earth 436 times. Use a mug.

Paper towels They waste forest resources and your money. Use a dishcloth.

Bleached coffee filters The dioxins used in the bleaching contaminate ground water and are linked to cancer. Use a cafetière.

Overpackaged food One-third of what we put in the rubbish bin is packaging. Buy in bulk; buy things with less packaging; take your own shopping bag with you.

Hardwood products Every year 27 million acres of tropical rainforests are destroyed. Use products made from sustainably harvested timber or salvaged wood.

Chemical pesticides They poison the soil and contaminate the ground water. Grow native plants and use organic pest-control techniques.

Household cleaning fluids Many of these release volatile organic compounds. Buy biodegradable non-toxic cleaners and washing powders, or make your own with ingredients such as vinegar and soap.

Higher octane petrol than you need The higher the octane, the more hazardous the pollutants. Drive less, drive a smaller car, and use lower-octane fuel.

Toys made with PVC Chemicals used to make PVC are known carcinogens; dangerous additives are often used; and PVC is the least recycled plastic. Use toys made from natural materials.

Plastic forks and spoons They are not biodegradable. Carry your own utensils with you.

June 1

Make a start

For more information visit:
Coop America:
www.coopamerica.org
The Ecologist:
www.theecologist.org

Never buy again

Make a commitment not to buy these items. It's a start towards creating a better world. Once you get into the swing of things you won't even notice the difference.

For more ideas, read:

- *50 Simple Things You Can Do to Save the Earth* and *The Next Step: 50 More Things You Can Do to Save the Earth* by Earthworks Group.
- *Save Cash and Save the Planet* published by HarperCollins in association with Friends of the Earth UK.
- *Go M-A-D: 365 Daily Ways to Save the Planet* published by *The Ecologist.*

Green funerals

Dying to save the world

Consider expressing a wish to have a green funeral. The Natural Death Centre will give you all the information you need.

***The Natural Death Handbook* is also available from them at www.naturaldeath.org.uk**

Funerals are environmentally unfriendly. Think of the wood used for the coffins, the land taken up for burial, the access roads needed for the site and the embalming chemicals that can leach into the soil. Funerals are also hugely expensive. The average UK funeral in 2000 cost £2,048, while the average cremation cost only £1,215, according to the Oddfellows friendly society.

There is an alternative to using the funeral industry – a green burial in a field or woodland. Natural burial grounds decompose very quickly; you're then left with an area of regenerated flora without the clutter of marble or granite memorial stones. To avoid legal complications and bureaucracy, green burial grounds are often not consecrated, but priests can bless individual plots. The legal requirement of marking each separate grave for the burial register can be fulfilled by planting a shrub, tree or even an electronic chip. Cardboard coffins with strap-down lids cost as little as £50, and these allow both them and their contents to decompose rapidly.

Along with a green burial, why not have an alternative funeral? Celebrate the life of the deceased as well as mourn their passing. Find out what to do by reading the *Natural Death Handbook*, which is a mine of ideas and practical advice.

How about a bamboo coffin?

The SAWD partnership is a UK company producing bamboo eco-coffins in Hunan Province, China. The bamboo is grown and cut under licence from the government – pandas do not live in the surrounding area. The coffins are hand-woven and then transported by sea Russian-doll-style (one inside another) to minimise transport costs. This type of coffin received a best-coffin award from the Natural Death Centre. Visit www.bamboocoffins.co.uk

Naked bike riders

When I see a person on a bicycle, it gives me hope for the human race. H G Wells

There are so many reasons to cycle rather than drive: You save a lot of petrol. You aren't giving your hard-earned cash to an evil oil company. Biking produces no harmful emissions. You will get a healthy heart and body, not to mention great legs. You can't get done for Driving Under the Influence. You can laugh and make faces at all the poor fools stuck in traffic as you sail past them. Your maintenance costs are close to zero. The bottom line is that cycling benefits both you and the earth.

See how many more calories you burn when you cycle:

Activity	Minutes	Calories burned
Cycling (15 mph)	30	360
Walking	30	144
Sleeping	30	32
Driving	30	71
Sex (vigorous)	30	53
Kissing	30	36
Watching TV	30	27

June 3

Go as bare as you dare

Take part in your nearest World Naked Bike Ride.

- **Date: early June – check the website for the exact date.**
- **Dress code: as bare as you dare.**
- **What to do: sign up at the World Naked Bike Ride website, then tell your friends to tell their friends that it's time to take off their kit and hop on their bikes!**

World Naked Bike Ride: www.worldnakedbikeride.org

Naked ambition

The World Naked Bike Ride is an annual global event. People ride as naked as they dare around town to protest against oil dependency and celebrate the power of the human body.

Every group has its own approach to cycling naked. Some focus on body painting. Some participate within the context of ancient cultural celebrations. Some use the day to promote cycling and a cleaner environment. Some use their bodies to call attention to political issues. Some riders choose to cycle throughout the night. Some during the day. Some skip the bicycles altogether and rollerskate or rollerblade.

Act now

Do some research. Then write, design and print a leaflet, including facts and figures, and a call to action. Print 100 copies and hand them out in the street or put them through letterboxes.

End Child Prostitution, Child Pornography and Trafficking of Children for Sexual Purposes (ECPAT): www.ecpat.org.uk

Anti-Slavery Society: www.antislavery.org

The Hearth

Albanian girls are being trafficked to Italy, where they are forced into prostitution. In 1997, Vera Lesko founded The Hearth of Vlora Women to try to end this, and the related problems of drug and child abuse. The Hearth raises awareness of the problem, and it provides counselling, and medical and legal help. The Hearth opened the first shelter in Albania in 2001 for women and girls. This provides a secure place to stay and an opportunity for them to rebuild their lives.

End child prostitution

In every continent, and in developed and developing countries alike, poverty, lack of education and parental pressure is forcing children into the sex industry. Some are sent by their families into what they believe is domestic service, but the children are then kidnapped, trafficked across borders and forced to work as sex slaves.

Commercial sexual exploitation of girls and boys exists in three main forms:

- Prostitution (which includes child sex tourism)
- Pornography
- Trafficking for sexual purposes

Commercial sexual exploitation of children is a multi-billion dollar industry. Over 1 million children worldwide are involved. Most children are aged between 13 and 18, although some are as young as five. In Vietnam, 30 per cent of the 185,000 prostitutes are under 16. A large proportion of child prostitutes catch sexually transmitted diseases. 70 per cent of child prostitutes in Thailand are HIV positive, and many girls have abortions. Most children suffer serious psychological problems.

Article 34 of the Convention on the Rights of the Child requires countries to act to prevent the inducement or coercion of a child to engage in unlawful sexual activity, and to prevent the exploitative use of children in prostitution, pornography or other unlawful sexual activities. Article 35 requires countries to act to prevent the abduction, sale of or traffic in children for any purpose or in any form. Despite this, child prostitution persists.

Child prostitution, like child slavery, should simply not be tolerated. It is a gross abuse of the human rights of those who are least able to do anything. Whoever you are and whatever you do, you must do something about it.

Help the environment

When it comes to saving the environment, every bit helps. To mark World Environment Day 2004, the Environment Agency came up with 60 ideas. Some of them are listed here:

Clean air

Drive intelligently – accelerate gradually, obey speed limits, combine several errands in one trip.

Limit how long your car engine runs when you stop.

Use a car with a three-way catalytic converter.

Water

Take showers instead of baths.

Limit use of garden sprinklers or hoses.

Collect rainwater to water your plants with.

Put a bag of water in your lavatory cistern to reduce the water flushed.

Turn the tap off when brushing your teeth.

Use full loads in dishwashers and washing machines.

Repair dripping taps and turn taps off properly.

Use environmentally friendly cleaning products.

Energy use

Buy local produce or grow your own.

Fly less frequently.

Use thermostats that switch off the heating.

Insulate your home and hot water tank properly.

Use a fan instead of air conditioning.

Turn off appliances and lights when not needed.

Fit energy-efficient light bulbs.

Heat small meals in a microwave.

Dry your clothes on a clothesline.

Waste

Use a doorstep recycling scheme.

Choose products with recyclable packaging.

Cook fresh food, which has less packaging.

Reuse plastic shopping bags or use cloth bags.

Use rechargeable batteries.

Print and photocopy on both sides of paper.

Reuse envelopes.

Environmental issues

For further information visit these websites:

- **UK Environment Agency: www.environment-agency.gov.uk**
- **World Environment Day: www.unep.org/wed**
- **Visit the New Dream Foundation to see the impact of your actions: www.newdream.org/ttoffline**

Make a pledge

Pledge to do at least ten of these – twenty if you want to be a superhero.

Why not begin by considering these actions to assist our wildlife:

- Put out a bird feeder or nesting box.
- Build a pond in your garden.
- Take part in a local tree planting.
- Buy products made from sustainably produced wood.

June 6

Gum on the streets

People in the UK spend an estimated £258 million on chewing gum, with half the population chewing the stuff (28 million according to Wrigley's). But gum seems to end up everywhere else but where it belongs – in the bin. An estimated £150 million a year is spent trying to clean up discarded gum, which is found on up to 91 per cent of busy high streets in England, according to an EnCams survey. The Government has decided to clarify the litter laws and is advising on-the-spot fines for gum throwers.

Gum chewing began in ancient Greece, where they chewed mastiche made from tree resin. Thousands of years and billions of gum chewers later, it appears that we still haven't figured out how to throw gum into a bin. Gum littering became such a problem in Singapore (which has the tightest litter laws in the world) that they banned chewing gum altogether. This has just been relaxed. Sugarless gum is now available on prescription from pharmacists. The penalty for smuggling gum into the country is one year in jail and a fine equivalent to £3,000.

Have a target

Don't be a litter lout.

Make your own 'target board' for gum disposal. Use a large sheet of cardboard, metal or plywood, and place a funny phrase or amusing picture on it to attract people's attention. Put it up at a school or on the street. You will hopefully make your streets a little cleaner .

Buy a Wrigley share. They own 50 per cent of the chewing gum market. You could attend Annual General Meetings and share your ideas on gum disposal with the Chair. Buy your share at www.oneshare.com or www.frameastock.com

EnCams runs the Keep Britain Tidy Campaigns: www.encams.org

DEFRA's chewing gum campaign: www.defra.gov.uk/news/latest/2005/local env-0601.htm. Also see www.parliament.uk/post/pn201.pdf

Solving a sticky problem

Gum cleaners seem to be fighting a losing battle. So another approach is being adopted. Gum boards are being fixed to lampposts and signposts where gum chewers can stick their used gum. In Huddersfield, the boards had issues of public concern where people were invited to stick their gum in a 'Yes' or a 'No' box. In Poole, they used pictures of celebrities whose popularity was in decline, such as Jeffrey Archer and Jeremy Beadle.

Fight fistula

My name is Talana Shabera. I'm an Ethiopian. I'm fourteen years old. I was promised in marriage when I was three years old, betrothed at ten years old, and pregnant at twelve. After three days of labour I was carried on a stretcher to a hospital where my baby died two hours later. The obstructed labour left me incontinent. I smell and I feel so ashamed. Talana Shabera

Talana is suffering from fistula – a tearing of the soft tissue between the vagina and the bladder – which occurs during a complicated childbirth. Over 9,000 women and girls in Ethiopia suffer this painful condition. But exact numbers are impossible to obtain, as women with fistula are often hidden away.

As long as poverty continues, so will fistula. Many expectant mothers in Ethiopia, perhaps as many as 70 per cent, live over two-days walk from the nearest hospital. They need access to obstetric care and a skilled person to be with them during the birth. While women in the West are having cosmetic surgery to hide signs of ageing, perhaps as many as 2 million women in the developing world are having their bodies destroyed, as a result of where they were born.

Love to help

Participate in the Fistula Hospital's Love-a-Sister programme. Help one woman obtain free, safe surgery to repair her devastating injuries of fistula and re-build her life. A £250 contribution will pay for surgery and postoperative care. If you don't have the money, go out and raise it.

Celebrate your fundraising success by downloading some of Nancy's wonderful photos from the Safehands website. Frame them and hang them on your wall.

The UNFPA's campaign to end fistula: www.endfistula.org

Safehands for Mothers: www.safehands.org

The Fistula Foundation, supporting the fistula hospital in Addis Ababa: www.fistulafoundation.org

Two feisty women

Dr Catherine Hamlin decided to do something about fistula. Forty years ago, she set up the Fistula Hospital in Addis Ababa. This has become a world centre of excellence. As well as trying to help women with fistula, the hospital provides training for obstetricians and gynaecologists from all over the world.

Nancy Durrell McKenna is a photographer who has taken some wonderful photographs of pregnant women. She founded Safehands for Mothers to do something for women who don't have access to obstetric care. Safehands produces training materials for health professionals.

World Ocean Day

Ocean clean-up

The International Coastal Clean-up takes place in September each year. On a single day, 300,000 volunteers in 90 countries help clean up over 11,000 miles of shoreline. Join in: www.coastalcleanup.org

Clean-up Day is also about pollution prevention. Volunteers record the different types of marine debris, and analysing this leads to a better understanding of the causes. Ocean Conservancy then uses this information to educate the public, business and government officials about the problem.

World Ocean Day: www.theoceanproject.org

The Ocean Conservancy: www.oceanconservancy.org

June 8 is World Ocean Day, a chance each year to celebrate the world's oceans and their rich diversity of life, to highlight the problems and action being taken to promote a healthy and productive ocean, and conserve marine resources for future generations.

Oceans cover 70 per cent of the planet's surface. Everybody on the planet is affected by the oceans – from the Gulf Stream which warms the European Atlantic seaboard to the El Nino and La Nina temperature fluctuations which create climate change in the Southern Pacific, and the Indian monsoons where moist ocean air condenses to water the otherwise dry land.

But ocean environments around the world are under severe stress, due to rising sea temperatures, over-fishing, destruction of coral reefs, the impact of cruise ships, entangled animals, marine debris, pollution, mercury contamination, offshore drilling, unsustainable coastal development and many other factors. The basic problem is humankind's greed and unconcern for what is a common resource.

Endangered fish

The stellar sea lion is the largest sea lion in the world found in Alaska and the Aleutian Islands. Once numbering 300,000, they are now threatened by loss of food due to over-fishing, entanglement and pollution.

The manatee was once mistaken for a mermaid by lonely sailors. They are found mainly in Florida, and only 3,500 survive. About 300 die each year, many run into by speedboaters. Get to know these beautiful fish and other endangered species, including: Beluga whales, Bocaccio, Bottlenose dolphins, Goliath groupers, Grey whales, Hawaiian monk seals, Harbour porpoise, Right whales, Sawfish, Sea otters, Sea turtles and Sharks. They all have a right to life. Find out more about them at the Ocean Conservancy website.

Bangladesh needs bees

Bees and honey played an important part in ancient civilisations. The founder of the kingdom of Sparta in Ancient Greece took ideas from bee colonies, with regard to discipline, organisation and administration.

Modern bee keeping in the Indian subcontinent started during the Gandhian self-reliance movement in the 1940s. Some refugees in West Bengal learned how to keep bees in wooden hives during the war of liberation in the 1970s, and they took their expertise back to Bangladesh after the war. The importance of honey is stressed in many religions. Prophet Hazrat Mohammad told his companions that honey is the best among all the drinks. The Bible mentions honey and the honey bee 60 times. In ancient Hinduism, bees were considered the companion of their holy God.

Bee products have important medicinal and dietary uses. The symptoms of colds, typhoid, constipation and dysentery can be reduced by eating honey; and the immune system can be strengthened. Honey is used to beautify skin and hair. Royal jelly is used as a tonic. Bee venom has many pharmaceutical uses.

Bee keeping does not require land (hives can be placed on a roof) or big investment. Anyone can do it in their leisure time and through it they can generate additional income for their family.

A better future

Support a rural community in the developing world to start bee keeping to generate livelihoods and improve health.

Donate £25 to Hunger-Free World, and they will help a family to start bee keeping.

Bees for Development helps people worldwide to create sustainable livelihoods with bees. They organise beekeepers' safaris in countries such as India, Trinidad and Tobago and Tanzania. The safaris combine travel with adventure, learning, making new friendships, and tasting exotic cuisine. Non-beekeepers as well as beekeepers are welcome. Visit: www.planbee.org.uk

Hunger-Free World Bangladesh: www.hfwbd.org

June 9

Creating new colonies

Hunger-Free World, in Bangladesh, is one of many NGOs around the world now promoting bee keeping as part of a strategy to raise the income levels of rural people. They provide farmers and families with:

The hives: three bee boxes and three iron stands, together with a colony of bees.

All the equipment needed: a division box, knife, musk, uniform, net, gloves, feeder, smoker, queen excluder and a honey extractor machine.

Sugar to feed the bees in the off-season.

Training in bee keeping.

June 10

Obesity - a growth area

Get into shape

If you are overweight or obese, get into better shape:
At work:
- **Get off the bus or train a few stops earlier and walk the rest of the way.**
- **Go for a walk at lunchtime.**
- **Use the stairs instead of the lift.**
- **Go and speak to colleagues instead of using the phone or email.**
- **Stand while on the phone.**
- **Schedule exercise time into your day.**

In your leisure time:
- **Plan outings and holidays that include exercise: run, walk, swim or fly a kite.**
- **Dance for fun.**
- **See the sights in a city by walking, jogging or cycling.**

Check the shape you're in by using the calculator at www.worldheartday.com/aheartforlife/Obesity.asp

The growing waistlines of Americans are eating into the profits of the airline industry. A study by the US Center for Disease Control calculated that $275 million has to be spent each year on 1.3 billion more litres of fuel needed to carry the extra 10 lbs weight that the average American gained during the 1990s. This adds an extra 3.8 million tonnes of carbon dioxide to annual greenhouse gas emissions.

Obesity is a major cause of disease, primarily heart disease and diabetes. And it is becoming a global problem. In the rich world, obesity is largely caused by lifestyle (increasing calorie intake and lack of exercise). The increasing quantity of processed foods means that fat and sugar now account for more than half the caloric intake, and consumption of refined grains has largely replaced that of whole grains. Snacking between meals is also becoming routine. In the developing world, the trend towards urban living and a Westernised diet is a significant factor. There are also cultural factors at work. For example, being overweight may be seen as a sign of power and success in countries where many people go short of food. In China, the one-child policy has created a generation of 'little emperors', spoiled rotten by their parents.

A weighty problem

In the USA 28 per cent of men and 33 per cent of women are obese, and 64 per cent of the adult population is overweight. Obesity levels are rising sharply, and are also increasing in Australia, Canada and Europe, although they are still lower than in the USA.

In South Africa (urban areas) 10 per cent of men and 33 per cent of women are obese.

In Brazil (urban areas) 8 per cent of men and 33 per cent of women are obese, more than double that of 22 years ago.

Prisoners in Guantánamo

I can recognise the conditions that prisoners are being kept in at the US camp at Guantánamo Bay because I have been there. Not to Cuba's Camp X-Ray, but to the darkened cell in Beirut that I occupied for five years. I was ... denied all human rights and contact with my family, and given no access to the outside world. Because I was kept in very similar conditions, I am appalled at the way we – countries that call ourselves civilised – are treating these captives. Is this justice or revenge?
Terry Waite

International law requires that people who are detained be formally charged, informed of their rights, and permitted access to legal counsel. This was not done for the Guantánamo detainees.

The prisoners are being denied due process of law. The law provides no basis for circumventing these requirements by labelling such persons 'enemy combatants'.

Human Rights Watch says that three categories of prisoners at Guantánamo should be released:

- Taliban soldiers detained in the now-concluded war between the USA and the Afghanistan government, unless they are being prosecuted for war crimes.
- Civilians with no meaningful connection to Al-Qaeda or the Taliban, who probably should never have been sent to Guantánamo in the first place.
- Suspected terrorists whose detention had nothing to do with the war in Afghanistan – they should be charged with a crime and prosecuted.

Amnesty International says:

- Allegations of abuses such as arbitrary arrests [and] ill-treatment ... are raised each year in the US State Department reports on human rights practices in other countries. Now they are ... made against the US government in the context of its War on Terror.

Not forgotten

Cageprisoners.com is a website raising awareness of Guantánamo, run by Muslim volunteers. Watch their video: www.cageprisoners.com/downloads/why.swf

Clive Stafford Smith, lawyer and Rowntree 'Visionary' has been campaigning on Guantánamo through Reprieve, the organisation he established to fight the death penalty in the USA: www.reprieve.org.uk

Liberty

In February 2006, of the 490 prisoners at Guantánamo, 463 had had their cases reviewed: 14 of these were released and 120 transferred. Eight British residents and one Australian claiming British citizenship remain at Guantánamo.

Liberty is an organisation that defends human rights in the UK: www.liberty-human-rights.org.uk

Make your views known

Rapid-response letter writing has developed with the internet. All the big campaigning organisations encourage it, whether the issue is human rights, conflict or the environment.

If you are concerned about an issue, join a Rapid Response Network. Sign up and start writing letters in your own words.

These two letter-writing websites are small ones run by committed individuals:

Global Response with 5,500 members from 92 countries: www.globalresponse.org

Earth Action Network campaigning in the US: www.earthaction network.org

ActionNetwork with over 750,000 activists taking action on mainly US issues: www.actionnetwork.org

Get letter writing

Dear Forest Service staff,
I am deeply concerned about the ... plans to remove Yellowstone's grizzly bears from the endangered species list. As the Forest Service revises the plan, I strongly urge you to select Alternative 4, which would protect important wildlands, restore degraded habitat and maintain habitat within and between grizzly bear ecosystems. Please ... do everything possible to ensure Yellowstone's grizzlies remain protected.
Yours faithfully ...

Protecting Grizzly Bears may not be your passion. Perhaps you really care about protecting areas of outstanding beauty, ancient monuments, heritage sites, other wildlife, campaigning against 4x4s ...

If you feel strongly about something bad that is being planned, or already taking place, you need to make your views known to those who are causing the problem, or who can help with a solution.

Letter writing is one way of doing this. Demos, publicity campaigns and lobbying are other things you can do. Sending a letter will let you get your views across. It may not make much of a difference. But lots of letters show that lots of people care.

Earth Action Network

Earth Action Network was started by Dr Mha Atma Singh Khalsa, a Los Angeles chiropractor. He wanted to help the planet, and read in an activist guidebook that a single letter received by a government or company was considered to represent the views of 100 to 1,000 people. As a result, he began writing letters to influential people, based on information he got from environmental newsletters and reports. A friend pointed out that others who felt as strongly as he did would love to do the same, and Earth Action Network was born.

Buy local, eat local

Food is travelling further and further, often hundreds or even thousands of miles from where it was produced to where it is consumed. This pollutes the atmosphere with greenhouse gases and other harmful emissions, and clogs up the highways with articulated lorries. But there are other problems too.

The local food chain is fast disappearing. Family farms, local abattoirs, small processing plants, local distribution systems and small shops are all finding that they can't compete in today's global market.

Centralisation of food distribution has meant the loss of local distinctiveness – traditional varieties, and a sense of belonging to the community.

Money leaks out from the local economy and into the bank accounts of multinational food businesses.

Much of this is our fault. As consumers we have a choice. If we use our choice to buy local, then shops will put more effort into stocking local produce.

Local produce

Farmers' markets are where farmers, growers and producers from the local area sell their produce directly to the public.

All products sold will have been grown, reared, caught, brewed, pickled, baked, smoked or processed by the stallholder. They offer freshly-picked fruit and vegetables, meat, fish, cakes, pies, jams, cheeses, drinks and other fare (though not necessarily organic produce). Plus a chance to talk to the stallholders.

Local Food Works: www.localfoodworks.org

Reduce food miles

Some simple things to do to help regenerate the local food chain:

- Buy from local shops and markets.
- For food that cannot be grown in your region, such as tea, coffee, bananas or chocolate, buy fairtrade products.
- Buy seasonal fresh produce.
- Avoid air-freighted products.
- Write to your supermarket's head office, and smaller retailers, asking them to stock more locally grown and made produce. Ask local restaurants to feature local produce on their menus.
- Consult a local food directory to see who's growing or producing what in your locality. If there isn't one, why not produce one yourself?
- Grow your own food – organically if possible – in your back garden, on an allotment or community garden, or even in window boxes and gro-bags.
- Write to your MP asking for a clearer labelling system that shows the distance the food has travelled and the country or countries of origin.
- Ask publicly funded canteens (schools, hospitals, prisons etc.) to buy more local, seasonal and organic food.

Share your car

Care and share

Just for the fun of it, go travelling to celebrate National Liftshare Day. Log in to a liftshare website, and find somebody who is going somewhere interesting. Share a ride with them.

Start liftsharing. Next time you have a spare seat in your car or want to go somewhere, share the ride.

Liftshare, for sharing a ride in the UK: www.liftshare.org

National Liftshare Day: www.liftshare.co.uk/nlsd.asp

World CarShare Consortium: www.ecoplan.org/carshare

Carplus: www.carclubs.org.uk

The average car commuter in the UK drives 19 miles a day. Cutting that by half through car sharing would save 648 kg of carbon dioxide over one year, the same as that absorbed by 216 trees. Liftshare

Commuting to work? Driving your children to school? Going shopping? Going to town? Going to a football match? Driving abroad? The chances are that there will be empty seats in your car. But other people might want to travel to roughly the same place at the same time and could share the journey with you.

It makes good financial and environmental sense to share the costs of a journey as it results in one less car trip, though it is better to walk, cycle or use public transport. The internet is a great mechanism for linking people to share a journey. Also consider car sharing, whereby people club together to jointly own and run a car. The benefits of sharing a journey:

- Saves money – you can save up to £1,000 a year.
- Reduces the number of cars on the roads – less congestion, pollution and fewer parking problems.
- Is especially beneficial for people in rural areas.
- Makes an enjoyable journey to work in the morning.

Liftsharing – halve the impact

Here are some simple rules for internet liftsharing:

- Decide if you are prepared to travel with a member of the opposite sex.
- Exchange telephone numbers and make arrangements over the phone, even if the first contact is by email.
- Meet in a well-lit public place.
- Give someone else your journey details plus contact details of who you are travelling with.
- Take basic safety precautions, ask for car details – make, model, colour and registration number. Ask the driver to bring along a driving licence, insurance and roadworthiness certificates.

Donate smart clothes

Imagine you are down and out, or simply very poor. All the clothes you own are shabby. But you've managed to get a job interview, and you want to look your best. You've got nothing nice to wear for your interview. This makes it less likely that you'll get the job. This is the Catch 22: no smart clothes, no job; no job, no money to buy smart clothes.

Dress for Success Professional Women's Group is an organisation that addresses this problem. Women are referred to it by government agencies and other organisations, including homeless shelters, domestic violence shelters, immigration services and job training programmes. Each client receives one suit for a job interview and a second suit when she gets the job. Dress for Success then provides ongoing support to help clients build a successful career.

Dress for Success needs a supply of clothes. Donate new or nearly new (and clean) office clothes. They are particularly in need of clothes in larger sizes:

- Co-ordinated, contemporary, interview-appropriate skirt and trouser suits
- Beautiful, crisp blouses
- Gorgeous blazers and jackets
- Professional shoes

Why not start a Dress for Success branch in your town? Their website tells you how.

June 15

Clothes for good causes

Charity shops would love the things that Dress for Success can't use. Donate your old clothes, jewellery you no longer wear, decorative items you are fed up with and unwanted presents. They will convert these into cash for a good cause.

Buy as many of your clothes as possible at charity shops and become the new home for someone else's perfectly good clothes. You'll be saving money and supporting a charity. And you'll also be dressing distinctively rather than being a boring old follower of fashion!

Dress for Success: www.dressforsuccess.org

A story of success

Nancy Lublin used a $5,000 inheritance from her great-grandfather to start Dress for Success, and put a great idea into practice.

Dress for Success now provides interview suits, confidence boosts and career development advice to more than 45,000 women in over 73 cities each year.

Most of its branches are in the USA, but there is a branch in London, as well as in cities in New Zealand and Canada.

Legalise it

Whether or not you are a user, you may feel that the criminalisation of cannabis use is the wrong approach to the drug problem. If so, join the campaign to 'Legalise It'.

Help drug users, volunteer on a drugs helpline.

Cannabis is not a monster, buy some cannabis seeds to decorate your home or office. Keep within the law!

If you smoke cannabis, assess your cannabis use at: www.knowcannabis.org.uk

If you want confidential advice, call the FRANK free helpline on 0800 776600 or go to The Site helpline: www.thesite.org/drinkanddrugs/helplines

Campaign to legalise cannabis use by joining: www.ccguide.org.uk or www.clcia.org.uk

Buy cannabis seeds at: www.skunk.co.uk

Cannabis - a problem?

The government believes that drugs are bad for us. Using and supplying drugs is a serious criminal offence, the seriousness depends on the class of drug:

- **Class A drugs** heroin, methadone, cocaine, ecstasy, LSD, injectable amphetamines and magic mushrooms when prepared for use.
- **Class B drugs** amphetamines and barbiturates.
- **Class C drugs** cannabis, anabolic steroids, benzodiazepines (tranquillisers) and amphetamines.

Possession of Class C drugs can result in two years in prison, and for supply or intent to supply up to 14 years imprisonment, plus a fine. Penalties for Class A and B drugs are higher – up to life in prison and a fine for supplying/intending to supply Class A drugs.

The upside of cannabis: Cannabis was first used medicinally in China some 5,000 years ago to treat malaria, constipation and rheumatic pains. Today it is more likely to be used as a recreational drug, although it is sometimes prescribed for medicinal use.

The downside of cannabis: Psychiatrists now believe that cannabis use can lead on to mental health problems in later life. Supply, possession and use are all criminal offences. Remember, you'll be less effective in changing the world if you're dopey!

Buying cannabis seed

In the UK, it is legal to purchase and possess cannabis seeds. But it is against the law to germinate the seeds or smoke the product.

The best selling cannabis varieties on the Skunk website are:

1. Skunk No. 1 seed
2. Lowryder seeds
3. Hawaiian Skunk seeds
4. Northern Lights seeds
5. Skunk Haze seeds
6. Hindu Kush Skunk seeds
7. Indian Skunk seeds
8. Durban Poison seeds
9. Afghani No. 1 seeds
10. Indian Haze seeds

Transform arid lands

Semi-arid land in Africa is turning to desert, partly due to poor land and water management. In areas where electricity is not available, the only fuel for cooking is wood. The daily search for wood is taking people further afield, and is resulting in whole areas being stripped of what meagre vegetation they had. Once the trees and scrub have gone, there is nothing to hold the topsoil in place. Rain quickly evaporates, the soil dries off and the wind simply blows it away.

In much of Africa rainfall is highly erratic. It is always possible that seasonal rain will just not arrive. And when it does, much of it drains off into rivers, and flows out to sea. If rainwater could be retained, it could be used during the dry season to increase food production. It would also impact on people's daily lives, as they would no longer have to walk long distances for water, and the water would be cleaner.

One answer lies in small-scale 'sand dams', which an organisation called Excellent Development has been helping to build for over 20 years. Started in 1984 by 18-year-old Simon Maddrell, it has worked with communities in East Africa to construct 50 dams, and aims to make that 300 by 2010.

Turn wine into water

Excellent Development has teamed up with Virgin Wines which is offering £20 off their first case of wine and a £5 donation towards Excellent Development's work. Visit www.excellentdevelopment.com/wine.php to find out how to take advantage of this special offer and turn wine into water!

If you don't live in the UK, buy a bottle of wine and drink a toast to Simon Maddrell and his vision.

Excellent Development: www.excellentdevelopment.com

SOS Sahel working with the Africa Drylands Alliance in Mali, Niger, Ethiopia, Kenya and Sudan to reclaim the desert: www.sahel.org.uk

Help build a sand dam

A sand dam is a reinforced concrete wall, 2–4 metres high, built across a seasonal river bed. A pipe is laid through the dam, and extended 20 metres back upstream. When the seasonal rains occur, sand is washed downstream and collects behind the dam. It traps water, which seeps out and runs through the pipe long after the soil in neighbouring valleys has dried up.

As well as helping to construct the dam, local people work to improve the land behind it, terracing the hillsides to improve water and soil conservation. The extra water enables them to grow vegetables, which improve their diets. They also grow trees in nurseries, eventually planting them out to further rehabilitate the semi-arid land.

June 18

Recharge your batteries

Do your bit

Reduce the environmental impact of battery use:
Use rechargeable batteries wherever possible. Some batteries can be recharged up to 1,000 times. But you will need a battery charger.

Purchase Nickel Metal Hydride (NiMH) batteries in preference to Nickel Cadmium (NiCd) batteries, as these are much less toxic.

Never throw used batteries away with your household rubbish, as some of their ingredients, especially cadmium, are highly toxic.

Recycle used batteries instead.

Find out everything you need to know about batteries at: www.batteryuniversity.com

Batteries are so much part of our lives that we rarely think about them until they need replacing. And that's precisely the time that we do need to think about them, because we have to address the problem of what to do with them, and what to replace them with.

Around 22,000 tonnes of batteries are sold annually in the UK and almost all of them end up in a landfill site. Many batteries contain some very nasty chemicals, such as cadmium, which can poison the environment. They also include zinc, which could be reused if the battery were recycled. Battery use is increasing, which means that battery waste is becoming an ever-bigger problem. The situation is similar in many other countries around the world.

The different types of rechargeable battery:

Lead-acid heavy but cheap; used for car batteries and for heavy equipment such as wheelchairs.

Nickel-cadmium long-life, used for power tools; contain toxic matter. Avoid if possible.

Nickel-metal-hydride used in mobile phones and laptops; contain no toxic matter.

Lithium-ion and Lithium-ion-polymer high energy and low weight; used in lightweight laptop and notebook computers and for mobile phones.

Reusable alkaline cheap rechargeable batteries used for torches and other consumer devices.

Don't let energy go to waste

Ask your employer, school or college to provide a battery bin for collecting and recycling used batteries. If they won't, build one yourself. Make it bright and colourful; produce a leaflet alongside it, explaining why it is important to recycle batteries. The battery bin should be situated in a prominent place.

Find out if your local council does anything about battery recycling. If yours doesn't, use your lobbying skills to persuade them that they should.

Put yourself in prison

Please, use your liberty to promote ours.
Aung San Suu Kyi, opposition leader in Burma and Nobel prizewinner

Burma is ruled by a brutal dictatorship, which uses murder, torture and rape to keep 50 million citizens under its thumb. Hence its nickname: 'The Prison without Bars'. The government has incarcerated over 1,000 political prisoners, 38 of whom are elected MPs. Millions of people have been forced into slave labour. Living conditions are horrendous. Yet the borders are sealed, and no citizen can leave.

Aung San Suu Kyi is the face of hope for the people. She is a renowned advocate for democracy and also the world's only Nobel Peace Prize recipient under house arrest. For decades she has been campaigning for liberation for the people. She is the leader of the National League for Democracy, the legitimately elected leader of Burma. Today is Aung San Suu Kyi's birthday, and has been designated 'Arrest Yourself Day'. People all over the world are invited to throw a 24-hour house party, to draw attention to her struggle.

Campaign for Burma

Arrest yourself and your friends in your own house for 24 hours to draw attention to the situation in Burma. Why not ask everybody to give £10 and use the party to raise money for the international struggle for freedom for the people of Burma? Have a great time, but make sure that you tell the local media.

Send a birthday card to Aung San Suu Kyi. Send your card to the US Campaign for Burma at 612 K St., NW Suite #401, Washington, DC 20006, USA to arrive by 1 June; the cards will be delivered in person on 19 June.

Aung San Suu Kyi's website: www.dassk.com

The Burma Campaign UK: www.burmacampaign.org.uk

Aung San Suu Kyi's story

Aung San Suu Kyi's father, General Aung San, led Burma's fight for independence from the UK in the 1940s and was killed in 1947. She studied at Oxford, married and had two sons, but returned to Burma in 1988 to tend her critically-ill mother. She became involved in the pro-democracy movement, which was gaining momentum, despite the murder of thousands of demonstrators by the 'State Law and Order Restoration Council' (SLORC). In the 1990 general election the party she headed, the National League for Democracy, won 80 per cent of the vote, but the SLORC refused to recognise the result, and arrested her. Since then, she has been under almost constant house arrest, speaking in public on a few occasions. She was awarded the Nobel Peace Price in 1991.

Anti-prejudice

Become part of the 365 Busted Myths to Change the World project. Identify a popular prejudice. Bust the myth with accurate factual information in c.80 words.

Send your Mythbuster to sola_arts@yahoo.co.uk. Visit www.solaarts.org

Challenging the Myths: www.refugeeaction.org.uk/information/challenging themyths1.aspx

Student Action for Refugees has lots of ideas: www.star-network.org.uk

Sola power

The Mythbusters Project challenges prejudices with accurate information circulated on business cards and via the internet. It is the brainchild of Adele Spiers, who runs Sola Arts in Liverpool. People reinforce their prejudices with inaccurate facts and figures. The first Mythbuster project challenges negative perceptions of asylum seekers. Future subjects will include gender, race, young people, unemployment, old age, disability, drug-taking.

Mythbusters

Q Why do all asylum seekers come to the UK?

A They don't. The majority of asylum seekers stay close to their country of origin. This means that some of the poorest countries in the world support the largest numbers of refugees. The UK received 33,930 applications for asylum in 2003 (as against 71,365 in 2001). That is less than 0.02 per cent of the world's refugees. Most people don't choose their country of asylum; where they end up depends on how quickly they fled and by what means. For those who can choose, important factors are existing communities, colonial bonds and knowledge of the language. A few are influenced by financial considerations. Most have little or no knowledge about the employment or welfare situation in the UK.

Q Do asylum seekers get more money than pensioners?

A No. Asylum seekers are only entitled to the equivalent of 70 per cent of basic Income Support. A single asylum seeker receives about £39 a week in vouchers, which they can now exchange for cash. Currently, the level of Income Support (a minimum income guarantee) for a single older person is £105.45, and the full state pension for a couple is £160.95 a week.

Q Won't they swamp our culture?

A Generally speaking, it is absurd for people in the rich world to claim that they are having their culture swamped by refugees: the numbers entering are small, compared to local populations. In some cases, though, local authorities have settled large numbers of refugees in a small area and this has created problems, especially if the area is already economically deprived or lacking services. Communities may then end up blaming asylum seekers, who aren't responsible for poor conditions.

Build a solar cooker

A few years ago, I woke up to the fact that half of the world's people must burn wood or dried dung in order to cook their food. It came as quite a shock ... especially as I learned of the illnesses caused by breathing smoke day in and day out, and the environmental impacts of deforestation – not to mention the time spent by people (mostly women) gathering sticks and dung to cook their food.

And yet, many of these billions of people live near the equator, where sunshine is abundant and free. As a University Professor of Physics with a background in energy usage, I set out to develop a means of cooking food and sterilising water using the free energy of the sun. Steven E Jones, Brigham Young University

Using a solar-powered cooker in a land where the sun shines nearly every day has to be a win-win situation. Some reasons why a solar cooker is a good thing:

- It helps prevent deforestation and desertification. In developing countries, the majority of rural people cook over wood fires or stoves. The year-round removal of so much vegetation contributes to soil erosion.
- It saves the time of the women whose job it is to collect the firewood, and might even free up young girls so that they can attend school.
- There is no smoke pollution, reducing the risk of the respiratory disease that affects women and their children who spend so much of their time breathing in the smoke from open fires.
- It reduces injuries.
- It reduces carbon dioxide emissions and makes a contribution to the reduction in greenhouse gases.
- It can produce safe drinking water as well as to prepare food, reducing the risk of disease.
- The sun's energy is free.

Cook dinner for free

- **Build a solar cooker yourself.**
- **Organise a solar-cooked lunch party for your friends on a sunny day.**
- **Become a passionate advocate for solar cooking and do what you can to spread the word.**

Plans for building a solar cooker can be got from: www.solarcooking.org

Steven Jones: http://en.wikipedia.org/wiki/Steven_E._Jones

Three types

Box style, which works like a mini-greenhouse.
Panel style, which directs sunlight into the cooking area using reflecting panels.
Parabolic, which focuses an intense beam of sunlight on the bottom of the cooking pot.
All can be made using simple materials, such as aluminium foil, cardboard, polythene, an inflated car inner tube, and a sheet of wood.

June 22

Global warming

It must be reversed

For further information:
Peter Sweatman:
www.ctt.org
www.marklynas.org
www.climateark.org
www.heatisonline.org
www.earthday.net/footprint/index.asp
www.co2.org/calculator/index.cfm

Our house is burning down and we're blind to it ... The earth and humankind are in danger and we are all responsible. It is time to open our eyes. Alarms are sounding across all the continents ... Climate warming is still reversible. Heavy is the responsibility of those who refuse to fight it.
Jacques Chirac, President of France

Peter Sweatman writes: 'Three years ago I met a successful lawyer who told me about the enormous problems we are creating through our reckless abuse of the environment. He said that the situation was as serious as a huge meteorite directly colliding with the earth ... I now believe that the single biggest issue humankind faces is global warming. The issue is not the amount of warming but the speed of the change, which will lead to massive species loss, population migration on a global scale, increased weather disasters, and rising sea levels – if nothing is done now.

I decided that individual action was vital, and set about planting trees and 'greening' my life. But I also felt that there were many people who did not have enough information ... With four friends, I founded Catalyst Climate Change Trust to pool our resources ... lobby and inform people about global warming.

Our first step was to commission research into how European companies, which are regulated to reduce their CO_2 emissions, can sue companies in non-Kyoto signatory countries; that is, those that are competing in the global market but are able to produce CO_2 freely. This research was launched at the international climate talks. It received huge media attention. We then arranged for 450 of our friends and colleagues to listen to a group of the best-informed climate specialists talk about global warming ... Many have offered to give money, take action or join CCT ... If five of us can do this, what could 50 or 500 people do?

Hot spots

Read *High Tide* by Mark Lynas. Mark visits some of the climate change hot spots around the world: the Peruvian Andes to examine the glaciers melting, northwest China to inspect desertification, the Pacific to watch islands sinking, the US East Coast to see the impact of hurricanes. He reports the situation as it is. If you've got the time, go and see for yourself.

And if you are now convinced by the seriousness of global warming, do something. Join with your friends and start campaigning.

Recycle your bike

Merlin Matthews was such a genius at fixing everyone's bikes when he was at university that he earned the nickname 'Dr Bike'. He would fix bikes in exchange for beers. He was even approached for advice about starting up a bike factory in Haiti. This made him realise that there are lots of bikes being thrown away that could be fixed. He decided to find a way of collecting old bikes in the UK and sending them to Haiti, thinking that he would be able to spend most of his time in Haiti's sunshine running a bicycle repair workshop. Sadly, he realised that his time would be better spent in the UK fundraising, and sorting out the bikes and shipping them. He linked up with Institute for Transportation & Development Policy, International Bicycle Fund and Bikes Not Bombs in the USA, and decided that, since US organisations were better able to help in Latin America, he would focus on supplying bicycles to Africa.

The charity he started, Re-Cycle, has so far donated over 14,000 bikes. Many people there have to trek four hours every day just to get drinking water, or walk eleven miles (each way) to get to school. A bicycle can make the difference between life and death, or a child gaining an education, or not. The charity also works with local African groups, teaching people how to repair and maintain bicycles.

Surplus bikes

Allow your old bicycle to improve someone's life in Africa. Dig it out and donate it. Someone will be grateful.

Bike recycling groups:

- **Re-Cycle: www.re-cycle.org**
- **Bike Recycling, a network of UK bike recycling groups: www.bikerecycling.org.uk**
- **Bikes for the World and Bikes not Bombs both donate bikes from the USA to the developing world: www.bikesfortheworld.org www.bikesnotbombs.org**
- **Afribike, an organisation providing South Africans with bicycles: www.afribike.org**

And these organisations promoting sustainable transport solutions globally:

International Bicycle Fund: www.ibike.org

Institute for Transportation and Development Policy: www.itdp.org

June 23

Help send bikes to Africa

Can you provide any of the help needed to recycle bikes internationally?

Storage space for collected bikes – needs to be 100 per cent secure, but infrequent access required.

Contacts in the haulage industry and the shipping world – to get good discounts.

Containers (40 or 20 ft) at the end of their seaworthy life – donated to be used for secure storage or turned into a cycle repair workshop in Africa.

Second-hand bikes, parts and tools.

Enjoy slow food

Make it last

Organise a dinner party for your seven best friends. Ask them all to prepare and bring something delicious using only the best ingredients plus a bottle of something special. Plan the menu together or leave things to chance.

Linger over your dinner, the longer the better. Have a really great time. Repeat as often as desired.

Slow Food: www.slowfood.com

The Slow Food movement was founded in 1988 by Carlo Petrini, an Italian journalist. He was protesting against the opening of a McDonald's next to the Spanish Steps in Rome, seeing it as part of a global fast-food culture. He believed that the world was forgetting the joys of good food and leisurely dining.

Eating something delicious will help sustain biodiversity by preserving food plants under threat from an industry demanding mass production of foods that look, rather than taste, good and which have long shelf lives. The pleasure in eating good food is itself a small but meaningful political act.

Eco-gastronomy isn't going to save the world, but if you can bring food politics and the pleasure of eating together, the Vesuvian apricot and Delaware Bay oyster won't be the only species to benefit.

The Slow Food Manifesto

... We are enslaved by speed and have all succumbed to the same insidious virus – Fast Life – which disrupts our habits, pervades the privacy of our homes and forces us to eat fast foods. To be worthy of the name, *Homo sapiens* (Latin for 'thinking man') should rid himself of speed before it reduces all of us to a species in danger of extinction.

A firm defence of quiet material pleasure is the only way to oppose the universal folly of Fast Life. Suitable doses of guaranteed sensual pleasure and slow, long-lasting enjoyment should hopefully preserve us from the contagion of the multitudes who mistake frenzy for efficiency.

Our defence should begin at the table with Slow Food. Let us rediscover the flavours and savours of regional cooking and banish the degrading effects of Fast Food. In the name of productivity, Fast Life has changed our way of being and threatens our environment and our landscapes.
So Slow Food is now the only truly progressive answer. But it is an idea that needs plenty of supporters in order to turn this (slow) motion into an international movement, with the little snail as its symbol.

Testing theories

Morgan Spurlock, a 33-year-old New York film-maker, was watching the news in West Virginia in November 2002, when he saw that two teenagers from New York were suing McDonald's for making them obese. He decided to test out the teenagers' claim that eating fast food could seriously damage your health, and film the process. For a whole month he would eat nothing but McDonald's food: for breakfast, lunch and dinner. There were three ground rules:

1 He had to eat every item on the McDonald's menu at least once.
2 He could only eat what was available over the counter (no special orders).
3 He had to order a SuperSize meal whenever a counter assistant offered him this option.

He would record the state of his health prior to this new diet and afterwards. The outcome was *SuperSizeMe*, an award winning 98-minute film.

In the first week he put on 4 kg. After a month he'd added a total of 11 kg. His cholesterol level rose by 65 points and was 33 per cent higher than when he started. His doctor also suggested that this diet of fast food was causing serious liver damage. It took Spurlock 14 months to return to his former physical condition.

Fat issues

Spurlock's film challenges the power of the huge food corporations to determine what we eat. It is not just their menus but their marketing clout, and the impact that this has on lifestyles and attitudes, which seems to be leading to an epidemic of obesity.

Complain to the Advertising Standards Authority (which oversees advertising to see that it is 'legal, decent, honest and truthful') if you see any advertising on TV and in magazines that is obviously untrue.

For the advertising codes of practice and how to complain: www.asa.org.uk.

If there is something you feel needs testing, test it out and see what happens.

SuperSizeMe: supersizeme.com

June 25

The food industry response

Since the first showing of the film *SuperSizeMe*, McDonald's has phased out its SuperSize meals and is testing a Go-Active Happy Meal with a salad, bottle of water and free pedometer!

However, in the USA, Hardees has launched its Monster Thickburger with 1,420 calories and 107 grammes of fat per portion. It consists of Angus beef (664 calories) and 4 rashers of bacon (150 calories) with 3 slices of processed cheese (186 calories) and mayonnaise (160 calories) in a sesame seed bun (230 calories) spread with butter (30 calories).

Torture is endemic

Do something

The Medical Foundation for the Care of Victims of Torture helps over 3,000 people a year. Support the Foundation, identify your worst fear and resolve to face it head on. You might, for example, be afraid of heights. Arrange to do a charity parachute jump.

Or try ethical banking. Open a Medical Foundation Saver Account at Triodos Bank. They will donate 0.25 per cent of your average account balance each year to the Foundation and you can choose to donate all or part of your interest. Visit: www.torturecare.org.uk

World Organisation Against Torture, an international coalition fighting arbitrary detention and torture: www.omct.org

If we fail to do anything about torture, we condone it. Michael Palin

Beatings, electrocutions, being suspended for hours, mock drownings, sleep deprivation, rape ... The ingenuity of humans to think up ways of torturing their fellow humans is limitless. Room 101 was dreamt up by George Orwell for his novel *1984*, as the place where each person confronted his or her own worst nightmare. For Winston Smith, the hero of the novel, it was rats. In Room 101, Smith had a cage containing starving rats strapped to his face until he 'confessed' that he loved Big Brother. Would you have been able to hold out? Or would you, like Smith, have 'confessed'? What would be your breaking point?

Horrendous stories are published almost daily about people being tortured. Don't run away from them. Often, people have had to go through a second form of torture, just to recount and relive their story. As a tribute to the courage they have shown in standing up for what they believe in, we can at least do them the honour of listening to them.

Case studies

Elizabeth is a 21-year-old student from Zimbabwe. Early one morning, a group of men, some in Zanu-PF T-shirts, barged their way into her house. A black hood was placed over her head and she was taken away, detained for two days, beaten, raped, and questioned about her political activities. All she had done was to participate in the youth section of a pro-democracy movement.

Edwin, from an English-speaking area of Cameroon, was 15 when he was caught protesting against plans to scrap the Anglo-Saxon education system. He was held for three weeks, beaten, kicked and whipped. Undeterred, Edwin joined an opposition group and co-founded the Student Parliament. His university branded him a dissident and refused to let him do postgraduate studies.

Start your own school

If you are planning for one year, plant rice, If you are planning for two years, plant trees. If you are planning for 100 years, plant education.
Old Chinese proverb

Only 37 out of 155 developing countries have primary education and have managed to enrol and keep all school-age children in a school until they have received a rudimentary education. This is helping to meet Millennium Development Goal No. 3: to ensure that, by 2015, children everywhere will be able to complete a full course of primary schooling. Another 32 countries look likely to achieve this goal by 2015. But in 70 countries, more needs to be done.

Ethiopia is a country that is still trying to address the problem. Nearly two-thirds of Ethiopians cannot read or write. But with more than half the people in the country under 15 years old, there is an opportunity to rectify this. Primary school is free, and is supposedly mandatory, but fewer than half of all children ever begin school and only one in ten continue to Year 9. It is also normal for a class to have up to 100 children, making teaching and learning very difficult indeed.

One class at a time

Asfaw Yemiru believes that education is the only way for the poor to achieve a better life. At only 14 years old, he opened a school for street children. That was in 1957. Four years later, he built the Asere Hawariat School for 2,000 children (classes 1–5). In 1972 he opened the Moya School for 2,000 children (classes 6–8), and their education is still free. Asfaw Yemiru won the World Children's Prize in 2001: www.childrensworld.org Canon Tim Kinahan has started a fund for Asere Hawariat School: http://gazette.ireland.anglican.org/090104/focus090104.htm

To support the School of St Jude: eol.habari.co.tz/st-jude.htm

June 27

Gemma's story

After finishing university, a young Australian, Gemma Sisia, travelled to Uganda to teach for three years. On her return, Gemma started taking $10 out of her pay packet each week to sponsor some Ugandan children she had met. Soon her family and friends were also sponsoring children's education.

This was the starting point for Gemma to build and run a school – St Jude's near Arusha, Tanzania. The 300 students currently range in age from 4–10 years old, and each year a new grade is added. Gemma has persuaded people around the world to donate money for tuition, books, uniforms and lunches.

June 28

Responsible travel

Plan ahead

For a more detailed explanation of sustainable tourism, see: www.uneptie.org/pc/tourism/sust-tourism/home.htm

International Ecotourism Society: www.ecotourism.org

Responsible Travel: www.responsibletravel.com

Good practice

Responsible travel conserves the environment and improves the well-being of local people. By being responsible you are likely to get a little bit more out of your travels – as well as putting something back.

Next time, travel more responsibly. Why would you want to do otherwise?

Here are some suggestions from Responsible Travel on to how to approach travel to foreign countries in a way that will bring benefits to the country, without diminishing the self-respect of its people:

- Read up on the countries you plan to visit. The welcome will be warmer if you take an interest and speak even a few words of the local language.
- Stay in B&Bs, village houses and locally owned accommodation, benefiting local families.
- Travel like Gandhi, with simple clothes, open eyes and an uncluttered mind.
- Check your tour operator's responsible travel policy.
- Help the local economy by buying local produce.
- Bear in mind that a small amount saved when bargaining to buy an item, could be extremely significant to the seller.
- Recognise cultural differences. The people in the country you are visiting may have different time concepts and thought patterns from your own. Respect local cultures, traditions and holy places.
- Cultivate the habit of asking questions and discover the enrichment of seeing a different way of life through other people's eyes.
- Use public transport, hire a bike or walk where convenient. You'll get to know the place better.
- Use water sparingly. Local people may not have sufficient clean water for their needs.
- Find out where locals go. Visit the main tourist sites, but get off the tourist trail too.
- Don't discard litter, take it home with you. Waste disposal is a major expense in poorer countries.
- Ask permission before you photograph people. In some cultures it can cause offence.
- Do not buy products made from endangered species, hard woods, shells from beach traders, or ancient artefacts (which may have been stolen).
- Take small gifts from home for your hosts.

More great ideas

In compiling this book, we invited people to submit ideas for ways of changing the world. Here is a selection of those we received, but did not have space to give them their own page:

- Organise a carnival to kick racism out of the community. Celebrate the diversity of all the different peoples who live in your neighbourhood.
- Do a litter walk with some friends. Pick a mile of road or beach, and pick up all the litter you find. Wear heavy-duty gardening gloves. Take great care of sharp objects. Start a 'Stop Litter' campaign.
- Make a banner to promote an issue (horizontally or vertically) and hang it up.
- Hold a swap-shop party. Everyone brings ten things to swap for something they like better. Everyone leaves with ten new things.
- Get people in your office to stop printing out emails – save up to 40 per cent of office paper.
- Make recycled paper. It's fun and it makes great gifts. All you need are scraps and a blender.
- Organise a 'I have a dream' contest to find the best ideas in your community for addressing some of its key problems and opportunities.
- Organise a Talk-to-your-Neighbours day. Or just invite your neighbours in for a cup of tea.
- Create a catalogue that features locally made items, to stimulate the local economy.
- Set up a local coffee shop that is cheap, fairtrade and healthy. Fill it with posters, publications and music on how to change the world. This could be the best franchise idea since Starbucks!
- Use pavement chalk as a protest tool – or just to brighten up the street. Create a floor mural. Unlike paint, chalk will wash away with the next rains.
- Petition Mr Kipling to reduce cake packaging. Do a survey of food packaging. Start a campaign to get manufacturers to reduce the amount they use.

Keep them coming

Campaign to get empty housing back in use. Do a survey. Think about who might need it. Homeless people? Asylum seekers and refugees? Students? Visitors and tourists? It's doing no good remaining empty.

Take any one of the ideas on this page and make it happen.

Or think of a better idea and send it to us.

Send your great ideas to us: www.365act.com

An old idea

Befriend an elderly person:

- Have tea with them
- Do their shopping
- Tend their garden
- Share experiences from the past and the present.
- Collect their stories of life long ago.

June 30

Purify water

Do-it-yourself

SODIS is a simple alternative to boiling water (which consumes firewood) and chlorination (which requires the availability of chemicals and also adversely affects the water's taste).

Try the SODIS process for yourself, as an act of solidarity with those who have no alternative.

Share the technology with anyone you think might be interested.

Solaqua Foundation: www.sodis.ch/Text2002/T-Howdoesitwork.htm

UNESCO Water Portal: www.unesco.org/water

About 1.1 billion people do not have access to safe drinking water – that is at least a third of people in developing countries. Two-thirds of these people live in Asia. In Sub-Saharan Africa, 42 per cent of the population does not have access to a clean safe drinking-water supply. This lack of water supply and proper sanitation facilities, causes serious health problems. The main dangers are diarrhoea and cholera. Together these kill 1.8 million people a year, 90 per cent of whom are children under 5 years old.

One of the UN's Millennium Development Goals is to halve, by 2015, the proportion of people who do not have safe drinking water and basic sanitation. The UN has declared 2005–2015 as the International Decade for Action, and plans to focus on water-related issues under the slogan 'Water for Life'.

There is a simple way of purifying water in emergencies (such as the post-tsunami period) as well as for everyday use. It's called SODIS, which stands for solar disinfection, and it is being promoted by Fundación Sodis in Latin America and by the Solaqua Foundation in other parts of the world.

How SODIS works

Get hold of a transparent plastic bottle. Wash well before first-time use. Use PolyEthyleneTerephthalate (PET) plastic bottles rather than PolyVinylChloride (PVC). Whereas PET bottles smell sweet when burnt, PVC bottles often have a bluish tinge, and produce smoke.

Fill the bottle three-quarters full with water from a local water source such as a stream or river. The water should not be too muddy. Shake to aerate the water – the dissolved oxygen helps in the purification process. Then fill completely and screw on the cap.

Place the bottle on a corrugated metal roof in strong sunlight for one full day. The heating of the water and the Ultra-Violet (UV-A) radiation together destroy the micro-organisms which cause water-borne diseases.

Set up a co-op

In 1844, twenty-eight craftsmen in Rochdale pooled their money to open a store that sold commodities such as flour, oatmeal, butter, sugar and candles. These 'Rochdale Pioneers' – Miles Ashworth (a weaver), James Bamford (a shoemaker), John Bent (a tailor) and the others – founded the co-operative movement. They wanted to achieve fair prices for essential goods they needed, and they wanted to ensure that the products they were buying were not being adulterated.

Co-operatives involve people working together, using the economies of scale for mutual financial benefit. They belong to the members, who control trading practice and distribution of any profits (as a dividend), and are run democratically – one member, one vote. Today there are 'producer co-operatives', jointly marketing members' products; 'consumer co-operatives', which jointly purchase what members need; 'credit unions', in which members pool their savings and obtain cheaper credit; 'giving co-operatives' through which members pool their donations to give bigger amounts to charities; 'housing co-operatives' that build and manage housing on behalf of owner-tenants; and even 'babysitting co-operatives' whereby parents share babysitting. Co-ops can be formally or informally run.

International Day of Co-operatives is the first Saturday in July

Work together

It only needs three of you to start your own co-operative. Here are two simple ideas:

- **A dog-walking co-operative, in which each person takes turns to walk everyone's dogs.**
- **A food co-operative, with each member going to the wholesale market once a week to purchase fresh fruit and vegetables.**

Work out your rules – set out what members are going to get out of it and what they are going to put in, as well as how it will operate. This constitution should be signed by all the members.

Co-op On Line: www.cooponline.coop

International Co-operative Information Centre: www.wisc.edu/uwcc/icic

Amul, milk-processing plant: www.amul.com

The National Dairy Development Board: www.nddb.org

Milk co-operatives in India

Dr Verghese Kurien is known as the 'father of the white revolution' in India. He started a milk processing plant, so small producers could get a decent price for their milk. This has now grown into Amul, which collects, processes and sells 5 million litres of milk a day on behalf of 2.36 million producers. The National Dairy Development Board was set up under Dr Kurien's leadership to spread the principles of co-operation in the dairy industry across India.

July 2

Mad pride

The numbers

According to the Mental Health Foundation:

- **1 in 5 women and 1 in 7 men have some mental problem, mainly anxiety, depression, a phobia or panic attacks.**
- **1 in 100 will suffer manic depression or schizophrenia.**
- **The total cost of mental health in England is about £23 billion per year.**

July is Mad Pride Month.

Mad Pride: www.zyra.org.uk/madpride.htm

MindFreedom: www.mindfreedom.org

MadNotBad: www.madnotbad.com

Mental Health Foundation: www.mentalhealth.org.uk

Mad Pride was formed in 1997 and is comprised of ex-psychiatric patients and enlightened others. Sick of the 'loony' tag, outraged by increasing stigma ... we campaign for urgent issues, risking our necks and the wrath of our shrinks. Mad Pride website

Mad Pride, in common with Black and Gay Pride, upholds the idea of people celebrating who they are, and campaigning for justice and equal human rights.

MindFreedom is at the centre of the psychiatric survivors' liberation movement. They have declared July as Mad Pride Month, when events are organised in Canada, France, the UK and the USA to promote self-determination for those deemed 'mad', and to highlight human rights abuses of people diagnosed with psychiatric disabilities. It documents the oral histories of survivors, in order to assist others.

In July 2005, activists pushed a psychiatric bed on wheels the 33 miles from Bradford to Manchester. A mannequin was strapped to the bed by four-point restraints in order to highlight psychiatric abuse.

Nutters with attitude

- Keep sane. Reduce the stress in your life. Do the ten simple things suggested by the 'Ways to look after your Mental Health' poster from the Mental Health Foundation. Download this from the publications section of their website.
- Understand those who suffer mental illness. Read their personal testimonies on the MindFreedom and MadNotBad websites.
- Wear a Mad Pride T-shirt, to show solidarity with the Mad Movement and find out what's happening for Mad Pride week this year.
- Go to the Mad Market section of the MindFreedom website, and buy a Hypodermic Highlighter for $3. This popular novelty stationery item also highlights the human rights issues in mental health. Buy lots, and give them to all your friends.

Bombard the gun lobby

There are 639 million guns in the world; 16 billion rounds of ammunition are manufactured each year – that's two bullets for every person on the planet. Every year throughout the world roughly half a million men, women, and children are killed by armed violence – that's one person every minute of every day of every year. Weapons fuel violent conflict, state repression, crime, domestic abuse, slaughter of school children and accidental death. If arms continue to spread, more lives will be lost.

The first week in July is Global Week of Action to Control Arms. The week culminates with International Gun Destruction Day, at which guns are publicly destroyed across the world. In 2004, 5,137 firearms were publicly destroyed in Togo, and in the UK, where guns are tightly regulated, 300 gun replicas were crushed by a steamroller to publicise the issue.

Take action to control arms, sign the Million Faces petition. This is the largest visual petition in the world. It will create a gallery of 1 million people who are prepared to take a public stand on gun control.

A safer world

If you sign the Million Faces petition, you will be asked to submit a photograph of yourself plus personal details and choose a slogan. How about:

- Get tough on arms
- It's time for an arms trade treaty
- Make me safe from armed violence
- Stop gun running

The International Action Network on Small Arms (IANSA), Oxfam and Amnesty International are campaigning for tougher arms control: www.controlarms.org

Brandon's Arms, an organisation which aims to reduce deaths by firearms: www.brandonsarms.org

July 3

Brandon's bid to save lives

When he was seven years old, Brandon Maxfield was shot in the face and paralysed. Someone in the house had heard a noise outside and started to load a gun, which accidentally went off. The gun, manufactured by Bryco Arms, had a faulty design that required the safety catch to be turned off before it could be loaded. Brandon sued the manufacturer and received $24 million in damages. The company declared itself bankrupt, and got permission from the Court to sell its factory near Los Angeles, equipment and a stock of 75,000 unassembled guns. Just one bid of $150,000 was received from the plant's manager. But the Court allowed 20 days for other bids. Brandon, now aged 17, raised $505,000 and made a rival bid, determined to 'melt down all the guns ...' Sadly, the plant's manager topped this with a bid of $510,000, and Brandon's bid to save lives failed.

Don't buy American

Make this your Fourth of July promise: Don't buy American. Boycott large US companies such as American Airlines, American Express, AOL, AT&T, Citibank, Chevron/Texaco, Coca-Cola, ExxonMobil, FedEx, Ford, Gap, General Electric, Heinz, IBM, Kelloggs, KFC, Kodak, Kraft, Levis, McDonald's, Maxwell House, Microsoft, Nike, Pepsi, Revlon, Starbucks, Timberland, UPS and Wal-Mart (Asda).

Boycott Bush's biggest funders: www.boycottbush.net

For more information on consumer boycotts go to: www.ethicalconsumer.org

Boycott the USA

The USA is the most powerful nation on earth. But instead of using its superpower status to uplift and liberate humanity, the USA often abuses its political, economic and military might. The US government has invaded sovereign nations and torn up international trade and arms control agreements. While lecturing others about the evil of weapons of mass destruction, it has huge stockpiles of nuclear weapons that could annihilate the entire planet. The US refuses to implement the Kyoto Treaty on global warming, and has rejected the right of the International Criminal Court to try war criminals and torturers.

American political and military power derives from its economic might and depends on international trade to sustain its wealth. It has to sell goods and services abroad to maintain the affluence that funds its global political and military hegemony. No one can force us to buy American. The people of the world, including US citizens, can use their collective spending power to change US policy and help shape a more peaceful and just world. If people stopped buying US products, corporate profits would begin to slide. The US government would then come under immense pressure from the major corporations to moderate its policies.

Why stop there?

The most successful country boycott was the Anti-Apartheid campaign against South Africa's white minority regime. Some other country boycotts advocated by pressure groups:

Burma for nullifying election results and imprisonment of elected leader.

Canada for slaughter of 1 million seals.

China for the jailing of dissenters.

Israel for refusing to withdraw from Palestinian territory seized in 1967.

Morocco for the occupation of Western Sahara and human rights abuses.

Turkey for persecuting the Kurds.

Reinvent the village fête

The Village Fête, or the School Summer Fair, can end up the same year after year: face painting, bouncy castle, guess-the-weight-of-the-cake competition. But it needn't be like that. Surely it's possible to come up with something a bit different. How about trying out some of the ideas dreamt up by some of the most creative minds in the country? Every year the Victoria & Albert Museum hosts a Village Fête at which artists and designers are invited to create their own stall and try to raise as much money as they can. These are some of the stalls that were created in 2005, all variations on the stalls that you would find at a traditional village fête:

Make a bread portrait Use peanut butter and chocolate on a slice of bread.

Bubble gum blowing Blow the biggest bubble and be videoed while you do it. The videos are then edited to blow and pop in time to music.

Bubble wrap mow down Just like a tug-of-war, two competitors race to pop all the bubbles on their side of a strip of bubble wrap.

Lucky Dip nail bar Put your hands through two holes in a screen, and two nail artists will paint your nails with colour and humour.

Smash 'n' grab An amusement arcade game where you direct a crane to pick up a gift item. But it never seems to work. In this game, the crane is a human hand that responds to the instructions you give by manipulating the control.

Make your own geodesic dome Use an office stapler and 30 postcards.

Letterpress scrabble Play Scrabble using wooden printing blocks instead of tiles for the letters. Your completed game is then printed out using a traditional handpress.

Flyaway paper planes Build an aeroplane and see how far you can get it to go with an elastic catapult.

Stalls with a difference

Be really creative and design your own stall. Make it quite wacky and really fun to do.

The V&A village fête is organised by Scarlet Projects: www.scarletprojects.com

The V&A is the UK's leading museum of arts, crafts, textiles and design from around the world. There are a huge range of things to do online. www.vam.ac.uk/activ_events/do_online/index.html

Jane's story

Charity Projects was set up by Jane Tewson in the 1980s. One of its first events was the Nether Wallop Festival – just an ordinary village fête, but with the difference that many celebrities came along, and the event was filmed for television. Shortly afterwards, Charity Projects went on to create Comic Relief, which raises money through its Red Nose Day telethon.

July 6

Stop poisoning yourself

WWF has created a list of actions you can take to reduce your consumption and use of toxic chemicals at home and in your life.

- **Buy organic.**
- **Thoroughly wash fruits and vegetables, and peel them whenever possible.**

Stop using pesticides. Green up your garden using natural methods:

- **Traps and biological controls such as parasites and natural predators.**
- **Disease- and pest-resistant plants.**
- **Plants that repel insects such as basil, chives, mint, marigolds, and chrysanthemums.**
- **Compost and mulch to improve soil health and to fertilise.**

www.worldwildlife.org/toxics/you_do.cfm

Don't buy

Use environmentally friendly cleaning products. Don't buy or use chlorine bleach. Use inexpensive cleansers such as soap, vinegar, lemon juice, and borax. Avoid air fresheners.

Say no to chemical soup

Toxic chemicals can be found in virtually all creatures and in every environment. Manufacturers are making enormous quantities for agricultural use, for industrial use and for the products we buy and use in our lives. Most of these will be released into the environment – and once there they can travel great distances, persist for years, and become concentrated in living things that we may end up eating.

An estimated 1,000 new chemicals are created every year, in addition to the tens of thousands already in commercial use. Very few have been tested properly for their effect on wildlife and humans. There is growing evidence that some of these chemicals can alter sexual and neurological development, impair reproduction, cause cancers and undermine immune systems. If we can reduce the amount of chemicals that pass through our hands and bodies, it will be a contribution to a safer world.

WWF recipes to help make your home toxin-free:

All-purpose cleaner

3 tsp liquid soap + ¼ cup vinegar + ¼ cup lemon juice + ¼ cup borax (per gallon of water)

Window cleaner

¼ cup vinegar (per gallon of warm water)

Stain remover

Soak fabrics in water mixed with borax, lemon juice, hydrogen peroxide or white vinegar.

Oven cleaner

Baking soda, vinegar, salt, steel wool.

Clean grease with rag and vinegar. Sprinkle salt on spills. Let it sit for a few minutes, then scrape the spill and wash the area clean. For stubborn spots, use baking soda and steel wool.

Controlling ants and cockroaches

Combine powdered sugar and borax in equal parts and sprinkle where they crawl.

Slow cities

All cities now seem to look and feel much the same. This is partly as a result of globalisation. Everywhere you go you will find a McDonald's and a Starbucks, and everyone is always in a hurry. Inspired by the success of the Slow Food movement, 32 Italian towns and cities joined together in 1999 to create the Slow City movement to try to reverse this trend.

A Slow City is a place where people care about their town or city, enjoy living and working there, and value the things that make it special. Over 100 cities in 10 countries have now joined the movement. Ludlow in England was the first city in the English-speaking world to join. The programme involves:

- Enlarging parks and squares; making them greener.
- Outlawing car alarms and other disruptive noise.
- Banning ugly TV aerials, hoardings and neon signs.
- Promoting recycling, alternative energy and cleaner greener transport.

These are specific things that can be done. Purchase of local produce, appreciation of the seasons, and a slower and more reflective pace of life are some of the less tangible aims of the Slow Cities movement.

For a town to become a Slow City, the mayor has to make an application to the Cittàslow Committee in Italy, submitting a presentation about the town, giving reasons for wanting to apply, identifying goals that have been met, and details of who is involved.

Vote for slow living

Towns and cities that subscribe to slow living ideals, and with a population under 50,000, can apply to join. Larger cities are considered to have become just too big to slow down.

Write a simple manifesto for slowing down the town or city where you live – even if the population is bigger than 50,000.

Try to get a debate going locally. Write a letter to your local newspaper asking people to contact you if they are interested. Tell your local councillors about the movement you are starting. And if your town or city is small enough, float the idea of it joining the Slow City movement.

Find out more about Slow Cities from: www.cittaslow.net and www.cittaslow.org.uk

July 7

Slow City principles

- Encouraging diversity not standardisation.
- Supporting local culture and traditions.
- Working for a more sustainable environment.
- Supporting local produce and products.
- Encouraging healthy living especially through children and young people.
- Working with the local community to build these values.

July 8

A new way to protest

Do your own Bare Witness demo. Get together a group of friends. Agree on an issue that you feel really passionately about. Think up a short slogan to spell out with your bodies. Then go for it – whatever the weather.

Download practical information on using this stunt to get your message across from the Baring Witness website.

In the UK, Bare Witness: www.barewitness.org

In the USA, Baring Witness: www.baring witness.org

Baring all for peace

Bare Witness and Baring Witness are not affiliated to any political group. They support all efforts to bring about peace and inject a dose of common sense into the world. They are people who decided they had to do something, anything, to show that they cared, and that war is not the answer.

Bare all for your beliefs

Peace – it's such a simple word, but it has many connotations in today's political climate. So, it takes a certain amount of courage to speak out against war these days. To speak out publicly, stripped of anonymity and clothing takes even more courage.
Bare Witness

In November 2002, 45 women stripped off in Marin County, California, and formed the word PEACE with their naked bodies as a statement against the 'naked aggression' of US foreign policy.

This was the starting point for Baring Witness, a new style of campaigning. Baring Witness simply spells out a word or words using nude or clothed human bodies. This provides you with a great photo opportunity, and can bring press wide coverage for your cause. Getting access to the media will make the existence of the campaign known. It will also educate, inform, increase awareness and gather support. By baring witness you will achieve all of this.

Similar actions are now taking place all over the world – not just for peace but also as protests against GM crops, the World Trade Organisation and other iniquities. In the UK, the first Bare Witness event took place in January 2003, when 30 people bared all for peace. They were sending a message to the UK government that invading Iraq was not the way to solve the problem. They could have stayed at home in the warmth and shaken their heads at the bad news streaming from their television set. But instead, they came out of their homes, and, in the middle of winter, they got out of their clothes in order to fight for peace.

Paint a mural

July 9

Does your local park need brightening up? Your office, or even your own garden? Why not paint a mural? You could paint an outdoor mural on a blank wall or a door, or an indoor one – anywhere there's a wall that's crying out 'Paint me!'

Murals can brighten up the environment. They can also assert the culture of a minority group, or promote a social or political message. People painted murals during the Great Depression in the 1930s as public art projects. Murals today are being painted on housing estates, in parks and in playgrounds. They can be painted indoors as well as outdoors. Murals can be painted by people from the community working together, or by a single artist as a piece of outdoor art.

If you're going to paint an indoor mural, why not do it with natural paints? Normal paints give off volatile organic compounds (VOCs), which can cause respiratory disease, and are stuffed with toxic chemicals and heavy metals. It is estimated that each household has several litres of leftover paint, and much of this will end up in the household rubbish, and then be dumped in landfill and leach out into the soil.

Brush up here

Find a wall that needs painting. It could be inside or outside. Remember to get permission, if you need it.

Draw a design for the mural you would like to paint. Do this with a group of friends, and discuss it with the local community where the mural will be painted. The theme could be something relevant to your community. It could celebrate a person or event. Or it could simply be a public work of art.

For information on eco-paints, go to: www.greenbuildingstore.co.uk

And go window shopping at www.ecomall.com

Be inspired! To see some great examples of mural painting, visit these two archives of mural paintings in the USA:

Social and Public Art Resource Centre: www.sparcmurals.org

New Deal Mural Archive: newdeal.feri.org/library

Paint it green

Natural paints are made with citrus-oil solvents rather than petrochemicals. They get their colours from minerals and clays. They may not be as bright, and are mostly for indoor use, but they are eco-friendly. A green mural will show that you care about the environment in two ways, both artistically and chemically.

July 10

Origami birds

Peace Pals has instructions for making a simple peace dove: members.aol.com/pforpeace/peacepals/project2.htm

For more information on how to create an origami bird and lots of links: www.paperfolding.com/diagrams

Livio de Marchi, an Italian artist, has created a huge floating dove of peace: www.liviodemarchi.com/uk main3.htm

Messages of peace

Create a flock of paper birds with your own peace messages and display them around your workplace or at school. Alternatively, hang them from trees in your neighbourhood.

Recruit as many friends as you can to help you with the project. You can make your bird display more eye-catching by using an array of coloured paper.

Bomb for peace

Thailand has suffered decades of intermittent violence from Muslim separatists. In February 2004, the separatist movement in the nation's three southernmost provinces stepped up attacks on police, government buildings, and other symbols of the mainly Buddhist Thai state. The government responded with force and declared martial law in the region. Around 450 people were killed.

On 5 December 2004, the government of Thailand dropped an estimated 100 million origami birds as an attempt to promote peace, in a campaign devised by Prime Minister Thaksin Shinawatra. The crane is a widely recognised Thai symbol for peace, so people across the country folded paper cranes and wrote peace messages on them. The 'peace bombing' was scheduled to coincide with the 77th birthday of revered King Bhumibol Adulyadej. About 50 military planes and helicopters lifted off from three air bases and released the paper birds at low altitude. The airdrop took all day, but was completed by sunset after more than 150 flights.

As the birds fell to their targets in the provinces of Narathiwat, Yala and Pattani, schoolchildren rushed out to collect them and read the notes inside. Some students constructed giant nets stretched across schoolyards to capture birds. There was great interest in finding the bird that the prime minister himself had signed. Mr Thaksin promised that any student who found it would win a scholarship. Local officials responded with creative ideas for preventing a massive litter foul up. The Governor of Narathiwat offered to exchange ten paper birds for an egg and 30 collected birds for a kilogram of rice.

There were critics of this campaign, who said that it would not solve the complex problems causing the violence. However, it was a way of highlighting the need for a resolution of the conflict in the region.

Ecological footprints

An ecological footprint is the area of productive land required to produce the food, energy and materials consumed by a person or a country, and to absorb the waste they produce, or cause to be produced.

A large footprint indicates a higher standard of living, but also a lifestyle that wastes resources. Differences between countries are also caused by factors such as the climate and the need to travel. Rich countries are mostly at the top of the list and poor countries at the bottom. The total footprint for all of humanity is 13.2 billion hectares – growth is mitigated to some extent by technological advance. The average footprint per person is 2.18 hectares; the average area of productive land available per person is 1.89 hectares; the global deficit per person is 0.29 hectares.

The global footprint exceeds the Earth's capacity. The human race cannot continue indefinitely to take more from nature than nature can provide.

Small steps

Reduce your footprint:

- **Walk and cycle if possible.**
- **Downsize your car or go electric. Share car journeys and use public transport.**
- **Avoid air travel.**
- **Eat less meat and buy fresh food locally.**
- **Recycle and reuse.**
- **Insulate your home.**

Measure your ecological footprint by taking the Ecological Footprint Quiz at: www.myfootprint.org

Redefining Progress: www.rprogress.org

For facts and figures: www.redefiningprogress.org/newprojects/ecolFoot.shtml

Doing the footwork

The organisation Redefining Progress has produced this table of footprints for each nation (in hectares of land per person).

10 largest footprints	
USA	9.57
United Arab Emirates	8.97
Canada	8.56
Norway	8.17
New Zealand	8.13
Kuwait	8.01
Sweden	7.95
Australia	7.09
Finland	7.00
France	5.74

10 smallest footprints	
Pakistan	0.67
Ethiopia	0.67
Tajikistan	0.65
Malawi	0.64
Burundi	0.63
Congo, Dem Rep	0.62
Haiti	0.62
Nepal	0.57
Mozambique	0.56
Bangladesh	0.50

Selected others: UK 4.72, Russia 4.28, Germany 4.26, Japan 3.91, South Africa 3.52, China 1.36, Nigeria 1.10

July 12

Doctor yourself

Books to save lives

Buy a copy of *Where There Is No Doctor* either direct from Hesperian, or from TALC. Use it yourself as a self-help health manual.

Make a donation to the Hesperian Gratis Book Fund.

Or, if you are travelling abroad to a poor country, buy a copy of one of the books in the local language. Donate it to a village library or information centre. It may help save someone's life.

Hesperian Foundation: www.hesperian.org

Hesperian's Gratis Book Programme: www.hesperian.org/projects.php

Teaching Aids at Low Costs (TALC): www.talcuk.org

I am a district pastor in Ghana with churches in 26 towns and villages. I started using the book Where There is No Doctor during my visits to these communities. With the help of the book, ailments such as headaches, diarrhoea, dysentery, skin diseases ... toothaches, constipation and dehydration have been treated at little or no cost at all.

In the 1970s, a group of health activists in Mexico compiled a notebook of treatment information for some of the common medical problems they found in their village. This grew into a much bigger healthcare manual covering almost every common health problem villagers were facing, and giving advice on what to do about the problem in the absence of a doctor. The manual was aimed largely at village health workers. It was initially published in Spanish as *Dónde no hay Doctor*. Through the Hesperian Foundation this book has now been adapted and translated into 90 languages from Amharic to Urdu, and used all around the globe. The Hesperian Foundation has now developed a range of other health materials, all of which are published cheaply and distributed worldwide.

Gratis books

The Hesperian Foundation has developed a Gratis Book Programme to provide free books to those who can't afford them. Donate $15 to pay for one book plus shipment. Around 1,500 free books are distributed every year.

- *Where There Is No Doctor* helps people with health problems, and to recognise problems that need to be referred to an experienced health worker.
- *Where Women Have No Doctor* helps women and girls to identify common medical problems and treatments.
- *Where There Is No Dentist* helps people care for their teeth.

Fight malaria

July 13

Malaria is one of the world's major killers, up there with HIV/AIDS and TB. Malaria causes over 1 million deaths a year, and it's on the increase. The majority of victims are children under five and pregnant women. The Roll Back Malaria Partnership, co-ordinated by the World Health Organisation, aims to halve the impact of malaria by 2010.

Malaria is caused by a parasite, and transmitted to humans through bites by the Anopheles mosquito. Here are some worrying facts about the disease:

- 300–500 million people suffer from malaria yearly, which is about 7 per cent of the world's population.
- Africa has 90 per cent of reported cases, and these account for around 10 per cent of hospital admissions, 25 per cent of doctor visits and 40 per cent of public health spending.
- Someone dies from malaria every 29 seconds.
- There are four types of malaria, all produce a severe fever. The most common can cause death and is becoming resistant to anti-malaria drugs.

Medicines for Malaria Venture has been set up to discover new and affordable anti-malarial drugs for treatment and prevention. MMV is developing a new drug, ACT, based on a herbal Chinese remedy, which could be the biggest breakthrough for a generation.

Use your PC

Anti-mosquito software has been developed by a Thai computer programmer. It generates sound waves through the computer's speakers that repel the mosquitoes, cockroaches and rats within a 2-metre radius. Fortunately, the frequencies that annoy rats and cockroaches are undetectable by humans. By 2005, there had been over 400,000 downloads, with an 85 per cent approval rating. This was one small step to dealing with malaria!

Anti-mosquito software: www.thaiware.com

Malaria Foundation International has information and lots of useful links: www.malaria.org

Medicines for Malaria Venture: www.mmv.org

Start to bite back

How to prevent the mosquito bites that may carry malaria:

- Screen windows and doors.
- Use mosquito nets on beds.
- Use biological control – some fish in small ponds and water tanks reduce the larval mosquito population.
- Stop mosquitoes breeding by closing off or removing stagnant water.
- Have drug treatment, both to prevent malaria and for malaria patients.
- Use insect repellents, including body lotions and mosquito mats and coils.
- Treat walls and bed nets with insecticide.

Unexpected places

Parties are a great way for like-minded people to get together and have some fun. A street party can encourage everyone to get together and bring colour and laughter into their neighbourhood. But what about holding a party in an unexpected place? It will be a memorable occasion!

Organise a public party in an unexpected place, and have fun!

It's Bastille Day so why not give your party a French flavour.

Reclaim the Beach: www.swarming.org.uk/recl/recl.htm

Space Hijackers: spacehijackers.co.uk

Step-by-step guide to organising a street party: www.streetparty.net

Throw a public party

London has its own beach on the Thames – a small sandy stretch of the foreshore outside the Royal Festival Hall that was created for the Festival of Britain. It is exposed twice a day at low tide. Technically, the beach is owned by the Port of London Authority, which inherited it from the City Corporation, which took it from George IV as payment for his gambling debts. But in reality it belongs to all of us – an unownable public space.

Reclaim the Beach holds free, non-commercial public events on this beach, ranging from afternoons of family-friendly seaside fun to late-night raves. The people who put the events on are all volunteers, and the performers and musicians all give their time for free. The success of the events depends largely on the active participation of everyone who comes, and a policy of benign neglect by the authorities.

The whole thing started in 2000 when a group of friends brought a ghetto blaster, a picnic and a few bottles of wine onto the beach. By summer 2001 there were full-scale parties with sound systems, DJs, live bands, lighting, fireworks and bonfires. Family-friendly daytime events have featured sandcastle competitions, boat rides and Punch and Judy shows. And when the tide rises, everyone goes home.

How about an underground party?

The group Space Hijackers campaign for public use of public spaces. In 1999 it 'hijacked' a London Underground Circle Line train and turned it into a moving disco. All the equipment was brought in suitcases and transformed on-site into a bar, a stereo deck, a nibbles counter and a disco light. Around 150 people attended, plus all the passengers who happened to be on the train at the time – all of whom were given free vodka, tequila and sweets. After one and a half laps of the Circle Line, the party-goers went to a pub to continue partying.

Harness energy

Solar electric power has become a realistic possibility, and not just for pocket calculators. It can change lives in parts of the world that are beyond the reach of conventional electricity, and it doesn't produce any greenhouse gases or damage the environment.

Greenstar, an organisation working to deliver solar power to villages in the developing world, has designed a portable community centre that uses solar power to operate a water purifier, a classroom, a small clinic with a vaccine cooler and a digital studio with satellite or wireless internet connection. Greenstar then works with local people to develop a website that the villagers can use to conduct trade.

Greenstar plans to install 300 similar centres around the world. It uses 'virtual volunteers' to undertake specific assignments such as researching online sources of practical books on solar power, which will be used to create a Solar Bookstore, and finding out what work is being done on community health centres by other international organisations.

July 15

Solar power

Find out as much as you can about solar energy: how much it costs; where to get it; and how to install it.

See if you can get a solar unit installed at home, school or your workplace.

Buy a solar LED torch and a solar battery charger from Solar Energy Alliance.

For information on solar electric systems in the UK, contact Solar Century: www.solarcentury.co.uk

For solar energy devices in the developing world: www.sustainablevillage.com

Solar Energy Alliance, a resource centre: www.solarenergyalliance.com

Greenstar: www.greenstar.org

The Barefoot College: www.barefootcollege.org

Barefoot power saving

The Barefoot College in Tilonia (near Ajmer in India) has set up a 'barefoot solar engineers' programme. This trains unemployed young people, and women with low literacy skills, to install and maintain home solar-lighting systems in their villages. These solar engineers have electrified 300 Adult Education Centres in India, 521 night schools, and 1,475 houses in Ladakh, which is 3,350 metres high in the Himalayas. It has saved 12,000 litres of kerosene and diesel a year.

The college also runs training courses on the use of solar systems in sustainable development. All the electricity for the training centre is supplied from a 40 kw solar unit. This project has received international acclaim and is worth a visit.

July 16

Take a stand for Sudan

Arm yourself

Make and wear an armband in support of the Sudanese:

Get an old sheet and a thick marker pen. Cut the sheet into strips the width of your thumb and length of your forearm. Write 'Ask me about Magboula' on the centre of the strip.

Prepare an information sheet on Magboula and a brief overview of the situation in Sudan.

Wear the armband to work or school, or just around town. Give armbands to people you meet, and ask them to wear these to show their support.

Southern Sudan news site: www.gurtong.org

Human Rights Watch reports: hrw.org/reports/2004/sudan0504

After the holocaust in Nazi Germany, the world said that it would never be allowed to happen again. But it has happened, repeatedly and with no sign of ending. Over the past few years in Sudan, millions of people in Darfur have experienced a daily hell that we can hardly fathom.

The first thing we can do to help is conquer our ignorance about what is happening. A snapshot of the crisis in Sudan:

- The Janjaweed Militia are perpetrating atrocities against African farmers. They burn down entire villages, killing and raping everyone they can reach.
- There is a severe water shortage that leaves people lined up at pumps, waiting for up to ten hours to get enough water to survive.
- Women are afraid to leave their homes for fear of being raped by the pillaging militias.
- With the onslaught of torrential rains, malaria will ravage the population.
- Over 1.2 million people have been made homeless.

Find out more about the situation in Darfur: www.darfurpeaceanddevelopment.org

Who is Magboula?

When people ask you about your armband, tell them about Magboula Khattar, a 24-year-old Sudanese woman. The Janjaweed Arab militia burned her village, murdered her parents and finally tracked her family down in the mountains. Magboula hid, but the Janjaweed caught her husband and his brothers, who were only four, six and eight years old, and killed them all. She escaped with her baby girl to a refugee camp in Chad. She is just one of the 1.2 million people who have been left homeless by the Janjaweed. Remember that when Sudan is old news, there's bound to be somewhere else where atrocities we can barely imagine are taking place.

Rescue a pet

Pets require a lot of care and attention, but they can be a fantastic addition to your life.

If you want a pet, there is no reason to go to a pet shop. Many puppies and kittens sold in pet shops come from pet breeders. Sometimes the animals are inbred and are not used to living in a home environment. Why not take care of an unwanted pet instead? Go and find a pet at your local animal shelter. Greyhounds, for example, make wonderful pets. Yet many are killed as soon as they are too old to race.

Find the pet that's just right for you. Understand the responsibilities of owning a pet (and the cost involved). And give your new pet a warm home and a lot of tender loving care.

If you don't want a pet you can still do something to help an animal. Go to the Animal Rescue website, and click on the icon. Your simple click will provide food for an animal in need. In 2004, over 4 million people clicked each month. This raised enough to fund 31.5 million bowls of food. Visitors who shopped at the on-site store funded an additional 3.1 million bowls of food. Like other 'click and donate' sites, your click costs you absolutely nothing. It simply triggers a donation by one of the site's sponsors.

Offer shelter

Next time you want a pet, get it from your local animal shelter or rescue centre. You'll be making a poor animal very happy.

Make sure your pet is neutered, otherwise you could end up with ten pets instead of the one you planned for. As a matter of course, many animal shelters will vaccinate, neuter and give a full battery of tests to your new pet in order to ensure that you take home a healthy animal. You won't get this five-star service if you buy a pet at the local store.

The Animal Rescue Site: www.theanimalrescuesite.com

Cats and Dogs Online: www.catsdogsonline.com

Battersea Dogs and Cats Home: www.dogshome.org

July 17

An online matchmaking service

Cats and Dogs Online was created when Jacqueline Holstead had to find homes for her three cats – BB, a lovely little black moggie; Rusty, a cuddly teddy bear of a cat; Beatie, the talkative Tonkinese cat. The process of finding new homes was logistically and emotionally difficult. It became clear that adopting an animal is not an easy task, and finding the right new home is even more difficult.

Cats and Dogs Online brings animal lovers together – people who wish to adopt a pet and people who find that they need to re-home their pet.

July 18

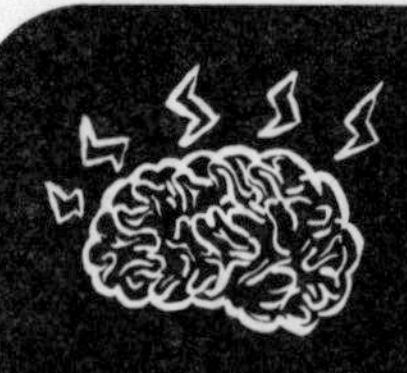

One day at a time

My 365 Ways to end violence against women: Submit your ideas for ending violence against women to the Violence Information and Education Centre, and help them compile a book of practical ideas. Violence Information and Education Centre: www.viec.org/my365ways.html

***Random Acts of Kindness: 365 Ways to Make the World a Better Place*; and *Join Me*, both by Danny Wallace: www.join-me.co.uk**

***365 Ways to Meet People in Cleveland* by Miriam Carey, Gray & Co., 2001: www.grayco.com/cleveland/365/**

365 more things to do

The idea of this book is to provide an idea for each day of the year for changing the world. But there are many other things to do for each day of the year.

365 ways to meet people Many people find it hard to meet other people. They may be too busy at work; a relationship might just have broken up; or they may have just moved into the area. A book published in Cleveland (Ohio, USA) suggests 365 ways to meet people. Here are a few of the suggestions:

Go social climbing Take a rock-climbing class. No previous experience needed. But a head for heights is a good idea. Meet other social climbers.

Join the full moon hike Go for a monthly walk with other lunatics in the Cuyahoga Valley National Park.

Help build a park The Park Works group builds playgrounds and restores existing parks and public spaces. They need volunteers.

Walk with other dog lovers On Saturdays at about 8.30 a.m. dog owners meet at Rocky River Elmwood Park to exercise their dogs and meet other humans.

If you don't live in Cleveland, start compiling a directory of ways to meet people in your home town.

Kiss in 365 different ways

Kissing may not make the world a better place, but it could make you happier. Two of the 365 ways to do it:

An ice kiss Chill your mouth by sucking an ice cube. When you have chilled out, spit out the cube, find someone you want to show affection, and kiss them.

An electric shock kiss Both people first rub their feet on a carpet for a minute or two. If the carpet contains synthetic fibres, then this creates an electric charge in your body. When you're charged up, slowly move your lips towards your partner's. If you've done it right, a spark will jump between the two of you. Immediately this has happened, kiss for real.

From *365 Ways to Kiss your Love* by Tomima Edmark. See more ideas at: www.theromantic.com/kissing/365.htm

Try out a wheelchair

The best way to understand the frustration that people with mobility problems face in their everyday lives is to experience it for yourself. You can do this easily by getting into a wheelchair for a day. The steps you did not notice become insurmountable barriers, the public transport you got around on is suddenly completely inaccessible to you, and you find that there are no disabled toilets at the meeting you are attending.

Your day will become dominated by all the things you can't do, by all the opportunities that the rest of the population takes for granted being denied to you. But for those who need a wheelchair all the time, this is what their whole life consists of. Only when all of society comes to realise the importance of disability access as a basic human right – and at whatever the cost of provision – will things begin to change.

A day out

Borrow a wheelchair for a day. Get in it and go for a day out. Make a diary of your experience. Take a camera to photograph what you find most aggravating.

Campaign with disabled people for better access throughout your neighbourhood or town.

Learn more about disability issues from these websites:

British Council of Disabled People: www.bcodp.org.uk

RADAR, the disability network run by and for disabled people: www.radar.org.uk

Disability Rights Commission: www.drc.org.ukl

July 19

An uphill battle

There are lots of 'wheelchair for a day' projects to promote accessibility awareness. This is one that took place in Vermont in the USA in 2002.

On the first day of the Wheelchair for a Day campaign, sixteen biology students and four faculty members spent the day in wheelchairs, obtained for the event. For the second and third days of the campaign, the wheelchairs were made available to staff and other faculty members at five points on the campus. Those who were interested signed up to use the wheelchair at a specific time.

All participants received a free T-shirt designed by the students. This had the image of a person in a wheelchair at the foot of the hill leading up to the college Chapel. The slogan was 'Accessibility: It's an Uphill Battle'.

The week also included a discussion on the final day at which participants discussed their experiences as wheelchair users and decided what to do as a result.

Guerrilla girls

Reinvent the f-word

Dubbing themselves 'the conscience of culture', Guerrilla Girls see themselves as feminist counterparts to the mostly male tradition of anonymous do-gooders such as Robin Hood and the Lone Ranger.

Guerrilla Girls fight discrimination with facts, humour and fake fur: www.guerrillagirls.com

Life of Florynce Kennedy: rwor.org/a/v22/1090-99/1095/flo_kennedy.htm

Fight testosterone power. Got any leftover oestrogen pills? Send an 'Oestrogen Bomb' to Bush, Cheney and Rumsfeld, with your own message suggesting a more feminine way of governing the USA and the world. Address: The White House, 1600 Pennsylvania Avenue, Washington DC 20500, USA.

Florynce Rae Kennedy, prominent civil rights activist and pro-choice campaigner, once famously said: 'If men could get pregnant, abortion would be a sacrament.' Maurice and Charles Saatchi, advertising gurus, sprang to public notice with a poster of a pregnant man, saying: 'If this could happen to you, you'd be more careful.'

The world looks different from male and female perspectives – not least when it comes to aggression and warfare. The architects of the Iraq war on both sides were all men. Would the situation have been different if the hormones coursing through their bodies had been oestrogen rather than testosterone?

Since 1985 the Guerrilla Girls have been reinventing feminism. Still going strong in the 21st century, they're a bunch of anonymous females who take the names of dead women artists as pseudonyms and appear in public wearing gorilla masks. They have produced posters, stickers, books, and organised demonstrations to expose sexism and racism in politics, the art world, film and culture at large. They use humour to convey information, provoke discussion and show that feminists can be funny. They wear gorilla masks to focus on the issues rather than their personalities.

Guerrilla Girls on feminism

We believe feminism is a fundamental way of looking at the world and recognising that half of us are female and all of us should be equal. It's a fact of history that for centuries women have not had the rights and privileges of men and it's time for that to end.

Despite the ... gains of women over the last hundred years, misogyny – the hatred or hostility towards women as a whole – is still rampant throughout our culture and in the larger world. We think that is the number one reason women need feminism. *Guerrilla Girls*

Campaign for Bhopal

At 12.05 a.m. on the night of 3 December 1984, the Union Carbide pesticide plant in Bhopal, India exploded, releasing a toxic gas that caused 8,000 deaths in a few days, and more than 20,000 in the years since. An estimated 150,000 people have suffered serious health problems. On the night of the disaster, six safety measures designed to prevent a leak were either malfunctioning, shut down or inadequate.

The site of the closed factory remains a toxic hotspot, with concentrations of carcinogenic chemicals and heavy metals. Chemicals continue to seep into the water supplies of an estimated 20,000 people who live in surrounding communities.

The Indian government charged Union Carbide's CEO with negligent homicide, but Warren Anderson has not been extradited from the USA to stand trial in India. Dow Chemical purchased Union Carbide in 2001, but has refused to take responsibility for the Bhopal cleanup. In 1999, fifteen years on, Bhopal survivors filed a class action suit against Union Carbide in the US courts, asking that the company be held responsible for violations of international human rights law and for cleaning up the environmental contamination in Bhopal.

Seek justice

Support the Bhopal People's Health and Documentation Clinic, which treats 1,000 victims each month and is documenting toxic death. It is funded entirely by donations and was awarded the Margaret Mead Centennial Award in 2002.

Join the International Campaign for Justice in Bhopal. It aims to bring justice to Bhopal survivors by keeping world attention focused on Dow Chemical's liability for the Union Carbide disaster. Visit: www.bhopal.net

Read more about Bhopal at the Greenpeace archive: www.greenpeace.org/international/footer/search?q=bhopal

The Bhopal People's Health and Documentation Clinic: www.bhopal.org

Compare the compensation figures

For the victims of 9/11

Congress authorised a $5,900 million compensation fund for the 2,963 deaths and about 4,400 injury claims arising from the disaster. The average death payment is just above $2 million, while the largest death payment to date has been $7.1 million.

For the victims of Bhopal

The disaster claimed 8,000 lives and an estimated 150,000 seriously injured people. Five years later Union Carbide agreed a compensation fund of $470 million. Each victim received less than $350 for injuries. The world's largest industrial accident cost Union Carbide just 48 cents a share.

July 22

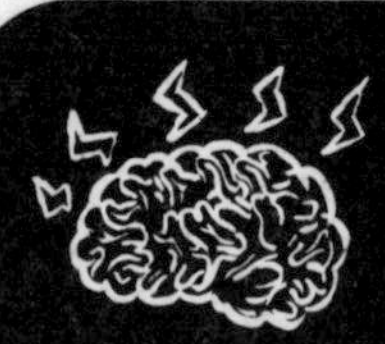

Finding facts

Take one of the following subjects and discover ten interesting facts about it:

- **Gender inequality in your country or in the world**
- **The growing inequality between rich and poor**

Or any other issue that particularly concerns you.

Make a poster to display your Killer Facts. Change people's attitudes. Suggest actions for people to take.

YouthNoise has an archive of facts and factoids on many contemporary issues: www.youthnoise.com

Wikipedia is an internet encyclopaedia: http://en.wikipedia.org

Compile a factoid

Trivia refers to bits of unimportant information. It can also refer to basic knowledge or information in history, science, current affairs, sport, popular culture. The word can also be used to refer to obscure bits of knowledge. In mediaeval universities, trivia were the things learned in the 'trivium', and comprised the three subjects grammar, logic and rhetoric.

Factoid is a spurious 'fact' invented to influence public opinion. The term was invented by Norman Mailer in his biography of Marilyn Monroe. He described a factoid as 'facts which have no existence before appearing in a magazine or newspaper'. The term is now also used to mean a small piece of true but insignificant information. For example, if the history of the earth lasted for only two days, human history would take up only the last two seconds.

Factlet refers to a tiny and trivial fact that is also correct. Ben Schott has made a fortune from facts in *Schott's Original Miscellany* and *Schott's Almanack.*

Ten facts about AIDS

- 42 million people worldwide are living with HIV/AIDS today.
- 25 million children will have been orphaned as a result of AIDS by the year 2010. Every 14 seconds another child is orphaned due to AIDS.
- 5 million people became newly affected in 2002.
- 3.2 million children under 15 are living with HIV/AIDS; 800,000 became infected and 610,000 died in 2002.
- 3.1 million adults and children died of HIV/AIDS in 2002.
- It can take ten years for HIV symptoms to show up. Sexually active, infected people spread the disease for years.
- Seven countries in Sub-Saharan Africa report 20 per cent or more of their population as HIV-positive.
- 55 per cent of the HIV/AIDS infected population in Africa are female.
- 50 per cent of the youth in developing countries cannot name any method that protects them against HIV/AIDS.
- One in three 15-year-olds will die prematurely of AIDS.

Create an axis of evil

Axis a main line of direction, motion, growth or extension
Evil morally reprehensible, causing harm

In 1982, President Reagan referred to the Soviet Union as the 'Evil Empire'. In his 2002 State of the Union speech, President George W. Bush echoed this when referring to North Korea, Iran and Iraq constituting an 'Axis of Evil' with respect to the war on terror: 'North Korea is a regime arming with missiles and weapons of mass destruction, while starving its citizens ... states like these, and their terrorist allies, constitute an Axis of Evil ... '

Whether or not you agree with President Bush's sentiments regarding the war on terror, one very real evil is the denial of human rights in North Korea. More than 4 million people have died of starvation since 1995, despite the fact that North Korea receives more food aid than any nation in the world. Article 3 of the Universal Declaration of Human Rights states that everyone has the right to life.

Fight for what's right

July 23

Create your own 'Axis of Evil' around an issue that you care passionately about. This might be greenhouse gas emissions, child labour, nuclear proliferation ...

Identify the 'baddies', those countries that remain out of line. Create a league table from the best to the worst. Find out about the organisations that are doing something about the issue.

US Committee for Human Rights in North Korea: www.hrnk.org

Human Rights Watch's Korea page: hrw.org/doc/?t=asia&c=nkorea

Free North Korea: www.freenorthkorea.net

North Korea Freedom Coalition: nkfreedom.org

The Korean paradox

Article 5 of the Universal Declaration of Human Rights states that no one shall be subjected to torture or to cruel, inhuman or degrading treatment or punishment. According to *The Hidden Gulag: exposing North Korea's prison camps*, published by the US Committee for Human Rights, North Korea has three types of labour camps, where 'the injustices and cruelty these prisoners suffer is almost unimaginable ... a starvation diet, torture, beatings, inhumane living and working conditions ... ' The report describes conditions in North Korea's six political penal labour camps, known as Kwan-Li-So, where tens of thousands of political prisoners work as slaves in mining, logging and farming enterprises.

This is the sort of future that a human rights activist in North Korea could face.

July 24

Private parts

Think about how your privacy is being threatened.

Is there is any person or any institution invading your privacy you would like to propose for an award?

Tell Privacy International. Nominate someone for a Big Brother Award.

Privacy International: www.privacyinternational.org

See also, a news site established by Privacy International and the Electronic Privacy Information Centre: www.privacy.org

Brotherly concern

Privacy International runs its Big Brother Awards in Australia, Austria, Bulgaria, Denmark, Finland, France, Germany, Hungary, Japan, Netherlands, Spain, Switzerland, UK and USA.

Awards are given to government agencies, companies and individuals who have significantly violated privacy. The judges comprise professionals, civil rights activists and others.

Big brother is watching

Government agencies and private companies are increasingly violating the privacy of people everywhere. Enormous amounts of personal data are being collected, stored and processed – often illegally – in the pursuit of more efficient marketing, greater social control, and more powerful mechanisms for monitoring of the citizen. Privacy International

Google uses a cookie that expires in 2038. This places a unique ID number on your hard disk. Any time you land on a Google page, you get a Google cookie if you don't already have one. If you have one, they read and record your unique ID number. About 75 per cent of internet searches are done on Google. For all searches they record the cookie ID, your internet IP address, time and date, your search terms, and your browser configuration. Google retains this data indefinitely, and they won't say why they need it or if they have ever been subpoenaed to disclose it.

In many countries, people are able to trace how you have voted. In the UK, for example, the number on your voting slip is recorded on the electoral roll used by the polling station to note down who has voted. It is then possible to find out the names and addresses of everyone who has voted for a particular party. A complete list of people voting for extremist parties could easily be compiled and handed over to the internal security services as a list of 'subversives'. The fear of being traced could deter people from expressing their true voting intentions.

Your mobile phone will show where you have made calls from, and soon satellite tracking systems for road pricing will record where your car has travelled. Your shop loyalty card and credit cards show what you have been purchasing. Video cameras are everywhere recording you walking in the street. You are being watched.

July 25

Open source cola

It's the real thing (almost)

Make your own cola. Drink it at home, at parties, or at festivals and fairs where you can promote the idea of open source sharing.

Opencola background and recipe: www.colawp.com/colas/400/cola467_recipe.html

Find out more about open source software and copyleft from the Wikipedia encyclopaedia: en.wikipedia.org/wiki/Open_source en.wikipedia.org/wiki/Copyleft

The ethos of the Open Source Software movement allows the free copying and modification of software while crediting the ownership of the original idea.

Opencola uses the same principles. It is a brand of cola and the instructions for making it are freely available and modifiable. It was originally designed as a publicity stunt to promote the Opencola software design company in Toronto. But the drink took on a life of its own. It sold 150,000 cans, and the company became better known for the drink than the software it wanted to promote. The cola website is now run from Japan. The success of Opencola partly stems from it being a quirky idea and partly from a widespread mistrust of big corporations. It provides you with a great opportunity to create a no-logo, no-brand product, and use this to explain the benefits of 'open source' sharing and issues of globalisation.

Opencola recipe

7X (Top-Seekrut™) flavouring formula
Mix the following oils together in a cup: 3.5 ml orange oil, 1 ml lemon oil, 1 ml nutmeg oil, 1.25 ml cassia oil, 0.25 ml coriander oil, 0.25 ml neroli oil, 2.75 ml lime oil, 0.25 ml lavender oil. Add 10 g gum arabic. Add 3 ml water and mix well in a blender. Keep in a sealed glass jar.

Opencola syrup
2 tsp 7X formula
3½ tsp 75 per cent phosphoric acid or citric acid
2.25 l water
2.25 kg plain granulated white sugar
½ tsp caffeine (optional)
30 ml caramel colour
In a 4-litre container, take 5 ml of the 7X mixture and add the acid. Add the water and then the sugar. While mixing, add the caffeine (optional), and make sure it dissolves completely. Then add the caramel colour. Mix thoroughly.

To prepare the drink
To finish, take one part syrup and add 5 parts carbonated water.
This recipe is licensed under the GNU General Public license. If you distribute modified colas, send an email to the recipe's author, Amanda Foubister at amanda@opencola.com

July 26

Become a puppy walker

Help turn Fido into a 'Florence Nightingale'. Puppy walkers have to meet certain criteria. To take on this role you need to:

- **Be at home most of the day (puppies cannot be left for more than three hours).**
- **Be over 18 years old.**
- **Live in a ground-floor dwelling with a securely fenced garden or yard that has speedy access to a 'spending' area (where the pup can relieve itself).**
- **Not have children under three.**
- **Have regular access to car travel.**
- **Be willing to take the puppy out as part of your daily routine – to the supermarket, for example.**

Guide Dogs for the Blind: www.guidedogs.org.uk

Hearing Dogs for Deaf People: www.hearing-dogs.co.uk

Guide dog training

Dogs can become canine superheroes. Guide Dogs are the eyes of the blind and Hearing Dogs are the ears of the deaf. These dogs are not born knowing hundreds of commands. They need to be trained. This is something you can help with. So why don't you help train a guide dog? The rewards will be enormous. The animal you help train will drastically improve the quality of life of a disabled person. You will be giving that person a constant companion, a best friend and the freedom to live their life in a more enabled way.

Guide dogs are generally from one of the following breeds:

- Labrador Retriever
- Golden Retriever
- German Shepherd
- Labrador/Golden Retriever cross

Guide dogs have to be trained to lead their partner in a straight line between two points and around any ground or overhead obstacles. The dogs can't read traffic signals, so are trained to stop at the kerb while their human partner listens for oncoming cars. But if the human partner begins walking and a car approaches, the dog is trained to stop. The dogs are trained to ignore all outside stimuli such as strange smells and sounds, other dogs and humans.

Walkies

Puppy walking is an important part of developing a future guide dog. A volunteer puppy walker takes a puppy aged around six weeks into their home and nurtures it for the first year of its life – teaching it basic commands and getting it used to as many different environments as possible. This is done under the guidance of a Puppy Walking Supervisor.

Cast out caste-ism

Discrimination on the basis of caste is a hugely important and worrying issue that is often ignored.

Caste-ism is most evident in Hinduism, which has four 'castes', based on occupation and ancestry. At the top are the priestly caste of the Brahmins; next the soldiers or Kshtriyas; then the merchants and farmers (the Vaishyas); finally those that serve them (the Shudras). Beyond these come the Dalits – who are completely outside the caste system ('out-castes' or 'untouchables'). In Hindu societies, many Dalit communities suffer extreme discrimination.

Dalits often have to live in huts outside the perimeter of the village; they may be denied access to water for fear of their polluting it; they often have the lowest-paid jobs, which also means that their nutrition and health is poor, and that their children have to work and are denied an education. Hinduism even denies Dalits advancement in the next life. They are condemned to return to the world as 'polluted' and 'outcast' people. There are 160 million Dalits in India and 260 million in Asia as a whole.

It's as bad as racism

Support the Dalits in their campaign for human rights.

Send Martin Macwan a letter of support: martin @icenet.net.

And why not raise some money for the Dalit rights movement?

There are equivalents to caste discrimination in other societies and cultures. Any discrimination based on the accident of birth should be fought against.

National Campaign on Dalit Human Rights: www.dalits.org

International Dalit Support Network: www.idsn.org

A Dalit website with lots of links: www.ambedkar.org

Martin's story

Martin Macwan is a Dalit. He began life as a child farmhand. He worked his way through school and went to college, graduating in psychology and then getting a law degree. In 1983, he began working with Pakistani refugees in Gujarat.

Macwan wanted to offer more than a social service. He started to work on Dalit rights. In 1986, four of his friends were shot dead, eighteen more wounded and several villages set on fire in an attack by feudal landlords who resented these 'uppity Dalit activists'. Macwan escaped death because he had gone home sick that day. He held a dead friend's body and vowed: '... your death will not be in vain.'

In 1989, Macwan started Navsarjan ('New Creation') Trust in Ahmedabad to mobilise and empower the Dalits. In 1996, he launched the National Campaign on Dalit Human Rights, which is working for the abolition of 'untouchability'.

July 28

Your credit rating

Join a Time Bank. See how much credit you can earn by helping others. Then start spending your credit by getting others to help you.

If there isn't a Time Bank in your community, start one. Five or six people will be enough to get going. These could be friends, people from a local tenants' association, people you meet in the doctor's waiting room, or parents and teachers from your local school. Show people what they can achieve immediately by doing something together for the community.

The Time Bank website explains how a Time Bank Works and gives you Ten Steps to creating your own Time Bank: www.timebanks.co.uk

Give time to others

A Time Bank enables everybody to give some of their time over to helping others, and at the same time receive other people's time for their own benefit. Time Credits are earned and then used to purchase what people need from other members of the Time Bank. This is a mechanism whereby everybody can help everybody else without anyone feeling that people are taking more than they are giving back. It is a mechanism for mutual aid within a community. Here are some of the things that can be converted into Time Credits, or which Time Credits can buy:

- DIY around the house – painting and decorating.
- Gardening and looking after houseplants.
- Cooking and organising a brunch party.
- Shopping or collecting a prescription.
- Listening, mentoring and giving advice.
- Dog-walking and babysitting.
- Teaching new skills – arts, crafts, music, sports.
- Practising a new language – conversation lessons.
- Organising community events.
- Professional assistance – IT support, accounts.

Almost any sort of time or skill can be exchanged.

The basis for calculating the exchange value is that one hour of time contributed equals one Time Pound. Everyone's time is worth the same. People should try to use up all their credits, or they can donate them to someone else or an organisation.

Banking on your time

Organisations can also participate in Time Banks. They can use the Time Bank to buy such things as help with:

- Door-to-door leaflet delivery.
- Getting repairs and decorating done.
- Answering the telephone.

They can earn Time Credits through offering use of their resources, such as computers and photocopiers, or providing meeting space and training.

Identify GM milk

Get active

Copy the 'model' letter from the Greenpeace website (under Campaign/GM/Get Active) and send it to the supermarket of your choice. Addresses are provided.

The Shoppers Guide to GM: www.greenpeace.org.uk/Products/GM/index.cfm

Greenpeace GM campaign: www.greenpeace.org.uk

Friends of the Earth's real food campaign: www.foe.co.uk/campaigns/real_food/index.html

July 29

There is an international debate raging about genetically modified foods. On the one side are the food manufacturers and the US government, who are pressing for free trade in GM products; on the other side are most consumers and the European Union, who want to restrict the trade. The real problem is that we don't know enough about the long-term impact of GM organisms in the environment, nor do we know whether eating GM products will have any adverse impact on our health. Those opposed to GM crops have the following concerns:

Health: including toxicity and allergic reactions.

Environmental: including the possibility that GM crops will contaminate nearby non-GM crops, increase pesticide pollution, damage soil, reduce biodiversity.

Economic: GM crops may hold a key to feeding the world – but their safety should be proved first.

The UK campaign to get GM out of food was led by Greenpeace and Friends of the Earth, and has been really successful. Food manufacturers and supermarkets have removed GM ingredients from their products and no GM crops will be grown in the UK in the foreseeable future. However, one problem remains – GM animal feed.

Direct your action

Despite the ban on growing GM crops, there is no ban on the import of GM animal feed, much of which is fed to the nation's dairy cows. Many consumers are unaware of this, but when made aware say that they would prefer it to stop. Marks & Spencer led the way, with a ban on milk produced by cows fed on GM feed. By late 2005 other supermarkets were considering following suit, but were clearly waiting to see whether customer power was going to force their hand.

Greenpeace is running a campaign, involving approaching shoppers outside supermarkets and offering to swap their GM milk for bottles of organic milk.

July 30

Love your neighbourhood

25 things

Photograph the 25 things that most please you about your neighbourhood. Then prepare a virtual exhibition.

Contact your local newspaper and offer to email your exhibition to anyone who is interested.

Common Ground, with rules for local distinctiveness: www.commonground.org.uk/distinctiveness/d-index.html

Your neighbourhood is special. Even if it's not perfect, you can learn to love it. Look around you and think about the things you really like. And do what you can to resist the way in which everything is becoming more and more uniform – the same shops, the same undistinguished new buildings, the same ways in which cars and parking are given precedence over people.

What's special could include parks and playgrounds, with people enjoying themselves, statues, architectural details such as a crazy chimney or interesting doorway, shop signs, road names, front gardens, trees and flowers ...

Some rules for local distinctiveness

- Change things for the better – not just for the sake of it.
- Let the character of the people and place win through. Kill corporate identity before it kills our high streets. Give local shops precedence.
- Defend detail. Respond to the local and the vernacular. New buildings or developments need not be bland, boring or brash.
- Enhance the natural features of the area – the rivers and brooks, the hills and valleys, the woods and heaths.
- Get to know your ghosts. The hidden and unseen stories of the area are as important as what is visible.
- History is a continuing process, not just the past. Don't fossilise places. Celebrate time, place and the seasons with feasts and festivals.
- Jettison your car whenever you can and use public transport.
- Know your place. Facts and surveys do not equal knowledge and wisdom.
- Buy things that are locally distinctive and locally made (food and souvenirs).
- Names carry resonances and secrets. Respect local names; add new ones with care. It is not good enough to call an estate 'Badger's Mead' when all the badgers have been destroyed.
- Reveal the past. Decay is an important process. Don't tidy things up so much that the layers of history and reclamation by nature are obliterated. Let continuity show.
- Use old buildings again. Find new functions for them.

Population pressure

There were 6,465,035,104 human beings alive on the planet on 7 September 2005, at 13.09 GMT, according to US Census Bureau estimates. The population has doubled since 1963 and increased by 74.4 million during 2005. By mid-2050, it is estimated to rise to 9.22 billion. Our planet has a limited supply of land, water and natural resources. Will it be able to support its increasing human population?

In the 1970s the world's two most populous nations took action to curb their populations. China instituted a one-child policy, and India introduced sterlisation camps and forced vasectomies. The side effects ranged from human misery to female infanticide.

Since poverty and gender inequality are key factors in population increase, the best way of slowing it down is by creating a social climate receptive to family planning. This means providing education for girls, so that they develop into women who have a much clearer idea of the options open to them. Literate women are more likely to act on information about how to limit their family and protect their children from disease and to generate extra income to bring up a smaller family in greater prosperity.

July 31

Trends

The world's population is made up of people with these age ranges:
Under 15: 29 per cent
15–30: 26 per cent
31–65: 38 per cent
Over 65: 7 per cent

Children under the age of 15 currently make up a large proportion of the world's population. With birth rates falling, and people living longer, children will decline as a proportion of the population.

World population information: www.census.gov/ipc/www/world.html

World Population/ Overpopulation Awareness: www.overpopulation.org

United Nations Population Fund: www.unfpa.org

Help relieve the pressure

Make a difference by helping families and communities to get out of poverty. Your financial support will help meet basic needs (such as health and sanitation).

- Sponsor a child, where your support will help a family and the wider community. ActionAid and Plan International specialise in child sponsorship. It costs around 50 pence a day.
- Adopt a village – this scheme aims to create a register of villages that would like to be adopted, and then to link these with individuals and agencies that would like to adopt them. Set up after the 2004 tsunami to create a 'tsunami of kindness', this project is still under development. Visit www.adoptavillageregistry.com

Lemonade for Alex

Fight cancer in children

Set up a lemonade stall in Alex's honour. Send the profits to Alex's Lemonade Fund at the Philadelphia Foundation: www.philafound.org/Alexslemonade.html

Or in the UK to CLIC-Sargent cancer care for children: www.clicsargent.org.uk

You will need:

- **A table, lots of lemonade, a jug and plastic cups.**
- **A sunny day (hopefully).**
- **A cheerful friend to keep you company.**
- **Posters and banners that say what you are raising money for.**
- **A cash box.**

Alex's Lemonade Stand: www.alexslemonade.org

Children's Cancer Web, information on childhood cancer: www.cancerindex.org/ccw

We have heard people say that Alex lost her battle with cancer. We believe that this could not be farther from the truth. Alex won her battle in so many ways – by facing her cancer every day but still managing to smile; by never giving up hope ... and by leaving an incredible legacy of hope and inspiration ... Jay and Liz Scott, Alex's parents

Alexandra Scott was an incredible eight-year-old. When she was only one year old she was diagnosed with neuroblastoma, an aggressive form of childhood cancer. At the age of four, she decided to set up a lemonade stand to raise money for her treatment. Her goal was to raise $1 million for paediatric cancer research. Now there are hundreds of lemonade stands all over the USA, raising money for Alex's cancer fund. Alex's fund has so far raised over $1.4 million.

Alex died on 1 August 2004. Her story is told in a book, *Alex and the Amazing Lemonade Stand.*

Some facts about childhood cancer:

- One in every 600 chlldren develops cancer before the age of 15. Leukaemia and brain tumours account for more than half the cases.
- The causes of childhood cancers are unknown.
- Childhood cancer occurs randomly and spares no ethnic group, social class or geographic region.

Make your own lemonade

1 Make a syrup. Add ten cups of sugar to ten cups of water in a saucepan. Bring slowly to the boil, stirring until the sugar completely dissolves. Allow to cool. Refrigerate.

2 Juice 50 lemons. Remove the pips. Add the lemon juice to the syrup.

3 Dilute to taste with still or sparkling water. Add approximately three times the quantity of water to syrup.

4 Decorate with a slice of lemon and a mint leaf. (Sufficient for 50 glasses)

Buy a share

Would you like to own Microsoft? When you buy a share in Microsoft, you become a co-owner of the company, along with all the other shareholders. You get these benefits:

- A share certificate, proclaiming your ownership.
- An annual report of the company's performance.
- Share dividends.
- The right to attend the company's Annual General Meeting and to vote on resolutions, including appointing Company Directors.

When you decide to sell your shares, you might even make a profit if the value of the shares has increased.

Of course, your share of the company is tiny – so your vote will only have any impact if it is part of a wider campaign. At the AGM, there will also be an opportunity to ask the Chair a question, such as does the company dispose of its waste safely, or does the company use child labour? Whatever your concern, you can ask the company for a response in front of a large audience with lots of journalists present.

Some companies find their AGMs become a forum where social and environmental issues are raised: companies such as Nestlé (which markets formula milk in the developing world) and Exxon (which is not doing enough to counter global warming).

Have your say

Is there a company you would like to confront over an issue? Buy one share in that company – through an online dealing service or a stockbroker.

Go along to the AGM. When the Chair asks for questions, stand up and have your say. All you need is one share in order to have the right to attend.

Information and ideas on shareholder activism: www.coopamerica.org/socialinvesting/shareholderaction

Humour is an excellent way of making a point. Read Isabel Losada's book, *A Beginner's Guide to Changing the World: For Tibet with Love.*

August 2

Use humour to make a point

Isabel Losada belongs to the Free Tibet Movement. They arranged for her to attend the AGM of BP to raise the issue of BP's investment in PetroChina, which was planning to build a pipeline through Tibet. Once she was in the meeting hall, Isabel changed into the costume of a Chinese soldier. Every time the Chair mentioned Tibet, she clapped and cheered. Every time her fellow Free Tibet protesters asked a question, she hurled abuse at them. And she congratulated the Chair on not letting terrorists disrupt the profits of the company.

August 3

Get your shoes shined

Next time you see a shoe-shiner, wherever you are, make sure that you get your shoes shined!

If you work in London, ask your Office Manager if it's possible to have StreetShine come in and clean people's shoes. Everyone will look smarter and feel happier.

Circulate information about StreetShine to organisations concerned with street children around the world. They might get inspired by the idea.

Streetshine: www.streetshine.com

StreetShine helps people

StreetShine is an exciting social enterprise that has just got started in the UK. It was founded by Nick Grant at the Thamesreach Bondway homeless project. StreetShine aims to provide homeless people with work and a regular income through operating a shoe-care service within office buildings. Its services include shoe-shining, a pick-up and drop-off point for shoe repairs, and selling accessories such as shoelaces.

The shiners get involved in three stages. They start by working part-time. As they gain self-confidence and improve their work skills, they progress to full-time employment. Finally, there will be franchise opportunities for those who wish to set up their own shoeshine business. This will give them independence, while at the same time they benefit from the StreetShine brand.

The objective of StreetShine is to break the vicious cycle of: no home = no job = no income = no home.

It does this by providing homeless people with real work and a sense of dignity. Once it has become established in London, StreetShine intends to expand to other major cities across the UK.

Shoe-shining is a job traditionally done by street children. A project such as StreetShine could turn this from 'street work' into a proper profession, complete with training, uniform and a brand image. The StreetShine principle could be developed in countries such as India or Brazil. Delhi or Rio could become the first cities where the shoe-shining is done by uniformed professional shiners, in partnership with shopping centres, government offices and leading hotels.

Full-time shiner

Andreas was StreetShine's first full-time shiner. He has built up a dedicated client base in offices he visits on a weekly basis all over the City and the West End in London.

Cleaning water

In February 2004 Coca-Cola launched Dasani in the UK. This bottled drinking water cost £1.69 (about $3.20). But its launch was followed by two fiascos. The first was when the press discovered that the water being used was actually London tap water, with impurities removed by a process called reverse osmosis. The second was when it was found that one of the minerals being added to improve the taste exceeded safety levels. The product was withdrawn.

In the rich world, water is a 'lifestyle product'. We will pay double the cost of a litre of petrol for a litre of water. In the developing world, lack of access to safe clean drinking water means disease and death. Clean water is a matter of life rather than lifestyle, and bottled water is bought at grossly inflated prices by those too poor to have a water source 'on tap'.

The technology that was used for Dasani has now been adapted for public use. Just digging wells is not sufficient if the ground water is contaminated with arsenic, fluorides or nitrates. The Bhabha Atomic Research Centre in Mumbai has installed small reverse-osmosis plants in a number of Indian villages. These plants can provide drinking water for up to 1,000 people. The cost works out at about 0.03 cents per litre. Dasani was 1,000 times more expensive!

Local tap

Buy a bottle of mineral or filtered water, but once you've drunk it, promise never to do this again! Put tap water into your empty water bottle, and nobody will know the difference. Refill as necessary.

When you go out to a restaurant, ask for 'local tap', with ice and a slice of lemon.

Calculate how much you are saving from both these actions. Donate this to WaterAid, which works to bring clean water to thirsty people around the world.

WaterAid: www.wateraid.org.uk

Pentair Water reverse-osmosis system: www.pentairwater.com

August 4

Water-purifying units

As well as the small reverse-osmosis units developed in Mumbai, other mobile water-purifying units using waste heat, diesel or solar power are also available. A domestic water purifier based on an ultra-filtration membrane has been developed that produces 40 litres of safe drinking water a day. This could be used by any household with access to a well.

The Pentair Water reverse-osmosis system costs $5,000, has a capacity of 500 litres per hour, and provides 1,500 glasses of clean water for just $1. Why can it not be used in villages, or slums?

Compost corner

Detailed instructions on composting: www.mastercomposter.com

Can-o-Worms, an easy to use vermicomposter where the worms do all the work: www.wigglywigglers.co.uk

Composting is easy

Build a compost bin and recycle your waste. If you have a garden or a yard, build a bin from old pallets or wood posts and wire-mesh netting, lined with old carpet or thick cardboard. Cover with a wooden lid or old carpet to keep rain out and heat in.

Buy a desktop wormery. This is an educational toy, artwork and desktop paperweight all in one. The kit contains bedding, drainage chips, sand and 12 worms, which you assemble in a small glass-fronted case. Give it to your green friends or worst enemies – £40 from WigglyWigglers.

Compost your waste

Composting decomposes organic matter into a growing medium full of nutrients. It takes place when organic matter is kept warm and dry for some months. It can be speeded up by using worms – called 'vermicomposting'.

A third of all household refuse could be composted, as well as most garden waste: grass mowings, hedge trimmings and plants that have flowered (but not weeds). Home-made compost makes an excellent soil conditioner and a rich source of plant food. The compost can be used in your garden and for your window boxes and pot plants. It cuts down on the need to buy peat-based products, thus saving the now nearly extinct peat bogs.

Do compost

- Kitchen waste – fruit and vegetable peelings, tea bags, coffee grounds, crushed eggshells.
- Garden waste – grass, hedge clippings, old flowers.
- Shredded card and paper (avoid heavily coloured).
- Wood ash.
- Human hair and animal fur.
- Autumn leaves. Put large amounts in bin liners to rot down for mulch.
- Old clothes – pure wool and other natural fabrics.
- Sawdust, bedding and manure from vegetarian pets.

Don't compost

- Cooked food, meat and fish.
- Droppings from meat-eating animals.
- Magazines and heavily inked cardboard.
- Nappies.
- Coal ash and soot.
- Diseased plants.
- Roots of persistent weeds such as couch grass.
- Synthetic fabrics.
- Glass, plastic and metal (recycle separately).

What's up Mac?

The McLibel Trial was a landmark court case between McDonald's, and Helen Steel and Dave Morris, a gardener and a postman from London. McDonald's issued writs on 20 September 1990, alleging that the pair had libelled the company in the Greenpeace factsheet 'What's Wrong with McDonald's?'

The two represented themselves in court. The trial began in June 1994, and three years later, after 314 days in court (the longest trial ever held in England), Mr Justice Bell ruled that McDonald's marketing 'pretended to have a positive nutritional benefit which their food did not match'; that they 'exploit children' with their advertising; that they were 'responsible for cruel practices regarding the rearing and slaughter of animals'; and that they 'pay low wages, thereby helping to depress wages for workers in the catering trade'. However, the Courts ruled that the 'McLibel Two' had libelled McDonald's over other points (starvation in the third world, destruction of the rainforest and selling food injurious to health) and ordered them to pay £40,000 damages. They refused. McDonald's did not pursue the matter.

In 2005, the McLibel Two won a ruling against the British Government from the European Court of Human Rights that they had been denied basic human rights by being refused legal aid to defend the case. This had left them at a real disadvantage. McLibel is seen as the worst corporate PR disaster in history.

August 6

Fast food

Buy a Big Mac and fries. Wash it down with a Coke. Become a restaurant critic and rate your Big Mac and fries for taste, appearance, ambience, affordability and enjoyment. Then think about the wider issues:

- **Nutrition – is a burger and fries healthy?**
- **Advertising – did the product live up to the image?**
- **Employment – what about pay and working conditions for the staff?**
- **Environment – what happens to all that litter?**
- **Animal welfare – do you think the animals enjoyed feeding you?**
- **Globalisation – is fast food a good or bad thing?**

If you feel strongly about the global food industry and its impact on our lives, visit the McInformation Network website. Volunteers are welcome: www.mcspot light.org

The McInformation Network

The McInformation Network is run by volunteers from twenty-two countries on four continents. It aims to compile and disseminate factual, up-to-date information, encouraging debate about the policies and practices of the McDonald's Corporation. It also provides fun and games on a McDonald's theme.

Chicken farming

Free range

Become a backyard chicken farmer. Buy an Eglu chicken coop. The complete package costs around £350. Every Eglu comes complete with its own private secure area, enclosed with animal-proof wire netting to keep hungry foxes away. You also get two chickens, organically reared to Soil Association standards, and at 'point of lay'. The Eglu is available from: www.omlet.co.uk

Adopt a chicken and find out about trade injustice in Ghana. Click on each chicken and hear their stories on this hilarious Christian Aid website: www.mailorderchickens.org

Information about battery chickens: www.downthelane.net/battery.html
Compassion in World Farming: www.ciwf.org.uk

There are 30 million chickens in the UK. Despite the public concern about their living conditions, 85 per cent still live in batteries and 70 per cent are kept in huge sheds containing upwards of 20,000 birds. Most farms keep four or five birds in a cage no more than 50 x 50 cm. The minimum legal requirement for one bird is just under three-quarters the size of an A4 sheet of paper. (This will be doubled by 2012 as a result of an EU directive.) The average hen lays 338 eggs per year. The chickens are kept for around 70 weeks before being slaughtered, mostly for pet food, although some enter the human food chain.

This is not just cruel to the birds, but dangerous for humans. Intensive chicken rearing makes diseases such as salmonella more likely. There are alternatives:

Better
Barn hens, with 25 birds per sq m on raised platforms. Deep litter, part-solid cage, just 7 birds per sq m.

Much better
Free range, with access to the outdoors, allowing 1,000 birds per hectare.

Best
Your very own backyard chickens. This is your chance to change the world – one egg at a time!

Creature comforts

The Eglu is a chicken coop for the 21st century, featuring spacious open-plan living for two medium-sized chickens or three bantams. Designed to be comfortable for the chickens, and effortless for you, the Eglu makes keeping chickens rewarding and fun. It is fitted throughout with wooden roosting bars and an integrated nesting box ... The chickens are kept warm in the winter and cool in the summer, thanks to modern twin-walled insulation. To make collecting your eggs easy, the Eglu has an eggport, which gives access to the nesting box.
From the Eglu sales blurb

Give it up

August 8

Giving up things is good for your soul. Hindus go in for renunciation. Christians give up things for Lent (the 40-day period before Easter). Muslims have the holy month of Ramadan (a month when they fast from dawn to sunset). Jews have Yom Kippur (a fast which lasts about 25 hours).

But here's another take on the idea of giving up. There must be things you could give up that would make only a tiny difference to your life. But using the time or money you save, you could then make a big difference to the world. Here are some ideas:

- Give up drinking bottled water. Drink tap water, there's nothing wrong with it, and it's free (once you are connected to the mains). And it doesn't involve lorries thundering down the motorway to bring it to you, or empty bottles to dispose of.
- Give up buying a cup of coffee on the way to the office each morning. There are cheaper ways of getting your morning caffeine fix. Buy a thermos flask (maybe an aluminium designer one if you care about being cool) plus a really nice cup and a teaspoon. Make your coffee at home using only the finest coffee – freshly ground, fairtrade of course. Take this with you to work. Then enjoy.
- Give up smoking. This is the single most sensible thing you can do for a healthier life. And it will make a huge difference to your finances.

Question your needs

Answer these two questions:
1 What can I give up that I will barely even notice?
2 What will this then enable me to do?
Give it up. And do it!

H2G2 is a website inspired by *The Hitchhiker's Guide to the Galaxy*. It is a guide to 'life, the universe and everything'. It is an open-source guide, with visitors to the website contributing, adding to and amending content. You can contribute your ideas on how to give it up and how to get a life: www.bbc.co.uk/dna/h2g2

Save time and money

Here are some more ideas for things to give up:

- Replace things with logos with things with no logo (read Naomi Klein's book *No Logo*).
- Give up deodorant, and smell like yourself rather than a perfume factory (and save the world from volatile organic compounds).
- Be alcohol-free at least one day a week.

Fairtrade tea

Bag some tea

The Just Change project promotes barter trading between poor communities in India, and markets tea to affluent consumers in India and overseas. Package and market tea from the Nilgiris. Sealed bags containing 25 tea bags can be purchased from Just Change for 90p. Design nice packaging and leaflets showing where the tea comes from. Sell as much as possible to friends and colleagues. Set up a thriving tea business.

Just Change: www.justchangeindia.com

AMS, the tribal community organisation: www.adivasi.net

ActionAid's Chembakolli tea pack: schools@actionaid.org.uk and www.chembakolli.com

A community of forest dwellers in southern India has embarked on tea growing. The people are 'adivasis' – indigenous forest dwellers who live about 5,000 feet up in the Nilgiri Hills. Over the years, the adivasis lost their rights over the forest lands, due to enclosure by powerful people who wanted to settle on the land and fell the trees, and the Forest Department, who wanted people out of the forests for conservation reasons. The Tribal Community Organisation (AMS) encouraged settled agriculture in order to make the adivasis economically independent and to protect tribal land rights. Tea cultivation made sense because it was the predominant crop of the area, would generate a regular income, and because planting tea would provide evidence that the adivasis had tenure of the land. Over the last ten years, more than 1,000 families have each planted tea on plots of up to one acre, and are now enjoying a steady income.

Tea growing provided the organisation with a base for building other enterprises including: a Tea Nursery to supply tea plants; co-operative tea marketing to negotiate a better price for curing the tea; a 300-acre tea estate owned by the community.

Fairtrade tea plantations

Unlike fairtrade coffee, which is produced by co-operatives of small farmers, fairtrade tea is produced mostly on large privately owned plantations in India, Sri Lanka and East Africa. To become fairtrade-certified, a tea estate has to provide its workers with fair wages and good working conditions, and ensure adequate housing and healthcare. Certified estates encourage sustainable farming, prohibit child labour, and the workers and managers together decide how the fairtrade premium will be used to benefit the workers (housing, education healthcare). There are around 50 fairtrade-certified tea estates in India, employing more than 120,000 workers.

Hug a tree

People do some weird and wonderful things to protect trees. When a 400-year-old giant oak tree in Southern California was threatened by the widening of a highway for a new housing development, John Quigley came to its rescue. With the support of others, he ascended into the leafy heights of 'Old Glory', as the beautiful tree was named by local children, and stayed there for 71 days during the winter of 2002–03. Eventually he was removed by police and the highway was built, but the tree was carefully removed and replanted on a new site where it is now thriving.

The Chipko Movement became world famous in the 1970s and 1980s. Local people on India's border with Tibet had used the forests in the foothills of the Himalayas in a sustainable way for many years. The forest had provided them with food, materials for shelter, medicines and fodder for their animals. Then the government restricted their access and sold licences to fell the trees. When a sporting goods manufacturer arrived to fell the trees, local people, including many women, went out and hugged the trees to prevent them being felled. This was the birth of Chipko Andolan (Hindi for 'Movement to Hug'). The leader, Chandi Prasad Bhatt, declared their aim: 'Let them know they will not fell a single tree without felling one of us first ... we will embrace the trees to protect them.' The loggers withdrew.

Go down to the woods

Go out and hug a large and lovely tree in your local park or wood. Think about the heroism of the Chipko pioneers and about what you can do to preserve trees and woodlands.

If you are too embarrassed to hug a tree, then go out and hunt one! And send the details to The Ancient Tree Hunt.

Read about Old Glory: www.landscapeonline.com/research/article/5502

For more information on the Chipko Movement: www.unu.edu/unupress/unupbooks/80a03e/80A03E08.htm

The Ancient Tree Hunt: www.woodland-trust.org.uk/ancient-tree-hunt/

Hunt for an ancient tree

Unless you know exactly what you've got and where it is, you can't really protect it. That is the principle behind the survey organised in the UK by the Ancient Tree Forum, The Woodland Trust and the Tree Register of the British Isles. But they are relying on you to go out there and find the trees, measure them, and send in the details. Check out the website and find out how to do it properly.

Civilian casualties

Facts and figures

Start creating a dossier of facts and figures on an issue that particularly concerns you. Save press cuttings and read official reports. Use the internet to help you. You may find yourself becoming an expert on the subject.

For every US death there have been 18 Iraqi deaths:

- **American servicemen killed in Iraq (April 2006): 2,377**
- **Iraqi civilians reported killed (calculated by Iraq Body Count, April 2006): 34,030–38,164**

To find out about the cost of the Iraq war to the US ($272 billion as of April 2006) go to: http://costofwar.com/index.html

Iraq Body Count: www.iraqbodycount.org

War has distressing consequences for civilian populations. Even if civilians are not directly killed or maimed as a result of military action, they may suffer long-term injury or illness as a result of radiation, post-conflict contact with unexploded munitions, or pollution caused by the spillage of toxic materials. Populations become displaced and many people suffer deep psychological trauma. Documenting and assigning responsibility for the side-effects of war is a hard task, requiring long-term on-the-ground resources. But direct deaths and injuries from military strikes can be much more easily identified, both in place and in time, and responsibility can readily be attributed to the weapon that caused that death or injury. Despite this, the military forces operating in Iraq, predominantly from the USA and the UK, make no attempt to keep a tally of the civilian deaths.

The Iraq Body Count project has been created 'to record single-mindedly and on a virtually real-time basis one key and immutable index of the fruits of war – the death toll of innocents'. It aims to promote public understanding and support for the human dimension of the 2003 Iraq war by providing reliable, up-to-date documentation of civilian casualties.

How the Iraq body count is conducted

The information is gleaned by surveying the reports of news-gathering services around the world. An incident must be reported by at least two agencies, and by logging the following information the organisation aims to ensure that an incident is never counted more than once:

- Date of incident
- Time of incident
- Location of incident
- Target as stated by military sources
- Weapon
- Minimum civilian deaths
- Maximum civilian deaths
- Sources (at least two sources)

If you're young

These are ways in which young people can link together to change the world:

The Freechild Project was set up to advocate, inform, and celebrate social change led by young people around the world. Their website is a great resource list for youth action.

iEARN describes itself as the world's largest non-profit global network that connects young people and encourages them to collaborate in changing the world. It brings them together from over 20,000 schools and youth groups in more than 110 countries. There are more than 120 iEARN projects, each trying to answer the question 'How will this project improve the quality of life on the planet?'

Peace Child International focuses mainly on the issues of sustainable development and human rights. Every two years, it organises a World Youth Congress for up to 1,000 young people (Scotland 2005, Bangalore 2007). It also runs a 'Be the Change' programme to encourage and support local youth-led initiatives for changing the world. You can get involved in 'Be the Change', attend a World Youth Congress or volunteer as an intern at their HQ near London, with full board and lodging provided.

TakingITGlobal is a global online community which inspires young people to make a difference. It provides a source of information on issues, opportunities to take action, and a bridge to get involved locally, nationally and globally. Membership is free and allows you to interact with various aspects of the website to contribute ideas, actions and experiences. There are profiles of 850 youth projects that TiG members are undertaking all over the world.

Young person's guide

If you're a young person (aged 16–25) check out all these websites. And become a member of TakingITglobal, which is closely linked to the Global Youth Action Network.

www.tig.org
www.freechild.org
www.iearn.org
www.peacechild.org
www.youthlink.org
www.freethechildren.org

If you once were a young person, you can still change the world!

Networking

Free the Children is an international network of children helping children at a local, national and international level through representation, leadership and action. It was founded by Craig Kielburger in 1995, when he was just 12 years old. The main goal is to free children from poverty and exploitation.

Surfers against sewage

Action for cleaner water

Here is a four-point action plan for safer beaches, rivers and lakes:

1. **Don't chuck rubbish down the loo – the only thing going down your toilet should be human waste and toilet paper.**
2. **Enjoy your beach, but remember to bin your rubbish or take it home.**
3. **If you notice a pollution incident, report it immediately.**
4. **Buy organic. Once pesticides get into the water cycle, they can persist indefinitely.**

Join Surfers against Sewage: www.sas.org.uk

Humans create a continuous supply of sewage that requires disposal. In many countries, sewage treatment and disposal methods are primitive: whatever goes down the toilet washes up on the beach or along the banks of rivers.

Toxic chemicals produced as by-products of industrial processes also require disposal. Most are discharged into rivers and run off into the sea. Products in everyday use at home contain a vast array of chemicals and organic compounds that are flushed, washed away after bathing or showering, or disposed of directly into the drains. There is no regulation of these discharges. Many substances will remain in the environment indefinitely, either in the water itself or in the flesh and fat of organisms.

Surfers against Sewage has been campaigning against sewage discharge and toxic dumping since 1990, when a wet-suited and gas-masked 'SAS hit squad' demonstration took place at the Royal Cornwall Show, with pollution fact sheets handed out to the public. From this small beginning, SAS has become a national campaign, highlighting the problem of sewage disposal into the sea, and monitoring compliance with legislation.

The recipe for faecal soup

Everything that goes into the drains – bleach, chemicals, paint, solvents, oils, fats – and everything that is flushed down the loo will end up in the sewers. You're making this 'faecal soup' every day. It's lucky you don't have to drink it. Make sure others don't have to swim in it! The ingredients of this soup are:

- Sewage-related debris
- Bacteria and viruses from human intestines
- Chemicals and heavy metals from household and beauty products
- Nutrients (nitrates and phosphates)
- Endocrine disrupting substances
- Oils, fats and greases

No flies on you?

Flies affect almost everybody. They may not be as much of a nuisance as mosquitoes, but they can be just as dangerous.

Trachoma is caused by *Chlamydia trachomatis*, a micro-organism that spreads through contact with eye discharge from an infected person. It is transmitted via towels, handkerchiefs and fingers, and also through eye-seeking flies, taking the infection from one person to another. After years of repeated infection, the inside of your eyelid may become scarred so severely that the eyelid turns inward and your eyelashes rub on your eyeball, scarring the cornea (the front of the eye). If untreated, this condition will lead to blindness.

It affects 84 million people, of whom 8 million are visually impaired. It is responsible for more than 3 per cent of the world's blindness, and is especially prevalent in many of the poorest areas in the world.

The buzz

We've all seen dying children in refugee camps with flies crawling all over their faces. We've also been infuriated by flies at home.

Why not make a fly trap for your kitchen.

Choose a country and circulate the instructions for making a fly trap as widely as possible in that country.

All about eye diseases, from the World Health Organisation: www.who.int/topics/blindness/en

Teaching Aids at Low-Cost (TALC), fly trap instructions: www.talcuk.org/free/html/fly trap/flytrap.htm

Build a fly trap

Go to the TALC website and download instructions on how to build a fly trap. You will need:

- Two large clear plastic bottles, preferably identical, one with its screw top.
- One smaller plastic bottle, made of smooth plastic.
- A small quantity of black or dark paint.
- A sharp knife.
- A small piece of string.
- A pointed instrument.
- A candle.

The flies fly into the lower bottle, attracted by bait. They then make their way through a narrow tube into the upper bottle, where they are trapped. Various baits can be used. Chicken entrails are OK but tend to dry up. Flies seem to like the smell of 250 g of yeast in a litre of water with 6 g of ammonium carbonate added two days later. The Maasai of Kenya use a mixture of goat dung and cows' urine – you could try this!

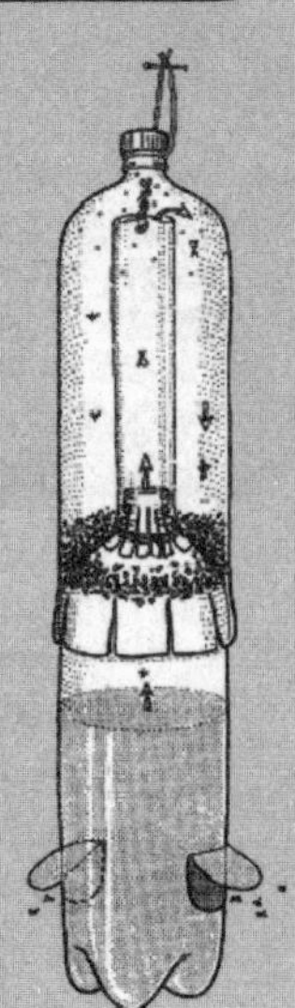

August 15

Stop child soldiers

Human Rights Watch provides a sample letter for you to email or fax to governments.

Let governments know that you care about the use of child soldiers, and that they should sign up or ratify the Ban.

Encourage Cambodia, Colombia, Jordan, Nepal and the Philippines to join the 35 countries that have already ratified the Ban.

Encourage Algeria, Eritrea, Fiji, Mozambique, Thailand and Yemen to sign up.

Coalition to Stop the Use of Child Soldiers: www.child-soldiers.org

The World Revolution, information on child soldiers: www.worldrevolution.org/guide/childsoldiers

Human Rights Watch, stop the use of child soldiers: hrw.org/campaigns/crp/index.htm

Guns in the hands of babes

> *They held a court and found her [a girl presumed to be a spy] guilty. They ordered me to lead her away and shoot her, and at first I hesitated; but then I did it. To [the guerrillas] it was a proof of my loyalty, but to me it didn't prove anything.*
> Gloria, who joined the FARC in Colombia aged 11

> *I killed another child. I did this three times. I felt bad but I knew what would happen if I disobeyed.*
> Bosco, who was abducted by the Lords Resistance Army from Gulu, Uganda at age 12

Over 300,000 children are involved in warfare. They are in the front line, carrying AK-47s and M16s. They go on suicide missions, act as soldiers, spies, sex slaves, messengers, assassins and human mine detectors. Child soldiers are used in more than thirty countries. They are cheap and expendable, so tend to receive little or no training. They suffer higher fatality rates than their adult counterparts. Some are abducted, some volunteer. The main reason for volunteering is their personal experience of ill treatment by government armed forces.

The 'Straight-18' Plan is trying to ratify an International Ban on Use of Child Soldiers, setting 18 years as the minimum age for conscription, forced recruitment and participation in armed conflict.

Child recruits

Burma has the largest number of child soldiers in the world, according to Human Rights Watch. The national army forcibly recruits children as young as 11. More than 20 per cent of active duty soldiers may be under 18. Armed opposition groups use children as well.

For a copy of HRW's report 'My Gun was as Tall as Me' go to: hrw.org/press/2002/10/burma-1016.htm

Anonymous generosity

The best way to cheer yourself up is to try to cheer somebody else up. Mark Twain

Think about the idea of giving freely to someone, without being asked or being expected to give, without you knowing them or them knowing you.

For example, you are crossing a toll bridge and you decide to pay not just your own fare but also the fare of the car behind you. You leave a card, saying that this is an act of generosity from a complete stranger. They could then do something that will make someone else happy and pass the card on. They put a £5 note with the card next to an ATM machine, to be picked up by someone who needs the money. That person then buys an extra ticket at the cinema for the next customer, who buys a drink in a bar for a person selected at random, and the process goes on.

Attitudes not just acts can make a difference. Making another person happy could be like a butterfly flapping its wings and causing a hurricane thousands of miles away. Your unattributable act of generosity could be the start of a wind of change.

A true act of charity

Perform two acts of generosity today.

Go to the Give It Forward Today (GIFT) website, created by 12-year-old Alex Southmayd. He gives lots of ideas, plus you can download GIFT Certificates for the recipients of your generosity.

Download two GIFT Certificates with the message: 'You have been GIFTed. Your mission (if you accept it) is to GIFT two human beings with an act of kindness. Please pass this on ...'

Give It Forward Today: www.giveitforwardtoday.org

The eight degrees of charity

Charity is a part of every religion. Moses Maimonides was a Jewish sage who lived in the 12th century. He suggested that there were eight degrees of charity:

Bottom level Giving to a poor person unwillingly. It is better not to give at all.

Seventh level Giving to a poor person with a glad heart and a smile.

Sixth level Giving after being asked.

Fifth level Giving before being asked.

Fourth level Not knowing who you are giving to, but allowing the recipients to know who their benefactor is.

Third level Knowing who you are giving to, but not allowing the recipients to know who their benefactor is.

Second level Giving to the poor, neither party knowing the identity of the other.

Top level Investing in a poor person, to solve their problem.

August 17

How do others see you?

Organise a Photograph a Day in Your Life project at your school, community centre or workplace. Or link your church with a mosque, or your temple with a synagogue.

Bring two groups of people together who ordinarily would not interact, or who are divided by conflict. All you need are some digital cameras.

After you've finished, upload your photos onto: www.fotolog.com.

PhotoVoice: www.photovoice.org

Capture a day in the life

Seeing the world through other people's eyes can be a big shock. Your neighbours may be living next door to you geographically, but your lives could be a million miles apart. Knowing more about their different life experiences could help you understand how they feel and even make you see things in a completely new light.

Misunderstanding can foster fear and hatred; unfamiliarity may become an obstacle to peace. The Photographing a Day in Our Life project aims to open your eyes to the perspectives and ideas of your neighbours, and to develop mutual understanding.

Here's how it works: people from adjoining communities who would not normally interact – or who interact minimally – are grouped into pairs. The two groups could be contrasted by, say, age, gender, religion, race, conflict, sexuality, income, domestic situations, or disability. Each pair is given a digital camera. They are asked to 'photograph a day in each other's life'. The photographer shadows the person they are paired with, and captures images of their daily routine – at work, play and home. Then the photographer becomes the photographed. Finally, each pair makes a short presentation about why they chose to show certain photographs.

Photographing life at the edge

PhotoVoice, set up by Anna Blackman and Tiffany Fairey, trains socially excluded groups in photojournalism to give them a voice and provide professional skills. PhotoVoice works with homeless people, refugees, street and working children, orphans, disabled groups and women living with HIV/AIDS in Afghanistan, Democratic Republic of Congo, Nepal, Vietnam and the UK.

So far, they have trained over 300 people. Their images offer insights into how people live, captured by the very people whose lives are a daily struggle.

Celebrate cycling

The Revolution will arrive on a bicycle. Salvador Allende, President of Chile, 1970–73

Critical Mass is foremost a celebration rather than a protest. It is a bunch of cyclists riding around together, from one point to another. It is a group of individuals who just happen to be doing the same thing at the same time. And because there's no organisation and nobody in charge, no permission needs to be obtained for arranging an event in a public place and no one person is held responsible.

It started in September 1992 in San Francisco as a festive reclaiming of public space. It originally had a less catchy name: 'The Commute Clot'. The first ride attracted 60 cyclists, and the numbers have grown over the years. The idea has also spread to other cities. Independent Critical Masses have sprung up all over the world. Critical Mass has become a self-propelling global movement.

Critical Mass is different in every city. Some groups are big, some small. There are different approaches to respecting traffic laws (or lack thereof), interacting with motorists and relationships with the police.

August 18

On your bikes

Join a Critical Mass ride. Have fun. Assert the power of the pedaller. Reclaim the streets for the most environmentally friendly (and often the quickest) form of urban transport.

If there isn't a Critical Mass in your city ... then start one!

Critical Mass groups in the UK: criticalmasslondon.org.uk/when&where

How to start a Critical Mass bike ride: www.criticalmassrides.info/howto.html

How to make a Critical Mass: www.critical-mass.org

How to Not Get Hit By Cars, 10 tips for safer cycling: bicyclesafe.com

A resource site for cycle commuters: www.BikeToWork.com

A Critical Mass happening

'What's this all about?' ask amused and bemused pedestrians on Market Street as hundreds of noisy, high-spirited bicyclists ride past, yelling and ringing their bells. There are a wide variety of answers: 'It's about banning cars. It's about having fun in the street. It's about a more social way of life. It's about asserting our right to the road. It's about solidarity.'

In riding around the city as part of a Critical Mass, many important questions come up. Why is there so little open space where people can relax and interact, free from the incessant buying and selling of ordinary life? Why are people compelled to organise their lives around having a car? What would an alternative future look like?

Get active

Organise a Politics 'n' Pizza, Politics 'n' Pancakes, or Politics 'n' Punk Brunch – whatever works for you. Make the invitation simple: 'Brunch this wknd?' or 'My house Sat' will usually be more appealing than 'League of Pissed Off Voters etc'.

Get together in small groups, and once everyone has had something to eat and drink, make a list of the issues that are important to all of you and the policies you would like to see implemented. Get in touch with the relevant candidates or MPs and extract some promises from them.

League of Pissed-Off Voters: www.indyvoter.org

EPolitix, online news plus links to MPs' websites: www.epolitix.com

Support democracy

If democracy is to mean anything, it should express the will of the people, and the ballot box is how the will of the people is manifested. There may not be an election this year or even next, but it is important that everyone prepares for next time. What issues concern you most? Are the political parties even addressing them, let alone adopting policies you think are sensible?

Now is the time to start getting a group of people together, discussing the issues with them, and planning how, together, you can make an impact when the next election comes. It is never too soon to start a campaign to encourage participation in the political process. Then, when the next election comes, you will be prepared. You will know the issues. You will also know how to get involved in the election campaign.

You can find out about your Member of Parliament, his or her voting record, how they stand on the issues on the They Work For You website. The website also profiles the political parties and their manifestos, and think tanks and what they are thinking. Visit: www.theyworkforyou.com

The League of Pissed-Off Voters

This was formed to encourage the younger generation to learn the nitty-gritty of politics and invent fresh ways of playing the democracy game on their terms. The League's intention is to transform thousands of young adults who have never messed with politics before, into savvy political players. The League is American, but their ideas can be used anywhere. They publish the following resources for participating in elections:

- A 90-day plan of action.
- How to host a Kickass strategy session.
- A sample survey for contact collection.
- The 'You get out the Vote' toolbox.
- How-to-get-out-the-vote in twelve easy steps.

Circles of Compassion

A 'Circle of Compassion' is a gathering at which people sit in a circle on the floor. It is also a tool to help people communicate honestly and openly. The Circle allows participants to:

- Listen without judging.
- Understand one another, bridge differences and try to reach a consensus.
- Devise and implement creative solutions to problems in a spirit of openness and collaboration.
- Settle disputes in a spirit of reconciliation.

The World Conference on Women held in Beijing in 1995 was a milestone in the development of international collaboration between women and women's organisations. Circles of Compassion are being promoted by the Women's World Summit Foundation as a mechanism for discussing some of the critical areas of concern that were identified there. The Foundation's target is to achieve one million circles.

Be creative

Create your own Circle of Compassion. Take one of the 12 Beijing issues. Invite friends, colleagues and acquaintances to contribute to the discussion. Think of a positive action you can take together to address the issue.

Women's World Summit Foundation: their website has information on organizing a Circle of Compassion: www.woman.ch

August 20

Addressing women's equality

The 12 areas of concern on women are:

1. The persistent and increasing burden of poverty on women.
2. Unequal access to education.
3. Inequalities in health and in access to adequate healthcare.
4. Violence against women.
5. The effects of armed and other conflict.
6. Inequality in economic structures, policy-making and production processes.
7. Inequality in power and decision-making.
8. Insufficient mechanisms to promote the advancement of women.
9. Lack of awareness of and commitment to women's human rights.
10. Insufficient coverage in the media of women's contribution to society.
11. Women's contribution to managing natural resources and safeguarding the environment is not recognised.
12. The girl-child.

Donate old computers

Recycle them

Donate your old computer through a computer recycling scheme.

Or you can take an old laptop with you when you are travelling to countries in the developing world, and find an organisation or a school and just leave it with them. These will be really useful in areas where the power supply is irregular.

Encourage your employer to donate all your company's computers when upgrading.

In the UK, contact: www.computeraid.org

UK directory of computer recyclers from: www.icer.org.uk

Advice for organisations receiving donated computers: www.digitalequalizer.org/practices.htm

More than 600 million perfectly good computers will be discarded by companies worldwide over the next five years. In the UK every year over three million computers are decommissioned and one million end up filling up landfill sites. Fewer than 20 per cent of old computers are recycled. Effective disposal of old computers is becoming increasingly costly, with stricter environmental regulations and declining residual values.

A great many old PCs are in good working order and could continue to be used by someone else. In the developing world, 99 per cent of schoolchildren graduate from high school never having seen or touched a computer. There are commercial organisations that take old PCs for recycling, and also specialist organisations, that refurbish PCs and then send them to charities, schools and low-income households in developing countries.

Prices are getting lower and specifications are rising year by year. Discarded computers have higher and higher specifications. What you no longer need can be a wonderful opportunity for someone else.

Computer Aid International

This is a specialist non-profit-making organisation that renovates and ships computers to developing countries at a cost of around £65 per unit, depending on the quantity shipped. The computers are shipped without a Windows operating system, but Linux can be installed at no extra cost.

Computer Aid International is now shipping 25,000 computers a year, mainly to Africa. These can be used for non-commercial purposes such as:

- Computers in schools.
- Setting up an IT skills training project.
- Creating a cyber café to generate income.
- A computer loan scheme for university students.
- For distribution to non-governmental organisations.

Build a skip sculpture

We live in a throw-away society:
7 million tonnes of paper are thrown away every year in the UK alone – it requires 80 million trees to make this paper;
8.5 billion cans, half for food, half for drinks, are produced each year in the UK – enough to reach to the moon and back and halfway there again.

Every year, an average European family with two children throws away 50 kilos of paper (six trees), 60 kilos of metal and 45 kilos of plastic. That last item may not sound a lot, but it's equivalent to 13,500 supermarket bags.

Here are three ways to deal with all this rubbish:
Reduce Throw away less. Make sure you buy products with as little packaging as possible.
Reuse Buy a proper bag for your shopping, instead of using plastic bags. Use both sides of a sheet of paper.
Recycle 80 per cent of domestic rubbish can be recycled, including paper, glass, metal and plastic.

August 22

Turn junk into art

Make your own sculpture with a message. Scavenge the local skips. Make a tour of your neighbourhood. See what people are throwing away. Retrieve bits and pieces that look interesting. Use these to build a sculpture in your front garden or a park.

Get a picture of your 'skip sculpture' in your local newspaper. Use the publicity to highlight the quantity of waste being generated. Produce a simple leaflet or poster telling people what to do about this.

See the WEEE Man at: www.weeeman.org

The WEEE man

WEEE stands for Waste Electrical and Electronic Equipment. To highlight the problem of this waste, the Royal Society of Arts commissioned Paul Bonomini to create the WEEE Man, a humanoid sculpture made out of all the electrical and electronic equipment that one person is expected to consume in a lifetime. It weighs 3.44 tonnes and stands 7 metres high.

To work out its weight, a calculation was made. The total electrical and electronic waste for the UK population (938,000 tonnes in 2003) was divided by the UK population (59,553,000), giving a figure of 15.75 kg per person per year.

Average life expectancy is 78.05 years. A 21-year-old in 2003 will live until 2060. Factoring in an e-waste growth rate of 4 per cent, this person will produce 3.44 tonnes of WEEE in their lifetime. A person born in 2003 will live until 2080 and produce 8.36 tonnes of WEEE. The WEEE Man would have to double its size.

August 23

Posters to download

Display your protest

Create your own art gallery of posters.

Visit the websites listed opposite and any others you can find. Download the posters you consider most effective, print them out (using A3 paper if you can), frame them and hang them up. Email them to your friends. Make and send your own postcards using these designs.

'All posters are public domain unless otherwise noted. Feel free to print them and use the messages for your own posters ... Wage peace my friends.' – extract from the Insta-Protest website.

Sometimes people are spurred into action by some event. The Sharpeville massacres in apartheid South Africa, the Vietnam war, and now the 2003 US-led invasion of Iraq as part of the 'war on terror'. All of these have led to an outpouring of protest.

Society may be divided on the issues, but it can produce great poster art!

There are a large number of websites where you can download, reproduce and distribute some great copyright-free posters that are critical of the Bush-Blair policy on Iraq. Here are some:

- Peaceposters: print or email a poster at: www.peaceposters.org
- Another Poster for Peace: www.anotherposterforpeace.com
- Over My Dead Body, with Iraq posters plus a make-your-own educational toy on the G8: www.overmydeadbody.org
- Community Re-education for the Advancement of Patriotism (or C-R-A-P if you prefer): www.c-r-a-p.org/reeducation.htm
- The Ronald Reagan Home for the Criminally Insane, also featuring a print-your-own $100 Hallibacon bank note: www.insanereagan.com/graphics.shtml
- Insta-Protest – 'In a better world I would have never had to make them. The sooner these posters become unnecessary the better': 64.70.140.219/feb15/
- Adam Nieman's website: www.adamnieman.co.uk/index.html

Design a poster

Add to your collection by designing and printing your own poster. The Insta-Protest website features a 'design-your-own-poster' function.

Cigarette litter

Cigarette butts are a major litter problem in our cities. Almost one in three end up on the streets. Globally, 4.3 trillion cigarette butts are 'littered' every year, and in many rich countries they account for around half of all street litter. In the UK, 200 tonnes of butts are discarded each year. In the USA it's over 250 billion individual butts. In Australia, the smokers of New South Wales discard enough butts to fill seven Olympic-sized swimming pools.

Indoor smoking bans have led to a dramatic increase in 'butt litter'. What's good for our health can be bad for the environment:

- It can take up to twelve years for a cigarette butt to break down.
- Cigarette butts can leach chemicals such as cadmium, lead and arsenic into the water table and the marine environment.

BUTTsOUT is a global campaign on cigarette-butt littering, now active in five countries. Developed by PlanetArk in Australia, its goal is to see smokers taking responsibility for the litter they create, and to develop solutions to the problem of cigarette butts. The campaign seeks to engage smokers and non-smokers alike. But in the end it is only smokers who can stop the problem by changing their behaviour.

Be a smoker's friend

If you want to be nice, buy your friends who smoke a BUTTsOUT funky, reusable, ashtray. Visit the BUTTsOUT website and select from a range of colours.

If you are not prepared to be quite so nice, buy an old tobacco tin (from a junk shop or car boot sale) and fill it with cigarette butts you have collected from the street. A pair of gloves and a face mask might be handy when you're doing this. Wrap up the box nicely and include a flyer from BUTTsOUT. Hey presto, a birthday present for a smoker.

Non-smokers can educate smokers to recognise that butts are litter, and suggest positive alternatives to stubbing them out in the street. BUTTsOUT: www.buttsout.net

Personal portable ashtrays

BUTTsOUT produce a funky, reusable, fire-resistant, personal ashtray that can be used outdoors; 82 per cent of smokers say they would use them because they are easy to operate. They trap most smell and smoke, fit into a pocket or clip onto a belt, and come in a range of colours.

Leeds City Council distributed a customised version as part of a campaign to improve its streets. In Croydon, litter wardens have handed out free personal ashtrays to cigarette litterbugs, and tobacconists are being encouraged to stock them.

August 25

Make an A-B-C

As easy as ...

Get together a small group of people. Decide on the theme and format for your A-B-C.

Choose an Art Director to organise who does what and to create an overall design as well as preparing the artwork for the printer.

Print and distribute it. Decide on the selling price. Look out for possible outlets (such as bookshops, cafès, restaurants), and offer a good discount so that it's in their interest to sell it.

England in Particular, a Common Ground initiative: www.england-in-particular.info

We all tend to take our surroundings for granted. When you have lived or worked in a place for a long time you cease to 'see' it. You stop noticing the architectural details or the natural environment.

Your neighbourhood has evolved over the years. Understanding what makes it different from everywhere else – what makes it very special to you, what gives it a sense of place, what stories are attached to it, and what makes it the great place that it is – is important. It may be a street sign, a shop front, a carving on the brickwork, a tree or the fruit piled high on a market stall that makes you feel that your neighbourhood is special.

Why not celebrate your neighbourhood and raise everybody's awareness of their surroundings at the same time by producing an 'A-B-C': a graphic representation in 26 parts, based on the letters of the alphabet, of what makes your area special.

How to make an A-B-C

Decide the theme of your A-B-C. Will it cover everything, or just focus on one aspect of your neighbourhood in particular? Will it have a purpose? Is it for local interest? For tourists? As part of a local campaign? For citizenship education in schools?

Decide on the format. Your A-B-C could take many forms. Some are made entirely from photographs. Others include illustrations, linocuts, engravings or a mixture of all of these. Some have short captions. Others have longer descriptions.

Identify 26 places, objects or signs, each one linked to or depicting a particular letter of the alphabet. Take photographs of them. Using the pictures and captions, make these into a small booklet or a large poster.

Use your A-B-C simply to show what delights you and what you care about – so that others will begin to see the neighbourhood in the same positive way. Use it as part of a campaign to save the area, or even use it to show what's horrible, abandoned and in need of a bit of tender loving care.

Give blood

It must be a wonderful feeling to save someone's life. Although medical professionals, firefighters, coastguards, experience that satisfaction time and again, it seems beyond the reach of the rest of us. But you too can save a life simply by donating about an hour of your time – and a pint of your blood.

Few of us can predict when we might need a blood transfusion. And if we are lucky enough never to need one, then it is almost certain that our children, our parents, someone we know will need one sometime in the future. Giving blood couldn't be easier. It's quick, simple and safe. And all that most people feel is the satisfaction that they are helping to save lives.

Most people can give blood. If you're generally in good health, between the ages of 17 and 59 and weigh at least 50 kg (7 st 12 lb), you could start giving blood today. And when you do, find out how easy it is to save someone's life. If you are pregnant or have just had a baby, are taking antibiotics, have contracted or think you may have contracted HIV, had malaria, inject drugs, are a hepatitis carrier, then you will not be able to give blood. There are other criteria you have to pass as well, so contact the National Blood Service in advance, and they will send you a simple health-check form to fill in.

When you arrive to give blood someone will go through your health-check form. If they consider that it is safe for you to be a donor, then a drop of blood will be taken from your finger and tested to make sure you're not anaemic. And if you're still okay, then just under a pint of your blood is taken – a procedure that takes about ten minutes.

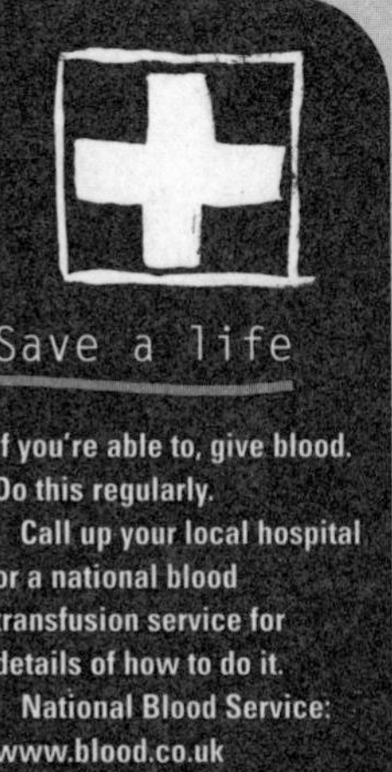

Save a life

If you're able to, give blood. Do this regularly.

Call up your local hospital or a national blood transfusion service for details of how to do it.

National Blood Service: www.blood.co.uk

Helen's story

Helen was premature when she was born and weighed only 1.9 kg. When she was a few weeks old she caught a chest infection and stopped breathing. She had to be put on a ventilator to keep her alive, and be pumped full of antibiotics.

A blood test revealed that she was anaemic, and a blood transfusion was needed. Just a small amount of blood, donated by one of the hospital's support staff, changed her from a pasty white to a healthy pink, and saved her life.

See RED to fight AIDS

RED products

Buy these RED products:

- **Get a Motorola RED mobile phone: a £10 donation and 5 per cent of your bill will go to the Global Fund.**
- **Use the American Express RED card, there is no annual fee: £5 if you use the card in the first month and 1 per cent of what you spend go to the Global Fund (1.25 per cent if you spend £5,000 in a year).**
- **Wear a GAP INSPI(RED) T-shirt, Armani wrap-around sunglasses (as worn by Bono) and Converse mudcloth leisure shoes; part of the cost will go to the Global Fund.**

(PRODUCT) RED: www.joinred.com

The Global Fund: www.theglobalfund.org

AIDS, tuberculosis and malaria are three killer diseases that are ravaging the world, and where the impact is greatest in the poorest countries. These three diseases need eradication or an effective remedy to be found. The Global Fund was established in 2002 to substantially increase resources to do this.

By June 2006, the Global Fund had committed US$5.2 billion to projects in 131 countries. It had provided:

- 544,000 people with treatment for HIV and AIDS
- 5.7 million people with voluntary HIV testing
- 1.43 million people with treatment for tuberculosis
- 7.3 million people treated for malaria
- 11.3 million families with insecticide-treated mosquito nets

(PRODUCT) RED was created by Bono, lead singer of U2, and Bobby Shriver, Chairman of DATA (the Debt AIDS Trade in Africa organisation that Bono set up in 2002) in order to raise awareness and money for the Global Fund by organising joint promotions with some of the world's leading brands. The money raised goes to AIDS projects with an emphasis on helping women and children. It will help prevent mother-to-child transmission of HIV, provide nutritional support to AIDS-affected families and anti-retroviral therapy.

Bono's story

Born in Dublin on 10 May 1960, Paul Hewson was originally nicknamed 'Bono Vox' (good voice) by a friend after a hearing aid advertisement they passed by regularly and because he sang so loudly that he seemed to be singing for the deaf. This was shortened to Bono.

He joined U2 in 1976 in response to an advertisement asking for people to form a band, later becoming lead singer. Bono along with his fellow Irishman Bob Geldof has played a leading role in campaigning for third world debt relief and a better deal for Africa.

Creative commons

Jill is a budding photographer who has put her portfolio online. Someday she might want to charge people for copying her photos. But while she is still trying to build her reputation, she wants people to copy her work as much as possible. Among her favourite photos are some dramatic black-and-white shots of famous skyscrapers.

Jack is making a digital movie about New York City. He wants to include a still photo of the Empire State Building. He searches the internet for 'Empire State Building' and finds a collection of photographic websites. But he isn't sure if the photos are copyrighted or not. He uses a search engine that helps him look for files without copyright notices on them. But he knows that even things without copyright notices can be copyrighted. He worries that if he uses the photos he has found and then posts his movie on the internet, the people who took the photos will find the movie, get upset and sue him.

Creative Commons was set up to make it easier for Jack and Jill to find each other online, and then to develop the creative collaboration they both seek.

Common knowledge

If you've created something that you want to share with the world – a photo, a film, a theory, an equation, a slogan, a recipe, a poem, or some music – put the best of what you've created online at Creative Commons. This will get your work distributed, and you can borrow the works of others.

Help create a 'world bank' of common property for the benefit of all, instead of tying your work up in copyright restrictions which make it difficult or expensive for others to use.

Creative Commons licences: creativecommons.org/license

Creative Commons: creativecommons.org

Fostering collaboration

In 2002, Creative Commons released a set of copyright licences to enable people to dedicate their creative works to the public domain. Their range of licences covers such things as who can use the material for free, whether it can be adapted or has to remain in its original form, whether the licence allows the material to pass to another user under the same conditions (share alike), and the nature of the attribution to the original source. These licences can all be downloaded for free. Creative Commons also wants to increase the amount of source material online, and to make access to that material cheaper and simpler. It provides a space for sharing work and accessing the work of others.

Seed the world

Feed the world

Become a seed donor. Grow plants, allow some to run to seed and donate the seeds to the Kokopelli Seed Foundation. Seeds produced by Kokopelli's seed-grower network are sent all over the world. If you haven't got a garden, then do it in gro-bags on your roof or balcony.

All seeds are welcome: tomatoes, melons, lettuces, beets, carrots, grains, pulses, peppers. Every species will find a home somewhere.

For more details, read Dominique Guillet's book, *The Seeds of Kokopelli.*

Kokopelli's website page devoted to seeds for the developing world: www.kokopelli-seeds.com/third-world.html

It's hard to understand how it feels to live right at the margin, if you have what you need. Having 'nothing' means having absolutely nothing for too many people. There are lots of reasons why 36,000 people are dying of starvation every day, two-thirds of whom are children: war, drought, overpopulation, AIDS, and poverty. Seed shortage is another reason.

The only seeds available to many farmers in some of the poorest countries in the world, where food shortage is chronic, are for varieties of vegetables that do not produce their own seed. There is nothing accidental about this. The varieties, known as F1 hybrids, have been bred to be like it. Who would do something so unnatural? Why, the companies selling the seed, of course. They claim that such varieties produce higher yields, but it locks the farmers into the need to purchase fresh seed each year.

The mission of the Kokopelli Seed Foundation, which started in France and has now spread around the world, is to create a 'Community-Supported Seed Fund' to provide poor farmers with the seeds they need. Anybody can grow and collect seeds. Gardeners and farmers were doing this for thousands of years before the emergence of commercial seed growers.

Become a Kokopelli seed grower

It's not as hard as you might think. Food plants provide plenty of seeds:

- A pumpkin or melon contains hundreds of seeds.
- A tomato contains around 70 seeds.
- A lettuce going to seed may produce up to 10,000 seeds.

A 10 x 10 metre garden is big enough for 150 tomato plants, which would produce 6 kg of seeds. This would be enough to provide 40,000 packets, each containing 30 seeds.

The Kokopelli Seed Foundation will advise you on what to grow and even provide you with starter seeds so that you can start up your 'seed factory'.

Invest in young people

Children living on the streets need to earn money just to survive. Many do this by begging or ragpicking. But it is difficult for them to keep the money they earn safe, and therefore impossible for them to use it to create a better future for themselves. In Delhi, a group of street children started their own bank, called Bal Vikas Bank (Children's Development Bank). It is a place to keep their money safe, it encourages them to save for their future rather than just live from day to day, and it makes loans to older children to help them set up a small business.

The bank gives them a chance to do something safer which will help them earn a better income, and get off the streets. For example, two boys started a mobile tea business. They strapped an urn to the back of a bicycle and sold tea to lines of taxi and rickshaw drivers who were waiting to refuel their vehicles with Compressed Natural Gas.

The amazing thing is that this bank is run entirely by the children. They make the rules, decide the loans, encourage saving and build the membership. The idea is spreading across India, and children's banks are also being started in Afghanistan, Bangladesh, Nepal, Pakistan and Sri Lanka. The children now want to spread the idea across the world.

Offer support

Organise a fundraising event to make a difference to the lives and futures of young people. Set yourself a target of £100. Send all the money you raise to support youth enterprise initiatives, without deducting anything for administration.

Help street children in South Asia set up a children's bank.

Help young people in Kenya become taxi drivers.

Help other young people in other countries set up an enterprise of their own.

The Bal Vikas bank programme: www.childrensdevelopmentbank.org

Child Savings International, an international network of children's banking schemes: www.childsavingsinternational.org

August 30

Taxi driving

A group of seven youths in Kisumu, Kenya, want to become taxi drivers. The 'taxis' are bicycles, which have been converted to include a pillion seat over the rear mudguard. This is an accepted form of transport in the town. As taxi drivers, the boys should be able to earn a decent income. The youths will be offered loans to purchase and modify a bicycle. They will repay the loans out of the money they earn, which will enable more youths to set up in business.

The vegan challenge

Try it for seven days

Will Poutney says: 'I am a serious meat eater ... but I accepted a challenge from a mate and went completely vegan for a week ... I've gone back to eating meat, but going vegan made me think about my choices much more carefully.'

Are you man or woman enough to give up meat? This will mean a change in your lifestyle. It's also a great way to see how meat affects the way you feel. Go vegan or vegetarian for a week, or a month. After that, do what you want. If nothing else, you can say you gave it a go.

A free Vegetarian Starter Kit: www.vegetarianstarterkit.com

30 reasons to go vegetarian: www.goveg.com/feat/chewonthis

A vegetarian is someone who abstains from eating any sort of meat or fish. A vegan doesn't consume or use any animal products at all. People become vegetarian or vegan for different reasons. They may believe it is cruel to kill and eat animals, or that it is a drain on the environment to rear the meat and to dispose of the remains, or simply for health reasons.

Eating a well-balanced diet, free from animal products is good for your health. Here's why:

Fat: Vegan diets are cholesterol-free and low in fat.

Heart disease: Meat-eaters are 50 per cent more likely to develop heart disease than vegetarians.

Impotence: Meat-based diets can lead to impotence, as fat can clog up the arteries going to all your organs, not just to your heart!

Life-threatening illnesses: Cancer, stroke, diabetes, osteoporosis, obesity and other diseases have all been linked to meat and dairy consumption.

Unwanted chemicals: Livestock, poultry and cows are often pumped full of chemicals, hormones and drugs that are absorbed by you when you eat meat.

Toxins in fish: The flesh of fish can accumulate toxins up to 9 million times as concentrated as those in the waters they live in.

What's the beef?

Want some veggie beefcake or cheesecake? 'Lettuce ladies' and 'broccoli boys', dressed in strategically placed vegetables, raise eyebrows and open minds as they travel the USA, educating people about vegetarianism, and serving up delicious veggie food. Apart from all the well-known health benefits of a vegetarian diet, this deliberately non-PC, humorous campaign places an emphasis on the improvement a veggie diet brings to your libido. Choose your favourite pin-up and join PETA (People for the Ethical Treatment of Animals). A signed photo comes with membership: www.peta.com

Waste is a burning issue

The problem of waste is twofold: creating less, and disposing of it in a safe and sustainable way. Most importantly, we must protect human health and the environment from toxic poisoning. Disposal is as important in the developing world as in the industrialised world, the latter exporting waste to the former for disposal where the rules are less stringent.

'We oppose incinerators, landfills, and other end of pipe interventions.' The Global Anti-Incinerator Alliance (GAIA) is an alliance of individuals, non-government organisations and academics working to end incineration and promote waste prevention.

GAIA works on municipal disposal, hazardous waste and medical waste. Each workgroup undertakes projects to prevent incineration and to promote alternatives. GAIA's first global campaign is to stop the World Bank funding incinerators. GAIA says:

'We recognise that our planet's finite resources, fragile biosphere and the health of people and other living beings are endangered by polluting and inefficient production practices and health threatening disposal methods. Our ultimate vision is a just, toxic free world without incineration.'

Stop it going up in smoke

Join in the Global Day of Action.

Here are some actions they suggest:

- **Draw the public's attention to local incinerators, waste facilities and landfills.**
- **Picket government agencies that support or promote 'burn' policies.**
- **Join in the fax and email action to demonstrate public opposition.**

Global Anti-Incinerator Alliance: www.no-burn.org

Recycling fun facts: members.aol.com/ramola15/funfacts.html

How incineration works

The waste is unloaded from a truck into a bunker area, transferred into a hopper and fed into the furnace.

Combustion of the feedstock takes place in the furnace.

Heat recovery cools the exhaust gases; the recovered heat is reused in the incinerator or used to generate more electric power.

A gas cleaning system, with a 'scrubber' to filter out pollutants, and electrostatic precipitator or a fabric 'bag filter' to remove particles and polluting gases.

A fan draws exhaust gases through the system prior to discharge into the air.

Solid waste and water residues are removed. Ash from the furnace falls into a tank forming a highly toxic sludge.

Deal with Islamophobia

Look at muslimyouth.net, produced by young Muslims, an alternative to how the press reports Muslim issues.

Find out about Nasim Ali, who set up Camden United, an antiracist football project in London, and is now, aged 28, Deputy Mayor of Camden.

And Hannah Al-Rashid, a European gold medalist for Pencat Silat, a Malaysian martial art.

Find out about the views of young Muslims on cultural identity, religious observance, the war on terror, and a whole lot more.

muslimyouth.net: www.muslimyouth.net

Muslims in the West

Islamophobia is currently a problem throughout the world. Since 9/11 and the start of the 'War on Terror', there has been a growth in Islamophobia (hatred of Muslims) in North America and Europe.

Young Muslims now feel vulnerable. They feel they might be picked up in a dawn raid, or be imprisoned without having a hearing. They feel that the society they live in wants them to hide their faith and become less visible.

In France, the government passed a law which banned people from wearing religious symbols in state schools. So schoolgirls can't wear a 'Hijab', even if they feel strongly that they should be doing this as a matter of modesty.

Muslims have come to our country and been offered citizenship. Their children have been born and educated here and English is their mother tongue. We will be better able to understand the terrorist threat and what to do about it, if we could better understand how young Muslims see the world.

Best of both worlds?

Here are comments from two young Muslims in the West:

> 'How hard can it be to live as Muslim in the West? To accept that with every tick of the clock, things change. Fashion changes and just as long as none of it clashes with the Islamic rulings on clothing, then we can change with it. Because sometimes we have to. Personally speaking, I like to mix-and-match. I love wearing Indian sequinned tops with English flare-bottom trousers. I like to get the best of both worlds.'

> 'It is clear that the events of 9/11 have had a major impact on the world and on Muslims in particular. And so practising Islam freely in Britain has become a lot harder. This has caused many Muslims to value their religion a lot more and their citizenship a lot less.'

Free software

Free software is a matter of liberty, not price – think of 'free' as in free speech, not as in free beer! When programmers can read, redistribute, and modify the source code for software, so it evolves. People improve it, adapt it and fix the bugs. This can happen much faster than conventional software development, for example the evolution of Microsoft's MS Windows operating system with Linux (free and open source).

Free software provides four kinds of freedom:

- The freedom to run the program, for any purpose (Freedom Zero).
- The freedom to study how the program works, and adapt it (Freedom One).
- The freedom to redistribute copies (Freedom Two).
- The freedom to improve a program, releasing your changes so everyone benefits (Freedom Three).

Access to the source code – 'Open Source' – is a precondition for Freedoms One and Three.

The Free and Open Source Software movement is built on the ideals of collaboration and sharing. It is also enabling computer users in the developing world to access software without having to pay an arm and a leg for it or pirate it.

Software Freedom Day is early in September

Open sources

MS Office has become the standard software package for office use. But try OpenOffice.org

Download Open Office from www.openoffice.org – read the licence conditions. Copy it onto as many CDs as possible. Distribute free to people who could use them.

Software Freedom Day is held each September to promote the idea of Free and Open Source Software: www.softwarefreedomday.org

Free Software Foundation has developed free software, created a Copyleft licensing system, and publishes an online directory of free software: www.gnu.org

Open Source Initiative promotes open source development of software: www.opensource.org

A free software flood

'I'm from Skopje, Macedonia, and Microsoft organised a conference to promote the opening of a Microsoft office in my country. Over 600 IT people attended (managers mostly). This is a lot of people for Macedonia which has 2 million citizens (only 4 per cent have access to the Internet).

Our organisation bought and recorded 1,000 CDs with free software (OpenCD/Knoppix) which we gave out. We called the operation 'Free Software Flood' because it was raining like hell that day and because all the participants where 'flooded' with free open software.'

Free/Libre Software Macedonia

Resources

The Open CD Project has free software to download. www.theopencd.org

International Open Source Network is an initiative of the United Nations Development Programme (UNDP) to bridge the 'digital divide' between rich and poor nations. It has a downloadable user manual for the Linux operating system, www.iosn.net

Free Software Magazine, which is free! www.freesoftwaremagazine.com

Best free anti-virus software, adware/ spyware/ scumware remover, browser, spam filter, software suite etc. Aloke Mullick is a practising surgeon who reviews free software. He circulates an e-newsletter with advice on what works best. Get on his mailing list: acmullick@yahoo.com

Find out more about Mark Shuttleworth at www.africaninspace.com

Software freedom

Ubuntu Linux is a complete desktop Linux operating system, freely available with community and professional support. The Ubuntu Manifesto states that software should be available free of charge, that software tools should be usable by people in their local language and despite any disabilities, and that people should have the freedom to customise and alter their software in whatever way they see fit.

'Ubuntu' is an ancient African word, meaning 'humanity to others'. The Ubuntu Linux distribution brings 'the spirit of humanity to the software world'. Ubuntu is funded by Mark Shuttleworth, a young South African entrepreneur who achieved fame as a space tourist, paying around $20 million to travel on a Russian Soyuz TM-34. Also from South Africa is www.translate.org.za which aims to localise Free and Open Source Software by providing translations in the 11 official South African languages. Translation from English is a key task for bridging the digital divide.

Find out more about Ubuntu from shipit.ubuntu.com and get 1, 5 or 10 CDs free of charge to install and share.

Save a ton of money

While you're enthused by the idea of Free and Open Source Software:

- Change your PC operating system to Linux.
- Use Open Office for computer work.
- Download and use lots of other free software.

Be free. Be open. Save money. Take a stand for sharing on the internet.

Wear a ribbon

Ribbons are used as symbols for promoting awareness, such as the red ribbon for HIV/AIDS awareness. Here are other colours being used, and related weblinks:
Gold Childhood cancer (www.cancerindex.org/ccw)
Grey Asthma/allergies (www.asthma.org.uk); Diabetes (www.diabetes.org.uk); Mental illness (www.mentalhealth.org.uk); Brain tumour (www.cancercenter.com/brain-tumors.htm)
Green Clean environment (www.greenpeace.org); Organ/tissue donation (www.uktransplant.org.uk); Missing children (www.missingkids.co.uk); Leukaemia (www.lrf.org.uk)
Light blue Prostate cancer (www.prostate-cancer.org.uk)
Orange Hunger (www.hungerday.org); Lupus (www.lupusuk.co.uk)
Peach Uterine cancer (www.4woman.gov/faq/cuterine.htm)
Pink Breast cancer (www.breastcancercare.org.uk)
Red HIV/AIDS (www.unaids.org)
White Alzheimer's disease (www.alzheimers.org.uk); Free speech (www.englishpen.org)
And a **Lace** ribbon for Osteoporosis (www.nos.org.uk)

Show you care

Build awareness of different causes in your own school, office, or community by organising a 'Ribbon Week'.

Make a different-coloured ribbon each day of the week, and encourage people to pin them on their dress, shirt or jacket lapel.

Make a poster or leaflet for each 'cause of the day'. Hand these out with the ribbons.

For a list of lots more colours and causes, check out: kiwijewels.com/awareness_colors_and_meanings.htm

How to make a ribbon

1. Cut a 7-cm length of narrow ribbon. Lay it down, the shorter edge on top.
2. Hold down the midpoint with one finger, moving the left end to point downwards at a slight inwards angle.
3. Fold the right end in the same way, so the ribbon crosses itself about 1.5 cm below the fold. Where it crosses itself, glue the top ribbon to the bottom ribbon. Or sew the ribbon at the crossover point, using a thread of the same colour.
4. Pin a safety pin to the back at the crossover point.

September 6

Footballs fairly traded

Buy three

Buy three footballs:
- **Use one to play football with family and friends.**
- **Kick one into a playground (as an unattributable act of generosity).**
- **Donate one to a youth football project in an African slum, where sport has a real role to play in engaging young people. Send it to National Youth Organisation (Bidii Foundation), PO Box 28838, 00200 Nairobi, Kenya.**

Fair Deal Trading in the UK offers three footballs. The 'Premier' (£19.90) and the 'Pro' (£34.80) both conform to FIFA international match standards. The cheapest ball is sold in aid of Stop the Use of Child Soldiers, £12.90. For more information, contact www.fairdealtrading.co.uk

Football production has a reputation for using child labour. This was brought to public attention in the late 1990s. The response of most big companies involved in the trade was to ensure that they could provide a 'no child labour' guarantee. As a result production was concentrated in large factory units and many women lost what had been a good home-based earning opportunity.

The challenge for Fairtrade was to develop a way of producing footballs in the villages whilst ensuring children were not involved in the production process, and that workers receive a fair wage and were covered by health insurance. The $2 'fairtrade premium' provides for this and also supports a micro-credit fund for the families of stitchers to help widen their opportunities for generating income.

How a football is made: The inner structure of a football is made from layers of fabric, which are glued (with latex) onto the outer skin of stitched panels. A design can be screen printed onto the panels. A latex bladder is glued onto one of the panels. A professional ball has an air mattress which helps reduce the time a ball needs to regain its shape after being kicked.

Alive and kicking

Although AIDS is one of the biggest killers in Africa, nine-year-old Alan Majisu has no idea what it is. Living in Karangware, a sprawling Nairobi slum, Alan loves football but misses out because his school lacks equipment. Instead, he plays on the streets with a ball made from plastic bags.

Alive and Kicking was set up by Jim Cogan to revive local production of leather footballs in Africa. The leather is supplied by Bata and stitched by young Kenyans. The footballs carry an AIDS message, and are sold at a small mark-up to schools and community projects. Contact: www.aliveandkicking.org.uk

Campaign for votes at 16

Here are ten reasons for young people to have the vote:

1 Young people suffer a double standard of having adult responsibilities but not rights.
2 Young people pay taxes, live under the law – they should have the vote.
3 Politicians will represent their interests if youth can vote.
4 Young people have a unique perspective.
5 Sixteen is a better age to start voting; 16-year-olds are less mobile than 18-year-olds.
6 Lowering the voting age will increase voter turnout.
7 If we let stupid adults vote, why not let smart youth vote?
8 Young people will vote well.
9 There are no wrong votes.
10 Lowering the voting age will benefit the lives of youth.

Download a petition

If you live in the UK, you can sign the petition for votes at 16 – and get all your friends to sign too.

You can download petition sheets from the Votes at 16 Campaign at: www.votesat16.org.uk

www.youthrights.org/vote10.html

Give young people a say

Women worldwide have fought for the same voting rights as men. Women were granted equal voting rights in 1928 in the UK and in 1920 in the USA. In the UK, it was the suffragettes who led a campaign to get votes for women. Emily Davison gave up her life for the cause; she ran in front of the King's horse in the 1913 Derby and was trampled to death.

Young people are now campaigning to get the voting age lowered to 16. The arguments against this are the same as those used by earlier generations to deny women and the working classes the vote, that they are too innocent of the world and others know what's best for them. Those arguments are as wrong now as they were then.

Save the tiger

Celebrate the tiger

Organise a Tiger Day Festival with a procession, plays, quizzes, games, face painting. Educate people on the issues of habitat conservation.

Never buy tiger products (anything made of tiger skin, or traditional medicines made from tiger parts).

Visit a wildlife sanctuary. This helps provide an economic pressure for tiger conservation.

The Campaign Against Tiger Trading: www.savethetigerfund.org/catt/catt_action.cfm

Global Tiger Patrol, supporting community initiatives to protect the tiger: www.globaltiger patrol.co.uk

Project Tiger India: http://projecttiger.nic.in

India is home to 60 per cent of the world's wild tiger population, but the tiger is under severe pressure from habitat reduction and poaching for Traditional Chinese Medicine. In 1900, there were thought to be 40,000 tigers in India. Today, just 2,000–3,000 remain. There is a distinct threat that the wild tiger could become extinct.

Efforts are being made to save the tiger. Reserves for tigers have been created, and significant financial resources are committed by government and international wildlife agencies to save the tiger.

The focus is on wild tigers. Big cats in cages would never survive if released into the wild. One of the most fascinating facts about the wild tiger is the extremely close bond between the tigress and her cubs. A tiger learns every survival skill from its mother, which can't happen when tigers are fed in cages. If we preserve their habitat, tigers will survive as they are at the top of the food chain. For a viable tiger population, a habitat should possess a good prey base, which in turn depends on an undisturbed forest vegetation. The tiger's survival means the survival of all other species living in its habitat and the preservation of a complex ecosystem.

International Tiger Day is held in the last week of September

Tiger reserves

The first 9 tiger reserves to be established in India were:

- Bandipur in Karnataka
- Corbett in Uttaranchal
- Kanha in Madhya Pradesh
- Manas in Assam
- Melghat in Maharashtra
- Palamau in Jharkhand
- Ranthambhore in Rajasthan
- Similipal in Orissa
- Sunderbans in West Bengal

Find them on a map.

The power of comics

Comics are a powerful medium. Words and pictures combine to tell a story or raise an issue. Comics can be serious or funny. They can stimulate, provoke and be used to urge people to action.

You don't have to be a professional artist to draw a comic strip. World Comics Finland and World Comics India have been running comic workshops with some of the world's poorest people to help them communicate effectively using comics; within their local community or to the wider world. The idea is spreading, and World Comic projects have been active in India, Tanzania, Mozambique, Lebanon, and also in some European countries.

A wallposter comic can be useful. A simple format is two sheets of A4 paper taped together. This provides space for a big headline and four panels, which should be enough to get a message across.

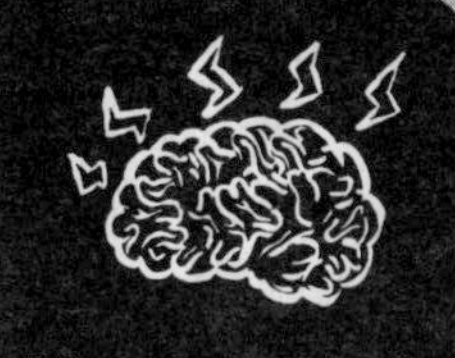

Picture power

Create a wallposter comic about an issue you feel strongly about. The World Comics Finland website gives advice on producing one. You don't need great drawing skill, but a good storyline and characters with which the readers can easily identify.

When you have finished, pin your comic somewhere people can see and read it.

World Comics Finland: www.worldcomics.fi

World Comics India: www.worldcomicsindia.com

September 9

Tips for producing a good comic

Write a very short story that gets your message over.

Four sentences is enough, one for each panel.

You can use captions as well as speech bubbles to show what is going on. Use as few words as possible.

The story should have an interesting beginning, some action and an ending that emphasises the point you want to make.

ZZZ

Draw in pencil first, until you get it right. Then ink it in.
Now your comic is ready for photocopying or printing.

Challenge it

Challenge sexual harassment or just sexist behaviour at the workplace.

Download a postcard from the I Spy Sexism website. Send it to the wrongdoer. Let them know you're watching and will continue to, and will take firm action if their behaviour doesn't change.

Ron Davies's website: www.ex.ac.uk/~RDavies/arian/scandals/behaviour.html

I Spy Sexism at the Third Wave Foundation: www.thirdwavefoundation.org

Sexual harassment and your rights at work, from the Equal Opportunities Commission: www.eoc.org.uk

Sexual harassment

Sexual harassment is 'offensive behaviour of a sexual nature'. It includes sexual innuendo about appearance or sex life; unwelcome physical contact; an unpleasant environment created by sexually explicit pictures being displayed; lewd emails being circulated or employees downloading internet porn.

These are two high-profile cases of 'Sexism in the City'. Both women won out-of-court settlements for alleged sexual harassment. In March 2001, Isabelle Terrillon, a trader working for Nomura Securities in London, alleged that an executive told her to wear short skirts, another asked her to strip and give him a massage, and male colleagues circulated degrading pornographic emails. In July 2004, Elizabeth Weston, a lawyer working with US investment bankers Merrill Lynch in London, alleged that a senior made lewd remarks about her sex life and caused red wine to be spilt down her front.

Ron Davies, author and librarian at Exeter University, has documented big financial scandals on his website, and allegations of sexist harassment made by female executives in the City of London.

Stereotyping

The word 'stereotype' was originally a printing term, and meant a duplicate impression. This developed into a metaphor for an identical idea used in different situations. A 'cliché' has a similar meaning, and also comes from printing; it expressed the sound of molten metal being poured to form the type to be used for printing. Today a 'stereotype' is a simplified image of an individual or a group that is perceived to share certain characteristics. It's often used to portray negative qualities – of women, homosexuals, ethnic and racial groups, old people, young people ...

The 'Don't Stereotype Me!' sticker from 'Bitches, Bimbos and Ballbreakers: The Guerrilla Girls Illustrated Guide to Female Stereotypes'. Download it from: www.guerrillagirls.com

Blow the whistle

Speaking out takes courage. If you witness wrongdoing at work or elsewhere, you must choose whether to remain silent or speak out. It's easier after the event to say that 'we should have spoken out'. But at the time, it can be a huge personal decision.

But whistle-blowing should be approached wisely. Is the wrongdoing substantial enough to warrant the risks of reprisal and the investment of time and resources to expose it? If you do decide to pursue the matter, then you should do so in a planned way, making a commitment to see it through, and not be put off by bureaucracy and stonewalling.

Here's how to blow the whistle:

- Before taking any irreversible steps, talk to your family and close friends.
- Find out if there are other witnesses and if they are upset about the wrongdoing.
- Consider first if you are able to make an effective complaint within the system.
- If you do decide to blow the whistle, decide whether you want to 'go public' or do it anonymously.
- Develop a plan of action, so you are in control of the process.
- Keep a careful record of events as they unfold.
- Identify and copy all supporting documents before anyone has suspicions about you.
- Get the support of potential allies, such as elected officials, journalists, activists and whistleblower networks.
- Do it in your own time and with your own resources, not your employer's.
- Invest funds to get a legal opinion from a competent lawyer.

Tell the truth; never over-egg your charges. You may find yourself and your own life investigated. Make sure you have nothing to hide.

Expose wrongdoing

If you see wrongdoing, have the courage and commitment to speak out.

Public Concern at Work: www.pcaw.co.uk

Government Accountability Project (USA): www.whistleblower.org

National Whistleblower Center (USA): www.whistleblowers.org

Smoke free

Jeffrey Wigand was Vice President, Research and Development at tobacco company Brown and Williamson. He blew the whistle on the industry in 1995, which had been minimising the health issues of cigarette smoking. His activities inspired the Hollywood film *The Insider*: www.jeffreywigand.com

Also watch *Erin Brockovich*, with Julia Roberts as a toxic waste whistleblower on: www.erinbrockovich.com

September 12

Listen here

Tune in to find out about what's happening in the world. Listen to BBC World documentaries on your computer. Go to: www.bbc.co.uk and click on 'Listen to shows you've missed' and then 'World Service'. If you don't have Realplay, you'll be told how to load a free version.

See the latest news in words and pictures at 10x10, where the top 100 words and pictures are shown every hour based on world news: www.tenbyten.org

Sign up to receive e-newsletters from BBC World to alert you to forthcoming programmes: www.bbcworld.com

Radio ga ga

It's not just TV, websites and newspapers that report on world events. Radio is also a great way to find out about current affairs. Listen to programmes on OneWorld Radio: radio.oneworld.net or seek out pirate radio stations for a unique take on the world.

Turn on and tune in

BBC World broadcasts excellent programmes on international development, health, environment, human rights, gender and other global issues. Programmes can be informative and inspiring.

Here are some good sources on what's happening, and what people are doing to change things:

New Internationalist reports on the issues of world poverty and inequality. It focuses attention on the unjust relationships between the powerful and powerless worldwide. It debates and campaigns for radical changes to meet the basic needs of all people: www.newint.org

Resurgence reports on environment and ecology, holistic science, creative living, spiritual well-being and sustainable agriculture, with articles written by theorists, visionaries, activists, scientists and artists: resurgence.gn.apc.org

Utne Reader reprints the best articles from over 2,000 alternative media sources. It contains 'Provocative writing from diverse perspectives ... Insightful analysis of art and media ... Down-to-earth news and resources you can use ... In-depth coverage of compelling people and issues that affect your life ... The best of the alternative media.' Some is available on the web, some you need to subscribe to: www.utne.com

WorkingForChange, a daily journal of progressive news and opinion published by Working Assets. Take action with ActForChange, part of the website: www.workingforchange.com

Third World Network, based in Malaysia, provides a Southern perspective on global issues. It publishes a daily SUNS bulletin, the fortnightly Third World Economics and monthly Third World Resurgence. It also distributes books published in the Third World: www.twnside.org.sg

September 13

Wood-burning stoves

Wood-burning stoves can change lives dramatically. The Escorts Foundation works with the people of the Changa Manga forest area in Punjab, Pakistan. Families there spent hours illegally pillaging the forest for the firewood needed for cooking. It was damaging the forest; out of 760 trees grown per acre, 600 were being stripped for firewood. And cooking meant that the women were spending hours near a smoky stove (a 'chulla'), causing respiratory and eye problems.

A new stove, using less wood, hadn't caught on. This was partly due to the cost of a local blacksmith making the stove's steel chimney. The Foundation modified the design with a simple mud chimney, and altering the stove so it could be made out of local raw materials (measured in units of tins and bottles) and using a cooking-oil drum as a mould.

This stove could be built by anyone anywhere with just mud, straw and clay. The challenge was to demonstrate to village women that it would actually work, and save them time. The stove uses up to 75 per cent less firewood, and can use smaller branches and twigs. Escorts then trained women to become 'chulla mechanics', who would go back to their villages and help other women make stoves. One stove takes a day to make, and costs virtually nothing. So far, 12,000 have been installed, with an average 70 per cent take-up in most of the villages.

Life-changing solutions

Support the Escorts Foundation in this work.

It costs just £2 to build a stove (including all the training and support). Raise a small sum and make a huge impact on people's lives.

The Escorts Foundation won a 2004 Ashden Award for projects bringing renewable energy to local communities in the developing world: www.ashdenawards.org

Benefits of wood-burners

An evaluation has shown the following benefits derived directly from the use of wood-burning stoves:

- Children attend school more regularly.
- Children are cleaner.
- There is a 70 per cent saving in time collecting firewood.
- There is a 50 per cent reduction in the use of firewood, thereby reducing carbon dioxide emissions.

September 14

Persistent pollutants

POP quiz

Understand what POPs are and the danger. Know what you are buying and using. Then reduce (or eliminate) your use of POPs.

For instance don't use toxic insecticides. Careful sanitation, door and window screens, fly swatters, flypapers and fly traps all help reduce the fly population.

From fleas to weeds, factsheets for pesticide-free solutions: www.pesticide.org/factsheets.html

Pesticide Advisor, alternatives at home, in the garden and on humans and pets: www.panna.org/resources/advisor.dv.html

Pesticide Action Network: www.pan-international.org

Fragranced Products Information Network: www.fpinva.org

Health Care without Harm: www.noharm.org

Persistent Organic Pollutants (POPs) are among the most dangerous chemicals ever created. They include many pesticides, industrial chemicals and chemical by-products. POPs break down very slowly in soil, air, water and living organisms, and persist in the environment for a long time. They get into the food chain, and then into the tissues of living creatures, including humans. POPs damage reproduction, the body's development and immune system, and create nerve disorders, cancers and hormone disruption.

Every living organism on earth now carries measurable levels of POPs. The pollutants travel long distances in air and water currents, and don't disperse in high-altitude, low-temperature regions of the globe. Peoples and ecosystems of the Arctic and Antarctic are at high risk. In 2001, a treaty banning the use of POPs was signed by 91 countries. It comes into effect when 50 countries have ratified it.

It's VOCs as well as POPs. Beauty comes at a price. Fragrances are chemicals which vaporise easily, that's why we can smell them. They are added to products to give them a scent or to mask other ingredients. The volatile organic chemicals (VOCs) emitted by fragrance and cleaning products contribute to poor indoor air quality, and are associated with headaches, allergic reactions and other side effects.

Eliminate chemicals

Chemicals in agriculture are not always essential to high productivity. 2,000 Bangladeshi farmers were trained to grow rice without insecticides and with reduced amounts of nitrogen fertiliser. The yield was not affected and the farmers saved money. This scheme is being replicated across the country. Around 12 million farmers could enjoy higher incomes and improved living standards, while creating environmental benefits for everyone. Visit www.irri.org

Promote breastfeeding

A mother has a right to independent information and freedom from pressure from companies. If she bottle feeds she should be aware of the risks and costs. International Baby Food Action Network

Breastfeeding is the best start in life: it is free, safe and protects against infection. Breastfed babies need no other food or drink for about the first six months of life, and have a reduced risk of diabetes, pneumonia, ear infections, and some cancers. It is extremely rare for a woman to be physically unable to breastfeed.

In the developing world, formula milk is expensive. Often mixed with unclean water, it can cause diarrhoea; and may be over-diluted to make it last longer, so leading to malnutrition. Where water is unsafe, UNICEF says babies are 25 times more likely to die if bottle fed, and reversing the decline in breastfeeding could save the lives of 1.5 million infants every year.

Nestlé, the world's largest baby food company, says that it's acting responsibly when it sells formula milk worldwide. 'Breastfeeding is best for babies. Chemist Henri Nestlé stated this in his Treatise on Nutrition soon after founding our company in 1867, and it is still true today. We are committed to ensuring that the best interests of mothers and babies are served by our employees around the world.'

Who is right?

Make up your own mind about breastfeeding. If you think that Nestlé needs to do more, join the boycott and bring pressure to bear:

- **Stop buying Nescafé coffee and other products. Tell your friends and workmates to do the same.**
- **Write to tell Nestlé that you support the boycott.**
- **Present signatures at the Nestlé AGM.**
- **Encourage support from community groups, unions, churches and so on.**
- **Hold a day of action in your community.**

Baby Milk Action, the UK campaign against Nestlé: www.babymilkaction.org/pages/campaign.html

International Baby Food Action Network: www.ibfan.org

For Nestlé's point of view: www.babymilk.nestle.com

Nestlé SA: www.nestle.com

Breast is best

Campaigners say that Nestlé:

- Provides information to mothers which promotes artificial feeding and discourages breastfeeding.
- Donates free samples to health facilities, boosting artificial feeding.
- Gives inducements to health workers for promoting its products.
- Does not provide clear enough warnings on labels of the benefits of breastfeeding and dangers of artificial feeding.

Try to improve

Get together with some neighbours and set up an Eco-Team. Over the next four months try to reduce your environmental impact from energy and water use, household waste, transport and shopping. Take a Green-Score test to measure your improvements.

GreenScore and Eco-Teams are projects of Global Action Plan: www.globalactionplan.org.uk

To set up an Eco-Team, email: ecoteams@globalactionplan.org.uk

To buy green: www.thegreendirectory.co.uk www.greenchoices.org or www.gooshing.co.uk

Green tips for everyday from Greenpeace Canada: www.greenpeace.ca/e/resource/green/everyday.php

Get yourself a greenscore

We can all live a greener, more environmentally sustainable life. But this will mean changing what we buy and how we live.

Some things will require a bit of effort. For example, reducing the number of car journeys we make or not buying cheap air tickets to get away on weekend breaks.

Some will require money: loft insulation, draught excluders, double glazing. Some will be a bit less comfortable until we get used to things: turning down the heating and switching off the lights and TV remote. Some will be a bit more expensive, such as buying organic food and drink. But on the other hand, we will save money in the long run on things such as long-life electric bulbs.

To help you become greener, take the GreenScore test to see how green you are. The questionnaire covers around 80 practical things you can do to become more energy efficient, reduce the impact of your travel, save water, shop sensibly, and reduce, re-use and recycle your rubbish.

How will you score? To take the GreenScore test, register at: www.greenscore.org.uk

Flintham Crusaders

Seven young people from the village of Flintham, aged between 12 and 17, formed a youth Eco-Team. They cajoled their parents into cutting down household waste, composting and saving energy and water. Their efforts saved their families an average of £19.28 per week and reduced the amount of waste going to the landfill by half. Tom, the youngest member of the team, was fired up by his experience. After completing the programme, he decided to expand his hobby of keeping ducks and chickens to provide eggs to sell to villagers. He produces over 200 eggs a week, which he delivers by rollerblade to 'increase the danger level'!

Speak up and speak out

Speak up for what you believe in. It's important for you to have your say. Here are some opportunities for you to get your voice heard:

- At conferences and public meetings you attend, don't just sit there thinking about what you might say. Stand up and say something. Mention who you are (and the organisation you represent). Then say what you need to say clearly and succinctly. And bring along lots of literature to hand out afterwards.
- Call into a phone-in programme with your point of view. They will ask you what you would like to speak about before they let you on air. So make sure that it's something sensible.
- Send your views by phone or email to viewers' and listeners' feedback programmes on TV and radio.
- Write a letter to the editor of your local newspaper.
- Write to your Member of Parliament or Congressperson. They often refer to their postbag, but in actual fact get very little correspondence except through orchestrated campaigns.

Your view may not be heard or be published this time. But try again. And keep trying. See yourself as an expert with something important to say on an important issue. And one day, perhaps, people will be trailing after you to get your point of view.

September 17

Get your voice heard

Make a list of ten things you could do to get your voice heard. Then try to do them all.

Make a diary of what you have done, with the dates and details of each approach. If you get no response, then telephone to ask why. It pays to be assertive.

Get something published or broadcast at least once during the month, if you can.

SpeakersBank provides training to non-profits, local communities and young people to encourage people to Speak Up and Speak Out about the issues they care about. See their publication for young people: Untie Your Tongue, and Get Life Licked! www.speakersbank.co.uk

Tips for public speaking

Breathing: give yourself enough air to get the words out
Eye contact: communicate personally
Straighten up: speak tall
Talk with your hands: gestures reinforce what you're saying
Volume: don't eat your words
Emphatic pauses: to make a point
Slow down: make each syllable count
Tonal variation: for emphasis and impact
Or **B-E-S-T V-E-S-T** for short. Give it your best shot!

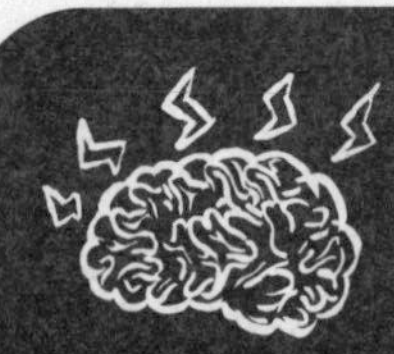

Tell tales

Call your local library, and arrange a time when you can go along and enthral a group of kids. Tell them stories about people who'll inspire them to great things. And why not persuade your local Talk Radio to give you a weekly storytelling slot.

For stories and information about storytelling, tips and networks: www.storynet.org and www.storyteller.net

For spooky stories from the American South: www.themoonlitroad.com

For folktales and legends from all over the UK: www.mysteriousbritain.co.uk

For stories for all ages from all over the world: www.dancingpony productions.com

Storytelling

The imagination is a place all by itself. A separate country. You've heard of the French Nation and the British Nation. Well, this is the Imagi Nation. It's a wonderful place. George Seaton

Storytelling is as old as humanity. 30,000 years ago, hairy, grunting cave dwellers threw down their tools to sit by the fire and share tales about the day's hunt. A millennium ago, entire fiefdoms and kingdoms gathered together to hear their storytellers perform.

Through stories, we are introduced to the rise and fall of empires, the world's great and passionate loves. We taste what it would be like to live in another time in the past or in the future or in another body. Entire cultures and histories have been passed down through the ages through oral tradition. Public libraries, schools, playgroups, day-care centres, women's refuges, after-school clubs and youth centres would all jump at the chance to have you come in and do some storytelling.

Opening sentences

'It was a dark and stormy night ... the rain fell in torrents, except at occasional intervals, when it was checked by a violent gust of wind which swept up the streets (for it is in London that our scene lies), rattling along the housetops, and fiercely agitating the scanty flame of the lamps that struggled against the darkness ...' from *Paul Clifford* by Edward George Bulwer Lytton (1830)

'It was a dark and stormy night ... ' is the most quoted opening of a story. The annual Bulwer Lytton Fiction Contest awards a prize for the worst opening sentence of an imaginary novel. Why not have a go? You might even win! Visit www.bulwer-lytton.com

Declare independence

Change often happens when people band together in common interest. Sometimes it's a planning issue which arouses local hostility, or because an individual feels enough is enough, something must be done.

In 1977, the 120 residents of Freston Road (in London) were threatened with eviction to make way for a giant factory estate. They held a referendum on declaring independence from the UK: 95 per cent were in favour. They applied for membership of the United Nations. Everyone could be a Minister. The Education Minister was a two-year-old, and the Foreign Minister was a dwarf, who wore a T-shirt saying 'Small is Beautiful'. There was no Prime Minister.

Media attention was worldwide. The *Daily Mail* printed a leader column and a report 'from our Foreign Correspondent in Frestonia'. Parties of tourists were shown the borders and received passport stamps. Frestonia applied to join the International Postal Union, printing its own postage stamps. It was eventually rebuilt to a community design with several million pounds of foreign aid from the UK.

Titles for sale

Become part of the joke. Purchase a Hay Hereditary Title:

- **Knight: £25**
- **Baron: £35**
- **Earl: £40**
- **Duke: £50**

You get a Certificate and a Hay Passport. You can attend an Investiture. Bed and Breakfast with the King is £70. Talk to him about declaring independence for your own community.

King of Hay: www.richardbooth.demon.co.uk

Frestonia: www.globalideasbank.org: search on Frestonia

September 19

King of Hay declares independence

The booktrade in Hay-on-Wye was started in 1961 by antiquarian bookseller Richard Booth, who lived nearby. Richard wanted to create a town full of bookshops with an international reputation. On 1 April 1977 he declared 'Home Rule for Hay' and appointed himself King. This started as a joke, but was taken seriously by the media and was given worldwide publicity. Richard's bookshop is now the biggest second-hand bookshop in the world. Hay's population is just 2,000, but there are 30 bookshops and an important annual literary festival. Hay has become the 'book capital of the world'. On Independence Day, the King ennobled two small boys who were in the crowd watching the ceremony. This marked the beginning of the 'Hay Peerage'. Following the success of Hay-on-Wye, twenty other book towns have been created in areas facing economic decline.

Become a net-jetter

During your trip, write a travelogue and take photographs recording your daily experiences and encounters. Email this to everyone you know, or put it on a website or a blog you have created for your trip.

Witness for Peace: www.witnessforpeace.org

Palestine Summer Encounter: http://travel.holylandtrust.org

School for International Training: www.sit.edu/studyabroad/index.html

Broaden your mind

Do you have any idea how many countries there are? There are currently around 190 countries in the world. How many have you seen? Probably not many, so get moving! It might even change your life. Here are some ideas to inspire you:

Witnessing war and peace Why not find out about countries that have experienced war and conflict? But check the security situation first. You can travel independently, but you could also join a peace tour.

From Fiji to Cyprus (and back again) The School for International Training allows you to engage with regional experts and work with local organisations.

Palestine The Palestine Summer Encounter, organised by the Holy Land Trust, aims to create a dialogue between overseas visitors and Palestinians. In two months, you learn Arabic and volunteer with a Palestinian non-profit organisation.

Colombia, Cuba, Mexico, Nicaragua In a Witness for Peace delegation you will address issues of peace, economic justice and sustainable development.

Bosnia Builders for Peace is a summer programme that includes restoration of historic sites damaged during the Bosnian war, plus teaching conversational English at a free summer school.

Travel fund

Get the money together to pay for your trip. Put a big jar on a table just inside your front door. Stick a label on it that reads 'BRAZIL' in big letters, or wherever you'd like to go to. Every time you enter or leave your apartment, 'BRAZIL' will be staring you in the face, reminding you of your plans.

Ask everyone who comes to your home (and that includes you) to put any change in the jar. It doesn't matter whether it's a pound or a penny. It's all going to add up.

As soon as you have enough money, you can pack your passport and take off to see the world.

Campaign for peace

... a day of global ceasefire and non violence devoted to commemorating and strengthening the ideals of peace both within and among all nations and peoples ... the observance and celebration of which makes in strengthening the ideals of peace and alleviating tensions and causes of conflict ... an invitation to all nations and people to honour a cessation of hostilities for the duration of the Day ... and an invitation to all Member States, organisations and individuals to commemorate in an appropriate manner this International Day of Peace. United Nations General Assembly

All over the world people campaign for peace. In 2001 the UN General Assembly made 21 September the International Day of Peace (Resolution 55/282).

The US government spends 25 times as much on the military as it does on overseas aid; the UK spends over eight times as much; France six times as much; Germany and Japan five times as much.

Seven things you can do for World Peace Day:

- Organise your own event. A fast, or a disco with apt music: 'All we are saying is give PEACE a chance'.
- Give £5 and get nine of your friends to do the same. Use the £50 to support a peace initiative.
- If a world leader could do something, what should they do? Write a letter to them with your idea, and send a copy to your local newspaper.
- Be inspired by Gandhi: 'Be the change you wish to see in the world.' If there is one small thing you could do for world peace, go and do it today.
- Measure smiles per hour. Today, World Peace Day, smile at people you meet and people in the street.
- Choose an issue or a region of conflict, try to hear both sides, and keep up to date with breaking news.
- Find a pen pal 'from the other side' and share your thoughts and ideas.

Find out more

International Day of Peace website: www.un.org/events/peaceday

Find out more about the Salt March from: www.saltmarch.org.in

Salt March

In 1930, Gandhi, with 78 followers, led a Salt March to protest the injustices of the British Empire. This became a turning point in India's fight for independence. They walked 241 miles in 24 days from Gandhi's ashram in Ahmedabad to the village of Dandi, where they proceeded to make salt from sea water (illegal at the time, as the British imposed a hefty tax on salt). The Salt March was re-enacted in March and April 2005 to reawaken the people of the world to stand up for peace and non-violence.

Pedestrians have rights

People first

Pay a parking meter for parking time and use it as a venue for a party, using a whole row of parking meters in the busiest area of town at the busiest time of day. Have lots of banners and placards so that everyone knows exactly what you are doing.

The World Carfree Network is a clearing house for information from around the world. Their annual World Carfree Day in September has over 1,500 cities in 40 countries participating: www.worldcarfree.net

Carbusters provides tools for taking on car culture: www.carbusters.org

Also go to carfree.com , a website linked to the book *Car Free Cities*.

We're all pedestrians and many of us also drive cars. As drivers we demand congestion-free roads and the right to drive as we wish; but when we are not in our cars, we hate the traffic noise, the polluted air, the dangerous driving, our streets jam-packed with traffic and parked cars, traffic signs everywhere. And when traffic is banned, we suddenly realise how much nicer our streets could be.

The car culture is not going to suddenly disappear. But we can fight to make it less dominant in our lives and landscapes.

Carbusters is an organisation which campaigns against traffic. They stage events and protests to cut down the use of cars. Carbusters organises pedestrian-crossing actions to contest the fact that cars always get the right of way, even when they are outnumbered by pedestrians. Protesters dress in solid black or white outfits, march into the middle of the road and lie down, creating a human zebra crossing.

Carbusters campaigns

Get hold of an old car, park it in the centre of town and invite people to destroy it. Whilst they are doing this, tell them about the destructiveness of the car.

Offer a free roadside counselling service for all car addicts. Give them the opportunity to undertake the 'Eight-step Programme to a Car-free Life' on the Carbusters website.

Hand out fake parking tickets, designed to look like the real thing, 'fining' drivers for hogging public space or contributing to climate change.

Sticker a car parked on the pavement or in a pedestrian zone with footprint-shaped stickers and leave a note saying: 'Warning, You have parked illegally in a pedestrian area. Next time your car will be walked over.'

Have a healthy heart

World Heart Day takes place at the end of September. It is held in more than 90 countries around the world and receives a great deal of positive publicity. The aim is to increase awareness of heart disease and encourage people to adopt healthier lifestyles. The World Heart Day slogan is 'A Heart for Life'.

Heart disease has become the Number One killer. This is not just in Europe and North America, but across the developing world, especially amongst the middle classes in urban areas. Cardiovascular disease accounts for one in three deaths each year, adding up to 17 million people. Changes in diet, involving the consumption of more pre-prepared and fast foods, which contain too much fat, sugar and salt, is one of the reasons for the growth. Smoking and lack of exercise are also important factors.

The main risk factors for heart disease include: high cholesterol, which furs up the arteries, high blood pressure, smoking, lack of exercise, unhealthy diet, being overweight or obese, drinking too much alcohol, stress, and genetic factors.

Life savers

First start with yourself. Try not to die young. Small changes to your lifestyle can bring big rewards.

Check the shape you're in by going to: www.worldheartday.com/heartforlife/Obesity.asp

If you smoke, stop. It is also important to have a smoke-free environment at work and at home, so make others around you aware of the dangers of passive smoking.

A balanced diet and regular exercise are both important. Even 30 minutes of moderate exercise every day will help.

World Heart Federation: www.worldheart.org

World Heart Day: www.worldheartday.com

Be fit for life

Some ideas for incorporating exercise into your daily routine:

- Get off the bus or train a few stops earlier and walk the rest of the way.
- Go for a walk during the workday break or at lunchtime.
- Take the stairs instead of the lift.
- Go and speak to someone instead of phoning or emailing them.
- Stand while on the phone.
- Schedule exercise time into your diary.
- Why not do salsa or go line dancing, or get together with friends to jog, play football or swim on a regular basis?

Food for thought

Marine action

Favour fish caught by the least wasteful fishing methods. The Marine Conservation Society lists 20 fish not to eat, and 25 fish that you can eat with a clear conscience. Follow this and you will know that you are not contributing (at least for the moment) to the extinction of a particular fish stock.

Campaign for government to give fishermen tradable rights to fish, with new responsibilities for marine conservation. And to create nature reserves in the oceans, where fishing is banned.

Read *Cod* by Mark Kurlansky: how a once abundant fish has come to be nearly extinct.

For information on the Marine Conservation Society and on what not to eat: www.mcsuk.org

While the human population grows, there is a crisis at sea. Nature's limits have been breached by too many fishing vessels catching too many fish, often in extremely wasteful and destructive ways. Over-fishing what is considered a 'free resource' is leading to a catastrophic decline in fish stocks. What was once found in abundance has or will soon become endangered species.

If nothing is done, the oceans will turn into fish deserts. The human communities around the world that depend on fishing will be forced to find alternative livelihoods. There will also be disastrous consequences for marine life.

In his book *The End of the Line*, Charles Clover suggests these actions: The fishing industry fish less, especially the giant trawlers that scoop up everything. Consumers eat less fish, or eat fish less wastefully caught. And we should all know more about how fish are caught and reject fish caught unsustainably.

Fish for the plate

Eat and enjoy these fish

Bream
Brill
Brown crab
Catfish
Clams
Cockles
Coley
Dab
Dover sole
Flounder
Gurnard
Herring
Langoustine
Lemon sole
Lobster
Mackerel
Megrim
Mussels
Oysters
Pollack
Poulting
Red mullet
Scallops
Turbot
Witch

Don't eat these fish

Atlantic cod
Atlantic salmon
Chilean seabass
Dogfish
European hake
European seabass
Grouper
Haddock
Ling
Marlin
Monkfish
North Atlantic halibut
Orange roughy
Shark
Skates and rays
Snapper
Sturgeon
Swordfish
Tuna
Tropical prawns

Make someone smile

Give other people a chance to do good

A priest in Indianapolis preached about kindness. Then she held up 50 envelopes. An anonymous donor had filled each with a $50 bill. Anyone could take one, no strings attached. All the donor asked was that the money be used for good. 'We can make this world a better place,' the preacher told her congregation. Those who picked up the envelopes spent weeks pondering how best to spend the money and make a difference. The donor had trusted them to use the money wisely. They took that trust and passed it on.

Be unexpectedly kind

Why not do something small that will make someone's day?

> *One time when I was at a bookstore, I noticed that the shop assistant was the only person working. She was trying hard to be really pleasant even though she was overwhelmed with waiting customers. I crossed the road and bought a potted plant, walked back to the bookstore, handed the plant to the shop assistant and said, 'I hope your day gets better.' She smiled and said, 'It just did. Thank you so much.'*

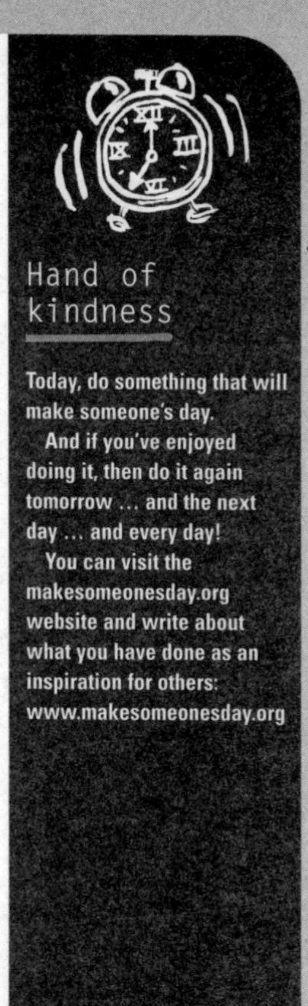

Hand of kindness

Today, do something that will make someone's day.

And if you've enjoyed doing it, then do it again tomorrow … and the next day … and every day!

You can visit the makesomeonesday.org website and write about what you have done as an inspiration for others: www.makesomeonesday.org

Make people feel good

Some other ways to make someone's day:

- Praise people and mean it: 'I saw what you did, and it was really great!', 'You're really important to me' and so on.
- Smile at people as you pass them in the street, when you are sitting opposite them in a subway or when you're stuck in a traffic jam.
- Lend a hand when someone needs it. Help an old person across the street, or someone with a pushchair trying to navigate some steps, or someone with heavy shopping. Do this without them having to ask.

And there are lots and lots of other ways to make someone's day!

September 26

School lunch rethink

Food matters

Download the 'Road Map' to a rethought school lunch from www.ecoliteracy.org/rethinking/rsl-guide.html and send a copy to the Headteacher of your local school. Join a Parents Jury. The Jury, co-ordinated by the Food Commission, works to improve the quality of children's food and drinks. It comprises 1,700 parents with children aged between 2 and 16. If you live outside the UK, set up your own Parents Jury. The Jury was originally called 12 Angry Parents.

Rethinking School Lunch: www.ecoliteracy.org

Feed Me Better: www.feedmebetter.com

Magic Breakfast: www.magicbreakfast.com

Parents Jury: www.parentsjury.org

Children are not eating well enough. Many children today have little understanding of how food is produced, how it gets to our plates and the connection between health and what we eat. School lunch should be seen as being more than just a meal.

Thinking outside the lunch box: Rethinking School Lunch is a programme developed by the Centre for Ecoliteracy in the USA to show that school lunches are more than just providing a plateful of food. Students visit local farms to understand farm economy and see local cottage-scale food production. They can compare this with the global market for foods run by international brands. Students work with kitchen staff to plan healthy meals. They also develop the messages that will persuade their peers to eat more healthily.

The most important meal of the day: Children concentrate less well if they arrive hungry at school in the morning. A quarter of UK children are turning up at school each morning without having had a proper breakfast. Magic Breakfast, the brainchild of Carmel McConnell delivers nutritious bagel breakfasts to children in London schools.

More than just a meal

Jamie Oliver, nicknamed 'The Naked Chef', is a young celebrity chef with his own TV cookery series and string of best-selling books. In 2004, he started a campaign to improve school dinners by showing that something could be done. Working in an area of South London in a TV series broadcast on Channel 4, Jamie developed new menus, worked with school catering staff to prepare more nutritious food within the budget, and persuaded the children to abandon junk food and start eating better. Side effects were: better concentration, better behaviour and better health. When the series ended, Jamie had persuaded the UK government to invest in feeding children better.

Fun lovin' criminals

Arthur Koestler, well-known author of *Darkness at Noon*, had the idea to stimulate prisoners to make creative use of their time inside. Their painting, craft, writing or music could be exhibited, and prizes given. This would help the prisoners' self-development and help prevent re-offending. The Koestler Awards Scheme was introduced into UK prisons in 1961.

Changing Tunes creates music in prisons. Whilst volunteering at Horfield Prison, rock musician Richard Pendlebury realised that there was a pool of musical talent amongst the prisoners. He put together a band of prisoners and began a music class, and he founded Changing Tunes to take his ideas forward.

Changing Tunes operates in six prisons. Each has equipment, and inmates choose the type of music they wish to learn or play; rock, pop, jazz, classical, or gospel. A musician organises the session. There'll often be a target, such as staging a concert or making a CD. Changing Tunes invites ex-prisoners to perform in its concerts, and none of the prisoners with whom it has worked closely have so far re-offended.

September 27

Listen to what they say

Go to www.prisonradio.org.uk and listen to these audio clips:

- **An inmate at Wandsworth reading his own poem.**
- **An atmospheric piece telling the story of former Wandsworth inmate Derek Bentley, the last man in Britain to be hanged.**
- **Is it possible to be happy in prison? A feature originally broadcast on Radio Wanno.**
- **An audio diary made by Mark Williams charting the lead-up to his release.**

Prison Radio: www.prisonradio.org.uk

Wanno be a part

Radio Wanno 999 is the first project of Prison Radio, devised by James Greenshields, Director of Radio for Development. This has four components:

A learning centre Prisoners study for a qualification in media production.

A broadcasting unit Prisoners run a talk-based radio station for the whole prison community.

A CD production unit Producing and distributing material of benefit to prisoners – including advice to new inmates.

A prison outreach project Helping prisoners after their release.

Radio Wanno's output is as varied as the people who produce it. A poignant piece on being a father in prison might sit alongside a comedy about cockroaches, and a dynamic vox pop package in which prisoners talk about the latest exploits of a Premiership football team.

Air pollution

Keep it clean

Wear a face mask whenever you go out into the street. It will protect you from pollution, and also make a statement that the air is not clean enough for people to breathe safely.

Most cycle shops sell face masks because cyclists are at more risk from vehicle pollution. They are in the street, with exhaust fumes all around them, at red traffic lights stationary vehicles pump exhaust fumes into their faces, and physical exertion means that their air intake is increased.

Department of Homeland Security's Ready America website has simple advice for making your own face mask: www.ready.gov/america/clean_air.html

Find out more from the National Society for Clean Air: www.nsca.org.uk

Every time we breathe in, dangerous air pollutants enter our bodies. These can cause eye and throat irritation, and more serious long-term effects such as cancer, and damage to our immune, neurological, reproductive and respiratory systems.

It's not just a city problem. Many air pollutants are dispersed hundreds of miles away from their source. Some remain toxic for a long time, and will affect ponds, streams, fields and forests for many years. Most air pollution is the result of energy consumption: the burning of fossil fuels for electricity or transport.

Pollutants in the air include:

Sulphur dioxide and nitrogen oxides, produced from the burning of fuel, and which cause acid rain.

Carbon monoxide, which is toxic, produced in vehicle emissions.

Particulate matter, such as smoke and vehicle exhausts. Legislation for cleaner air and substantial decreases in the amount of coal being burned have reduced this problem in America and Europe.

Lead, which is produced from a chemical added to petrol to make engines run more smoothly (lead tetra-ethyl); lead-free petrol has become the norm.

Other chemicals in petrol mean that many other pollutants are being released into the atmosphere.

Quality air

This is how one man brought clean air to Delhi. In 1986, environmental lawyer M C Mehta asked India's Supreme Court to protect constitutional rights by directing government to implement the 1981 Air Act in Delhi. In response, the Court pressed Delhi's administration to explain what it was doing to reduce air pollution. In 2002, all public service vehicles (buses, taxis and auto-rickshaws) had to convert to Compressed Natural Gas. The impact on air quality was marked and immediate. Visit www.cseindia.org

Crap towns

Readers of *The Idler* magazine were asked to write short pieces on awful places they knew. 'Crap Towns' is now a regular feature of *The Idler*, and the 50 worst towns are described in a best-selling book.

> Crap Towns *shows that Britain isn't just the place of warm beer, cosy bed and breakfasts and amiable locals that some travel books suggest. With burnt-out cars and housing estates patrolled by rabid dogs and feral kids, Britain can be just as challenging as the places gap year students and 'serious' travellers usually go for their poverty and misery kick.*

Hull, No.1 Crap Town in the UK

> In reality Hull is a sad story of unemployment, teenage pregnancy, heroin addiction, crime, violence, and self-neglect. I was born and brought up in this miserable shit-arsed excuse for a city and could not wait to leave the place. Why? Because my memories of 'home' are of the flat and boring landscape, the endless housing estates, the architecture – which is most flatteringly described as 'municipal' in style – and the narrow minded, bigoted attitudes of the vast majority of the populace. *Iain Robertson, Crap Towns website*

Is your town crap?

Look out for all that's worst. Snarled up traffic, graffiti, vandalism, decaying concrete, rip-off shops, little entertainment, dirty streets, no parks or playgrounds etc.

Write to the local newspaper or contact the local amenity society, to see if local people agree with you and are prepared to help make things better.

Get your town listed on the Crap Towns website. Most are in the UK, but some overseas towns are now beginning to appear.

Make a plan of action for what you are going to do about it. You don't have to put up with living in a Crap Town.

Crap Towns: www.idler.co.uk/crap

Terminology

'Crap' is a slang term for faecal matter, and used to refer to things of poor quality or inaccurate statements. It is a slightly less nasty alternative to the word 'shit', which has a similar meaning. The word crap probably derives from Middle English (c.1440) crappe 'chaff, or grain that has been trodden underfoot in a barn', deriving ultimately from Late Latin crappa, 'chaff' – although according to popular belief crap is thought to be derived from Thomas Crapper, a plumber who popularised the flush toilet from 1861. The flush toilet itself was invented by Sir John Harrington in 1595, which he called the Ajax – not the John.

Diarrhoea prevention

Teach yourself

How to rehydrate a child suffering from diarrhoea:

- **Wash your hands.**
- **Prepare a solution of one teaspoon of salt, eight of sugar and a litre of boiled and cooled drinking water.**
- **Give the child as much of the solution as it needs, in small amounts.**
- **Alternate with other fluids, such as milk and juice.**
- **Continue to give child solids if over four months.**
- **If child is still dehydrated after 24 hours, make up a fresh solution.**
- **If the child vomits, wait ten minutes and give more solution. Vomiting usually stops by itself.**
- **If problems persist, go to a health clinic.**

The Rehydration Project: www.rehydrate.org

How many have had diarrhoea today and how many have died?: www.rehydrate.org/diarrhoea/index.html

Most people will be affected by diarrhoea at some time in their life. But for many, especially babies and children, it can be deadly. Diarrhoea leads to dehydration, the main cause of death. Children are more likely than adults to die, because they become dehydrated more quickly. A drug that will stop the diarrhoea safely within a few hours does not exist. Yet the deaths of more than a million children a year could be prevented by a method that is cheap, safe and so simple it can be learned and used by anybody.

The treatment is Oral Rehydration Therapy, which is effective in most situations. Oral rehydration does not stop diarrhoea, but it does prevent the body from drying up by replacing the water and salts that help it retain water. This gives the body time and strength to do battle with whatever is causing the diarrhoea. ORT consists of salt and glucose. It is extremely cheap, costing as little as 5p per sachet (or you can make your own from these commonly available household ingredients). It does need to be added to clean water, however, which can prove problematic in areas where none is available. No other single medical discovery of the 20th century has the potential to prevent so many deaths at so little cost. It currently saves the lives of around 1 million children a year.

In the developing world:

- 1.8 million people die every year from a diarrhoea-related disease.
- 90 per cent are children under five.
- 88 per cent of diarrhoea-related disease is caused by an unsafe water supply, inadequate sanitation and poor hygiene.
- Better personal hygiene and improved drinking-water supplies would improve things greatly.

Become a philanthropist

Money is sitting in your bank account right now, waiting for you to spend it. It may be collecting interest but only very slowly. It is contributing to the profits of the bank and doing nothing for you. You could be spending it to change the world.

If you could do one thing to make a positive impact on the world, what would it be? Think minuscule, think mammoth, think traditional and think outrageous. If you have a vision, your money could help make that vision come true.

You could leave your money to charity in your will. But why wait? You could do something by yourself. Or you could join with others.

You could join The Funding Network, or you could set up your own network of like-minded philanthropists. Think of one thing that will make a real difference. It could address a problem, an issue or a cause which you care about passionately. This is a chance to put your money where your mouth is.

October 1

Give away your money

Set up your funding network. Find nine friends who would like to join you in giving money away. Agree how much you each will give. It could be a lot or a little. It could be the same amount for everyone, or everyone could give a percentage of their income. You decide.

Then look around for really interesting projects to support. Remember that your money will make much more of a difference by supporting a small initiative or giving direct to a project, than by giving it to a large charity.

The Funding Network: www.thefundingnetwork.org.uk

What a giveaway

The Funding Network is a group of people who meet regularly to give their money away. There are 100 or so active members of the Network, and most give at least £1,000 a year.

Members of the Network also suggest projects to support. This could be a disco run by and for people with learning disabilities, or an international Roma group lobbying for human rights, or a project that is making the Sahara green.

Funding days are held every three or four months, when members meet. Half a dozen selected projects are each given ten minutes to present their case and answer questions. Most come away with at least £5,000 given by those present.

The Funding Network is a chance for like minded people to get together, enjoy themselves, hear about some really interesting ways of changing the world and give away their money.

Conservation holidays

Get packing

Go on a conservation holiday. You will be asked to pay. But it will be a cheap holiday doing something really worthwhile. If you want to go to Albania, Australia, Bulgaria, Canada, Ecuador or around 20 other countries, or just stay in the UK, a BTCV conservation holiday may be just what you need.

Calculate the carbon impact of your air travel in getting there, and plant some trees to compensate.

BTCV conservation holidays: www.btcv.org

Biosphere Expeditions: www.biosphere-expeditions.org

Calculate your carbon emissions at Climate Care: www.co2.org/living/calculator_info/index.cfm

I spent two weeks in Romania on an eco tourism project in the delightful village of Salasu de Sus in the foothills of the Retezat Mountains. We came from England, Wales, New Zealand and even Malaysia to work with a group of local volunteers for a fortnight – and to gain a fascinating insight into a very different way of life. Our first challenge was the construction of a children's playground out of a few large logs. BTCV volunteer

The British Trust for Conservation Volunteers organises conservation holidays which last one to six weeks. Turtle monitoring in Thailand, Greece or Grenada, endangered primate surveys in India, footpath construction in Iceland, wetland management in Hungary; these are just a few of the things you can do. You'll work alongside local people, helping them to protect their environment. You'll do some physical work and get your hands dirty. But in return, the stress and routine of normal life will be replaced by beautiful scenery, a sense of achievement and new friends.

World Habitat Day is the first Monday of October

Survey elephants in Sri Lanka

This is just one of the conservation holidays organised by Biosphere Expeditions. You will survey the forests, jungles, grass plains and water holes around and within the Wasgamuwa National Park for elephants and help to build a database of individual movements and associations. You will interview local villagers outside the Park about elephant crop raiding, and assess any damage done. You will also spend time in tree-hut hides, attempting to observe elephant herds at water holes. All this in an effort to help resolve the conflict between humans and elephants and to gather data to promote the establishment of the first national park in Sri Lanka that crosses climatic zones.

Stay in an earthship

Earthships are solar-powered homes or work spaces. They're built from something that's causing a massive waste problem: used tyres. They work with the planet's natural systems, using the sun's energy and rain to provide heat, power and water. The use of earth-filled car tyres also provides excellent insulation.

Earthship living is autonomous: very cheap and cheerful. Living in an earthship means you don't need to make use of power stations emitting greenhouse gases, or rely on mains water or waste services. Tyres filled with compacted earth are strong, and require a low level of building skills.

At least 240 million tyres are scrapped each year in the USA and 150 million in the European Union. The UK generates 40 million used tyres each year, many of which end up in landfill sites. From time to time tyre fires have started in rubbish tips, releasing noxious fumes into the atmosphere.

But 20,000 new earthships could be built annually out of our used-tyre mountain. Earthships help reduce greenhouse emissions. Cement manufacture causes 10 per cent of greenhouse emissions worldwide. And in the developed world, other building materials create a further 10 per cent of emissions. Energy used in the home for heating, lighting, cooking, cooling contributes 30 per cent of total emissions.

World Space Week is the first week of October

Sustainable holidaying

Have a holiday in an earthship. Earthships were pioneered by Earthship Biotecture, which is based in Taos, New Mexico, USA. They have earthships available for holiday lettings at around $50 per person per night for a party of four. Experience recycled zero-emissions living.

Buy the T-shirt. If you're really committed, they will sell you 'how to' books, plans or even a fully built earthship.

Visit an earthship being built near Brighton by Low Carbon Network. This is an educational resource. They also run two- and four-day courses in earthship building skills.

Earthship Biotecture: www.earthship.com

Low Carbon Network: www.lowcarbon.co.uk

Make use of used tyres

John Dobozy, an Australian inventor, has developed a process by which the greatest amount of value can be extracted from a used tyre, turning it into a number of usable and saleable products, leaving practically no waste, and with the potential to generate around $3 of income per tyre.

Find out more from www.abc.net.au/catalyst/stories/s1185584.htm

October 4

Walk to school

Healthy kids

Three million children, parents, and community leaders from 29 countries around the world do something for International Walk to School Month.

Make sure all your friends and family know about it and participate. Go with them. Dress in fancy dress. Make a large placard with a catchy slogan. You'll be highlighting a major source of pollution and congestion.

International Walk to School Month: www.iwalktoschool.org

The UK Walk to School campaign: www.walktoschool.org.uk

Living Streets runs Walkability Workshops and has information on walking to school: www.livingstreets.org.uk

When I was about 10 years old, I used to walk to school, but was supposed to catch the bus home in the afternoon. My mother never knew that I used to spend the bus fare at the sweet shop. The walking journey home was always more pleasurable knowing that I'd got four fruit salad chews and a couple of sherbet flying saucers for the price of a bus fare. A grown-up, reminiscing

The school run adds considerably to morning rush hour traffic. It causes congestion, pollution and danger outside schools.

Children can walk to school on their own if they're old enough, or with their parents. Or you can organise a 'walking crocodile', parents and children meeting at an agreed point, walking to school together.

There are also crocodiles in the jungle. In Gudalur, in the South India Nilgiri hills, children from tribal settlements in the forests walk together with a community worker two or three kilometres to school each day along forest trails. As a result, more children (and especially more girls) go to school.

October is International Walk to School Month

Use shoe rubber not tyre rubber

Ten reasons for walking to school:

1 Pushchairs park easier than cars.
2 You save money.
3 You cut down on pollution.
4 You see more of your neighbourhood.
5 You meet and make friends on the way.
6 You can chat with your children about this and that.
7 You can put road-safety theory into practice.
8 You're making life easier for those who need to use the road.
9 It can be fun.
10 It keeps you and your children fit.

African school link ups

School link ups are a great way for teachers and pupils to see a different world perspective. It can teach children about the wider world and help them develop into active global citizens. It's an opportunity to make lasting friendships, and also makes the curriculum more interesting and immediate.

Link Community Development pioneers school links between the UK and Africa. It supports over 300 links between schools in the UK and schools in Ghana, South Africa and Uganda. A key aim is to improve the African school, so more children have a better education. Headteachers are provided with training and given help to produce a school development plan.

The school raises some money from its local community. It is then given a grant to spend on one of the priorities in the development plan. The link provides a chance for pupil and teacher exchanges, and for shared educational projects. The UK link school also helps with fundraising and support in kind. If every school in Africa had a link, it would transform education for millions of young Africans.

Learn more

Get your local school linked up. Find out as much as you can about school linking.

Choose a country and find a school that is interested.

Arrange to give a talk in your local school to the students as well as to the teachers.

Link Community Development: www.lcd.org.uk

North-South School Linking, an EU resource: www.schoollinking.net

Windows on the World: a free, easy to use British Council resource for schools and colleges seeking international links: www.wotw.org.uk

School children share their lives

Upper Culunca is a remote rural secondary school in South Africa. The infrastructure of the area is poor: no electricity, no water supply, dirt roads impassable at certain times of the year. Unemployment is around 70 per cent, and people leave to get jobs in the cities. Upper Culunca has three classrooms, as many toilets and a staff room.

Ken Stimpson School near Peterborough has a diverse mix of pupils, and decided to take part in the link-up project. At Ken Stimpson, students did a sponsored run to raise money. Another group, stunned by how little their African peers had to live on, started recycling; and a World Citizenship conference for young people was held. Over £1,000 has been raised in the UK to buy water butts to save rainwater and build two new classrooms. And a school farm is being developed, supported by the Rotary Club.

October 6

For positive messages

Dream about liberating a billboard! Think about what you would write. Billboard Liberation Front offer these tips:

Consider just altering it by adding a symbol, a word, or a thought bubble.

Plan escape routes. Check the site out day and night for activity. How will you reach the billboard safely? Do you need a ladder?

Go up on the billboard prior to your 'alteration'; make sure you feel safe.

Have a ground team to assist you and to alert you to danger.

Billboard Liberation Front: www.billboardliberation.com

Adbusters, a global movement fighting consumerism: www.adbusters.org

Billboard liberation

A can of spray paint, a blithe spirit, and a balmy night are all you really need. The Billboard Liberation Front

When was the last time you read a billboard with a positive message? Corporate giants have enough cash to bombard you with any message they want. Everywhere you look billboards (advertising hoardings) send out complex messages to sell you something. No one spends £20,000 to put up a billboard that just says 'Perform an act of kindness today'.

It's time to turn billboards into a tool for good. As most of us don't have £20,000 to put up our own advertising, groups like the Billboard Liberation Front 'adjust' someone else's message. But you must understand that liberating a billboard is completely illegal, you will get arrested if you are caught.

The opening to the Billboard Liberation Front's manifesto reads:

> In the beginning was the Ad. The Ad was brought to the consumer by the Advertiser. Desire, self worth, self image, ambition, hope; all find their genesis in the Ad. Through the Ad and the intent of the Advertiser we form our ideas and learn the myths that make us into what we are as a people. It is now clear that the Ad holds the most esteemed position in our cosmology.

Not so dumb

'This website is intended for entertainment purposes only. No one involved in the production and hosting of this website encourages any action which would violate state, federal, local or international statutes and treaties. We may be stupid, but we're not dumb.' Extract from the Billboard Liberation Front website Obligatory Disclaimer.

Harmony for humanity

Daniel Pearl was an American journalist working for the *Wall Street Gazette*. In January 2002 he was in Pakistan, investigating the links between fundamentalism and terrorism. He was captured and beheaded. The video of his beheading was circulated by his murderers and shocked the world. His widow, Mariane, told her story in her book, *A Mighty Heart*.

Mariane has now set up the Daniel Pearl Foundation in memory of her late husband. In the spirit of Danny's love of music and commitment to dialogue, she has created Daniel Pearl Music Days which are held during the first ten days of October each year (10 October was Danny's birthday).

Concerts for peace are organised around the world. The number of events has been doubling each year. Tens of thousands have already joined this global community, celebrating the ideals for which Daniel Pearl stood: cross-cultural understanding, mutual respect and tolerance. Small bands of amateur musicians to international stars, drum ensembles to big symphony orchestras have all participated. Over 400 concerts were held in 39 countries in 2004.

Play music for peace

Stand up to hatred and intolerance in the world; play music for peace!

Have some fun. Give fun to others. Organise your own gig for Daniel Pearl Music Day, or persuade your favourite venue to dedicate a performance.

Participation is open to anyone who wishes to promote tolerance, understanding and global harmony. You are not expected to raise funds.

Daniel Pearl Foundation: www.danielpearl.org

For participation guidelines in Daniel Pearl Music Day, please go to: www.music-days.org

Just Vision: www.just vision.org/profile

October 7

Just a vision

Just Vision website presents the stories of Israeli and Palestinian civilians who are working for peace. By the end of 2005, there were 180 such stories. This is a fraction of the Israelis and Palestinians whose peace-related efforts receive too little media attention. There are four criteria for being included. They must be engaged in work involving people on both sides of the Green Line; they must be living permanently in Israel or Palestine; they are pursuing non-violent approaches to peace building; and they are civilians, not elected officials. Just Visionaries include people like Inas Radwan, from Jenin, who organises summer camps in the USA for young Israelis, Palestinians and Americans. And Gershon Baskin, from Jerusalem, founder of IPCRI, an Israeli-Palestinian think tank.

TV needs help

An address that's cool

Get a .tv internet address. It's simple ... and it's cool.

If your email or website address is yourname.tv or yourorganisation.tv, this will look different and it will get you noticed.

To register, go to www.tv and it'll cost you US$50 for one year or as little as US$300 for ten years.

Find out more about Tuvalu by going to www.tuvaluislands.com

Get a 'dot tv' internet address, and support a threatened nation. All internet and web addresses end in a 'suffix': .com .org .biz .gov .coop .net .info, which show the nature of the organisation that is registering (a company, a civil organisation, a business, a government body, a co-operative, etc.). Or .uk .fr .pk .in, which show where the internet address is registered (UK, France, Pakistan, India, etc.). Each country has a different suffix, apart from the USA, the heartland for the developing WorldWideWeb.

Tuvalu, a group of islands in the South Pacific, has .tv as its suffix. This is a real asset for the country, as the letters 'TV' are recognised all over the world as having media glamour. But Tuvalu is so small that it doesn't even have its own TV station. Get a .tv web or email address and contribute to the economy of one of the smallest countries on the planet. The .tv suffix has been leased to the VeriSign corporation under a profit-share agreement with Tuvalu.

But also think about global warming and what you could do to bring the plight of the Tuvaluans to the attention of a gas-guzzling complacent world.

Natural Disaster Reduction Day is the second Wednesday of October

Tuvalu under threat

There are 11,500 Tuvaluans living on nine islands and atolls in the South Pacific with a total area of 26 sq km. The place is remote and really small. The islands are no more than 5 metres above sea level. Global warming and the melting of the polar icecaps, means that the sea is rising. The islands are in danger of disappearing; they get flooded not from waves, but through water bubbling up from the ground, and the flooding is becoming more frequent. Tuvalu is likely to disappear off the face of the earth; it is likely to be either the first or the second victim of global warming.

Send a letter

We've stopped writing letters. We now send emails instead. But finding an email in your inbox is not the same as getting a letter through the post. A letter has a personal touch; and it can be a real pleasure to get a letter which is not a bill or a piece of junk mail. So what can we do to encourage letter writing?

Letter Writing Day is held in Japan in July each year. The Japanese postal service issues a commemorative 80-yen stamp to mark the day. July has traditionally been known as 'Letter Month' in Japan, possibly because 7 July is Star Festival, when people write letters of wishes to their God. Letter Writing Day builds on this tradition.

International Letter Writing Week is held each year in October. This is the date when the Universal Postal Union was founded in order to facilitate international mail. The week encourages worldwide cultural exchange and friendship as a contribution to world peace. The Union organises a letter-writing competition for young people to mark the week. Each year, there is a different theme for the competition. The national postal services promote the competition and choose a national winner. UNESCO then chooses three overall winners. The competition is open to young people under 16. Letters must be between 500 and 1,000 words in length.

Past themes have included 'How to build a better future' (2003), 'My views on human rights' (1998), 'A letter to the person I admire most' (1997), 'How young people can help the children of a country at war' (1993). Themes are not always serious. In 2005, contestants had to write a letter to their favourite fairytale character.

Snail mail

Write two letters. And send them by snail mail.

Letter 1: To all your friends, to say hello or urge them to do more to change the world.

Letter 2: To your Prime Minister or the Secretary-General of the UN, urging them to act for a fairer world.

Universal Postal Union: www.upu.int

Japan Letter Writing Day: www.post.japanpost.jp/english/kitte_hagaki/stamp/tokusyu/2002/0723_letter

Amnesty's advice on letter-writing for campaigners: www.amnesty.org/campaign/letter-guide.html

Red letter

International Letter Writing Week Winner Anuar Yasin, a 13-year-old Ethiopian, won first prize in 2004 for a letter about how young people can help reduce poverty. He stressed that young people can play a pivotal role, and set out a number of actions that all young people could take to combat poverty around them.

Conduct a survey

Download suggested questions from Bullying Online, including an open-ended question for respondents to tell you how the bullying affects them.

Survey school students, or adults, asking them about being bullied at school.

Bullying Online: www.bullying.co.uk

Kidscape: www.kidscape.org.uk

Two Canadian anti-bullying websites: www.bullying.org and www.cyberbullying.ca

The Center for Safe and Responsible Internet Use cyberbullying website: http://cyberbully.org

Bully awareness

Question What do Ms Dynamite, Tom Cruise and David Beckham have in common?
Answer All of them were bullied at school.

Bullying can happen at school, the workplace or within families. It's particularly bad when the bullying is homophobic or racist. If you are being bullied, tell someone, though it may be easier to write a note explaining how you feel. Keep a diary of what's happening, so that you have a record if you need it. If you know someone being bullied, do something to stop it. Anti-bullying websites give information on what to look out for. The Wikipedia encyclopaedia gives these as some examples of bullying:

- Spreading (negative) gossip and rumours.
- Constant criticism for unspecified allegations.
- Taking the victim's possessions or exerting control of their work.
- Making the victim act against their will, with a threat of violence or discipline if they refuse.
- Actually following through with a threat to ensure the victim will comply with all future orders.

Stamp out cyberbullying

Cyberbullying is sending or posting harmful or cruel text or images using the internet or other digital communication devices. Cyber-bullies:

- Send cruel, vicious, and sometimes threatening messages.
- Create websites that ridicule others.
- Break into email accounts and send vicious or embarrassing material.
- Engage someone in instant messaging, trick the person into revealing sensitive personal information, and then forward it to others.
- Take embarrassing pictures of people using a digital phone camera and then send these pictures to others.

The Center for Safe and Responsible Internet Use provides advice and guidance on online cruelty.

The gift of sight

There are an estimated 45 million people in the world who are blind. The majority of these are poor people in the developing world. This year nearly 2 million people will lose their sight. If no action is taken, there will be 75 million blind people by 2020. More than two-thirds of blindness is treatable and preventable; 30 million people could see, if we could address the problem.

Restoration of sight is one of the most cost-effective interventions in health care. It costs surprisingly little to make a blind person see, and it brings enormous benefits to those who are enabled to see again.

'2020 Vision' means perfect sight. 'VISION 2020: The Right to Sight' aims to eliminate needless blindness by the year 2020. This initiative has been jointly launched by the World Health Organisation and the International Agency for the Prevention of Blindness, working with more than 20 international NGOs involved in eye care and the prevention and management of blindness.

World Sight Day is the second Thursday in October

Cost effective

Organisations that run eye camps, setting up a 'production line' for treatment, all need money. Project Orbis (a US agency) and SightSavers (an international agency) seek support. For example:

- **£3 protects 25 villagers from river blindness**
- **£5 buys a lens needed to replace a cataract**
- **£10 treats 8 people suffering from trachoma**
- **£17 restores sight to a cataract sufferer**

Or buy the Gift of Sight from www.goodgifts.org

20/20 Vision: www.v2020.org

SightSavers International: www.sightsavers.org.uk

Project Orbis: www.orbis.org

Main causes of blindness

Corneal blindness caused by malnutrition.

Cataract a clouding of the lens; 100 million people could benefit from a simple operation.

Glaucoma caused through malfunction of the eye's drainage system.

Trachoma an eye infection caused by poor hygiene, transmitted by flies. Trachoma can lead to blindness.

River blindness endemic in Sub-Saharan Africa and parts of South America, can be treated with drugs.

Childhood blindness usually caused by Vitamin A deficiency. There are 1.5 million blind children worldwide.

Retinal detachment due to ageing or accidents.

Refractive error and low vision usually corrected by providing spectacles.

Building a library

Start now

Think of some small part of today's civilisation that particularly fascinates you.

Start photographing it, keeping cuttings of newspaper articles about it, and buying all the books you can find on the subject.

Begin to build up a library. Some time in the future this could become a valuable archive, preserving for future generations knowledge of this special interest of yours.

National Yiddish Book Center: www.yiddishbook center.org

Books document the ideas of a culture and a generation. For example, Jews settled in Calcutta (now known as Kolkata) at the end of the 18th century, and developed a vibrant community with its own culture and lifestyle which was significantly different from Jews in other parts of the world.

Today only a handful of Jews remain in Kolkata, and they are very elderly. Tomorrow their presence will be forgotten, their synagogues abandoned, their graveyards fallen into disrepair. All that will remain will be the memoirs, the genealogies and the cookery books published by this community. And if these are lost, so will all memory of the Jews of Calcutta.

Collecting and preserving books is a way of preserving a heritage. Whether it is the Jews of Calcutta, the antics of the hippies of the 1960s or the early history of the Beatles.

Over a million books recovered

This is how one man saved 1.5 million books and an entire culture from extinction. In 1980, 23-year-old student Aaron Lansky was alarmed that all over North America thousands of Yiddish books that had survived Hitler and Stalin were being thrown away. The older generation was passing on, and their children and grandchildren were unable to read Yiddish.

This was an entire literature from a vibrant Jewish civilisation from central Europe that existed until the Pogroms and the Holocaust led to mass emigration and genocide. If the literature was destroyed, so would be knowledge of the civilisation that created it.

Lansky took a two-year leave of absence from graduate school, rented an unheated factory loft, and issued a public appeal for unwanted and discarded Yiddish books. He has now recovered 1.5 million books and established the National Yiddish Book Center, which translates books and supplies Yiddish books to libraries around the world. Read Lanksy's story – hailed as the 'the greatest cultural rescue effort in Jewish history' – in his book, *Outwitting History.*

Minimise toxic waste

Digital equipment causes toxic waste. Underneath beautifully designed music players and computers are poisonous chemicals like lead, mercury and cadmium that can cause birth defects and disabilities. Every computer manufacturer, every mobile telecoms provider, every digital download system is developing ever-newer products, and this is making the older models obsolete. These are then discarded.

About 40 per cent of heavy metals in landfills comes from electronic equipment discards. Just 1/70th of a teaspoon of mercury is sufficient to contaminate a 7-hectare lake, making the fish unfit to eat. Silicon Valley Toxics Coalition estimates that up to 600 million computers in the USA alone will soon be obsolete. These would create a pile 1.6 km high covering 2 hectares – the same as a 22-storey pile covering the entire 1,275 km^2 of Los Angeles. E-waste is growing three times faster than municipal waste, less than 10 per cent of discarded computers being recycled. Most are either stored in basements and garages, or tossed out with the rubbish.

October 13

At your disposal

Use your computer for as long as possible. Donate your old computer to a charity when you do change.

Find out how to dispose of your computer safely if it's just too old or broken down.

The Computer Take Back campaign: www.computertakeback.com

Silicon Valley Toxics Coalition, calling to account the global electronics industry: www.svtc.org

A letter to Apple

Send a letter to Steve Jobs, CEO of Apple Computer. Jobs has already agreed to take back iPods. This letter, from the Computer Take Back website, could encourage him to do more:

> Recycling iPods at Apple stores is a great thing; but why not go all the way and accept all obsolete Apple products at your retail outlets?
>
> If you can do it with iPods, you can do it with all your products! Old computers like the Apple II, IIe, and the Mac Classic contain toxics like lead, mercury, and cadmium, and end up in landfills or incinerators, polluting our land, air and water.
>
> By offering free recycling for all Apple products, including to those who don't happen to live near an Apple store, you can be the real innovator and green leader I thought you would be.

Grand health challenges

Your targets

Define your challenge. It may be to solve a problem, or to come up with good ideas.

Get some money together. See what you can afford to contribute; badger your friends; write to rich people, big companies, newspapers, telling them about your dream. Ask them to contribute. Set a target, and see if you can better it!

Set up a judging panel (of illustrious people) to decide the winner.

Use websites, blogs and newsgroups to spread the word. If the challenge is interesting and there's a cash prize, then lots of people might reply.

Grand Challenges: www.grandchallengesgh.org

Bill and Melinda Gates Foundation: www.gatesfoundation.org

Most medical research is directed towards diseases of the rich. If similar efforts could be made towards the poor, this could save millions of lives. In 2003, the Bill and Melinda Gates Foundation challenged researchers to come up with solutions for some of the world's major health problems. A number of 'Grand Challenges' were selected from more than 1,000 suggestions to address these goals, including:

- Create childhood vaccines that don't need refrigeration, needles or multiple doses.
- Use the immune system to guide the development of new vaccines for malaria, TB and HIV.
- Find ways of preventing insects from transmitting diseases such as malaria.
- Grow more nutritious staple crops to combat malnutrition.
- Discover ways to prevent drug resistance.
- Develop methods of treating latent and chronic infections such as TB.
- More accurately diagnose and track disease in poor countries, where sophisticated laboratories or reliable record keeping systems are not available.

In 2005, the Foundation gave $436 million for 43 projects.

Crops play a part in malnutrition

Many people's diet consists of a single 'staple food', which in many cases doesn't meet nutritional requirements:

Cassava A starchy root crop, it's a staple for more than 250 million Africans. Providing less than 30 per cent of protein for a healthy diet, it can be toxic if not prepared properly.

Rice The primary source of food for more than half the world's population, but it is deficient in many essential micronutrients.

Sorghum More than 300 million people in arid regions of Africa rely on sorghum, but it is low on essential nutrients and difficult to digest.

World-changing women

Did you know that women:

- Produce 60–80 per cent of basic foodstuffs in Sub-Saharan Africa and the Caribbean.
- Undertake over 50 per cent of the labour involved in rice cultivation in Asia and perform 30 per cent of the agricultural work in industrialised countries.
- Head 60 per cent of households in parts of Africa.
- Meet 90 per cent of household water and fuel needs in Africa.
- Process 100 per cent of household food in Africa.
- Contribute $15-trillion-worth of unpaid work in the home and the community.

But that:

- Women don't have equality with men in any country.
- 866 million women live below the poverty line; two-thirds of all poor people.
- 75 per cent of all refugees (20 million) are women.
- Two-thirds of illiterate adults are women.
- 86 million girls are not in school.
- Women earn three-quarters of the pay of men for the same work, outside the agricultural sector.
- In the 20th century, only 24 women were elected heads of state or government.
- Only 7 of 185 high-rank UN diplomats are women.

A force for development

Take part in Women's Rural Development Day. Reflect on and learn from the extraordinary contributions that women are making.

Read about the winners of the Prize for Women's Creativity in Rural Life, and what they have achieved. Select some favourite stories. Tell other people about their achievements.

Women's Creativity in Rural Life: www.woman.ch/women/1-laureates.asp

Women making a difference

Amina Bio Yau Bio Nigan from Gomparu, Benin, created her own micro-enterprise: transforming local produce into syrups, jams and cosmetics, selling at affordable prices. Her products are now well known and even sold in neighbouring countries.

Betty Makoni from Harare, Zimbabwe teaches English. Most of her girl students have been sexually abused so she created a club where they could encourage each other to sue the guilty. Betty's 'Girl Child Network' now consists of 166 clubs representing more than 3,000 girls.

Feed the world

Fight global hunger

Download the World Food Programme's video game, 'Food Force'. Play and enjoy it. Distribute copies. You will learn about the problems of hunger and the difficulties of delivering food aid. There are six missions to complete.

Go to the FightHunger site. Click and trigger a 19-cent donation, which is the cost of feeding one child for one day.

Food Force: www.food-force.com

FightHunger: www.fighthunger.org

Facts about hunger: www.bread.org/learn/hunger-basics

The good news: progress is being made on the war on hunger. The number of hungry people dropped from 959 million in 1970 to 791 million in 1997. **The bad news:** between 1995 and 2005, the number increased by almost 4 million a year. In 2002, there were 852 million underfed people (one in seven of the world's population): 815 million in developing countries; 28 million in transition countries; and 9 million in industrialised countries.

Hunger is the main health risk worldwide. Its impact is greater than AIDS, malaria and TB combined. The hunger hot spots in the world are: Haiti, West Sudan (Darfur), Afghanistan, North Korea, Colombia, Democratic Republic of Congo, Bangladesh, Nicaragua. The main reason is poverty; war and natural disaster account for 8 per cent of the problem. Causes include overpopulation and land degradation; population movements; drought; floods; locusts; severe temperature; natural disasters; man-made emergencies. The UN World Food Programme gives aid to refugees in emergencies, improves the nutrition of vulnerable people and helps build infrastructures through food for work programmes.

What is hunger?

Hunger a signal that the body is running short of food.

Undernourishment food intake does not provide enough calories to meet the body's minimum needs. This results in chronic hunger.

Malnutrition food intake is insufficient to support natural bodily functions such as growth, pregnancy, lactation, and resistance to and recovery from disease.

Wasting substantial weight loss usually associated with starvation or disease.

Stunting shortness for age, which indicates chronic malnutrition.

Underweight a low weight compared with a well-nourished, healthy person of the same age.

Reaching the aid target

When people tell you that aid and debt relief don't work, you say that what doesn't work is doing nothing. Gordon Brown, UK Chancellor

In 1970, rich nations promised 0.7 per cent of their gross national income for development. The intention was to raise the level to 1 per cent. By 2003, only six of 19 OECD countries had managed to achieve more than half the 0.7 per cent target. The USA was giving just 0.15 per cent, the UK 0.34 per cent. But Sweden, Netherlands, Luxembourg, Denmark and Norway were all exceeding 0.7 per cent. In 2005, a pledge was made by the European Union that member states would achieve 0.56 per cent by 2010, and reach the 0.7 per cent target by 2015. But this is too little and too late.

The Millennium Goals were agreed by the international community in 2000 to address poverty, hunger, universal primary education, health care, access to clean water and proper sanitation; all problems that the people of the rich world do not have to face, but which are part of the daily struggle for most of the people living in the poor world.

An immediate annual injection of at least $50 billion per year is required. This figure would ensure progress towards the Millennium Development Goals. For the goals to be met, $94 billion a year is needed.

Name and shame

Build on the Make Poverty History campaign and Live8 (July 2005), when 2 billion people listened to concerts aimed at raising awareness of global poverty.

Shame your government into moving towards the 0.7 per cent commitment by setting up your own 0.7 per cent campaign.

Pledge to give 0.7 per cent of your income, and use the Pledge Bank to challenge others to join with you: www.pledgebank.com

Send your cheque to the International Development Minister saying you are giving them 0.7 per cent of your income as a voluntary contribution to help them address poverty.

Global Call to Action Against Poverty: www.whiteband.org

Organisation for Economic Co-operation and Development (OECD): www.oecd.org

Living on less than $1 a day

Whilst you drink a cappuccino at Starbucks, consider that one sixth of the world's population live on a dollar a day.

Meanwhile, every cow in the European Union (one of which will have made the frothy milk for your coffee) receives a subsidy of more than $2 per day – which is more than the income of half the world's population.

Increasing awareness

Participate in this global water monitoring initiative. Not just this year, but next year too.

Order a water monitoring kit. Go out and measure the water quality of all the lakes, rivers, streams and estuaries near you.

Water on the Web, all you need to know: www.waterontheweb.org

World Water Monitoring Day: www.worldwatermonitoringday.org

Young Water Action Team: www.ywat.org

Water monitoring

Millennium Development Goal 7 pledges to ensure environmental sustainability. One of its targets by 2015 is to halve the proportion of people lacking access to clean water and sanitation. Water monitoring, providing data on the world's water resources, is essential if progress to this goal is to be measured. A water monitoring kit costs $13 plus shipping. This includes everything you need plus a step-by-step guide to using the kit. Each kit includes one set of hardware and enough pH and dissolved oxygen tablets to perform 50 tests. The kit is suitable for all ages, but a large group will require more than one kit.

Annual World Water Monitoring Day was created with the following aims:

- To promote the importance of water monitoring.
- To connect people with efforts to protect local watersheds, and get them involved in doing this.
- To monitor the health of each watershed.

On 18 October, people all over the world go out and test four key indicators of water quality:

- Temperature
- Acidity (pH)
- Dissolved oxygen
- Turbidity (how clear the water is, the amount of suspended particles)

They assess the health of local rivers, lakes, estuaries and other waterbodies. Everyone is invited to join in.

The Young Water Action Team

YWAT is a network of young water professionals, activists and students, aged 18 to 30. Their mission is to increase awareness and commitment of young people to water-related issues. There are members in more than 40 countries. If you are in the right age range, and interested in helping tackle problems regarding water, sanitation and hygiene, join YWAT.

October 19

Go on a pilgrimage

We went into the depth of the bush in Highgate Cemetery. When the highest tombstone came into view, we saw the familiar statue: an amiable old man, wise scholar, fearless fighter and giant who predicted and created a new world. On the tombstone was inscribed: 'Proletarians of the World, Unite!' Xue Baosheng

Karl Marx, founder of communism and author of *Das Kapital*, is buried in Highgate Cemetery, North London. Pilgrims from all over the world come to visit his grave. The idea of pilgrimage is found in almost every religion. The 'In the Steps of the Magi' tour organised by the Holy Land Trust aims to develop better understanding between people from different regions, with first-hand opportunities to explore the culture of the Middle East. The journey begins near Jerash in Jordan, ending in Bethlehem and visiting Petra, Jericho, Jerusalem, Hebron, Nazareth and Ramallah. Travel is by car, camel and walking – so allowing for good interaction with local people and communities.

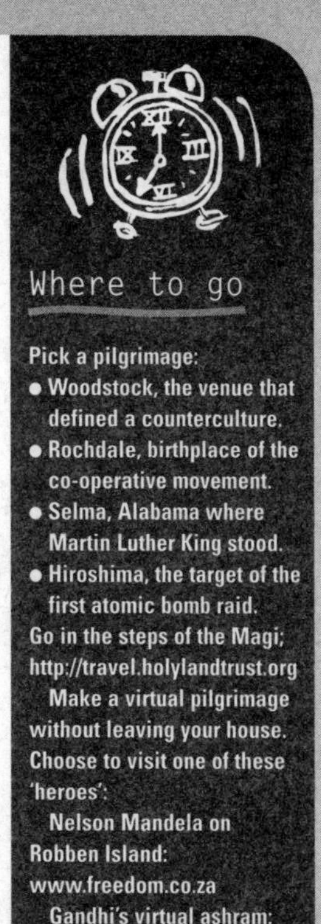

Where to go

Pick a pilgrimage:

- **Woodstock, the venue that defined a counterculture.**
- **Rochdale, birthplace of the co-operative movement.**
- **Selma, Alabama where Martin Luther King stood.**
- **Hiroshima, the target of the first atomic bomb raid.**

Go in the steps of the Magi; http://travel.holylandtrust.org

Make a virtual pilgrimage without leaving your house. Choose to visit one of these 'heroes':

Nelson Mandela on Robben Island: www.freedom.co.za

Gandhi's virtual ashram: www.nuvs.com/ashram

Karl Marx in Highgate: www.redrocks.net/travel/london/image23.html

In the Buddha's footsteps

Shantum Seth is an advisor to the UN Development Programme on volunteering and livelihoods, and is also involved in Ahimsa Trust working on peace and development. Shantum is a Buddhist: 'In the footsteps of the Buddha provides an opportunity to explore areas that few tourists visit and to understand some of the structures and subtleties of Indian life. We go for country walks and visit villages that have changed little since the Buddha's time 2,500 years ago. We visit schools, stop at mango groves for picnics, take a boat ride along the Ganges and even shop for silk! We go at a slower pace than tourists usually do, which allows us to be mindful, have discussions and time for ourselves. At each of the sacred sites I tell stories of the Buddha's life and teachings'. Visit travel.vsnl.com/footstepsofbuddha/shantum.htm

Opportunity to learn

Help Room to Read provide communities with schools and literacy.

Go to the website. See a slide show about their work.

Adopt a project. Raise money to help a community build a school or library. It's an achievable target. And you'll be proud of having done something really worthwhile.

Become a virtual volunteer, anything from website development to speaking at local schools.

Room to Read: www.roomtoread.org

Make room to read

World change starts with educated children. John Wood, Room to Read

School is unaffordable in many parts of the world, where people survive on less than a dollar a day. Even if there's a school nearby, some children may be two hours' walk away, and there may not be a teacher in attendance. Or the child may have to look after the family or work in the fields. Over 100 million school-age children are not in primary school.

The situation is worst for girls, often the last in line when it comes to allocating family resources. She may be looking after younger children in the family, doing housework and fetching water; and in some societies she will get married whilst still very young.

Room to Read creates educational opportunity in Asia, building schools and libraries. Villages raise part of the overall expenditure via donated land, labour, materials and cash. In just four years, Room to Read:

- Helped over 510,000 children.
- Built 110 schools and 1,475 libraries.
- Published 33 children's books in local languages.
- Donated 300,000 new books.
- Established 48 computer and language labs.
- Funded 975 long-term scholarships.

School building

The story of two young girls:

- Eight-year-old Karpali in Tennessee organised a read-a-thon, which raised over $6,000 for Room to Read to build a school in Nepal.
- Eight-year-old Renu lives in Phutung Village in Nepal. She wants to become a doctor – a big ambition for a daughter of subsistence farmers. When her parents could no longer afford school fees, Room to Read provided a scholarship. Now Renu's goal of becoming a doctor is back on track.

Free Nepalese children

When most people think of Nepal, they think of trekking and Mount Everest. They don't picture thousands of young people who are ignored and ostracised from society. Nepal is a land of extremes, a land where there is tremendous natural beauty alongside grinding poverty. The south of the country is just above sea level and in the north you will find the highest mountain in the world. If you cannot visit Everest for yourself, then why not build your very own Mount Everest to help the young people of Nepal have a better future?

The Esther Benjamins Trust was started by Philip Holmes in memory of his first wife. It is a small organisation working with Nepali children who have been trafficked across the border into India to work as performers in travelling circuses.

Aim high

Create a mountain for the Esther Benjamins Trust. Build as high a mountain as you can, using whatever items you like and stuck together with glue, tape or pins. Ask friends to sponsor you, paying an agreed amount per item. Turn the idea into a competition at work or school, with prizes for the highest or the one made from most items.

Send the Trust photos of your mountains, together with the money you raise. Young people in Nepal will thank you for your efforts.

Esther Benjamins Trust: www.ebtrust.org.uk

Rescuing child slaves in circuses

Circus children are denied the most basic rights, suffering physical and often sexual abuse. They are kept in wretched conditions, and given little food and rest. They have no schooling and minimal (if any) remuneration. They can work 18 hours a day, rehearsing and performing difficult and often dangerous acts. They are effectively kept as prisoners. Many lose contact with their family.

The Esther Benjamins Trust Circus Children Project began with an undercover survey in 2002, which revealed more than 200 children working in 29 Indian circuses. Most were Nepali, 82 per cent were girls, some as young as five. All the children wanted to go home, but were bound to the circuses by illegal contracts of up to ten years' duration.

The project aims to get the use of children in Indian circuses made illegal by 2007. It retrieves children by engaging with circus owners or via direct action. The Esther Benjamins Trust provides education, work skills and emotional support for the rescued children.

You can make a difference

Register as an official participant for Make A Difference Day. Or you can just do something independently.

Do something big or small, with lots of people, by yourself or with a friend; such as picking up the litter in your street, planting a few flowers around the base of a tree or helping old people across a busy road.

In the UK: www.csv.org.uk/Campaigns

In the USA: www.usaweekend.com/diffday

Go Mad in October

Make A Difference Day started in the USA in 1992 with a simple idea: 'Put your own cares on hold for one day to do something for someone else or for your local community.' It is the USA's largest single day of volunteering, with 3 million people doing their bit. It has been copied successfully in the UK, and other countries are now beginning to do it.

Make a Difference Day is always the fourth Saturday in October. But if you can't make that day, just do something that week or that weekend. For example, after a drug-related murder, young people on a Sheffield housing estate wanted to prove that they were not all 'vandals' and 'druggies.' The young volunteers created an inter-generational book, profiling children's and grandparents' experiences, in order to bring the young and older people of the estate closer together.

And disabled members from a Surrey-based charity, Reach Out Youth and Disabilities, joined forces with local police to renovate the house of a fellow volunteer and her disabled daughter, while they were away on holiday. They laid a new carpet, carried out repairs, and spring-cleaned the house. They also revamped the exterior, paving and landscaping the garden, laying a new lawn and installing a water feature.

Best in show

Cinnamon Trust held a 'Fun Dog Show' for Make a Difference Day 2003. It attracted 200 people and 71 dogs. The six categories in the show included 'waggiest tail', 'prettiest bitch' and 'most appealing eyes.' Organiser Pat Sanderson said: 'The event was great fun. The dogs got a lot of attention and the phone hasn't stopped ringing since, with people wanting to find out more about our organisation. We've already recruited half a dozen new volunteers!'

Sleep rough

There is no single reason why children run away from home. It may be because of abuse, loneliness, feelings of failure or low self-worth. According to ChildLine, the free helpline for children in distress: 'Many of the children and young people who call us about running away or being homeless have argued with their families; most desperately want to re-establish good communication, and get on again with their parents and siblings.' Others may have been released from child-care institutions with nobody they can turn to.

In the UK more than 100 children and young people run away from home every day. That is 35,000 each year, according to estimates from The Children's Society. Most go on the streets because there is nowhere else to go. Street life then lures them into crime, drugs and prostitution.

Most of us will never experience homelessness. If we could understand it better, we might deal with it more effectively. MuslimYouth.Net devised a project for young people to experience homelessness (under controlled conditions) and report on it.

Try to end homelessness

Organise your own homeless experience. Sleep out with limited funds for as long as you dare.

Get a friend to photograph you. Write up a record of your experience.

You must think about your personal safety before you embark on this.

The MuslimYouth.Net online magazine for young Muslims: www.musliyouth.net

October 23

Two days of street life

In March 2005 a group of six young people took part in the 2 DAYZ OF STREET LIFE project. Each participant was given £3, which had to last them two days (the duration of the event). The following were not allowed:

- Additional funds or credit/debit cards.
- Mobile phones or similar equipment.
- A change of clothes or personal hygiene items (like toothbrush or soap).
- Sleeping bags or other bedding.

They could only contact family and friends through a payphone (paid out of their spending money), and all food had to be bought from their allocated money.

The group was asked to keep in contact with a Project Manager during the two days. Participants were photographed and videoed discreetly. They had to submit a detailed diary, which was published on the MuslimYouth.Net website.

Solve world poverty

Organise a 'Penalty Shoot Out'. Invite your friends along, Get them to pay a fee for each kick. Give it to solve world poverty:

- **Players aim at eight hoops hung from a crossbar, one for each Millennium Goal.**
- **When someone 'scores' play stops for a discussion of the relevant Goal.**

Millennium Development Goals: www.development goals.org

The Millennium Campaign: www.millennium campaign.org

Global Call to Action Against Poverty: www.white band.org

Voice activation

The Millennium Campaign aims to ensure the eight goals are met. A number of celebrities have dedicated their support for the cause; actors like Angelina Jolie and Richard Gere, and singer Shakira have joined the 'Only with Your Voice' campaign and spoken out on these issues.

The Millennium goals

The world community came together in 2000 to agree a plan to solve world poverty. They would work together to achieve eight goals by the year 2015. They set themselves 18 targets, so that they could measure their success.

The Eight Millennium Goals are:

1. Extreme poverty and hunger must be halved. Halve the number of people living on less than $1 a day, and the number who suffer from hunger from the 1990 level.
2. Universal primary education must be achieved. All boys and girls must have proper schooling at primary level.
3. Promote gender equality and empower women. Eliminate gender disparities at all levels of education by 2015.
4. Child mortality must be reduced by two-thirds. Reduce the under-five mortality rate by two-thirds from the 1990 level.
5. Maternal mortality ratio must be reduced by three-quarters. Reduce the maternal mortality rate by three-quarters (from the 1990 level).
6. The spread of HIV/AIDS and malaria must be halted. Halt and begin to reverse the incidence of HIV/AIDS, malaria and other major diseases.
7. Environmental sustainability must be ensured. Reverse the loss of environmental resources. Halve the proportion of people who lack access to clean water and proper sanitation. Improve the lives of at least 100 million slum dwellers.
8. A global partnership for development must be developed. Rich and poor countries must work together. All rich countries should increase their development aid to 0.7 per cent as a minimum. There must be equitable rules of trade. Heavily indebted poor countries should be helped.

War on the arms trade

I watched a Hawk attack a village in the mountains. It used its machine guns and dropped incendiary bombs ... They have a terrible sound when they are coming in to bomb, like a voice wailing ... They fly in low ... and attack civilians, because the people hiding in the mountains are civilians. Four of my cousins were killed in Hawk attacks near Los Palos. Jose Gusmao, refugee from East Timor

Since the 1970s Indonesia has waged a brutal war in East Timor, involving bombings, arbitrary arrests, torture, kidnapping, sexual abuse and extra-judicial killings. Since 1994, over half of Indonesia's weapons have come from the UK. These have included the Hawk jets described by Jose Gusmao, and British Scorpion tanks used in attacks on demonstrations in 1998, which killed peaceful protesters. These are just two examples of the impact of the arms trade which fuels wars and consumes vast amounts of money.

Money spent on arms is money not being spent on development. In 2004, wealthy countries sold arms worth US$22 billion to the developing world. Half of this would enable countries in Africa, Asia, the Middle East, and Latin America to put every child in primary school. The deadly trade continues via massive government support to the arms industry, providing large financial subsidies, promoting arms sales abroad and watering down export controls.

The Campaign Against Arms Trade suggests three ways of reducing the arms trade:

- Genuine export controls, putting human rights, development and an end to conflict before arms company profits.
- Ending government subsidies to the arms industry.
- Converting arms production to civilian industries.

Disarmament Week is last week of October

October 25

A deadly trade

Stopping the supply of arms in conflict zones and to dubious regimes should be a part of the ethical dimension to any country's foreign policy. Write to your MP asking that she or he presses the Government to end arms export subsidies.

The next time a newspaper reports a massive arms deal, write to the editor pointing out the potential suffering to the recipient country.

Get involved in campaigning for an end to the deadly trade in weapons – join a local CAAT group in your area.

Campaign Against Arms Trade: www.caat.org.uk

Power play

The major exporters of arms are all wealthy countries.

In 2004 the value of the arms being exported was:

USA	$18.6 billion
Russia	$4.6 billion
France	$4.4 billion
UK	$1.9 billion

October 26

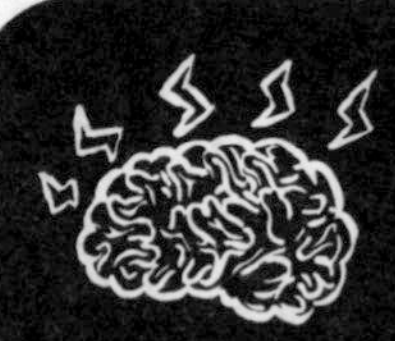

Invent a word

Invent a new word for a new idea or innovation. That's the easy bit. Now try to get it in the Wiktionary. It's a free online dictionary of words in every language, including definitions and data on origins and pronunciation. It is a companion to the Wikipedia encyclopaedia. To get in, a word needs to satisfy at least one of the following criteria:

- **It is in widespread use.**
- **It has been used in a well-known work.**
- **Common usage of the word has been confirmed in a reputable work.**
- **It has been used in at least three recorded instances over a period of at least a year in publicly available written texts or in audio-visual productions.**

If your word qualifies, write the Wiktionary entry for it. Wiktionary: en.wiktionary.org

McSweeney, publishers of Future Dictionary: www.mcsweeneys.net

Words for the future

New words and phrases are added to our vocabulary every day. As society evolves, as new technologies are developed, as new ideas become current, so new words and phrases are created and existing words and phrases acquire new meanings. For example:

Spam, once a brand of canned meat, is now used to describe junk email.

Bootylicious, an amalgamation of beautiful or rather 'bootiful' and delicious.

Nuke and **Mutual Assured Destruction** (MAD), part of Cold War speak.

Text messaging and **ringtone** are part of our mobile phone society.

The 'Future Dictionary of America' lists words compiled in 2004. Intended to be read as though it was produced 30 years in the future, and to reflect the social and political issues of our times, the Dictionary comes with The Future Soundtrack of America, a musical expression of current policies. Nearly 200 contributors, mostly famous writers, have invented words. For example:

Wolfowish Hoping for that which is highly unlikely. Believing that the residents of Sadr City would greet the approaching Humvees with rose petals and chocolates was, in hindsight, probably indulging in a bit of wolfowishing.

Errorgance A feeling of smug superiority over those who do not share one's own erroneous or misguided convictions.

Theofandtoainthatiswas ...

WordCount is an interactive presentation of the 86,800 most frequently used English words, ranked and scaled in order of commonness and displayed side by side as one very long sentence. www.wordcount.org

Change your name

You might want to change your first names or family name for many reasons, for example because you:

- Are getting married or are making a commitment to live with a partner.
- Are getting divorced.
- Want to reclaim an old family name now unused.
- Are fed up with the name your parents gave you.
- Want to be noticed.

Names can be changed in two ways. You can pick a new name and consistently use it. This is called 'common usage', used for stage names and aliases, but you will still have to use your original name for official documents. Or you can get a Court Order to change your name – in the UK this is called Deed Poll.

You might want to change your name to spotlight a cause. Is there an issue that you feel absolutely passionate about? Then answer the following:

- Do you want to draw attention to this cause by giving yourself a new name?
- Do you want to be seen as being intimately identified with that cause?
- Do you want to give up your existing name (though you can change your name back using the same process)?
- Do you have the courage to have a name which people will notice, comment on and even laugh at?

If the answer to all these four questions is 'Yes', then start making plans for a new name. What's it going to be? You can be sensible or silly. For example:

- Edward Goldsmith, an environmentalist, could become Edward Going Green.
- Emily Pankhurst could have become Emily Votesforwomen.
- John Potter, a cycle activist, could become Free Wheeler.
- Hans Blix, a UN arms inspector, could become Guantánamo Sucks.

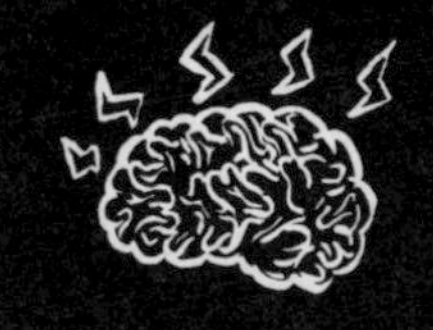

Changing names online

Type 'change your name' into Google, and you'll find a lot of online name-change services which will do the necessary.

The soyouwanna website will tell you more: www.soyouwanna.com/site/syws/changename/changename.html

Do the deed

These are the Deed Poll Limitations:

- You can't change your name with 'fraudulent intent,' for example to avoid bankruptcy or impersonate someone.
- Your new name should not be blasphemous, offensive or vulgar.
- You should use only letters, hyphens and apostrophes.
- Use of your new name should not result in a breach of a trademark (a singer calling himself Mick Jagger to promote his music would not be allowed).

Low impact T-shirts

Buy a hemp-cotton-mix T-shirt. Plain T-shirts in sand, black, navy, natural, olive and dark red, from The Hemp Store, £15: www.thehempstore.co.uk

With hip-hop inspired designs from top graffiti artists, from the Urban Shop, £24.95: www.headstrong.co.uk

Buy 3 juggling balls stuffed with hemp seeds (£12). If you can't juggle, you can always eat the contents: www.hemp-union.karoo.net

Hemp rules okay?

Cotton grows best in a hot dry climate, but requires a lot of water. In countries like Egypt, Pakistan and the central Asian republics of Uzbekistan, Tajikistan and Turkmenistan, cotton is a major export crop and growing it is leading to serious water problems. The Aral Sea has shrunk and is in danger of disappearing altogether, the mighty Indus has become a trickle, and the intensively irrigated fields are becoming salty which will lead to desertification of the land. All of this is due in large part to cotton growing.

The cotton needed to make just one T-shirt requires 1,170 litres of water – that's more than a tonne. So next time you buy a T-shirt promoting fairtrade tea, just remember to balance the good of getting a message out that helps tea workers earn a fair wage with the impact that the purchase of your T-shirt is having on the world's water problems.

Switch to hemp

Hemp is the cannabis plant – *Cannabis Sativa* – used for non-drug purposes. Hemp seeds are a common ingredient of 'healthy' seed mixes. Hemp is a coarse linen-like fibre used for sacks and floor coverings because of its strength and durability. Hemp was used to make ropes, but to prevent rotting it was tarred. This is the origin of 'A Jolly Tar' as a nickname for a sailor. Hemp is also used as a clothing fabric. Garments with a rougher finish can be made from 100 per cent hemp. It is too coarse on its own for T-shirts; the usual mix is 55 per cent hemp, 45 per cent cotton.

Hemp

- Grows well in cooler climates.
- Needs little or no irrigation.
- Grows easily, and in just 120 days.
- Smothers weeds.

Cotton

- Consumes 22 per cent of the world's pesticides, though it is planted on only 3 per cent of the world's fields.
- One T-shirt needs one cupful of fertiliser and pesticide.
- 30 per cent by weight of a cotton garment is chemical residue; what we put next to our skin is easily absorbed by the body.

Live on less

The average person requires 2,500 calories a day to survive. People in the developed world (and the rich in the developing world) are consuming 40 per cent more than this norm. Obesity is fast becoming an epidemic, whilst 600 million people in the developing world, mainly the rural poor, are badly malnourished.

Plenty and waste are taken for granted in the rich world, whilst hunger and need exist in the poor world. Could you live on less? Doing this will make you more sensitive to what many of your fellow human beings are experiencing, simply because of where they happened to have been born.

Live on less. Try some of these exercises in marginal living:

- Go without having your rubbish collected for a month, and analyse what you normally throw away.
- Confine your water consumption to 10 litres a day, equivalent to one flush of the toilet.
- Live without electricity for a day or a week.
- Do without motorised transport. Walk or cycle if you need to travel.
- Spend as little as you can for three months. Make a diary of everything you spend.
- Buy only basic food, no convenience foods, and with as little packaging as possible.
- Entertain yourself for a week; no TV, no radio etc.

What would you miss most?

Examine the things you did to make do. What were the things you most missed? How much reduction in consumption could you bear without feeling excessively inconvenienced? What can you do about global inequality?

Living on Less, reflections of a blogger: livingonless.journalspace.com

Human Development Reports: hdr.undp.org/statistics/data

Less than a dollar a day

The following figures show the percentage of the population living on less than $1 a day (2004 selected countries):

Burundi	58.4 per cent
Central African Rep.	66.6 per cent
Gambia	59.3 per cent
Mali	72.8 per cent
Niger	61.4 per cent
Nigeria	70.2 per cent
Sierra Leone	57.0 per cent
Zambia	63.7 per cent

October 30

Show your support

Go to Shawn's website to see what it's like to live with HIV/AIDS.

Wear a red ribbon to show your support for people with AIDS.

Never put yourself at risk of contracting HIV.

**Shawn's two websites:
www.aboyagirlavirus.com
www.mypetvirus.com**

Love on the web

Shawn Decker and Gwenn Barringer's websites give an engaging, honest look at two people in love. Shawn has HIV and Gwenn doesn't. They answer all the questions you can think of, and then some.

Gwenn has her own site (aboyagirlavirus.com), and she makes one excellent point; if she can stay HIV negative, then anyone should be able to.

Living with AIDS

Shawn Decker has a story to tell about living with HIV/AIDS:

I'm a positoid. In the early 1980s I was infected with HIV through the use of tainted blood products. At the age of 11, after being diagnosed HIV positive, I was expelled from the 6th Grade because local school officials thought I was a danger to other students. That was in 1987, a time when certain communities believed that HIV/AIDS was something that could not happen to them.

Eventually I was readmitted to high school, and graduated as 'Homecoming King'. In part, I think this gesture was my classmates' way of showing that they not only liked me, but they supported me as well. Even though I wasn't speaking openly about HIV at the time, they respected me for being 'goofy, wisecracking, HIV positive Shawn'. Later, when I came out of my AIDS closet, I used that humour as my main tool in educating others about life with HIV. Nearly 20 years later, I'm healthy, happy and in love.

One way that I try to raise awareness about HIV/AIDS issues is through public speaking. My partner, Gwenn, shares my passion for HIV education, and we travel the US through CAMPUSPEAK, talking to college students about our relationship – I'm HIV positive and she is not. Much of the conversation has to do with our sex life, and by 'opening our bedroom door', so to speak, we give people a chance to learn that those with HIV are normal beings with normal emotions.

My advice to young people is to be open and honest about the topic of sex. Know that you cannot tell that someone is HIV positive by looking at them, and in many instances people who are HIV positive themselves do not even know; so how could they tell you?

Elect a woman President

US elections don't only affect Americans, decisions of the President affect people around the globe. Non-US citizens might have views about the candidates. Yet they can't express these through any ballot box.

The next US Presidential Election is in 2008. Non-Americans can express their preferences at the Leader of the Free World website. The 2004 US Presidential Election gave George W Bush a second term. The Leader of the Free World election voted in Ralph Nader. John Kerry came 32nd, and George W Bush 65th.

The Leader of the Free World website is available in over ten languages, for a truly global election, and:

- Lists all possible Presidential candidates, and provides information on each
- Provides a Candidate Matcher, which will find the candidate most closely reflecting your own views
- Gives you a chance to 'vote' for your preferred candidate, and decides the 'winner'
- Includes Voter Verifiable Paper Trail and Voter Verifiable Ballot Tabulation (a more accountable mechanism than what is used in many US States)
- Enters voters into a lottery; prizes in 2004 included a trip to Washington DC and a T-shirt each week.

October 31

Write to vote

A pro-Kerry letter-writing campaign run by the UK *Guardian* newspaper aimed at Ohio, most important swing state. US outrage included these two letters:

'Hey England, Scotland and Wales, mind your own business. We don't need weenie-spined Limeys meddling in our presidential election.'

'Real Americans aren't interested in your pansy ass, tea-sipping opinions. If you want to save the world, begin with your own worthless corner of it.'

Leader of the Free World: www.leaderofthefreeworld.com

Condoleeza Rice: www.rice2008.com

Hillary Rodham Clinton: www.votehillary.org

Who will get your vote in 2008?

There is a real chance that a woman could become President. Whichever your political affiliation, Vote Condi or Vote Hillary!

Condoleeza Rice Appointed Secretary of State in 2004, responsible for foreign policy. From 2001, National Security Adviser to President George W Bush. And from 1993 to 1999, Provost of Stanford University, responsible for 14,000 students and a budget of $1.5 billion.

Hillary Rodham Clinton First Lady during her husband's tenure of the Presidency from 1993 to 2001. Elected Senator in November 2000 for New York State, serving on the Armed Services, the Health, Education, Labor & Pensions, and the Environment & Public Works Committees.

RAWA power

Read *Meena, Heroine of Afghanistan* by Melody Ermachild Chavis. Buy some music to support RAWA. Choose between two CDs:

- *Azadi*, a compilation for RAWA: www.museumfire.com/azadi.htm
- *Dropping Food on their Heads is not Enough*: www.gcrecords.com/benefit.html

RAWA: www.rawa.org

Working closely with RAWA:
In France, FemAid: www.femaid.org
RAWA Supporters UK: rawasupporters.co.uk
In the USA, Afghan Women's Mission: afghanwomensmission.org

Support women in Afghanistan

We work hard for women's rights in Afghanistan. We need the solidarity and support of all people around the world. RAWA

The notion of Afghanistan as a country where women are most oppressed was reinforced under the rule of the Taliban (which ended in 2001), when women were only allowed out in public dressed in a burka, many suffering abuse to their human rights.

RAWA, the Revolutionary Association of the Women of Afghanistan, was founded in 1977 by Meena, then aged 21, for Afghan women to fight for their rights. Meena was killed ten years later in Pakistan by Afghan KGB agents, in connivance with fundamentalist warlord Gulbuddin Hekmatyar.

RAWA runs education, health and income-generation projects alongside political campaigning. Since the end of the Soviet-backed regime in 1992, RAWA's struggle has been focused against religious fundamentalism and its male chauvinist attitudes.

FemAid all over the world ...

USA: A large number of kites were donated and distributed to two RAWA orphanages. Kite flying had been banned by the Taliban. A jazz musician gave a concert for his 40th birthday and sent the proceeds.

UK: A charity football match was organised, and supporters of both teams raised money. Stella McCartney sold signed and numbered T-shirts for a RAWA orphanage. For FemAid UK Sadie Brinham filled 150 shoe boxes for Afghan orphans with necessities such as school supplies and toothbrushes, plus New Year's presents. Sadie then set up a UK branch of FemAid (sadiebrinham@yahoo.co.uk).

France: Schools in the Bordeaux area collected school supplies to send to Afghan refugees in Pakistan.

Canada: Funds were raised for medical aid for a Quetta hospital (in Pakistan near the Afghan border) and for training midwives.

A shoebox giftbox

Christmas is still weeks away. But you may already be finding the commercialisation distasteful, while worrying what to buy your family and friends. Why not put together a box of small items for someone who will appreciate them? There are several schemes that distribute gifts, packaged in shoeboxes, to children who are living in such poverty that a toothbrush, a packet of crayons, or a skipping rope will be a treasured gift. But why wait until Christmas? This really simple idea was found on the www.honduras.com website:

> When you pack your luggage, please include a shoebox full of school supplies. Also take an extra $20 along. When you arrive in Honduras, keep an eye out for a small, poor school, and give your box to a teacher. Then as you continue your vacation, look out for an obviously poor person (preferably a woman). Walk up to her and give her the $20.
>
> The reason for giving to a woman is because it is usually a woman who has to feed and clothe the children; so your money will more than likely go where it is desperately needed. *Gringo Jak*

November 2

Box clever

Remember to keep the shoebox next time you buy a pair of shoes.

Wrap the box with some bright wrapping paper. Wrap the lid separately. Collect things to fill up your shoebox: assorted supplies for a school, or gifts for a child in an orphanage.

Get a group of friends to join you in filling a shoebox.

Samaritan's Purse is a Christian organisation that runs a shoebox scheme in North America, Northern Europe and Australia: www.samaritanspurse.org

The Rotary Club distributes shoeboxes year round: www.rotary1280.org/shoebox

Get packing

If it's a gift box, indicate whether it's for a boy or a girl and approximate age.

About 14 items fill a box. For schools, pens, pencils, solar-powered calculators, geometry set useful. Other popular items include non-mechanical toys, toothpaste, toothbrushes, soap, comb, sunglasses, caps, socks, T-shirts, hair clips, watches, small books.

Don't include used items, knives, electrical equipment, perishable items, medicines, breakable items, flammable or caustic materials or religious items.

Tie your box with string so that it can be opened easily in case of enquiries at customs. Take it with you when you travel abroad. Or deliver it to a charity running a gift-box scheme.

November 3

A peaceful night in

Challenge the culture of violence. Invite your friends to join you in a Non-Violent Movie Marathon.

Get some popcorn, fluff up the couch, and enjoy several movies that do not contain explosives, car chases, guns, bombs or kick punches. Explain to your guests the idea of your movie marathon, which is to think about the impact of violent images on society.

Challenge your guests to come up with ideas for addressing this issue.

An online magazine for movie buffs: www.movies.go.com

For film reviews, consult *Halliwell's Film Guide*.

Non-violent movies

Every day, we're bombarded with images of violence and death in video games, TV shows and movies with 'heroes' like Rambo, Spiderman and James Bond.

Some alternative movies you could watch:

Gandhi (1982) This film won 8 Oscars in 1983 including Best Picture, Best Actor (Ben Kingsley), Best Screenplay, and Best Director for Richard Attenborough. It is the awe-inspiring story of how a diminutive lawyer stood up to the British Empire and became an international symbol of non-violence.

Martin Luther King Jr: The Man and the Dream (2004) A look at the life of Martin Luther King, one of the most loved and influential leaders in American history. Writer and director Tom Friedman explores how Dr King's ideas evolved in the face of the rapidly changing climate of the Civil Rights Movement.

Free at Last: Civil Rights Heroes (2004) The heroic story of the Civil Rights struggle played out in the small acts of peaceful defiance by individuals such as Emmett Till, Medgar Evers, The Birmingham Four, Viola Liuzzo and others.

A thought-provoking movie marathon

Amandla! A Revolution in Four Part Harmony (2003): The role music played in the struggle against apartheid in South Africa.

Apocalypse Now (1974): Possibly Francis Ford Coppola's greatest work, a saga of the Vietnam war based on Joseph Conrad's *Heart of Darkness.*

Hotel Rwanda (2004): A hotel manager shelters more than 1,000 people faced with genocide.

The Killing Fields (1984): The true story of *New York Times* journalist Sydney Shanberg, who stayed on in Cambodia after the US withdrawal, in the face of the genocide being conducted by the Khmer Rouge regime.

Schindler's List (1993): Steven Spielberg's Holocaust epic of factory owner Oskar Schindler who loses his fortune whilst saving 1,100 Jews from Auschwitz.

Theatre of protest

A simple play reading can become an act of protest. In Aristophanes' ancient Greek play *Lysistrata*, women organise a sex strike to stop the endless warfare that their menfolk are pursuing. On 3 March 2003, the Lysistrata Project organised 1,029 readings of the play in 59 countries to protest against the war in Iraq. A secret reading in northern Iraq was organised by members of the International Press Corps. A reading in Patras, Greece, was held by Greeks and Kurdish refugees in a Kurdish refugee camp. There were secret readings in China. The readings raised $125,000 for peace and aid in the Middle East and elsewhere.

How they did it: The organisers wrote a letter that said: 'Are you frustrated by the build up to war? Do you feel like there isn't anything you can do? Well, here's something you CAN do ... ' They emailed this to everyone they knew. And they forwarded it to everyone they knew. The next day the organisers started hearing back from people all over the world. Within two weeks, they had been interviewed on national radio, readings were scheduled in over 70 cities, a documentary team started filming, and a couple organised an internet auction to raise money.

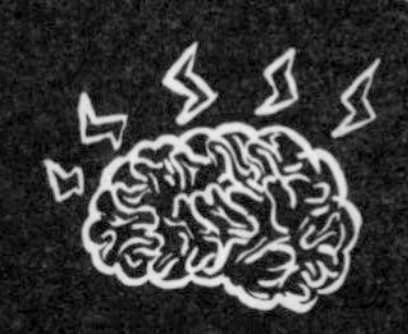

Playing up

Try a play by Richard Norton Taylor: *The Colour of Justice*: racism and police; *Bloody Sunday*: civil rights in Northern Ireland; *Justifying War*: the invasion of Iraq.

Or read: *The Accidental Death of an Anarchist* by Dario Fo; *Execution of Justice* by Emily Mann; *Fires in the Mirror* by Anna Deavere Smith; *The Syringa Tree* by Pamela Gien.

The Lysistrata Project: www.lysistrataproject.com

Kathryn Blume's account of how it was all organised: http://kathrynblume.com/AcAc.htm

'Put the Act back into Action', a Friends of the Earth how to guide to using street theatre: community.foe.co.uk/resource/how_tos

November 4

Ten steps for a successful play reading

1. Clarify your aims: Why are you doing it? What do you want to achieve? Be realistic, but also be ambitious.
2. Get a location: in a living room, at a community centre, anywhere!
3. Pick a time.
4. Pick a charity to benefit.
5. Get the script: online, from a library or a bookshop.
6. Cast the roles: friends, celebrities, whoever's willing.
7. Ask for volunteers via email. Give everyone who offers something to do.
8. Make the project visible: Get as much publicity as you can.
9. Put up a website.
10. Be green: Use recycled paper for programmes and fliers.

Landmine adoption

Casualty count

Host an Adopt A Minefield dinner. Find out this year's date from the Adopt A Minefield website, invite your friends and download some of the recipes donated for the occasion.

Raise lots of money. It costs about £1 to clear a square metre of minefield, and about £50 to help an amputee child walk again.

Adopt A Minefield passes 100 per cent of donations to projects clearing landmines and helping survivors. And it tells every donor what impact their money has made.

Adopt A Minefield: www.landmines.org.uk

Canadian Landmine Foundation: www.canadianlandmine.com

International Campaign to Ban Landmines: www.icbl.org

Each year, 26,000 people are killed or mutilated by landmines. 8,000 of these are children. The lives of 71 people each day are being damaged or destroyed. They didn't lay the mines; but they suffer the consequences. And their lives are at risk with every step they take.

There are between 60 to 100 million landmines in the ground worldwide. It costs between $3 and $30 to purchase an anti-personnel landmine. It can cost as much as $1,000 to remove it. Landmines destroy livestock and prevent the cultivation of arable land. They are an ever-present menace to those who live in affected areas.

Rebuilding war-torn communities and economies is difficult in any circumstances. But in many communities, recovery, reconciliation and long-term development are all but impossible because of landmines. The 'Ottawa Convention on the Prohibition of the Use, Stockpiling, Production and Transfer of Anti Personnel Mines, and on their Destruction', has now been signed by 136 nations. But not by China, Russia and the USA, three of the world's most powerful nations.

The Night of 1,000 Dinners

Co-ordinated by Adopt A Minefield, it takes place on or around the first Thursday of November each year, although people can hold dinners whenever it is convenient for them.

Thousands of people around the world host dinners in their homes, at work or in community venues to raise funds to clear landmines and help landmine survivors.

Dinners have been hosted on the sand dunes of the Sahara, in bedsits in Balham, in embassies in all sorts of weird and wonderful places.

Plant a peace pole

Peace is a daily, a weekly, a monthly process, gradually changing opinions, slowly eroding old barriers, quietly building new structures.
John F Kennedy

Peace poles are a memorial to peace. Wherever a peace pole has been planted, it is an indication that that place has been designated a place of peace. A peace pole ceremony can serve as a memorial to a tragedy that has taken place. The mayor of New York City, Michael Bloomberg, planted a 9/11 Memorial Peace Pole. A peace pole can be a symbol of a community making a commitment to peace, or of a new start between two previously warring factions.

Over 200,000 peace poles have been planted in over 180 countries on Earth. There are peace poles at:

- The Pyramids of El Giza, Egypt
- The Magnetic North Pole in Canada
- Sarajevo
- The Allenby Bridge between Israel and Jordan
- Baghdad
- Robben Island, South Africa
- New York
- Gorky Park, Russia
- Confucius burial site, Taiwan

Get planting

Plant a peace pole in your community. Pick a spot such as a public space or park; or even someone's backyard. The more people who pass by and see it, the better. You can make your peace pole. But make sure it is solid and durable in sun and rain.

Or if you prefer, buy a ready-made peace pole. The Peace Pole Project publishes a list of suppliers in countries all over the world. Outdoor poles cost between £200 and £750. A miniature version for a flower pot costs £7.

Organise a dedication ceremony.

The Peace Pole Project, a project of the World Peace and Prayer Society: www.worldpeace.org/peacepoles.html

Peace Pole Makers (USA): www.peacepoles.com

Reserve a space for peace

Peace poles are usually 2.5 metres tall. They can be made out of a sustainable material; for example, in North America they are often made from the Western Red Cedar cut from renewable forests. And they can also be constructed of metal or plastic.

They're planted in the ground or placed on stands if indoors. Desktop models, 50 cm high, are also available.

Every 'official' peace pole has the words 'May Peace Prevail On Earth' written on one side, often repeated on the other sides in different languages.

Recycle your mobile

You know how it is, you're now with the latest model. And your old mobile phone, the one you used to love and take everywhere with you, is left at home, unwanted and abandoned. It doesn't have to be like this. Your old mobile can have a new life, full of meaning and purpose ... but with someone else ... Oxfam, Bring Bring

Millions of mobiles are obsolete, broken or otherwise unused. And more are discarded every year. Most are put into the household waste. They end up in landfill sites, where the toxic material contained in the battery and LCD display leak out. Your old phone really does need to be disposed of safely. The best thing to do is recycle it.

The developing world is taking a technological leap into the mobile phone age. A really interesting Village Phone scheme is run in Bangladesh by Grameen Telecom, in partnership with the Grameen Bank. Rural women are given mobile handsets, which they pay for with a small Grameen Bank loan, and they are taught to use them. They then sell phone services to villagers, and this provides affordable telephone access to the village and contact with the outside world. It also provides the women with a livelihood.

Cell it on

Make sure that your old mobile is recycled.

Fonebak is a scheme endorsed by the mobile phone industry whereby you can return your old phone to a collection point or put it in an envelope and FREEPOST it to them: www.fonebak.com

Oxfam does something similar through its 'Bring Bring' Scheme. Take it into any Oxfam shop: www.oxfam.org.uk/what_you_can_do/recycle/phones.htm

Three small charities have set up www.cartridge4charity.co.uk

The Campaign to Recycle Unwanted Mobile Phones supports Child Advocacy International: www.childadvocacyinternational.co.uk/fundraising/recycle.htm

Grameen Telecom: www.grameenphone.com

Turn an old mobile into a sunflower

Researchers at Warwick University have developed a mobile-phone case that can transform into a flower of your choice.

It's made from biodegradable plastic, and when placed in a compost heap, a seed, embedded behind a small window in the case, germinates. The prototypes have used dwarf sunflower seeds. Watch a film about this: www.research-tv.com/stories/technology/mobilephones

World kindness

No act of kindness however small is ever wasted.
Aesop

Glen Bornais from Ottawa, Canada writes:

Despite my preoccupation with the big problems of the day (perhaps because I've studied political economy at a critically spirited institution) and despite my natural tendency towards the dramatic, I've recently come under the power of one truly simple idea: we could improve our lives, our communities, our families, our friendships, our world simply by engaging in a random and unsolicited act of kindness every day.

This approach to life will not likely resolve or reverse the unequal distribution of wealth, nor the damage we do to our planet, nor third world debt, nor suffering and hunger of the deepest kind, but acts of kindness as unsolicited compliments, smiles, simple charity, community trash pick up can help us regain faith in each and every person, and sometimes even in ourselves.

World Kindness Week is the second week in November and one day in that week is World Kindness Day

A kinder life

In 1997, the World Kindness Movement was set up.

Perform an act of kindness right now to the person you next see. Think of this as a start for leading a kinder life.

Join the Coinspiracy campaign and experience for yourself the multiplier effect of kindness and its endless possibilities. To participate contact: www.investinakinderworld.com

Inspiring quotations on kindness: www.kindness.com.au/quotations.htm

Calendars and bookmarks with ideas for acts of kindness from Random Acts of Kindness Foundation: www.actsofkindness.org/inspiration/graphics.asp

Or send an e-card: www.actsofkindness.org/inspiration/ecards.asp

Join the Coinspiracy ...

The Coinspiracy is an initiative of the KindActs Network Association of British Columbia in Canada. It uses a coin called a 'UNI', short for the universal nature of kindness. To participate, the 'Coinholder' does three kind acts: one for him or herself, one for the environment and one for someone else. The coin is passed on to the recipient of the kind act who in turn commits three acts and passes it on. In the first Coinspiracy in 2002, over 100,000 kind acts were performed, and about $30,000 raised in donations. On World Kindness Day 2003, 77 schools and youth groups in Australia, Bermuda, Canada, India, Italy, Nepal, New Zealand, Nigeria, Scotland, Singapore, South Africa and USA took part in the Coinspiracy.

Foundations for change

Give it away

Become a grant-maker. Give out money to change the world.

Get hold of a directory of foundations, make a list of those you like the look of. Write to them, telling them about your area of expertise and why you think you would make a great trustee. Most will not bother to reply. Others will say 'No'. But you might get a letter from one of them suggesting a meeting, and even end up having a say on how millions of pounds are distributed.

YouthBank: www.youthbank.org.uk

For directories of Foundations:

Directory of Social Change (for the UK): www.dsc.org.uk

The Foundation Center (for the USA): fdncenter.org

Philanthropists endow foundations, enabling them to donate money to good causes. When Henry Wellcome died he put the shares of his Wellcome pharmaceutical company into a foundation to give money to medical research. His company, which is now part of Glaxo SmithKline, invented the AZT AIDS drug. The Wellcome Trust is the UK's largest grant-making foundation. Bill Gates has said that he wants to give everything back by the time he dies. As founder of Microsoft and the world's richest man, he has set up the Bill and Melinda Gates Foundation with his wife to do just that.

All over the world, people are setting up foundations to give money to good causes. Some, like those of Gates and Wellcome, are huge, others quite small. All appoint people called 'Trustees', who decide how the money is spent.

Maybe you should write to a foundation offering yourself as a trustee. If you are young, they may need your experience as a young person. If you are a Muslim, gay, black, working class, a woman, they may want to have your perspective to inform their decision making.

YouthBank

YouthBank is a foundation that makes small grants to projects organised by young people. A YouthBank is run by a board of young people aged between 14 and 25. They make the decisions on how the foundation's run, what sorts of things to give to, how to encourage people to apply and which applications to back. This is real money given to real people to make a real difference. YouthBank members are responsible for seeing that their funds are well spent. YouthBanks have funded all sorts of projects, such as expeditions to Brazil, computer equipment, launching a magazine, funds for a monthly disco, a skateboard park, mural painting and yoga classes for disabled young people.

Dying to help

Are you dying to go to medical school? But perhaps the examinations are too hard and you can't manage the grades. Or you've set your hopes on a completely different and more fulfilling career. But here's an easy way for anybody to get into medical school without having to study to become a doctor.

Donate your body! Medical schools need it to help teach their students the principles of anatomy. You will be embalmed and frozen.

In England, about 600 people a year donate their bodies, but the 6,000 medical students who get into medical school each year need around 1,000 bodies to dissect. The government's Chief Medical Adviser recently wrote to all doctors in England asking them to encourage their patients to leave their bodies to a hospital. So why not decide to do this?

Medical school

Decide to donate your body to a medical school. It will add an extra dimension of meaning to your life! You won't feel a thing. And don't be embarrassed. You won't be recognisable. The embalming will have turned you a colourless grey – something like a pumice stone.

Further information from HM Inspector of Anatomy, Room 611, Wellington House, 135–155 Waterloo Bridge Road, London SE1 8UG.

November 10

How to donate your body

Contact a hospital or medical school to tell them you plan to donate your body.

Put your request in writing. Sign and date the letter, and get it witnessed. Tell your friends and family what you have done. If you do this, your family is legally obliged to hand over the body after your death. This is not the same situation as for organ donation, where carrying an organ donor card is only an expression of your wishes, and your executors can make their own decision on whether to donate your organs.

Immediately your death has been registered, your executors should hand over your body to your chosen hospital or medical school. They will then assess whether they can use your body. Not all bodies are accepted (which is the ultimate humiliation). Your body needs to be intact and disease free.

Once your body has been accepted it will be embalmed and frozen. This needs to be done within three days of your death. Your body can then be used for up to three years.

Around four medical students will work on your body, dissecting an arm and a leg, then the head and the neck, and so on until they've finished with you. Then your body can be returned to your family for burial or cremation.

Time to commit

Sign up to JAMOP and make a gesture to advocate peaceful solutions to international conflict. And join together with others on 07/07/07.

One minute of silence gives a time for reflection, for you to think about what part you can play to end war. Take a minute now to think about it, and commit yourself to one simple action for peace. Sit down; stand up; write a letter; lobby your elected representative.

See what conflict took place in the world during the 20th century by exploring the Conflict Map: nobelprize.org/peace/educational/conflictmap

Peace Pledge Union: www.ppu.org.uk

Just a Minute of Peace: www.jamop.com

Peace for a moment

After catastrophic events there is now a tradition of people gathering together, or just pausing in their daily routine, in silent contemplation.

Armistice Day or Remembrance Day is 11 November. On this day at the eleventh hour, two minutes' silence is observed in the UK to remember those who died in WWI, and in subsequent wars. As well as red poppies, distributed by the British Legion, there are white poppies, distributed by The Peace Pledge Union, symbolising that there are better ways to resolve conflicts than killing strangers.

On 6 August 1945, the first atom bomb used in war was dropped on Hiroshima, followed by a second on Nagasaki on 9 August. On 9 August 2005, Pax Christi Ireland observed One Minute for Peace at 10.02 GMT.

Global Minute for Peace Day takes place on 22 December, the Winter Solstice. On the first Global Day, the voice of J F Kennedy speaking at the UN was broadcast, saying: 'Together we can save our planet'. GMPD was initiated by John McConnell, who also began International Earth Day on the Spring Equinox.

Just a Minute of Peace (JAMOP) is a Canadian initiative, linked to an international concert for peace. People are urged to spend a minute in silence on 7 July 2007 at 23.59 GMT.

The world death toll

These are the total deaths in the 20th century from war and oppression:

Genocide and tyranny 83 million

Military deaths in war 42 million

Civilian deaths in war 19 million

Man-made famine 44 million

Taken from Matthew White's *Historical Atlas of the 20th Century*: http://users.erols.com/mwhite28/20centry.htm

Compile a directory

Right under your nose, there are things going on you probably don't even know about. There may be:

- A club that sails model boats on a nearby lake.
- A kite-flying group.
- People learning salsa, yoga, karate, tai chi, or flower arranging.
- Poker or bridge clubs.
- Reading circles, amateur dramatics and music groups.
- One o'clock clubs for young mothers to meet and share their experiences.
- Tea dances for senior citizens.
- The local soccer or baseball team that's about to make it big in the Local League.
- Self-help groups such as Alcoholics Anonymous, WeightWatchers.
- Local chapters of Greenpeace or Amnesty.
- Church groups, school groups, youth groups

... and much more.

Groups are a good indicator of how the community is functioning. The more the better. If people knew about what was happening when and where, or if organisers had a place to advertise what they were doing, then many more people might join in. It would become easier to find what to do, and easier to attract people for something you want to organise.

Local hero

Create a Neighbourhood Yellow Pages for your local community or town.

Make a list of all the activities and services taking place in your neighbourhood. Provide enough information on each for people to know if it is something they might be interested in.

Provide contact details for people to find out more.

Publish your list. Set up a website, which will cost little or nothing.

Produce a printed directory, and try to recoup your money from sales of a hard copy or from advertising.

Saturday Walkers Club: www.walkingclub.org.uk

Find out more about DoBe: www.globalideasbank.org

Walk this way

Nicholas Albery, a UK social inventor, created two initiatives to foster participatory activity. He needed to take regular exercise, due to a medical condition, so he created a Saturday Walkers Club. Walkers meet at a time and place specified on the website to take part. Walks are free; everyone is welcome. Nicholas also created DoBe, as an electronic community noticeboard for local communities to post news of participatory events being organised in the area. You can use the software to create your own noticeboard.

Food not bombs

Be prepared

Prepare meals to serve on the street. This is hard work, but also fun. Pick central locations, as this will make the problem of homelessness more visible.

You've just started a Food Not Bombs group. The Food Not Bombs Handbook on their website will tell all you need to know.

Food Not Bombs groups have been started in nearly 50 countries. Join or start a group in your city: www.foodnotbombs.net

Food for Life: The International Society for Krishna Consciousness runs free vegetarian food programmes in around 16 countries. www.ffl.org

Many homeless projects organise soup runs, going out in the evenings to provide free meals to people on the streets. Contact Homeless Link for details of local projects: www.homeless.org.uk

It is a scandal that there is hunger in the midst of plenty. Hungry people include: single-parent families, low-waged employees, the unemployed, the elderly and those unable to work through illness or disability. Before you eat the meal in front of you, your food has gone through a chain of farmers, distributors, manufacturers, wholesalers and retailers. At every point in the chain, perfectly good food is discarded. The USA wastes 20 million tonnes of food a year (about 80 kg per person). Just one tenth of this would end hunger in America.

Food Not Bombs started in 1980 with two ideas: militarism and war are a bad thing, and no person should go hungry in today's world. It provides free food to hungry people. They recover food that would otherwise be thrown out, fresh produce near the end of its shelf life, turning it into hot meals, served in city parks to anyone who wants it. It also campaigns against war and poverty worldwide. You can help.

To collect food for distribution to the hungry you will need a vehicle and a small group of committed volunteers. Approach supermarkets, grocers and greengrocers, markets and restaurants, asking them to donate food on a regular basis. Deliver the food you collect to night shelters, day centres and soup kitchens. Find out what they need and arrange a regular delivery schedule.

Crisis management

Crisis organises Christmas shelters for homeless people, with accommodation over the festive season, plus food, entertainment and health services. The biggest in 2004 was at the Millennium Dome, attended by 1,500 people. These projects need volunteers to collect, cook and distribute the food. If you've got the time, why not give it a go? Visit www.crisis.org.uk

Become an entrepreneur

Social entrepreneurs do for society's problems what entrepreneurs do for business, providing practical solutions through innovation and resourcefulness. They innovate by finding a new product or service to meet a need, or by developing a new approach to a problem. They get started immediately, confident that they will find a way of succeeding.

The Ashoka Foundation supports social entrepreneurs around the world by providing them with three-year bursaries. Veronica Khosa was a nurse in South Africa. Around her she could see sick people getting sicker, elderly people without a doctor, and hospitals with empty beds that wouldn't admit HIV patients. Veronica started Tateni Home Care Nursing Services, pioneering 'home care' in her country. Starting with almost nothing, her team took to the streets providing care to people in their homes. A few years later, the government adopted her ideas, and home-care schemes are now spreading beyond South Africa. Social entrepreneurs are unstoppable people with great ideas, people who get things done.

If you're UK-based and have a good idea for change in your community, or the world, apply for a grant from UnLtd. Grants range from £250 to £20,000.

November 14

Do it yourself

These organisations support social entrepreneurs. Visit their websites to see the sorts of people and projects they are supporting:

Ashoka Foundation: www.ashoka.org and www.changemakers.net

Skoll Foundation: www.skollfoundation.org

Schwab Foundation: www.schwabfound.org

Social Capitalist Awards: www.fastcompany.com/social

Apply for a grant to UnLtd: www.unltd.org.uk

Join these networks to meet other change makers:

Pioneers of Change: www.pioneersofchange.net

International Young Professionals Foundation: www.iypf.org

An Ashoka success story

Rodrigo Baggio wanted to help the poor make use of information technology to improve their communities and their own lives. In 1995, he set up a technology school in a Rio de Janeiro slum. The venture worked so well that his Committee for Democracy in Information Technology has set up over 900 schools in Latin America, South Africa and Japan. Students learn how to use computers and discuss issues facing their communities. They then devise a project involving computers – a local newspaper, a small business or a civic group – which they make happen. In 10 years, over 600,000 people graduated from CDI schools.

In-your-face politics

The Biotic Baking Brigade is a movement that actually moves: a network of political pranksters who literally practise in-your-face politics. They target assorted greedheads, hitting them right in the smacker ... with pies! But it is worthy work. The BBB's pies are the Boston Tea Party of our modern day, sending a serious message softly to the corporate oligarchy. Jim Hightower

Humour is an important weapon in the armoury of an activist. What do Bill Gates, Milton Friedman, Sylvester Stallone, Canadian Premier Jean Chrétien, Swedish King Carl Gustaf, Ronald McDonald, Timothy Leary, Eldridge Cleaver, World Trade Organization Director Renato Ruggiero and Andy Warhol have in common? They've all been 'pied' by the Biotic Baking Brigade. The Brigade consists of activists involved in ecology, social justice, animal rights and feminism, with a sense of humour and 'in your face' courage.

The art of landing a freshly baked cream cake in the face of a reactionary, pompous but otherwise deserving person has a long tradition. As a way of highlighting a cause with spectacular media attention, or merely bringing a lofty demeanour down a crust or two, there's nothing as good as a pie.

Target practice

Why not try the following:

1. **Get hold of a copy of *Pie Any Means Necessary: The Biotic Baking Brigade Cookbook*. Order from AK Press: www.akpress.org**
2. **Choose a recipe from this or another cookbook, and bake your pie. Sloppy is good!**
3. **Choose your target, and go for it.**

Biotic Baking Brigade: www.bioticbakingbrigade.org

Watch *The Pie's the Limit*, a documentary featuring pie throwings in San Francisco and beyond; plus interviews with real underground pie tossers. Watch half a dozen demagogues being served up their just deserts! View it or download it at: www.whisperedmedia.org/piepage.html

Pie any means necessary

Pie Any Means Necessary: The Biotic Baking Brigade Cookbook is an anthology that cooks up an intoxicating melange of history, tactics and recipes for this most edible of direct action techniques. Tips on the best way to slip into a meeting unobserved, ammunition in hand, blend deliciously with recipes for delectable pastries (perfect for throwing, or dining upon). Generously sprinkled with some witty communiqués explaining why those responsible for environmental destruction might be in line for their just deserts.

People mixing

You are probably missing out. There are interesting people everywhere, but most of us tend to stick with the groups of people we're used to. Almost everyone remains locked into their small group.

The reality is that people can't really be slotted into 'types'. One of the human race's greatest virtues is its diversity. You might share the political opinions of your bank manager, or a favourite food with your boss at work. You really don't know until you ask. There may be lots of really interesting people out there whom you never get to talk to.

Some people are more dedicated to mixing up their social groups. On Tuesday 16 November 2004, more than 4 million students at nearly 8,000 schools across the USA participated in the third annual Mix It Up at Lunch Day. They stepped out of their comfort zones to meet someone new.

So try mixing it up. Organise a day where everyone gets to meet new people. It's a great way to break down social, economic, racial, gender, ability, disability and even age barriers. You could allocate tables according to birth month, or the first letter of last names. Break down the barriers, and you might find people have more to talk about than they realise.

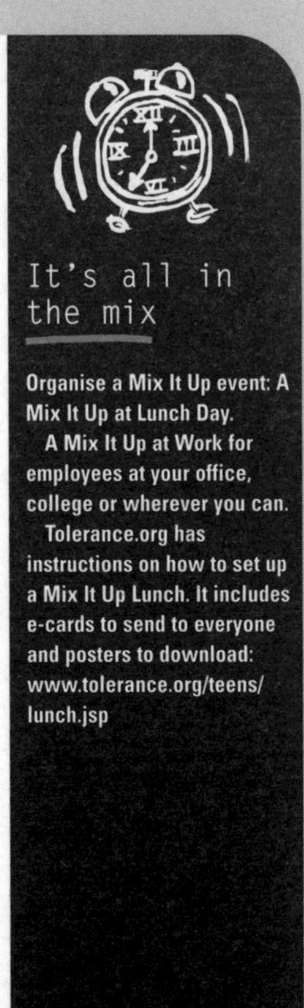

It's all in the mix

Organise a Mix It Up event: A Mix It Up at Lunch Day.

A Mix It Up at Work for employees at your office, college or wherever you can.

Tolerance.org has instructions on how to set up a Mix It Up Lunch. It includes e-cards to send to everyone and posters to download: www.tolerance.org/teens/lunch.jsp

Meet someone new

Where else can you mix it up? Here are some leads:

- In bars and restaurants, make a point of sitting next to strangers and chatting to them.
- At parties, go and talk to all the interesting looking people you don't know.
- Using a telephone directory, invite everyone in town with the surname 'Rice' or 'Bush' or whatever to meet for a drink one evening after work.
- Mix It Up encourages people to cross lines and meet new faces. You want to make a difference, so start by meeting someone new.

November 17

Jump to it

To find out more on knitting a penguin jumper and instructions on how to do it go to: www.tct.org.au/jumper.htm#Tasmanian

Send your jumper to Pet Porpoise Pool, PO Box 532, Coffs Harbour, NSW 2450.

See also:

Tasmanian Conservation Trust: www.tct.org.au

The Innocent Drinks Supergran project: www.innocentdrinks.co.uk/supergran

Two organisations helping the elderly: www.extracare.org.uk www.ageconcern.org.uk

Perk up a penguin

You can help to keep Australian penguins warm. Some penguins in Australia are now wearing knitted woolly jumpers. These have been knitted to keep the penguins warm after they have been exposed to an oil spill, when their feathers are cleaned (which removes the natural oils). If the birds aren't cleaned, the oil that clogs their feathers reduces the insulation and waterproofing. If the penguins try to clean themselves by preening, they will get poisoned. So a woolly jumper is the answer.

Over 15,000 jumpers were knitted by volunteers from all over the world in response to an appeal by the Tasmania Conservation Trust. Pet Porpoise Pool, a visitor attraction in Coffs Harbour, is also collecting jumpers for the same purpose.

Some jumpers are unsuitable for the penguins because of very loose knitting or greasy wool. Pet Porpoise Pool sells them on toy penguins in their souvenir shop. The proceeds are shared between the Penguin Rehabilitation Centre and the South Gippsland Native Animal Rescue.

More knitting

Innocent Drinks make delicious smoothies, thickies and juicy waters. To promote their drinks, they teamed up with the EAT snack bar chain to sell Innocent drinks dressed in knitted hats. For every bottle sold, 50p went to two charities working with the elderly, Age Concern and Extra Care.

Here's where you come in. Knit a hat and send it to Innocent. They put it on a bottle and sell it to a customer. The 50p pays towards outings for the elderly and activities in old people's homes.

Knit a fancy Santa, or a designer beret, or a floppy bunny hat for a smoothie bottle. If you're stuck for ideas, there's a pattern at: www.innocentdrinks.co.uk/supergran/how_to.htm.

Send your hats to: Little Woolly Hats, Innocent, The Goldhawk Estate, Brackenbury Road, London W6 0BA.

Combat terrorism

In August 2004, the International Commission of Jurists adopted a 'Declaration on Upholding Human Rights and the Rule of Law in Combating Terrorism', while condemning terrorism. Human rights violations carried out in the name of national security include:

- Government interference with the judicial process.
- Suspension of human rights where government has no power to do so, or where it is 'disproportionate'.
- Use of torture and cruel treatment or punishment.
- Secret detention or denying detainees access to lawyers, family members and medical personnel.
- Failure to produce charges or evidence.
- Denying detainees the right to challenge the lawfulness of their detention.
- Not providing a fair trial in an independent court.
- Using evidence obtained by torture.
- Not providing reparation to any person adversely affected by counter-terrorism measures.
- Expelling persons suspected, or convicted, of acts of terrorism to a state where they will be subjected to human rights violations including torture, enforced disappearance, unfair trial or execution.

Uphold human rights

Be vigilant of human rights. There seems to be a resigned acceptance that a significant loss of our human rights is necessary after 9/11 and the London bombings. But this need not be the case. The War on Terror should be conducted within a framework that upholds fundamental human rights.

Report any significant or disproportionate violation of human rights to Amnesty and to the International Commission of Jurists.

Amnesty International: www.amnesty.org

International Commission of Jurists: http://icj.org

November 18

The rights stuff

The Declaration on Upholding Human Rights in Combating Terrorism states that:

> In adopting measures aimed at suppressing acts of terrorism, states must adhere strictly to the rule of law, including the core principles of criminal and international law and the specific standards and obligations of international human rights law, refugee law and, where applicable, humanitarian law. These principles, standards and obligations define the boundaries of permissible and legitimate state action against terrorism. The odious nature of terrorist acts cannot serve as a basis or pretext for states to disregard their international obligations, in particular in the protection of fundamental human rights.

Help close the market

Support the campaign. Save the Children Sweden ('Radda Barnen' in Swedish) is campaigning to end the use of the internet as a marketplace for child pornography.

Join them in their fight against child pornography on the internet. They need our help.

Report any instances of child pornography on the internet you come across.

Radda Barnen's Child Pornography Hotline: www.rb.se/hotline/ehome.htm

Stop child pornography

The internet can be a dangerous place for children. A University of Cork research group collected more than 50,000 child pornography pictures involving 2,000 children via the internet over a two-year period. On average, two children are added each week. Up to 70–80 per cent of the pictures are as much as 30 years old. For the children involved, this violation continues as long as the pictures circulate.

Complaints about child pornography are on the increase. Between 1997 and 1998 Save the Children Sweden received three tip-offs, the following year it rose to more than 700. New sources of internet child pornography include Russia, Romania, the Baltic states and the Czech Republic. Live webcasting of sex acts involving children is now being reported.

Paedophile organisations and networks are becoming more daring and cunning in using the internet. Not only do they use it to display images of children but also to make contact with children through chat rooms. Police appear to lack the resources to deal adequately with the problem – despite the distribution of pornography in any form being illegal virtually everywhere.

Netting the paedophiles

In Sweden 53 paedophiles created a net community where members could post photographs and film clips. There was also a message site and chat room, where members could discuss pictures and fantasies. The members used nicknames and anonymous email addresses.

A technical oversight allowed an intruder to listen in to their exchanges. This person tipped off the Child Pornography Hotline, and the police were able to investigate and take action.

The pictures and film clips on view were rapes involving children as young as 4 years old and even a 3-month old baby. The paedophiles included an unemployed 27-year-old, a university faculty head and a female farm worker.

Rights for children

2.2 billion of the world's population are under 18. Almost all are protected by the Convention on the Rights of the Child, apart from 80 million children who live in Somalia and the USA, neither of which has signed the Convention, which was launched on 20 November 1989 with these basic ideas:

- Every child has a right to have basic needs fulfilled.
- Every child has a right to protection from abuse.
- Every child has the right to express an opinion.

Some important children's rights:

- The right to have a name and be registered as a citizen. Of 132 million born each year, 53 million children are never registered.
- The right to a home, food, clothing, education, health care and security. Around 600 million children live on less than $1 a day, 900 million on less than $2. Three-quarters of the world's children are very poor.
- The right to be protected from work exploitation. Children under 12 years may not work at all, but over 100 million children under 12 do work.
- The right to go to school. Elementary school should be free of charge to all.

Defend young people

Enlist your local school or young people's group as a Global Friend of WCPRC. They will then receive the prize magazine (which, as well as the prize web, is published in nine languages) and can vote from January to April for who has done the most for children's rights.

The World Children's Prize for the Rights of the Child: www.childrensworld.org

Information on the Convention on the Rights of the Child: www.unicef.org/crc

Eyes on the prize

The World Children's Prize for the Rights of the Child invites all schools and children to be part of an annual forum. Only children vote to choose the laureates. In 2005, 2.3 million votes were cast from 7,821 schools and groups in 73 countries.

Past laureates have included:

Maggy Barankitse (Burundi), for child welfare work.

Barefoot College and Children's Parliament (Rajasthan, India), where the Prime Minister is just 12 years old.

James Aguer Alic (Sudan), for fighting to free slave children.

Nelson Mandela (South Africa) and **Graça Machel** (Mozambique).

Hear their inspiring stories on the WCPRC website.

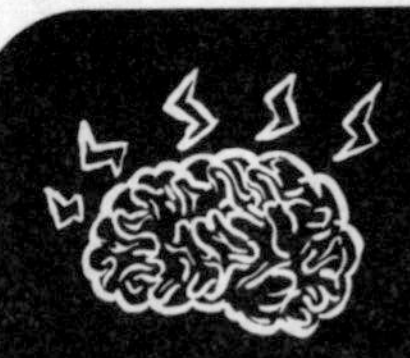

Turn it off

Spend less time watching TV. US children spend more time each year viewing (1,023 hours) than in school (900 hours). A BBC survey in 2004 showed UK 4-year-olds spending four hours a day in front of TV. Turn off your TV. Reduce viewing by half, and cut the number of TVs in your home to just one.

The TV-Turnoff Network encourages children and adults to watch less television in order to create healthier lives and communities: www.tvturnoff.org

White Dot, international campaign against TV. Read their survival guide 'Get a Life' for what to do after you've turned your TV off: www.whitedot.org

TV-B-Gone: www.tvbgone.com

Make a TV-free zone

Bhutan is a Buddhist sanctuary, a refuge from the world and its ills. In the 1930s all that was known of Bhutan in the West was from James Hilton's novel, *Lost Horizon.* He called Bhutan 'Shangri la'. The King of Bhutan decided that happiness was the most important thing, and in 1998, defined Bhutan's key aim as 'Gross National Happiness'.

Bhutan was the last country in the world to have TV. It came in 2002, with 46 cable channels, throwing Bhutan headlong into the global culture of the 21st century. Everyone underestimated the impact that TV would have on local life and culture. One third of Bhutan's girls now want to look more American (whiter skin, blonde hair). A similar proportion of girls also aspire to a new approach to relationships (boyfriends not husbands, and sex before marriage).

An editorial in a Bhutanese newspaper warns: 'We are seeing for the first time broken families, school dropouts and other negative youth crimes. We are beginning to see crime associated with drug users all over the world, shoplifting, burglary and violence.' Swapping Gross National Happiness for the joys of *Big Brother, Baywatch* and *I'm a Celebrity, get me out of here*, may not be such a good thing after all.

Technology to the rescue

TV-B-Gone is a universal remote control device that hangs on your key chain. It enables you to 'turn off virtually any television' at home or in a public place from a distance of about 14 metres. Point, press, keep pointing for just over a minute. It's that easy. Launched in October 2004, the TV-B-Gone device was sold out in just two days, and the suppliers have been battling to keep up with demand ever since.

It must have been a useful tool in late April 2005, when TV Turn-Off Week was celebrated in countries as far apart as the USA and Australia, the UK and Brazil.

Say thank you

Giving thanks is traditionally associated with autumn. Throughout history and all over the world, people have celebrated the harvest each autumn with some sort of thanksgiving ceremony. Demeter, the ancient Greek goddess of grain, was thanked at the festival of Thesmosphoria. On the first day of autumn, married women built leafy shelters. The second day was a fast day, and the third was a feast with offerings to Demeter. The Romans had Cerelia on 4 October, when the fruits of the harvest were offered up to Ceres. Cerelia was celebrated with music, parades, games and a feast.

The Chinese harvest festival is Chung Ch'ui, held at full moon in the 8th month. This is the moon's birthday, celebrated with special 'moon cakes', stamped with a picture of a rabbit (the Chinese see a rabbit, not a man, in the moon). The harvest festival of the Jews is called Sukkoth, the feast of tabernacles. They build small huts out of branches and foliage, which are decorated with the fruits of the harvest. Thanksgiving in the USA commemorates the first year in the New World of the founding Pilgrims, and a harvest that was plentiful. This is a day of family get togethers and turkey dinners.

Thanksgiving Day is the fourth Thursday in November

Keep in touch

Thanksgiving is a great day to say 'Thank You'. Today's the day to reflect on all that's good in the world.

Say thank you to all your funders and supporters. To be good at fundraising, you need to build good relationships with those who give you their money or time. This means thanking them nicely. Keep in touch, tell them what you have been able to achieve with their help, share your successes.

And say a special thank you to Tim Berners-Lee who devised the World Wide Web, which has profoundly changed all our lives.

View the Wellcome Medical Photographic Library: www.wellcome.ac.uk

Find out about Tim Berners-Lee: www.w3.org/People/Berners-Lee

Counting our blessings

Healthcare achievements in the 20th century to be thankful for:

- **Antibiotics**, **vaccines** and **anaesthetics**, which have transformed medicine.
- **Insulin** which saves the lives of diabetics.
- **Anti-retroviral drugs**, which mean that you don't need to die of AIDS.
- **The understanding of malaria**, which means that it can be treated.
- **The Human Genome project**, fighting to eliminate hereditary disease.

November 23

Stick 'em up

Help to shape your habits

Make some stickers. Buy a pack of large blank labels. Cut them into interesting shapes. Think up some provocative slogans and use marker pens (non-water-soluble will be best for obvious reasons) to write and illustrate your slogans.

Put them next to taps and light switches as a reminder to everyone (including yourself).

Put your stickers up at home, at work and in public places.

A bath and a washing machine both use 80 litres of water, a power shower uses 70, a dishwasher 35, flushing a toilet 9. A garden hose will use 450 litres an hour. This water is delivered to your door. It's high-quality stuff too, clean enough to drink. It's usually available on demand. And although you may be charged for the amount you use, it's almost free. This is amazing when you consider that people in other parts of the world may need to walk several kilometres each day to get a few gallons from the local water source.

Turning off the tap should be a reflex action. But people often forget to do it. They leave the water running when they are brushing their teeth, when they are staring at themselves in the mirror, when they are combing their hair ... or even after they have left the bathroom. This is a waste of a precious commodity – especially in long hot summers or in areas where demand is threatening to exceed supply. The same is true for turning off the lights when you leave a room. It's so basic, but your laziness or forgetfulness will translate into higher electricity bills, more pollution and more greenhouse gases contributing to global warming.

Ideas that might stick

Sticker slogans to put next to taps:

- Don't be a drip drip drip
- Save water. Turn off the tap
- Turn me on, baby! But turn me off!

Sticker slogans to put next to light switches – never place them over the switch itself or cover up a power point:

- Why burn up your cash?
- Save the earth with a flick of a switch
- Turn off the taps. It's the bright thing to do
- Have more fun in the dark

Information is power

The Open Directory describes itself as 'The Republic of the Web'. The project is the most comprehensive human-edited directory of the internet, maintained by a global community of volunteer editors.

The World Wide Web continues to grow at staggering rates; instead of fighting the explosive growth of the internet, the Open Directory provides a means for the internet to organise itself. Editors each organise a small section, culling out the bad and the useless, and keeping only the best content.

So far the Open Directory has catalogued over 4 million websites: 590,000 categories in 76 languages, using 66,849 editors. Just as the Oxford English Dictionary became the definitive book on words through the efforts of volunteers, the Open Directory aims to become the definitive catalogue of the Web. The Open Directory, founded in the spirit of the open source movement, is free. There is no cost for submitting a site to the directory, and use of the data is free, subject to terms of the Copyleft licence.

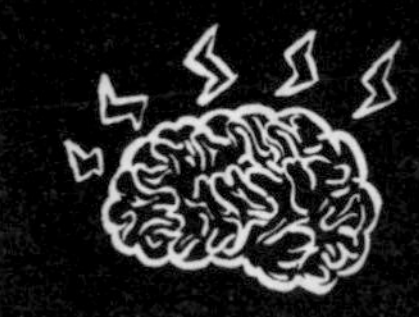

An open book

Join the Open Directory Project. Apply to become an editor using the form on the website. Editors select, evaluate, describe and organise the websites to be included in the Directory. Indicate a category that corresponds with your interests.

All you need is an interest in the subject area, plus a computer, a genuine interest in building a global directory that is objective in its outlook and free from commercial interests.

Open Directory Project: dmoz.org

Damn it!

The Open Directory has a number of entries in English for 'Curses': **Breaking curses from our lives** Biblical curses, and how to be free of them: www.bible.com/answers/acurses.html **Curses: Definition, history, modern usage** www.themystica.com/mystica/articles/c/curses.html **Generational curses** Curses carrying down a family line: hometown.aol.com/godswaitn/genealgy/index.htm **Global psychics, the truth about curses** Fraudulent practitioners claiming to remove curses for cash: www.globalpsychics.com/lp/Tips/curses.htm **Gypsy curses incorporated** Free curses or individually tailored curses for a fee: members.tripod.com/~Curses _Inc **An tinneall Mallachtai,** the curse engine Generate a curse in Irish: hermes.lincolnu.edu/~focal/scripts/mallacht.htm **Understanding curses** The effect of curses in a biblical context: hermes.lincolnu.edu/~focal/scripts/mallacht.htm dmoz.org/Society/Folklore/Magic/Curses/

Defend yourself

Use the F word

Download and photocopy the four 'Fighting Back' posters on self-defence for women and girls published by *the F word*, an online magazine on feminist issues: www.thefword.org.uk/static/fightingback/page1

Girls' Leap, a community programme in the USA to help girls understand and deal with violence: www.girlsleap.org

AWARE: arming women against rape and endangerment: www.aware.org

There are all sorts of situations where we may be in physical danger of attack – mugging, sexual assault or a random act of violence – whether we are in Houston or Harare, Moscow or Manila. Girls are particularly vulnerable to assault. In the USA:

- Women and girls represent 86 per cent of all victims of sexual violence.
- Children aged 6–17 years old account for 53 per cent of all victims of sexual assaults.
- A young woman is at greatest risk of sexual assault at age 14.
- 40 per cent of all young people have witnessed violence.

These startling facts should shock us all into finding ways to make life safer for ourselves, our families and communities. We need to understand the best course of action in a violent situation. We need to think about acquiring basic self-defence skills, which will help to conquer fear and boost our confidence.

What would you do?

Question 1 You're walking to your car in a deserted car park after working late, and hear someone behind you. You realise that they can reach you before you can get to your car. What would you do?

a Don't look back, walk faster, try to get into your car before they reach you.
b Put your hand on whatever defensive tool you are carrying, turn your head so you can see who is approaching.
c Stop and turn around, pull out a weapon if you are carrying one.

Question 2 You stop at a fast-food restaurant late at night. As you return to your car, a man with a knife orders you to go with him. What would you do?

a Scream.
b Co-operate, looking for a chance to escape.
c Try to talk him out of it.
d Refuse to go with him and resist in the strongest way possible.
e Pretend to faint.

Find the answers at: www.aware.org/quizzes/quizindex.shtml

Stop spending money

Around 20 per cent of the world consumes over 80 per cent of its natural resources. This is partly because we buy stuff we don't need. World Buy Nothing Day is when 'you can turn the economy off and talk about it'. It gives you a breather to think about whether you need to buy the things you feel you need. It will focus your mind on the environmental and ethical consequences of consumption: who you buy from and whether they are socially responsible.

There is only one rule: don't spend a single penny all day for the whole day. It all started with No Shop Day in 1994, organised by Ted Dave, a Canadian advertising executive, as a collective protest against the unrelenting calls to over consume.

These are some of the things that people do to support Buy Nothing Day:

- Ask friends to bring stuff to swap.
- Create a shopping-free zone, hanging out with friends in a public space.
- Interview shoppers on video about what they are purchasing and why.
- Get people to pledge to shop responsibly for a month.

Buy Nothing Day is held near the end of November each year

Buy nothing today

Buy nothing on Buy Nothing Day. Throw a Buy Nothing Day Party. Spend the whole of the day with friends instead of spending hard-earned cash.

World Buy Nothing Day: www.ecoplan.org/ibnd/ib_index.htm

Buy Nothing Day UK has a toolkit for organising a Buy Nothing Day, including posters, ideas on how to celebrate the day, and ways to get people involved: www.buynothingday.co.uk

Buy Nothing Christmas: www.buynothingchristmas.org

Adbusters: www.adbusters.org/metas/eco/bnd

Busy doin' nothing

More things to do instead of buying:

- Turn your mobile off and chill out.
- Go to the top of a tall building and look at the view.
- Paint your fridge a bright colour.
- Collect wild food: windfall apples, blackberries, mushrooms.
- Have a bath in candlelight.
- Learn to count to ten in ten languages.
- Grow your own beansprouts.
- Go out in the evening looking for bats.
- Take up jogging.
- Take your toaster apart and try to mend it.

November 27

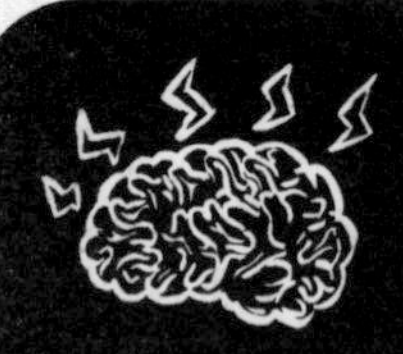

Dear diary

A weekly task

Buy *This Diary Will Change Your Life* and make sure you do each of the 52 tasks – one for each week of the year. You should find it a life changing experience. Find it on Amazon or at your local bookstore: www.thisweb sitewillchangeyourlife.com

Give the Likabula community a chance to become really rich. Instead of trying to change the whole world, jut give 100 people a better future. Send your cheque payable to 'Benrik Likabula Fund' to Benrik Ltd, PFD, Drury House, 34-43 Russell Street, London WC2B 5HA, UK. 'It's for charity, so it's compulsory!'

Mental preparation ... before embarking on your new life, take a moment to reflect. Focus on how pathetic your life has been until now. How dysfunctional your family is. How miserable your friends are. How much you hate your boss. How much your boss hates you. How thin the ozone layer is becoming. This Diary Will Change Your Life

Take the above advice then get started. *This Diary Will Change Your Life* is full of wonderful, zany things to do. Here's an example.

This week, play God with other people's lives. The village of Likabula is one of the poorest in Malawi, with roughly 100 villagers surviving on an average of $15 a month. Population: 104; Language: Chichewa/ English; Currency: Kwacha; Life expectancy: 37; Economy; tea, Mt Mulanje guiding, forestry.

If every diary reader donates £5, the village will be rich, and you will have changed the fortunes of an entire community. Go on, play God.

Ask a billionaire for money

Here is a sample letter to Lakshmi Mittal (age 55, worth $27 billion, steel), 18-19 Kensington Palace Gardens, London W8 4QQ:

Dear Mr Mittal,

Who would have thought that there was so much money to be made from steel! Well I guess there is, and you've got most of it, well done. Now I am a businessman of sorts, and I have a business proposition for you. In exchange for a very small proportion of your fortune (0.01 per cent max), I would devote my waking hours to spreading the word about your generosity. Billionaires get a bad rap for being greedy exploitative fat cats. Only the other day in the pub, someone was slagging you off, and so I smacked him for you, for free. Believe me, you need my help! Call me soon.

Freedom of expression

Writers play a critical role in countries where freedom of expression is denied. They can write about what's happening, and get their writings smuggled out and published in the free world. But if they remain true to their convictions, they lay themselves open to imprisonment. In *The Gulag Archipelago*, Nobel prize-winner Alexander Solzhenitsyn exposed the barbarism of the Gulag system in the Soviet Union. He was imprisoned and exiled for many years, before being allowed to seek refuge in the USA.

Václav Havel, a prominent Czech playwright, spoke out against Soviet oppression. His plays were banned, and he spent five years in prison after co-founding Charter 77. In 1989 he was elected his country's first post-Communist President.

Writers need to speak out. It is important to show solidarity with those who do, and who are imprisoned for doing this. PEN is an international campaign against the persecution and imprisonment of writers anywhere in the world. PEN has 130 branches in over 100 countries.

Join the campaign

English PEN organises a Writers in Prison campaign. Each month one writer is featured. Find out as much as you can about that writer by searching on the web. Go to www.amazon.com, and see if any of that writer's books are available. If so, order copies. Read as an act of solidarity.

Join PEN's Rapid Response Network to campaign against the oppression of writers.

English PEN, which founded the worldwide movement: www.englishpen.org

International PEN: www.internationalpen.org.uk

November 28

Two who spoke out

Raul Rivero Castañeda, poet and journalist, founded the news agency Cuba Press in 1995. With nine others he called on Castro to free prisoners of conscience and reform the socialist regime. In April 2003 he was charged with 'Crimes against the State' and given a 20-year sentence, after a one-day trial. He was released in November 2004, after being transferred from prison to a military hospital.

Naushad Waheed, cyber-dissident and a prominent artist in the Maldives, has been a critic of his government for many years. His most recent arrest took place in 2001. He was held for five months before being transferred to house arrest. In October 2002, he was tried without the chance to defend himself, and sentenced to 15 years in prison. In an account smuggled out of jail, Waheed described the torture inflicted on himself and others.

Help oil the peace process

Buy olive oil from Palestine. Zaytoun sells pesticide-free fairtrade extra virgin olive oil and high-quality soap made from olive oil in the UK as an act of solidarity with Palestinian farmers: zaytoun.org

Go olive picking in Palestine next October with Gush Shalom: www.gush-shalom.org/english/index.html

Holy Land Olive Oil sells Palestinian extra virgin olive oil in the US and Canada: www.palestineoliveoil.org

Another idea – Peace Oil, produced by Arabs, Bedouin, Druse and Jews in the spirit co-operation: www.peaceoil.org

Palestinian olive oil

Olive oil is the backbone of the Palestinian agricultural economy. Since the 2000 Intifada, farmers have had great difficulty in picking their olives. Many can't reach their fields without a special permit, as they are cut off by the so-called 'separation wall' (the barrier Israel is building between Israel and Palestine). In other villages, the olive groves are near to Jewish settlements, and access is hazardous or impossible.

Ironically, the olive branch is a symbol of peace in a region where olive picking is racked by conflict. As part of the 'Olive Picking Coalition', 255 peace activists from the Gush Shalom peace movement (in Hebrew, this means 'The Peace Bloc') took part in the olive picking at Yassouf and Jama'een villages in Palestine, where the villagers feared harassment by the settlers of neighbouring Tapuakh.

Gush Shalom staged a peaceful protest. Together, the families who own the groves and the activists shook the trees and climbed to the highest branches, talking in Hebrew, Arabic and English. The olives were collected on nylon sheets and taken away by tractor.

Gush Shalom's aims

- An end to the Israeli occupation.
- An acceptance of the right of the Palestinian people to establish an independent state in all of the territory occupied by Israel since 1967.
- Jerusalem as the capital of both states, united physically for municipal governance.
- A recognition of the right of Palestinian refugees to return, allowing each refugee to choose freely between compensation and repatriation, with a fixed annual quota for those able to return to Israel.
- The security of both peoples, ensured by mutual agreement and guarantees.
- An overall peace between Israel and all Arab countries, and the creation of a regional union.

Buy a good gift

There are many occasions when you may need to buy a present: a birthday, Christmas, Mother's Day, Valentine's Day ... or just because you feel like giving someone something. And how often do you find that you can't think what to give?

Here's a really great alternative: buy a good gift. Choose a gift from the Good Gifts Catalogue and your gift is actually delivered by a charity to a person, family or community in need. The recipient gets a card with details of the project and a badge to tell them that they are 'Gifted'. They can take pleasure in their gift, which is doing something positive; and they do not need to worry about how to get rid of yet another unwanted and unneeded present. You feel good, and your gift will make a difference to someone's life.

November 30

A catalogue of ideas

Buy a Good Gift for someone's Christmas present.

Once you've done it once, do it again for someone else. Giving will never be the same with a Good Gift.

If you're getting married, put Good Gifts on your Wedding List. Everything you're given is sure to be wanted.

The Good Gifts Catalogue: www.goodgifts.org

A selection of gift ideas

The gifts are fun to give and fun to receive. You can even give your worst enemy a brain cell – for medical research!

Life Cycle Give a bike for a midwife in places like Cambodia and Ethiopia. This will enable her to get around more quickly when she's needed. **£35**

Swords into ploughshares Help a village blacksmith turn a Kalashnikov or a tank into farm implements in war-torn Sierra Leone. **£25+**

Adopt a vegetable Save it from extinction. **£12**

Pedal power in Kigali Give a young Rwandan a bicycle with a pillion seat, and he'll earn an income by giving people rides around the city. **£55**

A nomadic camel To provide transport, milk and good company for a nomadic family as it wanders between Ethiopia and Somalia. **£125**

Ducks for peace Cows, goats, bees are all given to families to generate more income. The latest good idea is ducks. **£15**

Erase the tax

The high price of condoms acts as a disincentive to consistent use. Condoms in the UK are almost twice as expensive as in the USA, and dearer than elsewhere in Europe. They can be obtained free of charge on the NHS, but clinics ration them and they are hard to ask for. Ask your MP to write to the Secretary of State for Health, requesting he/she remove VAT from condoms.

Play the Tony Blair drugs test game at: www.actionaid.org.uk/1394/hiv_aids.html and Supershagland at: www.kikass.tv

United Nations Programme on HIV/AIDS: www.unaids.org

Terrence Higgins Trust, the UK's first AIDS charity: www.tht.org.uk

AVERT: www.avert.org

AIDS is preventable

AIDS is a global challenge. It is having a huge impact on the world's most vulnerable and poorest people. The HIV virus infects 13,500 people every day, swelling the total number infected with HIV to 37.2 million adults and 2.2 million children at the end of 2004. 95 per cent of these people live in the developing world. 3.1 million people died of AIDS in 2004, which means that, on average, somebody died every 10 seconds. 25 million people have died since AIDS was first diagnosed in 1981, 6 million of whom were children. More than 15 million children have been orphaned by AIDS.

There is hope for the future. The political will exists. The resources are there. Medicines that inhibit new infections now allow many to survive with the disease – and they are becoming more affordable through pressure on the drug companies and the wider availability of generic drugs. The UN has set up UNAIDS to encourage global action, and the Global Fund to mobilise funds. The Apathy is Lethal campaign promotes awareness and encourages action. Visit www.apathyislethal.org

Major challenges

- Women account for 57 per cent of the people living with HIV in Sub-Saharan Africa, largely as a result of gender inequality, violence and ignorance.
- Young people (15–24) make up nearly half of all new HIV infection worldwide.
- Prevention programmes currently reach only 1 in 5 people at risk.
- Only 1 in 10 pregnant women in poorer countries is offered services for preventing mother-to-child HIV transmission.
- Anti-retroviral treatment is available for only 7 per cent of the people who need it in developing countries: a total of 400,000 people at the end of 2003.

Have another chocolate

Child slaves may have made your chocolate. According to the BBC television programme, *Slavery*, made by Kate Blewett and Brian Woods of True Vision, thousands of children in Central and West Africa are being stolen from their parents, shipped to the Ivory Coast and sold as slaves to cocoa farmers. These children earn no money for their work, and are barely fed. They are beaten if they try to escape, and most will never see their families again. Nearly 50 per cent of the world's cocoa supply is grown in the Ivory Coast. Steven Millman saw the television programme and was so appalled he had to act:

> Suddenly I could taste every bit of chocolate I'd ever eaten in my life, a taste so sour at the thought that child slaves had produced it that I thought I would vomit. Since then I've done some research to see where chocolate might safely be purchased ... This information takes two forms. First, I've written over 200 letters to many of the world's chocolate manufacturers to find out who is making sure that their chocolate has no slavery involved and I am posting their responses. Second, I have compiled a links page with relevant information about news sources and organisations.

Avoid slave chocolate

Go to Steven Millman's website: www.radicalthought.org Click on the Companies Page to find out whose chocolate is made with child slavery. Don't eat it. One easy way of identifying slave-free chocolate is to buy chocolate made organically. There are no organic farms in the areas where slavery is used. Any chocolate bearing a 'Fairtrade' or 'Max Havelaar' logo will also be free of slavery.

If you are inspired by what Steven did, then do something similar about an issue close to your heart.

True Vision website: www.truevisiontv.com/

How to avoid slave chocolate

This is the letter that Steven Millman sent to over 200 chocolate manufacturers:

> Hi! – There has been a ton of information in the news over the last few months about the child slavery used in the harvesting of cocoa in the Ivory Coast. I love your chocolates, but I can't bear the thought of eating chocolate made by child slaves. Do you guys do anything to ensure that no child slavery is used in the production of your cocoa?
>
> Thanks, Steven

All replies and a list of the companies that didn't reply are posted on Steven's website.

Disability access

It's a basic right

Download the symbols and print them onto sticker paper.

Design a second version with a diagonal red bar superimposed on the symbol contained within a red circle to indicate that these facilities are NOT available, but should be made available in order to provide disability access.

Use your stickers to praise good practice and publicise a lack of proper access.

The symbols can be downloaded from: www.disabilityjobsite.co.uk/accessible/disability symbol.php

It is part of a modern, humane society that people with physical disabilities should have proper access to the offices, public buildings, events, and the streets and public transport they might wish to use. The Graphic Artists Guild Foundation in New York designed 12 symbols to promote and publicise accessibility of spaces and activities, including:

- An event or location accessible to people who are blind or have low vision.

- Availability of a text telephone.

- Large print books, pamphlets, guides and programmes for the visually impaired.

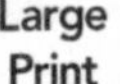

- Availability of telephones for the hard of hearing.

- Open Captioning, where captions are available all the time.

- Audio-description at performances for people who are blind or have low vision.

- Amplified listening systems, such as loop systems to amplify sound via hearing aids.

- Availability of printed material in Braille.

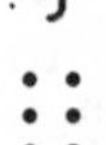

Access all areas

The most universally-known symbol for disabled accessibility is the wheelchair. It means that a facility is accessible to people with limited mobility, including wheelchair users: step-free access, disabled toilets and low public phones.

Stand up for your rights

> *Now, I say to you today my friends, even though we face the difficulties of today and tomorrow, I still have a dream. ... I have a dream that one day this nation will rise up and live out the true meaning of its creed: 'We hold these truths to be self-evident, that all men are created equal.'*
> Martin Luther King from his speech at a Civil Rights March on Washington, 28 August 1963

Is there an issue you feel really strongly about? Is there an injustice that is so outrageous that you boil with rage and feel that you have to do something about it? Take your inspiration from Rosa Parks. This previously very ordinary woman did something that was both very simple and very extraordinary. Her single action changed the course of her own life and was a trigger for the Civil Rights Movement in the USA. It also brought a young Baptist minister, Dr Martin Luther King Jr, to world prominence. So, stand up for your beliefs by starting a campaign or undertaking some sort of non-violent direct action.

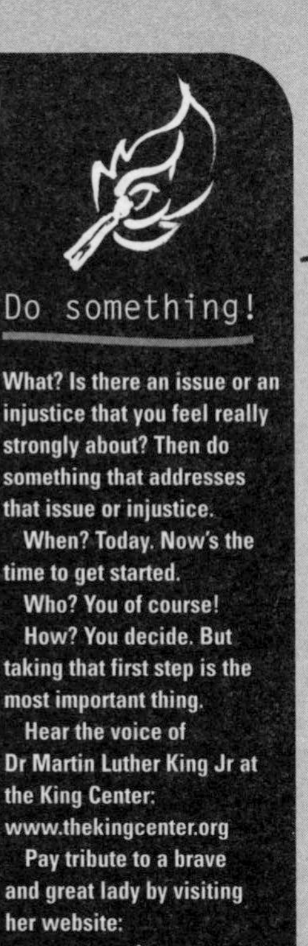

Do something!

What? Is there an issue or an injustice that you feel really strongly about? Then do something that addresses that issue or injustice.

When? Today. Now's the time to get started.

Who? You of course!

How? You decide. But taking that first step is the most important thing.

Hear the voice of Dr Martin Luther King Jr at the King Center: www.thekingcenter.org

Pay tribute to a brave and great lady by visiting her website: www.rosaparks.org

Find out more about Rosa Parks: http://en.wikipedia.org/wiki/Rosa_Parks

Rosa Parks, civil rights pioneer

Rosa Parks worked as a seamstress in Montgomery, Alabama, at a time when the southern states of the USA operated a kind of apartheid. She was arrested on 1 December 1955 for refusing to give up her seat on a segregated bus to a white male passenger, as demanded by the bus driver. She was convicted of violating a local ordinance. Her act sparked a city-wide boycott of the bus system by blacks.

The Montgomery Bus Boycott started on 5 December 1955 and lasted 381 days. Rosa's courage catapulted her into world history, and she is now referred to as the 'Mother of the modern-day Civil Rights Movement'. Up until her death in 2005 aged 92, Rosa continued the work with young people that she started with her husband through the Rosa and Raymond Parks Institute for Self Development.

Make a pledge for change

Some examples

- Jeff edited 100 pages for Project Gutenberg (www.pgdp.net); 50 others agreed to do the same.
- Andy installed low-energy long-life bulbs throughout his house; 20 other people had agreed to do the same.
- Matthew bought only Fairtrade tea, coffee and chocolate bars during July 2005; 20 others did this.
- Ellie did all her shopping locally and not in a supermarket chain in July 2005 along with 20 others.

Other pledge requests include displaying posters on 'How TB kills 1,500 Africans a day' in your car; planting 10 trees to offset your carbon dioxide emissions; giving 1 per cent of your salary to charity; refusing to register for an ID card but pledging £10 to a legal defence fund; make a switch to green electricity.

Pledge Bank: www.pledgebank.com

Changing the world all on your own might seem an impossible task. And indeed it would be. But it's okay, because there are others out there just like you: they feel the need to act, but don't want to do it alone. And the way to make contact with them is through the Pledge Bank.

The idea is simple. You enter a pledge online, promising to do something but only if a certain number of other people do the same. When enough people have signed up, everyone undertakes their pledge. This is a really good way of multiplying the impact of your actions to change the world. Here are some tips for successful pledges:

- Keep your ambitions modest. Why ask for fifty people when five would be enough? Every extra person makes your pledge harder to meet.
- Think about how your pledge reads. Will an outsider understand it? Read it to someone else. If they don't understand it, you'll need to rewrite it.
- Make your pledge imaginative, worthwhile, fun, and reasonably easy to complete.
- Don't imagine that your pledge will sell itself. Tell the world. Email your friends, print leaflets and stick them through your neighbours' doors. Get some publicity in the local newspaper.

Get others signed up

Pledge to do something to change the world. Put your pledge on Pledge Bank. Persuade family, friends, colleagues and complete strangers to sign up. Achieve your target by the cut-off date:

I will ... (enter your pledge), but only if ... (enter number) of other people will do the same. The other people must sign up before (enter date by which the pledging has to be completed).

Dress a tree

We need to care for and protect our trees, take them into our lives and look after them. They are the lungs of our planet, breathing oxygen into the air. Without them, we would die. Tree Dressing Day encourages the celebration of trees in the city or in the country, in your garden or in a park. And not just at Christmas.

Trees have been honoured and decorated throughout the ages, and still are in many parts of the world. Here are some examples from the past:

- Xerxes, the famed ruler of Persia, on discovering a plane tree that he considered beautiful, is reputed to have honoured it by dressing it with jewels.
- The prophet Mohammed, on his night journey along the Axis Mundi with the Archangel Gabriel as a guide, encountered a tree glowing with emeralds, rubies and sapphires, perhaps the miraculous Tuba Tree which stood at the heart of paradise.
- Alexander, explorer and conqueror of ancient times, found a talking tree with the heads of animals and people growing in its branches, which rebuked him for his ambition and forewarned him of his death.

All dressed up

Go dress a tree. Use anything you feel like: lights, big hanging numbers cut out of card, cloth, huge rosettes, objects for recycling.

You can use the decorations to put across a specific message, or just make your tree look so beautiful that people notice and appreciate it.

Tree Dressing Day is the first full weekend in December. The Tree Dressing Day Manual from Common Ground: www.commonground.org.uk/trees/t-dress.html

See examples of tree dressing at: www.england-in-particular.info/trees/t-dress.html

What we do now

- In Mexico during December, *pinatas* (bags full of sweets) are suspended from the trees as a treat for children to celebrate the riches trees provide.
- In Provence, South of France, on May Day may trees (hawthorn) are decked with flowers and ribbons.
- In some parts of Russia on Maundy Thursday, villagers will select a young birch tree and dress it in women's clothing or with ribbons and beads.
- At Chir-Ghat in India, local women, as an act of devotion, tie pieces of clothing to the branches of the ancient tree that reputedly witnessed the appearance of the god Krishna to the cow-girls.
- On the North American prairies, the Lakota, Oglala and Dakota Sioux put rags in trees as part of an ancient ritual connected with spiritual purification. Red is an offering to the sun, blue to the sky and green to the earth.

Light up a message

Night lights

Get one or several strings of lights.

Spell out a message for night-time drivers and midnight amblers to see.

Be as political, as fun, as serious, or as silly as you want. You are only limited by your ideas, your spelling, the space you have available, and how many lights you can afford.

Hang it up in your front garden, a window or a balcony facing the street.

Don't be surprised when people all over your neighbourhood pick up on your idea.

Do you want to change the world while you sleep? You can be curled up in your warm bed, dreaming of desert islands and exotic fruit cocktails – and still be sending out a message to passers by. We all have our own ideas about how to improve the state of the world. Why not write up a message in lights and hang it up outside your house or apartment?

Change your message whenever you feel like it, or when you think up an even better slogan. This is a great way of spreading a message in an innovative way. Here are some ideas for messages:

- **PEACE**
  If you're anti-war, or just as a seasonal message.
- **VOTE**
  At election time.
- **WALK TO WORK**
  To reduce greenhouse gas emissions.
- **SMILE**
  Because tomorrow will be a nice day.
- **SAVE WATER**
  When there's a drought.
- **SMOKING KILLS**
  A dear friend has just died of lung cancer.
- **FAIR TRADE**
  To support fairtrade, of course.
- **USE A CONDOM**
  Do your bit to combat HIV/AIDS.

Matching lights to messages

There are lots of 'novelty lights' on sale. Match your lights to your message. Here are one or two examples:

- Yellow ducks for a watery theme.
- Pink elephants to give people a laugh.
- Red chilli peppers for a particularly spicy slogan.

Why not try some 'rope lights'? These are especially easy to 'write' with and come in a range of colours.

Get street smart

It's the season of goodwill. Christmas is coming very soon. You've gone out to a restaurant to have a meal with some good friends. Do you feel a warm glow of satisfaction? If you do, then this would be a really good time for someone to persuade you to give to the homeless – to help people who are living a very different life from your own, who wouldn't be able to afford the meal you've just eaten, and who certainly wouldn't even be allowed into the restaurant.

This was the starting point for StreetSmart, a simple fundraising scheme whereby participating restaurants add £1 to the bill for each table as a voluntary donation. The restaurant passes on the money raised to StreetSmart, which then distributes it to local charities for the homeless. London diners help the London homeless, and Newcastle diners help out in the Northeast. The costs of running StreetSmart are sponsored by Bloomberg and all the money raised goes directly to the people who need it.

The donation is voluntary. The scheme is publicised through a small card placed on each table. Diners have a chance to say they don't want to pay the donation. But almost everyone is happy to do so, and most don't even notice.

Diners support the homeless

If StreetSmart is operating in your city and you're eating out, pay your £1 and think of the good it is doing. Discuss the scheme with other diners. If you notice that the restaurant hasn't signed up, then talk to the manager. Ask them to agree there and then to sign up to StreetSmart.

If there is no StreetSmart scheme in your area, contact StreetSmart and ask if you can tell restaurants about it and get something started.

And if you live in another country, this could be a great opportunity for you to start your own version of StreetSmart. Find out as much as possible about how the scheme works, and then get going on setting up your own scheme.

StreetSmart: www.streetsmart.org.uk

StreetSmart – a brilliant idea

StreetSmart started in London in 1998. It has now spread across the UK to thirteen cities. In its first seven years, it raised and distributed over £1.8 million to 149 projects.

The projects all aim to get people off the streets, and back onto their feet again. Some of the money goes to basics such as a bed, a shower, or a pair of shoes. But money also goes to rehabilitation – helping homeless people through crucial stages in their progress from vagrant to valued community member.

Preserve our culture

Around 10,000 people around the world have already made a time capsule.

International Time Capsule Society (Oglethorpe University, Georgia, USA): www.oglethorpe.edu (then type name of society into website search engine)

Smithsonian Centre for Materials Research and Education tells you how to make your own time capsule with a contact list of suppliers: www.si.edu/scmre/takingcare/timecaps.htm

The British Library advises on time capsules: www.bl.uk/services/npo/faqtime.html

Ideas for what to put in a time capsule: www.appliedhistory.com/suggest.html

Make a time capsule

To understand the present it is important to know about the past. We can do this through documents and what is written in books (personal memoirs as well as great histories), but also through the buildings, landscape and historic artefacts that survive.

How will future generations get a balanced view of our age if the great events of our time are remembered, but the experience of ordinary people living ordinary lives is forgotten? Each of us has a responsibility to ensure the preservation of contemporary cultural objects, and to use them to tell our story. One way of doing this is by making a time capsule:

- It needs to be airtight and watertight. You can buy one in lead (around £250) or plastic (around £50).
- Include in it some of the things that you think best represent life on earth as it is now – photographs, recordings, CDs, DVDs, newspaper articles, magazines, predictions about the future, clothing, equipment, seeds, identity documents, whatever.
- Produce a guide for your collection, explaining what the objects are, how they work, their significance and why you selected them.
- Bury it, but not too deep, in the hope that someone in the future will unearth it and discover the secrets of the early 21st century.

The rescue game

Gather a group of friends and ask them to imagine that they have been given a ten-minute warning that their house is in imminent danger of being flooded. Invite everyone to make a list of ten things they would rescue, and a brief explanation of why they would save them, and what they mean to them.

Compare lists and examine each other's choices. The aim is to give you all a better understanding of the meaning of the objects in your world.

Stand up for your rights

Human rights provide a foundation for building a just and peaceful world. Every human being has the right to dignity, respect, and freedom – whatever their race, colour, gender, sexual orientation, religion, political opinion, or social origin. On 10 December 1948, the General Assembly of the United Nations adopted and proclaimed the Universal Declaration of Human Rights. This has been translated into over 300 languages and dialects – from Abkhaz to Zulu. It is the holder of the Guinness World Record for the document that has been most translated. But, unlike the US Constitution or the European Convention on Human Rights, the Declaration has no legal force.

The Declaration contains 30 articles, including:

Article 1 All human beings are born free and equal in dignity and rights ...

Article 3 Everyone has the right to life, liberty and security of person.

Article 4 Slavery and the slave trade shall be prohibited in all their forms.

Article 5 No one shall be subjected to torture or to cruel, inhuman or degrading treatment or punishment.

Article 18 Everyone has the right to freedom of thought, conscience and religion ...

Article 19 Everyone has the right to freedom of opinion and expression ...

Article 20 Everyone has the right to freedom of peaceful assembly and association ...

World Human Rights Day is a time to reflect on how lucky we are to have our rights enshrined in a UN Declaration, and to pledge to do something for the people who are denied these rights.

Get some friends to each choose a right from the Declaration. Find a T-shirt screening shop to design colourful shirts. Assemble in a public space wearing your T-shirts and advertise your selection of rights to promote World Human Rights Day.

Celebrate human rights

Make a series of Tibetan prayer flags, each one focusing on a different human right. Visit the website of an Amnesty International group in Pasadena, whose idea this is: www.its.caltech.edu/ -aigp22/flags/home.shtml

Information on the UN and human rights: www.un.org/rights

Read the Declaration in almost any language: www.unhchr.ch/udhr

Singled out

Ngawang Gyaltsen is a monk from Drepung monastery, Lhasa. He was imprisoned for a year in 1987, and in 1989 was sentenced to 17 years in prison. He was singled out as leader of a group of monks accused of producing literature critical of the Chinese government. The group published a Tibetan translation of the Universal Declaration of Human Rights.

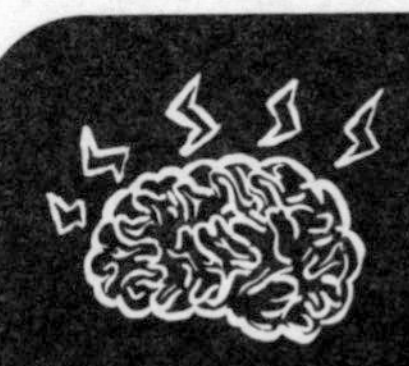

Help create a public library

Sign up as a member of BookCrossing.

If you happen to find a BookCrossing book left by someone else, read it, enjoy it and pass it on.

Each reader can put comments about the book on the BookCrossing website.

The person who originally supplied the book can keep track of its journey.

Encourage all your friends to join. The more BookCrossing grows, the better it will get!

BookCrossing: www.bookcrossing.com

Share your books

bookcrossing n. the practice of leaving a book in a public place to be picked up and read by others, who then do likewise. Added to the *Concise Oxford English Dictionary* in August 2004

You probably have lots of books on your shelves, gathering dust. Why not share them with others? Select one that you really like. Nobody is reading it at the moment. Register it on the BookCrossing website, and start its journey into the unknown.

BookCrossing is a book-lovers' community. It's a global book club that crosses time and space. It's a reading group that knows no geographical boundaries. It has 300,000 members, sharing 1.5 million books, all over the world. And it's completely free. A BookCrossing member leaves a book around for someone else to pick up and read; and registers this book on the BookCrossing website. The person who finds the book reads it and then passes it on to another reader. The book continues from one reader to another, until it gets lost or someone breaks the chain by not passing it on.

The three Rs of BookCrossing

- **Read** a good book – a book that you would recommend to others.
- **Register** the book with BookCrossing. First log in your details. This takes a couple of minutes. You will be given a BookCrossing ID number and the URL of the BookCrossing website. Label your book with these references, and put in a note asking the reader to pass it on after they've finished reading it. You can buy printed labels from the BookCrossing website.
- **Release** the book for someone else to read. Give it to a friend, leave it somewhere for someone to pick up – a park bench, a coffee shop, etc. – or release it 'into the wild', and people will have to search for it. The website enables you to say you have left it or gives clues to help people find it.

Bring cheer at Christmas time

December 12

Saint Nicholas lived from around AD 270–345 (or 352). Born in Patara (in modern-day Turkey), he is the patron saint of seamen, merchants, archers, children, students, prostitutes, pharmacists, lawyers, pawnbrokers, prisoners and Russia, and is the original Santa Claus.

Father Christmas as we know him today dates back to the 17th century. Pictures of him from that era show him as a well-nourished bearded man dressed in a long, green, fur-lined robe. He typifies the spirit of good cheer at Christmas time.

Father Christmas lives somewhere near the North Pole and flies round the world on Christmas Eve on his reindeer-driven sleigh delivering presents to children, climbing into people's houses through the chimney. Children leave an empty stocking at the end of their bed. Sometimes they write to him telling him what they would really like to be given. Adults may leave a glass of rum waiting for him in case he's thirsty. This will probably have mysteriously disappeared by the morning.

Play Santa for a day

You will need to:

- **Hire a costume. Go to a theatrical costumiers and rent one. Drop in at the North Pole and borrow one. Make your own.**
- **Learn how to be a really great Santa. You can do this by going to Santa School. Check out the Ministry of Fun.**
- **Hang about on the High Street dispensing good cheer to children.**

Ministry of Fun (UK): www.ministryoffun.net

When you wish upon a Star: www.whenyouwishuponastar.org.uk and www.thesantarun.org.uk

Worldwide Christmases

A 1.2 mile Santa run takes place in Edinburgh in December each year to raise money for the When you wish upon a Star Foundation, which grants wishes to terminally ill children. In 2004, 3,445 Santas took part (a world record for the number of Santas present at one time) and raised £1.25 million to help more than 1,000 wishes come true. The participation fee includes the loan of a Santa suit. Go to Edinburgh next December and give this a go.

Christmas is celebrated in most countries. Ways of saying 'Happy Christmas':

In Cantonese: **Gun Tso Sun Tan'Gung Haw Sun**
In Dutch: **Gelukkige Kerstmis**
In French: **Joyeux Noel**
In German: **Froehliche Weihnachten**
In Italian: **Natale Felice**
In Japanese: **Kurisumasu Omedeto**
In Portuguese: **Christmas Feliz**
In Spanish: **Navidad Feliz**
In Swedish: **God Ju**

Organise a hunger banquet

Life's lottery

Organise a Hunger Banquet. Each person attending is randomly assigned a role.

15 per cent of the people are in the high-income group; they sit at a table and enjoy a three-course meal.

25 per cent of the people are in the middle-income group; they sit on chairs and eat rice and beans (delicious and nutritious).

60 per cent are the world's poor; they sit on the floor, and get only rice and water.

www.hungerbanquet.org

Oxfam America's Hunger Banquet website gives you a chance to learn about hunger from the point of view of those who experience it every day:

www.oxfamamerica.org

Our planet produces enough food to feed every woman, man, and child – and with some left over. The problem is that the food does not reach everybody who needs it. And we're not talking here only about those who go hungry as a result of drought or conflict, but about people who are just too poor to buy enough food to keep them alive and healthy. Children are particularly at risk. Malnutrition stunts their physical and mental development and makes them more prone to disease.

Millennium Development Goal no. 1 is to halve the number of people suffering poverty and hunger by 2015. But if hunger is not really about an overall shortage of food, but about its unequal distribution, we should be able to do much better than that. We should be able to abolish malnutrition altogether.

You can use a Hunger Banquet (see left) to raise money to fight global poverty. But make sure the rich pay more!

Gloria's story

Gloria Narua is surviving but it wouldn't take much for her life to fall apart. She lives in Mozambique, where she grows crops on a small plot of land called a mashamba. Most years she can produce enough maize, groundnuts, eggplant, carrots, and kale to feed three children. She even owns a few chickens.

Sadly, she doesn't earn enough to send her children to school. Her oldest, Eduardo, is nine years old and desperate to learn how to read and write. She simply can't afford to educate him. Besides, this year, she'll need his help in the field to bring in the maize. Last year, her husband gathered the harvest with her, but he died in the spring. People say it could have been AIDS.

She misses her husband. As she looks forward to the harvest, she's worried. The rains were not good this year. It could be a tough year ahead.

Go on a sex strike

Sometimes there is nothing for it but to show you mean business. If you want to bring about change, or at least persuade your partner to see your point of view, you may just have to hit them where it hurts.

In Sudan, Samira Ahmed, a university professor, launched a sex strike in 2002 to try to end 19 years of civil war. She called it 'alHair', Arabic for 'women sexually abandoning their men'. The action (or rather the inaction) began with 20 women from the Lou and Jekany tribes, who were most involved in the fighting.

In Turkey, Birsel Lemke campaigned against a proposal to develop highly poisonous cyanide-based gold mining in sites across the country. Inhabitants of one village near the site of a proposed mine ran naked, bearing signs with the slogan, 'Before Eurogold strips us, we'll strip'. The women refused to have sex until the men had expelled the gold mining company.

Sex strikes have been used around the world:

- In Colombia, to protest against the drug wars.
- In Poland, to fight for legal abortion.
- In Amsterdam, by sex workers to protest against harassment.

Not tonight!

If there's an issue you care passionately about, write to the partners of those who are causing the problem urging them to go on a sex strike. Get as much publicity as you can for your campaign.

If there is something your own partner is doing that is causing harm to others or to the planet, why not start your own sex strike to persuade him or her to desist.

The Global Women's Strike held on 8 March each year highlights how much of the world's work is done by women, and the difference it makes when their contribution is withdrawn: www.globalwomenstrike.net

December 14

No water, no sex

In 2001, a group of women in Sirt, Turkey banned their husbands from their bedrooms in an effort to get a mains water supply to their village. The 27-year-old water system had broken down, and the women were having to collect and carry water over long distances.

The strategy had an immediate effect. The men petitioned the authorities to repair the water system, and offered their labour free. The local authority provided pipes to bring a nearby water source to the village. The women protested until water actually started gushing out of the taps. Islam requires people to bathe after sex, so there was a connection between the method of protest and what was being fought for.

Stop shopping

Real retail therapy

Shopping? We're spoiled for choice. We have enough, and we buy too much. When we feel down, we just go out for a bit of 'retail therapy'. Then we get home, and the buzz wears off. How about trying something really therapeutic: Stop Shopping.

Reverend Billy is the Arch-Priest of the Stop Shopping movement. His followers buy nothing whenever they go shopping. His particular targets are Starbucks and Wal-Mart. Visit his website for fun and ideas at: www.revbilly.com

'Twenty of us walked into Wal-Mart ... We each took a shopping cart and walked silently and slowly in an unbroken line up and down, pushing our empty carts through endless canyons of products. Sometimes the line got split up, by a real shopper, or a curious child, or a near convert; but the line always reformed, rejoined, moving randomly, inexorably toward what ... the religious fervour of sheer not-shopping.

The cop finally approached us – and we were tentative with our entreaties. He came to understand that we had simply and lawfully worshipped in a Wal-Mart. Maybe we were Odd. Maybe we put the Odd in our God! But he understood we were just celebrating buylessness ...

We heard him murmur something to himself. Then he said "Well our founding fathers did say that every healthy democracy needs a little revolution once in a while". Revolution? Who said anything about a revolution? Let's just Stop Shopping! Amen.' (Bill Talen, *Ecologistonline* 1/11/03)

Reverend Billy's playlet

Perform this at your local Starbucks.

Two actors walk in and start the action at the shelves near the cash register. Support actors walk in with them to distribute literature when the play is climaxing.

Ex-prisoner Oh gosh look at this place.

Friend It's just a Starbucks.

Ex-prisoner Well it beats the penitentiary cafeteria, I'll tell you.

Friend Yeah it's a beautiful coffee shop, everything is real ... arty.

Ex-prisoner That's the thing about prison. They don't let graphic designers in there.

Friend Well, prison is supposed to be depressing.

Ex-prisoner Just look at those packages over there, everything looks so ...

Friend What?

To find out what happens, download the full script from www.revbilly.com

Support the clown doctors

The clown doctors have become shooting stars in my life. I can count on them when I need some cheering up. Thank you for your smiles, your jokes, your fun. No words could ever describe what you have done for me! Brooke

Humour relaxes people, reduces pain and stress, makes people laugh and feel good and generally promotes a positive outlook. All in all it's a good medicine. And it doesn't have the side effects of some more potent drugs. This is where clown doctors come in. Imagine being in hospital, away from the comfort of your home, and feeling sad, anxious, frightened, lonely or in pain. Clown doctors treat children in hospital with a dose of fun and laughter. The clown doctors project was developed by the Humour Foundation in Australia, where 40 clown doctors entertain around 60,000 patients a year. A similar scheme was set up by the Theodora Foundation all over Europe. In the UK, the Theodora Trust recruits and trains special clowns to work in selected hospitals in England and Wales.

Humour works

If you think you have what it takes to become a Clown Doctor, make enquiries with the Theodora Children's Trust. Or you could make a donation.

If you know a child who is ill and could do with some cheering up, download the Clown Doctors Activity Book from www.humourfoundation.com.au

Bring a little happiness into an old people's home or a day centre for homeless people, and organise a Christmas entertainment for them.

Theodora Children's Trust: www.theodora.org.uk

Humour Foundation, Australia: www.humourfoundation.com.au

Juggling their skills

Clown doctors receive considerable training in the very special skills needed to divert children's attention during painful procedures, help calm them in emergency, or just brighten up their day. They learn how to develop their mastery of magic, storytelling, acting, mime, balloon sculpture, and juggling, and adapt these skills to each child's needs in various situations. When working on the wards, they have to behave with sensitivity, only approaching children when it is clear that they will be welcome. As one parent remembers:

> 'It was an extremely stressful time, but as if by magic the clown doctors would always arrive on the ward at the right time and brighten everyone's day. The children would perk up, parents would have their minds taken off the awful and often harrowing situations ... even the staff would smile!'

December 17

Streetwise

Remember George Bernard Shaw's wise words: 'The worst sin towards our fellow creatures is not to hate them, but to be indifferent to them; that is the essence of inhumanity.'

Read *Trash* by Gita Wolf, a book which shows the life of a group of ragpickers in South India.

Contact the Consortium for Street Children to find out about organisations in countries you plan to visit. When you get there, visit a night shelter and meet some of the children. Take some old toys to leave with them.

The Consortium's website: www.streetchildren.org.uk

Children on the streets

Children are living on the streets for many reasons. They have run away from physical or sexual abuse at home. Their families are too poor to feed an extra mouth. They are physically disabled and unwanted. Some are attracted by the idea of 'the bright lights'. In the developing world, they are 'street children'. In the rich world, they are 'runaways'. The causes may be different, but the result is the same: vulnerable children living on the street, fending for themselves.

Once on the streets, they need to earn money to eat. Some beg. Some sell. Some do shoe-shining. Many are ragpickers – recycling cloth, plastic, glass, metals, often in dangerous conditions. And some work is traditionally done by gangs of street children, such as erecting wedding tents in India. It is hard to comprehend what life for children on the streets must be like. When we encounter street children, we see them as a nuisance. But they are human beings who are being denied access to some fundamental human rights we take for granted.

The children speak out

Street children have their own ideas about the world and its problems:

With unity amongst ourselves, we can do anything! Mannar

We should work to protect all children and uphold their rights. We should see that the police who make the lives of street children so miserable are punished. Suresh

Education is the most important thing to bring about change. With education comes respect. And with respect we can build our lives.' Papu

Employment is the big issue. Every young adult should have the opportunity to earn a living. Anuj

After a brainstorm on how to change the world, a group of children in Delhi aged 9–17 decided to organise a National Street Children's Day, when they would do things for other people for free, which would challenge the stereotype that street children are parasites who are up to no good.

Make friends with Africa

The state of Africa is a scar on the conscience of the world. But if the world as a community focused on it, we could heal it. And if we don't, it will become deeper and angrier. Tony Blair, British Prime Minister, 2001

People are the real wealth of nations. The United Nations Development Programme (UNDP) defines 'human development' as much more than the rise or fall of national incomes. It is about creating an environment in which people can develop their full potential and lead productive, creative lives in accordance with their needs, interests and choices. Economic growth is only one means, although an important one, of enlarging those choices.

Many Africans now live and work in Europe and North America. Some are passionate about 'doing something' for Africa and have started organisations to raise money and support development programmes.

The Human Development Index is a 'league table' compiled by the UNDP. It tries to reflect the wider view of human development by taking into account life expectancy, adult literacy rate, education enrolment, gross domestic product per capita.

Help Africa

Elsie Nemlin, from the Ivory Coast, founded Stand Up For Africa (SUFA) in 2003:

- **To raise funds for the disadvantaged in Africa and facilitate their self-sufficiency.**
- **To provide volunteers from the African Diaspora to share skills for African development.**
- **To lobby for justice and fairness.**

SUFA's first programme addresses the child slave trade in West Africa: www.standupforafrica.org.uk

Volunteer to help one of the development initiatives.

The African Foundation for Development (AFFORD): www.afford-uk.org

News from all over Africa: www.allafrica.com

UNDP human development website: hdr.undp.org

The Human Development Index

The bottom 19 nations in the 2002 index were all in Africa:

Country	Index
Rwanda	0.431
Guinea	0.425
Benin	0.421
Tanzania	0.407
Côte d'Ivoire	0.399
Zambia	0.389
Malawi	0.388
Angola	0.381
Chad	0.379
Democratic Republic of Congo	0.365
Central African Republic	0.361
Ethiopia	0.359
Mozambique	0.354
Guinea-Bissau	0.350
Burundi	0.339
Mali	0.326
Burkina Faso	0.302
Niger	0.292
Sierra Leone	0.273

A blinding experience

Is a blind restaurant a good idea? Could the idea catch on? Might blind restaurants spring up in other cities? What do you think?

If you go to any of the cities featured opposite and below, make a point of going to dine at a blind restaurant, and find out for yourself.

Back home, contact an organisation for blind and visually impaired people active in your town or city, and suggest that you work together to organise a blind evening (with masks) at a local restaurant.

Die Blinde Kuh: www.blindekuh.ch

Dans le Noir?: www.danslenoir.com

Unsicht Bar: www.unsicht-bar-berlin.de

Eat in darkness

The idea of eating in total darkness may seem strange if you are sighted, but of course is perfectly normal to an unsighted person. In 1999, a blind clergyman, Jorge Spielmann, had the idea of opening a restaurant in Zurich staffed by blind waiters. It is called Die Blinde Kuh (The Blind Cow), and the waiters wear bells on their feet, so you can hear them approaching. Diners are met at the entrance and led to their tables. The toilets are lit, but diners have to be guided there by a waiter. The venture has a serious purpose – to give blind people work, and at the same time to teach sighted people what it is like to live in a blind world. Before opening his restaurant Spielmann sometimes used to blindfold guests at his home to encourage them to pay more attention to the food and the conversations going on. 'I just want people to experience the world on our terms.'

Dans Le Noir? (In the Dark?), which has branches in Paris and London, is run on much the same lines. The venture was established by the Paul Guinot Association, which helps France's blind and visually handicapped. 'We hope the restaurant will serve as a bridge between people who can see and people who can't.' The idea is certainly of interest to experimental psychologists, who are keen to find out how lack of vision affects our experience of taste.

Tasting blind

Adapting a building to make it totally blacked out is an expensive and time-consuming process. It also runs into difficulties when it comes to health and safety regulations. However, The Unsicht Bar (Invisible Bar) in Berlin gets round the problem by requiring diners to wear masks over their eyes. The restaurant was started by an organisation of blind and visually impaired people, and most of the staff are blind.

Become an encyclopaedist

Thanks to the internet, you can play a part in creating the world's most ambitious information project. Wikipedia is an internet encyclopaedia ('wiki' means 'quick' in Hawaiian), which is being created entirely by volunteers, who contribute new articles and update and revise existing ones. Everything is copyright free. Contributions have to comply with Wikipedia's 'neutral point of view' policy, so that there is no bias in what is published. Articles can be edited by anyone (except by banned users and there are a few protected pages).

Wikipedia is the world's largest and fastest-growing encyclopaedia. It was started in 2001 and in its first year over 20,000 entries were created. By September 2004, over 1 million articles had been completed (350,000 of which are in English). There are articles under active development in over 100 languages. Nearly 2,500 new articles are added to Wikipedia each day, along with ten times that number of updates to existing articles. Wikipedia is one of the ten most popular internet reference sites.

Related projects supported by the Wikimedia Foundation include: Wiktionary (dictionary and thesaurus); Wikiquote (compendium of quotations); Wikibooks (manuals and textbooks); and Wikisource (a repository of public domain documents).

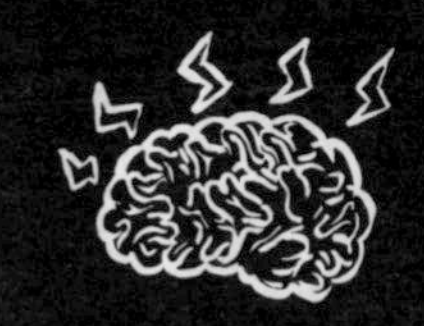

Contributions welcome

Write an article for Wikipedia on some obscure subject that you are an expert on. Start by finding out whether the subject already has an entry and what related subjects have entries.

Open your article with a concise paragraph, defining the topic and mentioning the most important points. The reader should be able to get a good overview by only reading this first paragraph. Then write the rest of the article. Guidance for contributors is published on the Wikipedia website.

Or, take a subject that you are really interested in and know something about, find the article in Wikipedia, and then edit it, adding all the bits that are missing: en.wikipedia.org www.wikimediafoundation.org

Translators wanted

In France, between 1751–72, a remarkable book was published that attempted to put all human knowledge between two covers. This was the *Encyclopédie*. Compiled largely under the direction of Denis Diderot, it comprised 28 volumes, 71,818 articles and 2,885 illustrations. A second, edition, in 66 volumes, was published from 1782–1832.

You can help translate the *Encyclopédie* into English: www.hti.umich.edu/d/did/call.html

Brighten up your community

Ray of light

Spend time walking around your neighbourhood. Make a note of all the things you would like to improve.

Think about: things that can be done easily, with little or no money; two or three things that are really important. Talk to neighbours and try to get a consensus for your improvement plan. Try to get at least one thing on your list done within the next three months.

For information on SAD: www.sada.org.uk

The Community Planning Website: www.communityplanning.net

Planning for Real: www.nifonline.org.uk

Christopher Alexander's famed *Pattern Language*: www.patternlanguage.com

It's the middle of winter. The days are short. Around 500,000 people in the UK suffer from Seasonal Affective Disorder (also known as SAD), which is the most common winter depression. It is caused by a biochemical imbalance in the hypothalamus (the gland responsible for regulating body temperature and food intake) caused by the shortening of daylight hours and the lack of sunlight in winter. The symptoms include a general lassitude and depression.

Many of us find the winter months bring us down, even if we are not as badly affected as sufferers of SAD. Our surroundings never look as good under grey skies as they do in the summer sunshine. But maybe this is the time to take a fresh look at the community we live in – when it is at its worst. What can be done to improve it? Remove the graffiti? Paint a mural? Hang up banners? Encourage window boxes? Plant trees? Tidy up the road signs, and other street furniture? Banish the motor car? Build sitting-out areas? Encourage live music? Provide more sunlight? Whatever it is, if you want it done by the end of the summer, you had better get started now.

From SAD to happy

On one side of a valley is the Austrian village of Rattenberg (population 455), which sits in the shadow of a high mountain, depriving it of sunlight for four months of each year. On the other side of the valley is Kramsach, which basks in the winter sun.

An array of computer-guided solar reflectors known as 'Heliostats', each 6.5 m^2 and programmed to adjust their direction according to the sun's position, bounces the sun's rays from above Kramsach to a rocky outcrop close to Rattenberg, where a second bank of mirrors directs light to the village.

There is not enough reflected light to brighten the whole village. But selected streets, buildings and public spaces are lit up, and the villagers now feel much less sad during the long winter.

Don't buy cocaine

For once the politicians and the police are actually right – cocaine is bad news. But not just for the reasons you might be thinking. You've probably heard all about how coke rots your nose, causes heart attacks, is highly addictive and fuels cartels and corruption.

But there's another reason not to buy cocaine that people don't talk about. It is that cocaine isn't 'fairtrade'. Far from it. Although many farmers initially turn to growing drugs because low commodity prices mean that they can't make a decent living from more traditional crops, less than 1 per cent of the profits from cocaine go back to the producer.

Every time you purchase a gramme of cocaine the people who cultivate coca leaves are being completely ripped off. They are breaking their backs and employing child labour just so you can get high for a few hours. It must be a bit of a downer knowing that kids have had to work themselves to the bone just so that you could indulge yourself.

For fairtrade

Stop using cocaine. And tell your friends to stop. Spread the word.

The Drug Policy Alliance website explores the drug war, and is a good source of information on every drug under the sun: www.lindesmith.org

Educate yourself. HuumeBoikotti is a Finnish website with lots of interesting information on the drugs trade: www.huumeboikotti.org/english.htm

Eat fairtrade chocolate, unzip a fairtrade banana, have a fairtrade cup of tea instead. It's better for you, and better for the world.

For fairtrade products: www.fairtrade.org.uk

Drug facts

Share these facts with your friends:

- Opium was being cultivated from 6,000 BC.
- In the 19th century, the opium business was one of the most profitable businesses of the British Empire.
- When Coca-Cola was first produced, the 'health tonic' contained small amounts of cocaine in the recipe.
- According to rough estimates, there is more money in circulation annually in the drugs trade than in the oil refinement industry, and almost as much as in arms trafficking.

Did you know that in the UK:

- 3 million people use illicit drugs (5 per cent of the population).
- Of 280,000 people using Class A drugs, only 20 per cent are receiving treatment or are in jail.
- The annual cost of crime by cocaine and heroin users is £16 billion.
- Drug users commit 36 million crimes each year – 56 per cent of total crime.

PC power

Decide to join in. It's not a huge decision to make. You are not using your computer up to its full capacity. If you want to use your employer's computer, get their permission.

Check whether your computer meets the minimum requirements. If it's less than 5 years old, it probably will. The operating system can be Windows, Mac or Linux.

Go to climateprediction.net, which should answer any questions you might have.

Register and accept the licence agreement.

Run the program; the results will be sent back automatically to: climateprediction.net.

Computing power

Two heads (or in this case tens of thousands) are better than one. Some problems are so complicated that it is difficult to find enough computer power to solve them. To get over this, a mechanism has been developed for harnessing together the unused computing capacity of PCs all over the world so that they can work together.

One very complicated problem is predicting climate change. The climateprediction.net project has over 95,000 computers in 150 countries. They work together to investigate how sensitive the different climate change models are to small changes in the underlying assumptions that have been used to create them, and also to changes in climatic conditions.

You can link your computer to the 95,000 others around the world that are already working on the climateprediction.net project.

To run a simulation will take between 10 and 22 days, depending on your computer power. If you switch your computer off and then back on again, the simulation will continue from where it was left off until it has been completed.

Climate prediction

This is the world's largest climate modelling experiment. It will provide decision makers with a much better scientific basis for creating policies to address global warming.

Each simulation divides the globe into thousands of sectors, and estimates the future temperature, based on certain assumptions such as cloud coverage, the rate of heat movement and rainfall rates.

The first results suggest that average temperatures could rise by as much as 11°C by 2050 unless deep cuts are made to greenhouse gas emissions. This is double the warming predicted by the Intergovernmental Panel on Climate Change. Visit www.climateprediction.net

Forecast your future

Christmas Eve is make-or-break time for children fortunate enough to be expecting gifts. Has anyone paid attention to their wish-list? Will Santa Claus bring them that much-desired gift? Over 750,000 children a year in the UK alone write a 'letter to Santa' in the run-up to Christmas. His address and special postcode is Reindeerland, SAN TA1. What happens to these letters? The Royal Mail replies to all such letters, and the process is covered on a webcam at www.royalmail.com/santamail

What is on your wish-list? Maybe you don't care too much what you receive by way of a Christmas gift, but would dearly love to see a more caring society, a more peaceful world, or a healthier environment. Well, these certainly aren't going to be brought by Santa Claus – or by any single individual. They are problems that you are going to have to help sort out yourself.

Write a letter to yourself, which you will open and read at some time in the future. It will be fascinating to read your letter then. You will be able to compare how things are now, with the world as it will be then. And your current aspirations and emotional state with those of the person you will have become.

Write now

Write a letter to yourself and read it in 10 or 25 years' time.

Write about the issue that you want to do something about. What impact do you think you will be able to make? How would you like things to be in the future?

You could add some personal thoughts – your current state of mind, how you spend your time, if you are in love with anyone, how you see your life evolving, your ambitions ...

Hide the letter or give it to someone to keep for you.

The Letters to Santa website was inspired by NY's Operation Santa Claus. You can download Christmas carols, stories, and even track down Santa's progress on Christmas Eve: www.operationlettertosanta.com

Operation Santa Claus

At the New York Post Office in the 1920s, postal clerks started opening some of the letters to Santa and, touched by some of the requests, dug into their own pockets to pay for presents. This has now become Operation Santa Claus, and the idea has been copied by other post offices in the USA.

The idea is simple. Postal staff volunteer to sort through the mail (c. 200,000 letters to Santa are received each year) and select those from needy inner-city children. Members of the public come to the Post Office, read through the mail and take away letters they would like to reply to with a gift.

Band Aid

Do they know it's Christmas?

Buy the various Band Aid, Live Aid and USA for Africa CDs. Live Aid: www.liveaiddvd.net

The 20th anniversary version of 'Do they know it's Christmas': www.bandaid20.com

Live8: www.live8live.com

The unofficial Live Aid site: www.live-aid.info

All about Band Aid at: en.wikipedia.org/wiki/Band_Aid

All about USA for Africa: en.wikipedia.org/wiki/USA_for_Africa

25 November 1984: There was widespread famine in Ethiopia. Images of people starving to death were being shown on TV. Bob Geldof, a rock singer with Boomtown Rats, felt he had to do something. So, with Midge Ure, he wrote a Christmas song, called up his famous singer friends to help record the song, and produced 'Do they know it's Christmas?' It was the first single to sell over 3 million copies in the UK. All proceeds went towards African famine relief.
28 January 1985: Inspired by Geldof, 45 musicians got together in New York to record 'We are the World', written by Michael Jackson and Lionel Richie. The group called itself USA for Africa – United Support of Artists. This was also a Number One hit.
13 July 1985: Geldof organised Live Aid: a rock concert held simultaneously at Wembley Stadium, London and at the JFK Stadium, Philadelphia, and broadcast around the world. (Geldof estimated that nearly 85 per cent of the world's TVs were tuned into it.) It raised nearly $100 million.

Geldof raised millions for Africa. But he also invented two big fundraising ideas: the pop single produced entirely for free, and the mega-concert broadcast globally. He went on to help set up the Commission for Africa and organise ten Live8 concerts on 2 July 2005 to get the G8 rich nations committed to eliminating poverty in Africa.

Band Aid Charitable Trust

'Do they know it's Christmas' was re-recorded in 1989 and 2004. The Band Aid Charitable Trust continues to receive income from sales and royalties, which it donates as aid for Africa.

In 2003, it supported food security, fresh water, eyecare and healthcare projects in west and east Africa. The 2004 recording helped victims of famine in Darfur, Sudan.

Make a will

Almost everyone has some assets, and everyone is going to die sometime. Your life expectancy might be high, but the unexpected can happen – today, tomorrow, whenever. It is important to make a will, because it allows you to:

- Choose how to dispose of your assets. If you die without a will, there are rules that dictate how your assets are distributed. This may not be in the way you would wish.
- Inherit from an unmarried partner. Unmarried couples (same sex or not) cannot inherit from each other without a will.
- Make arrangements for your children. Couples with children under 18 may want to consider arrangements if either or both die.
- Minimise tax payments (even inheritance tax).

It is your most recent will that determines what happens. So if your circumstances change, for example, if you separate from your partner or you hit the jackpot in the lottery, then make a new will.

Why not include a charitable bequest in your will? This could be a simple gift, or you might establish a fund for a specific purpose, which will continue for many years (for example, a bursary fund to provide school fees to a child in the developing world).

Give something to charity

Go and write your will today. Type 'make a will' into Google, and you will find many online will-writing services.

Include a charitable bequest in your will. Think about how much you would like to give and what you would like to support. Remember that a small bequest to a large charity will be almost unnoticed, but the same money could support really interesting work by a smaller organisation.

Remember that the charity will get nothing until you die, and that the gift will cost you absolutely nothing and may save tax when you die. So be generous!

Take the Make-a-Will quiz at: moneycentral.msn.com/retire/home.asp

Living Wills

A Living Will sets out how you would like to be treated as you near death, when you are unable to make decisions for yourself. It covers such things as the degree of medical intervention, pain management, feeding that should be administered, and where you would like to die. This can take the burden of decision away from your family.

A Living Will is an expression of wishes, rather than a legally enforceable instruction. Buy *The Natural Death Handbook*, or download from: www.globalideasbank.org/natdeath/ndh0.html

Do we need stuff?

Stuff it!

Make a catalogue of everything you own. Think about each item on your list: about how and why you came to acquire it, whether you still use it (or indeed ever used it), whether you still need it (or think you need it), and whether you really do want to keep it.

Set aside everything that you don't need or want. Then either take these to a charity shop or sell them on eBay. Or, if they are completely worn out or of no use to anybody, then throw them away (in a recycling bin, of course).

Keep your list. In five years' time, repeat the exercise and see if you have continued your consumerist ways, buying more than you need.

Find out more about Michael Landy at: www.tate.org.uk/magazine/issue3/michaellandy.htm

Michael Landy, a British artist, catalogued and destroyed all 7,226 of his possessions in a 2001 art installation called Break Down, held in a vacant C&A clothes store on Oxford Street, London. Landy stood on a platform overseeing a production line staffed by ten assistants. Every single one of his possessions was first catalogued and then destroyed – his passport, his keys and his credit cards, right down to a last dirty sock. The objects were shredded or ground up, and then put into plastic trays and sacks for disposal.

The things Landy valued most he left until last. One of the last objects to be destroyed was his father's sheepskin coat. Over 45,000 people visited the art installation, and the final day attracted 8,000 people:

> *When I finished I felt an incredible sense of freedom, the possibility that I could do anything. But that freedom is eroded by the everyday concerns of life. Life was much simpler when I was up on my platform.*

The event got a huge amount of publicity. Sermons were preached on the morality of consumerism. Landy was attacked for wanton destruction. Some saw it as an attack on capitalism; others as an act of madness and offered counselling. Landy described the event as an 'examination of consumerism'. Since then, he has been drawing street flowers. These are flowers that live in the cracks in paving stones.

Are we better off without?

We live in a consumerist society. We are urged to purchase much more than we need. And when fashion changes, we just buy something else – whether or not the thing we have is still functioning. Maybe, like Michael Landy, you could experience a sense of freedom by ridding yourself of possessions – maybe not all of them, just those you no longer need.

Auction it on eBay

If you no longer need it, someone else might really want it. And they may be prepared to pay good money for it. So why not auction it on eBay? You will find a new user, liberate some space in your home and raise money to help you change the world – all in one go!

eBay was created in 1995 by Pierre Omidyar as an online marketplace for buying and selling. He wanted to create an efficient internet trading space for individuals and small businesses. eBay pioneered an auction format with a simple, easy-to-understand mechanism that lets buyers and sellers decide the true value of items, build relationships with others, and become part of the eBay community. Pierre and co-founder Jeff Skoll are now major philanthropists.

eBay now has 114 million registered users, trading in more than 50,000 different categories in 29 different countries. At any time there will be more than 25 million items for sale. 3.5 million new items are added each day. People have auctioned everything from genuine Glastonbury mud (sold for a staggering £490) to a 40 lb buffalo head (complete with detachable horns). If you are not already hooked on eBay, there are simple instructions on the website on how to buy and sell. You can also buy a guidebook to help you through the process.

De-junk

Go through your possessions, identify all the things you no longer need, which someone else might want to buy from you. Then start selling.

In the UK, eBay has a Charity Page. Selling fees still have to be paid, but this provides some free additional publicity for non-profit making organisations.

Approach celebrities, and see if they will give you things to sell. Dave Rowntree, drummer with Blur, offered two hours of his time for a drumming lesson and a glass of champagne.

eBay Charity Page: http://pages.ebay.co.uk/community/charity/index.html

Download an eBay factsheet: www.harriman-house.com/ebay/factsheet.htm based on *The eBay Book* by David Belbin.

For charitable foundations funded by Omidyar: www.omidyar.net and Skoll: www.skollfoundation.org

The Great Chicago Fire Sale

This was the first charitable eBay auction, organised by a municipality to raise money for the arts.

The items donated for the sale included: a 1960s Playboy bunny costume; a dinner party prepared by Art Smith, who is the personal chef to Oprah Winfrey; the unusual opportunity to dye the Chicago River green: and much more.

Do some good

Think about the good you could do before you die.

Make a list of things you could do to address some of the world's problems. Your list can be as long or as short as you like. The problems are those you believe are important. The actions are what you want to do to address them.

Put the list somewhere where you can see it. Make sure you do at least one thing on the list each month – and try to do everything before you die.

A list of 100 simple things to do: brass612.tripod.com/cgi-bin/things.html

Grow a Brain is a website about things to do before you die: growabrain.typepad.com/growabrain/things_to_do_before_you_die/

Become a diamond

LifeGem of Chicago, Illinois, will take a few grains of your cremated remains and subject them to high pressure and temperature. After 18 weeks, you emerge as a sparkling one-carat diamond.

Things to do before you die

In this world, nothing is certain but death and taxes. Benjamin Franklin

The rest of your life is up to you. But, remember that you have only a limited amount of time before you go.

So start making a list of all the things you want to do before you die. Then start doing them. Right away. You never know how much longer you have left ...

Some things you simply must do:

- Scour the night sky for comets, with the chance of following Halley or Donati and having a comet named after you.
- Extract your own DNA. Spit gargled salt water into diluted washing-up liquid and slowly dribble ice-cold gin down the side of the glass. The spindly white clumps that form in the mixture are, basically, you.
- Measure the speed of light by melting chocolate in a microwave oven. You measure the distance between globs. Various calculations produce the answer. You can still eat the chocolate afterwards.
- Write your name in atoms at IBM's Almaden research laboratory, San Jose, California. While you're saving up to go there, simply go and see an atom by visiting a university lab with equipment to trap and cool atoms. Barium is best.
- Help nail a murderer. Register ahead with Tennessee's body farm and donate your corpse. It will be left out in the open to decompose before a trainee forensic scientist gets to work on it. An estimated 100 murderers have been convicted as a result of this training.

From *100 Things to Do Before You Die*, ideas from scientists brought together by Valerie Jamieson and Liz Else, Profile Books.

World social justice

The World Social Forum is a huge annual event, attended by people from NGOs, community groups and civil society movements from all over the world who are 'opposed to neo-liberalism and world domination by capital'. The WSF is an open meeting place for creative thinking, for democratic debate of ideas and issues, for free exchange of experiences, and for networking and linking up with other people in order to plan effective action for a better world.

The first WSF was held in January 1998 to coincide with the annual World Economic Forum in Davos, when 192 organisations from 54 countries launched a 'Declaration against the Globalisers of Misery'. The next year, in 1999, a Davos Forum aimed to show that the economic issues addressed by the World Economic Forum only served a small group of interests, and that other mechanisms were needed for addressing issues of social justice and world development. This led to the first World Social Forum held in Porto Alegre, Brazil in January 2001. Some 20,000 participants came together around the slogan 'Another World is Possible'.

Over 55,000 people from 131 countries came to the second WSF in 2002, and 100,000 attended in 2003. In 2004, the WSF was held in India, attracting around 250,000 participants. There are also regional and thematic WSFs, which explore specific issues.

Another world is possible

Change your plans for January. Take a trip to the next World Social Forum. It will open your eyes to what people are doing to create a better world. It could inspire you. And you should have a great time.

The World Social Forum is held in January: www.forumsocialmundial.org.br

There are a number of Regional Forums linked to the World Social Forum. In 2005, these included Forums for Europe, the Mediterranean, the Pan-Amazonian Americas and the Caribbean. Details of future forums are posted on the WSF website.

What it's like at the WSF

The programme includes lectures, presentations, workshops, films and videos, cultural events, marches and demonstrations, the issuing of declarations and much more. If you go, you will learn about the world and its problems, what is being done to address these, new ideas for development, and new skills for making change. You will meet old friends and make new friends – and you should come away believing that another world is possible.

Light up the future

Say goodbye to the old year and welcome in the new with an outdoor celebration, even if it's only in your street or garden. Use some kind of illumination – home-made lanterns, torches, tea-lights – anything you can lay your hands on at short notice to symbolise your hopes for a bright future.

And next year, think about involving your whole community in a lantern parade.

Bethesda Arts Centre: www.bethesdafoundation.org

New year's resolutions

Never doubt that a small group of thoughtful committed citizens can change the world. Indeed it is the only thing that ever has! Margaret Mead, Anthropologist

New Year's Eve is a time to look back and to reflect on all that has happened in the past year. What have you been able to achieve in your efforts to change the world? What has been your most successful action? What was most fun? What had most impact? What have you learned? What new friends have you made? How have you changed?

But it is also a time to look forward – to make a commitment to continue your efforts into the future. Through your actions, you can do your bit to change the world. You can also inspire others to action. Congratulations on what you have done so far. Keep up the good work. And best wishes for an enjoyable and successful New Year of making a difference!

Celebrating the Nieu Bethesda way

Nieu Bethesda is a poverty-stricken township in semi-arid desert of South Africa attached to the town of Bethesda. It has become a popular tourist attraction because of 'The Owl House', a tiny museum devoted to the work of the eccentric sculptor Helen Martins, who lived and worked there. The township also has underground pools from which the local people draw water with windmills.

The New Year of 2005 was welcomed in by a choir and a procession of lantern bearers, who walked through the streets and alleyways. Before the event, workshops were held to involve as many local people as possible in lantern making. Some of the lanterns were geometric and others were in the shape of wild animals and birds.

When night fell, candles were placed inside the lanterns and the procession started off. The local police and volunteers were there to ensure safety. It was a great night, which will be long remembered.

and 52 ways ...

And if you're just too damn busy to do all 365, why not try these 52?

1 Make amends
January 2
Bury the past by making amends with the person that you've done a wrong to, had a huge argument with or insulted. Not only will you have done good – it will be one less thing to worry about.

2 Coffee at a fair price
January 4
Buy and drink fairtrade coffee. It provides greater security for small producers than the fluctuating world market. The current fairtrade price is more than double the market price.

3 Start drinking
January 5
Support the local economy and help the environment when you have a drink with your friends. Reduce your beer, whisky and wine miles; choose bottles that have natural cork stoppers; and recycle all your bottles and cans.

4 Uncover your hidden bias
January 15
Try Project Implicit's Association Tests (see www.implicit.harvard.edu). You may try to behave fairly but you might still possess strong hidden negative prejudices, which these tests aim to detect.

5 Give money a voice
January 18
Make your money speak to the world. Inscribe some hard-hitting facts on your notes, which will be passed from person to person: for example, over one billion people have to survive on less than a dollar a day.

6 Fight the 4x4 menace
January 29
SUVs or 4x4s are the most polluting form of transport. Visit www.stop urban4x4s.org.uk to download fake parking tickets which describe everything that's wrong with a 4x4. You can put these under their windscreen wipers.

7 Give up apathy
February 1
Thrown into apathy by the sheer weight of the world's problems? Try www.antiapathy.org, a website which provides 'one-stop shopping'. Express an interest in some of the key organisations listed and act on the information they send you.

8 Collect small change
February 10
Empty your pockets or your purse each night and bung it in a jar –

you'll be amazed at how quickly your spare change mounts up. At the end of the year (or whenever the container gets full) you'll have the pleasure of deciding which project to donate it to.

9 Meeting up is fun
February 17
Meetup.com helps people find others who share their interest or cause, from Elvis fans to Environment savers. Meetups are usually informal, held monthly, open to anyone and held in public places, although some take place in offices or private houses.

10 Say adios in Ainu
February 21
Help save a language – without words to express things, knowledge and ideas begin to disappear. Investigate the languages in your region or take a course in an endangered language. Go to www.word2word.com/coursead.html or the Foundation for Endangered Languages (www.ogmios.org).

11 Say NO to plastic bags
February 22
Plastic bag litter creates huge problems, harming wildlife, blocking waterways and causing other environmental hazards. Use reusable bags when you go shopping. Recycle any plastic bags you take home with you as bin liners or freezer bags.

12 Freecycle for fun
February 27
Whether it's a chair, a fax machine, a piano or an old door, your local Freecycling group will provide you with an opportunity to recycle things, rather than throw them away. Check if there is a local group – if there isn't start one. See freecycle.org for guidance.

13 Save the rainforest
March 7
The rainforest continues to shrink rapidly at the rate of almost two acres a second. But you can do something to help – either save it for free by visiting www.therain forestsite.com or visit some of the click to donate sites such as www.worldlandtrust.org

14 Reason to dream
March 13
As Gandhi said 'be the change you wish to see in the world'. The Otesha Project website (www.otesha.ca) suggests examining the choices you make in the morning, from water use to transport etc. See what you can do – this morning and every morning – to help create a better world.

15 Check out the Ideas Bank
March 17
The Global Ideas Bank (www.globalideasbank.org) contains a mixture of weird and wonderful ideas for changing the world. You can send in your own, or vote on existing ideas and add your own comments.

16 Dubble Agents for chocolate
March 24
Ghana was the world's leading cocoa producer but its production is now suffering, affecting around 1.6 million people. The Kuapa Kokoo co-operative is trying to change this by selling cocoa to the European fairtrade market. Support them by buying Divine fairtrade milk chocolate or Dubble Bars.

17 Flushed with success
March 28
Why not build your own composting toilet? They use little or no water; are not connected to a sewage system; cause no damage to the environment; and produce compost as a by-product, which you can use in your garden – or sell.

18 Guerrilla gardening
April 2
Guerrilla Gardeners (www.publicspace.ca) plant herbs, flowers and vegetables on vacant land and by the roadside. Join them and start to sow the seeds of change. All you need is some seeds, a small bag of soil, a trowel, a watering can, some friends, and as much creativity as you can muster.

19 Remember Rwanda
April 6
Work to prevent the tragedies of Rwanda and other genocides from happening again. Remember Rwanda preserves the memory of the genocide, and aims to educate people on this and other genocides. See www.visiontv.ca/RememberRwanda/index.htm

20 Supercomputing
April 16
Join your computer up to a distributed network and help solve some of the world's big problems, which are too large or expensive for a supercomputer to manage on its own. For example, new cures for AIDS and cancer. Go to http://distributedcomputing.info/projects.html

21 Slow down
April 21
Why not swap your high-octane, stressed-out existence for a more relaxed one? Try downshifting (www.downshiftingweek.com) or read Carl Honore's *In Praise of Slow* (www.inpraiseofslow.com).

22 Happiness manifesto
April 24
Despite growing affluence, happiness levels are remaining fairly constant in the developed world. Why not look at other ways to increase your happiness? Try downloading the 'Happiness Manifesto' (www.bbc.co.uk) and following the suggestions.

23 Petition online
April 27
A petition is an effective way of getting attention and gathering support for an issue and the internet provides a fast and easy mechanism for collecting thousands of signatures. See The Petition Site (www.thepetitionsite.com/create.html) or PetitionOnline (www.petitiononline.com/petition.html) for more advice.

24 Join the sex workers union
May 1
Sex work is big business but it comes with many inherent dangers. Sex workers have banded together in the International Union of Sex Workers to promote health and human rights. Why not join as an act of solidarity (www.iusw.org)? It's free – and, no, you don't have to be a sex worker.

25 Plant your birth tree
May 6
Find out what species your birth tree is and plant one to commemorate your next birthday. Look for a location that desperately needs a tree – your own garden, a plot of vacant land etc. Or commemorate someone else's birthday by planting their birth tree.

26 Unwanted Styrofoam
May 18
Persuade manufacturers to stop using environmentally damaging Styrofoam (polystyrene) packaging by sending it back to them. Address your parcel to the Chairman at Head Office (the name and address will be on the company's website) with a polite letter about its impact. Styrofoam is very light, so it won't cost much in postage.

27 Publish it yourself
May 23
Publish your own book for as little as $6! See www.lulu.com, the website where you can publish and sell books, music, comics, photographs and movies. There is no set-up fee or minimum order and you, the author, retain complete control over content and design.

28 Go unshopping
June 1
Embrace the principle of unshopping – it involves unlearning all the bad habits of our consumer society, shopping more responsibly and thinking about the future of the planet. See www.coopamerica.org for a list of the ten items you should never buy.

29 Green funerals
June 2
Conventional funerals are environmentally unfriendly and very expensive. Why not consider a green burial in a field or woodland instead? The Natural Death Centre (www.naturaldeath.org.uk) will give you all the information you need.

30 Share your car
June 14
Although it is better to walk, cycle or use public transport when possible, if you are using a car it makes financial and environmental sense to share your journey. The internet is a great mechanism for linking people to share a journey. See www.liftshare.org

31 Donate smart clothes
June 15
Imagine that you've managed to get a job interview but because you're very poor you have nothing to wear. Dress for Success (www.dressforsuccess.org) addresses the problem by giving clients suits and smart clothes. They need a supply of new or nearly new (and clean) office clothes – why not donate yours?

32 Purify water
June 30
About 1.1 billion people do not have access to safe drinking water, something the UN plans to rectify over the next decade. Check out their plans at www.unesco.org/water or try the SODIS method (solar disinfection) www.sodis.ch/Text2002/T-Howdoesitwork.htm for yourself.

33 Reduce your ecological footprint
July 11
The Earth can no longer cope with our global ecological footprint (the area of land required to produce the food, energy and materials we consume and absorb the waste we produce). Test your own at www.myfootprint.org and follow the easy suggestions to reduce it.

34 End violence against women (365 more things to do)
July 18
Submit your ideas for ending violence against women one day at a time to the Violence Information

and Education Centre (www.viec.org/my365ways.html), and help them compile a book of practical ideas.

35 Open source cola
July 25
Promote the open source movement by making and sharing your own cola at parties, festivals etc. It allows the free copying and modification of software while crediting the ownership of the original idea (see wikipedia for more details). Download the Opencola recipe at www.colawp.com/colas/400/cola467_recipe.html

36 Give it up
August 8
Giving up things seems to be good for the soul (eg Lent, Ramadan, Yom Kippur). Why not see if there's something that you could give up – but make sure it's something that makes only a tiny difference to your day but potentially a big difference to the world (for example, stop buying bottled water, be alcohol-free two days a week).

37 Celebrate cycling
August 18
Join a Critical Mass bike ride where a bunch of cyclists take to the street – it's more of a celebration than a protest. Look for a group in your city (ww.critical-mass.org) or start your own following the tips on their website.

38 Tell a story
September 18
Follow in a tradition that is 30,000 years old and tell a story. Public libraries, schools, playgroups, and day-care and youth centres will probably jump at the chance of having you go along to do some storytelling. See www.storynet.org, www.storyteller. net and www.mysteriousbritain. co.uk for stories and information.

39 Harmony for humanity
October 7
Following the brutal murder of her husband, Mariane Pearl has set up a foundation in his memory (www.danielpearl.org) and has created Daniel Pearl Music Days, held during October. Why not organise your own gig or persuade your favourite venue to dedicate a performance?

40 Get a .tv address
October 8
By leasing a .tv email or web address you can help the economy of Tuvalu, a South Pacific nation whose islands are threatened by the rising ocean as a result of global warming. Go to www.tv and help draw attention to their plight.

41 Hemp rules
October 28
Cotton crops are very water, fertiliser and pesticide intensive. Also up to 30 per cent of a cotton garment is chemical residue ... and what we put next to our skin is easily absorbed by the body. Switch to hemp-cotton-mix T-shirts instead (www.thehempstore.co.uk).

42 Shoebox gifts
November 2
If you are on holiday in a developing country, take along a shoebox (tied with string so that you can open it at customs) filled with items useful for a school – for example, pens, pencils and solar-powered calculators. When you spot a small school, hand it over to a teacher.

43 Recycle your mobile
November 7
Rather than sending your old mobile to a landfill site where it will leak toxic material, recycle it. Both Oxfam (www.oxfam.org.uk) and Fonebank (www.fonebank.com) will accept phones which they send on to the developing world.

44 Donate your body
November 10
Why not donate your body to science? Medical schools in England need around 1,000 bodies a year but are making do with 600. Contact a hospital or medical school to tell them you plan to donate your body. Put your request in writing. Sign and date the letter, and get it witnessed.

45 Stick 'em up: stickers for the environment
November 23
It's easy to forget to turn off the tap or the light – but it all leads to higher electricity bills, more pollution and more greenhouse gases, contributing to global warming. Make some reminder stickers with provocative logos to stick next to taps and lights.

46 Buy a Good Gift
November 30
Rather than the same old tat, why not give a gift that will make a difference to someone's life – such as a nomadic camel or a duck for peace – from the Good Gifts Catalogue (www.goodgifts.org) in your recipient's name? They get a card with details of the project and the article is delivered to the person or community in need.

47 Pledge to change the world
December 5
Multiply the impact of your actions by making a pledge online through Pledge Bank (www.pledgebank.com). Promise to do something if a

certain number of people sign up – then persuade family, friends and complete strangers to do so. Once you meet your target number you can all go ahead and change the world.

48 Make a time capsule
December 9
Preserve contemporary objects for future generations by making a time capsule. A number of organisations offer advice on doing this – the International Time Capsule Society (www.oglethorpe.edu), the Smithsonian Centre (www.si.edu) and The British Library (www.bl.uk).

49 Share your books
December 11
Sign up as a member of BookCrossing (www.book crossing.com). Take a good book that you no longer want and register it on the website. Leave it somewhere for someone else to read, enjoy and pass on. You may be able to track its progress on the website.

50 Organise a hunger banquet
December 13
Get a taste of how the world lives by organising a hunger banquet (www.hungerbanquet.org). Invite guests and assign them a role – 15 per cent are the high-income group (they sit at a table and enjoy a three-course meal); 25 per cent the middle-income group (they sit on chairs and eat rice and beans); and 60 per cent are the world's poor (they sit on the floor, and get only rice and water).

51 Things to do before you die
December 29
Make a list of all the things you want to do before you die. Then start doing them. Right away. Include things that you could do to address some of the world's problems. Make sure you do at least one each month – and try to do everything before you die.

... and lastly

52 Change the world at random
Generate a random number between 1 and 366 on the internet at www.random.org/nform.html, go to this specific page in *365 Ways to Change the World*, and do the action for that day.

Index

Index

Index

Index